THE SPIRITUALISTS

THE
SPIRITUALISTS

The Passion for the Occult in the Nineteenth and Twentieth Centuries

RUTH BRANDON

 **Prometheus Books**

700 East Amherst St. Buffalo, New York 14215

Published 1984 by
Prometheus Books
700 E. Amherst Street, Buffalo, New York 14215

Copyright © 1983 by Ruth Brandon
All rights reserved
Published by arrangement with Alfred A. Knopf, Inc.
Library of Congress Catalog Card No. 83-47853
ISBN 0-87975-269-6

First published in the United States by
Alfred A. Knopf, Inc., New York
Originally published in Great Britain by
George Weidenfeld & Nicolson Ltd., London

Manufactured in the United States of America

For Phil and Nick, with love

Contents

Illustrations

PHOTOGRAPHS

Acknowledgements

A great many people helped in one way or another with the writing of this book. I should particularly like to thank: Professor J.O.Baylen; Diana Vincent-Daviss and Megan Elias, whose hospitality made working in New York not only possible, but fun; MrA.H.Wesencraft, the infinitely knowledgeable librarian of the Harry Price Collection at the University of London; and Nick Humphrey and Philip Steadman, whose generous encouragement and enthusiasm helped make the writing of the book such a pleasure. I should also like to thank the staffs of the American Society for Psychical Research; the New-York Historical Society; the New York Public Library; the Cambridge University Library; and the London Library.

THE
SPIRITUALISTS

1
Knock, Knock, Who's There?

Here's a knocking indeed!...Knock! Knock! Knock! Who's there, i'
the name of Beelzebub?...Who's there, i' th'other devil's name? –
MACBETH II, 3

Winters are long in northern New York State. They begin early, the
first snows often coming well before Thanksgiving, and linger on long
into what is, in kinder climates, the spring. For a poor and isolated
family like the Foxes there must have been times when the bleak
greyness seemed endless. They came originally from Canada where
(Mrs Fox later asserted) they had owned a sizeable estate. But that
had gone; and in 1848 John and Margaret Fox and their two youngest
daughters, Katherine, aged 11, and Margaretta, 13, were living in a
two-roomed cottage on a small piece of land at Hydesville, in the
township of Arcadia, New York. The family lived and ate downstairs
and slept upstairs, all together in the same room.

The rappings must have marked a break in the monotony, welcome
to the little girls, if not to their parents. During the month of March
1848, strange sounds began to plague the sleeping Foxes, raps and
knockings which disturbed their nights. On the evening of 31 March
they determined to go to bed early to make up for the lost sleep. The
girls went up soon after six, and their parents were to follow not much
later.

It was not, however, to be a restful night. Far from leaving them in
peace, the raps were heard with redoubled force as soon as the girls had
gone to bed. The feelings of John and Margaret Fox may be imagined.
What was causing the rappings?

The conclusion to which any parent would immediately jump was
that some naughtiness was being perpetrated by the little girls.

Certainly the rappings were indivisible from the children, occurring only around them. And indeed, forty years later, Maggie was to give a detailed description of how it had all been done.[1] They had begun, she said, by dropping apples tied to strings, naturally denying any knowledge of what had caused the ensuing bumps. They had been amazed at the effect these apparently disembodied noises had on others, their parents (if, in fact, this was the truth of the matter) evidently being both easily taken in and highly suggestible. Clearly their next step must be to improve their act.

It was Katie who first discovered that they could make very effective rapping noises with their fingers, and even better ones by cracking their toe-joints against any surface which would conduct sound. The girls practised, first with one foot and then with another, until 'we got so we could do it with hardly an effort'.

Hearing the noises coming from the top room, Mr and Mrs Fox rushed upstairs, where they stood transfixed as showers of raps resounded through the room. Katie now addressed the source of the mysterious sounds. She ordered the apparently discarnate entity to follow her as she snapped her fingers, giving her (as it were) rap for snap. It did so.

It seems that Mrs Fox had already been tending towards a spiritualist conclusion to the mystery. 'We were led on unintentionally by my good mother,' Maggie said. 'She used to say when we were sitting in a dark circle at home: "Is this a disembodied spirit that has taken possession of my dear children?" And then we would 'rap' just for the fun of the thing, you know, and mother would declare that it was the spirits that were speaking.'[2] At any rate, it was clear that whatever was causing the raps was intelligent. The thing was apparently a miracle. Feeling that others should witness this miracle and, possibly, the need of some moral support in this strange situation, Mrs Fox hurried to call in the neighbours.

On 12 April, just over a week later, one of these, William Duesler, wrote down what happened that evening. He wrote:

> The first I heard anything about them [the noises] was one week ago last Friday evening (31st day of March). Mrs Redfield came over to my house to get my wife to go over to Mrs Fox's; Mrs Redfield appeared to be very much agitated. My wife wanted I should go with them, and I accordingly went. When she told us what she wanted us to go over there for, I laughed at her, and ridiculed the idea that there was anything mysterious in it. I told her it was all nonsense, and that it could easily be accounted for. This

was about nine o'clock in the evening. There were some twelve or fourteen persons there when I got there. Some were so frightened that they did not want to go into the room. I went into the room and sat down on the bed. Mrs Fox asked questions, and I heard the rapping which they had spoken of distinctly. I felt the bedstead jar when the sound was produced.

The intelligence, then, however disembodied, was able to exert a definite physical force. But time was not left for reflection.

Mrs Fox then asked if it would answer my questions if I asked any, and if so, rap. It then rapped three times. I then asked if it had come to hurt anyone who was present, and it did not rap. I then reversed the question, and it rapped. I asked if I or my father had injured it (as we had formerly lived in the house), there was no noise. Upon asking the negative of these questions the rapping was heard. I then asked if Mr — (naming a person who had formerly lived in the house) had injured it, and if so, manifest it by rapping, and it made three knocks louder than common, and at the same time the bedstead jarred more than it had done before. I then inquired if it was murdered for money, and the knocking was heard. I then requested it to rap when I mentioned the sum of money for which it was murdered. I then asked if it was one hundred, two, three, or four, and when I came to five hundred the rapping was heard. All in the room said they heard it distinctly. . . . I then asked it to rap my age – the number of years of my age. It rapped thirty times. This is my age, and I do not think anyone about here knew my age except myself and family. I then told it to rap my wife's age, and it rapped thirty times, which is her exact age; several of us counted it at the time. I then asked it to rap A.W.Hyde's age, and it rapped thirty-two, which, he says, is his age; he was there at the time and counted it with the rest of us. Then Mrs A.W.Hyde's age, and it rapped thirty-one, which, she said, was her age; she was also there at the time. I then continued to ask it to rap the age of different persons (naming them) in the room, and it did so correctly, as they all said.

I then asked the number of children in the different families in the neighbourhood, and it told them correctly in the usual way, by rapping. Also the number of deaths that had taken place in the families, and it told correctly. I then asked it to rap its own age, and it rapped thirty-one times distinctly. I then asked if it left a family and it rapped. I asked it to rap the number of children it left, and it rapped five times; then the number of girls, and it rapped three; then the number of boys, and it rapped twice. Before this I had asked if it was a man, and it answered by rapping, it was; if it was a peddler, and it rapped.[3]

So spiritualism began.

The sensational news of spirit manifestations at Hydesville was not long in spreading. Crowds of people besieged the Fox home day after day, demanding to see the marvel. Familiarity, it seemed, in no way lessened the sense of wonderment felt by all. The girls' elder brother David Fox, who was married and who lived about two miles from his parents, had meanwhile devised a way of extending the spirits' hitherto rather limited conversational range. As William Duesler had shown, they were able to assent, dissent and count; but although they could clearly understand English it was hard to see how they would ever speak it, limited as they were – or seemed to be – to rapping. Then David hit upon the device of going through the alphabet; the spirits were to rap when the appropriate letter was reached. In this way words could be spelt out; and although the method was undeniably cumbersome, it has, *faute de mieux*, remained in use ever since.

Extraordinary as the Hydesville happenings were, they might well have remained a purely local sensation. After all, this was not the first time that spirits of the dead had communicated, or purported to communicate, with the living, using very similar techniques. For example, in 1534 some monks in the French town of Orléans had held just such conversations with the spirit of a citizen recently deceased, who had identified himself by rapping when his name was mentioned, giving two raps for yes and three for no, and making dispositions of his estate very much in favour of the monks, as the congregation could testify. The person actually doing the rapping was in fact found, later, to be a local conjurer (but who, asked the monks, might *he* not have been in touch with?).

More recently there had been the Cock Lane ghost, in London at the end of the previous century. This had attracted the attention of no less a person than Dr Johnson, and had been responsible for getting a man sent to the pillory on an accusation it made. But such cases, although they might become internationally famous, remained isolated incidents, and certainly did not give rise to new quasi-religions. It seems likely that such would have been the fate of the Fox sisters and their rappings, had it not been for their ambitious sister Leah.

Leah Fish lived some way from her parents, in the town of Rochester. She was a lot older than her sisters, being at this time in her mid-thirties, with a daughter, Lizzie, the same age as her sister Maggie. Mr Fish, who had taken her to Rochester, had proved an unsatisfactory husband, and had by this time left his wife and daughter. Leah, being (as later events were to confirm) a woman of resource, decided she would make her living by teaching music, and soon made herself independent in this way.

One day, early in May 1848, she was at the home of a friend of hers, a

Mrs Little, whose husband was a printer and whose daughters were among her pupils. The music lesson was in full swing when Mrs Little burst into the room, closely followed by her husband, clutching the proof sheets of a pamphlet that was just being printed. The pamphlet was by one E. Lewis, of Canandaigua, N.Y. He had called at Hydesville on 11 April, and had interviewed Mr and Mrs Fox and David, as well as the neighbours. He had then got them all to sign their statements, had made the whole into a pamphlet, and brought it to Rochester for printing.

Reading the pamphlet, Mr Little had recalled that Leah came from near Hydesville, and that her maiden name was Fox. Now he began to ask her questions. Was her mother's name Margaret? Did she have a brother David? Leah, understandably, was at a loss to know what could be going on. 'For mercy's sake, what has happened?' she cried. And in reply, they gave her the pamphlet to read.[4]

It must have been hard to know what to make of such a story; but Leah was giving nothing away, then or ever, as to her real thoughts. She contented herself by averring that if her parents and brother said it was true, then true it must be. Then she returned home, told her friends what was happening, gathered up her daughter Lizzie, and set off for the Erie Canal, where she could catch a boat for Newark, Wayne County, near her parents' township of Arcadia.

They arrived in Hydesville to find the family home deserted. There had been, as one friend put it, 'such a raffle constantly in and about the house' that life there had become intolerable, and the family had moved in with David. Here Leah found her parents and sisters in considerable confusion. Nobody was quite clear exactly what the rapping meant, and indeed the parents were inclined to wonder whether this was not some curse which had been visited upon them. Leah and Lizzie stayed about two weeks in Hydesville, and then decided to return to Rochester, taking Mrs Fox and Katie with them. And at this point the accounts given by Leah and her sister Maggie diverge.

Leah said they decided to leave Maggie with David because they hoped that if the girls were separated the rappings would cease and leave them all in peace. But no sooner were the Rochester party on the canal boat than the rappings began again. 'Perfect consternation came upon them; they kept by themselves as much as possible, but when they went to the dinner table with the other passengers, the spirits became quite bold and rapped loudly, and occasionally one end of the table would jump up and nearly spill water out of our glasses; but there was so much noise on the boat going through the locks, and other disturbances, that only we, who recognized the special sounds, knew of them.'[5]

Maggie's account of the same period is rather different. According to her, almost the first thing Leah did on her arrival at Hydesville

> was to take both her and Katie apart and cause them to undress and to show her the manner of producing the mysterious noises. . . . So interested was she in the matter, that she insisted upon taking back with her to Rochester, at the end of a fortnight, her daughter Lizzie and Katie, her sister – Maggie not being inclined to go with her. And in the interval, she practised 'rapping' herself, with her toes, after the manner illustrated by the girls. She found great difficulty in producing the same effect, however, as the joints of her feet were no longer as pliable as in childhood. The effort required was also much greater, and never during her whole lifetime did she succeed in attaining to much proficiency in this method of deception. The pronounced movement necessary in her case to cause even a faint sound to be heard, was easy to detect.[6]

Naturally enough, spiritualists did their utmost to discredit Maggie's confession, which, by the time she made it, was not all that difficult to do. It was by then 1888, and in the forty years which had passed since the events she was describing, the mischievous little girl had become a broken, alcoholic woman. And Kate, who had at first associated herself with the confession, soon after denied it. In fact Kate herself had made an equally detailed and circumstantial confession, not forty but three years after the Hydesville events. This was to a Mrs Culver, who lived nearby in Arcadia and was David Fox's sister-in-law. In 1851 Mrs Culver made a deposition about what Kate had told her.

> The girls have been a great deal in my house, and for about two years I was a very sincere believer in the rappings [she wrote], but some things which I saw when I was visiting the girls in Rochester, made me suspect that they were deceiving. I resolved to satisfy myself in some way, and soon afterwards I made a proposition to Catharine [sic] to assist her in producing the manifestations. I had a cousin visiting me from Michigan, who was going to consult the spirits, and I told Catharine that, if they intended to go to Detroit, it would be a great thing for them to convince him. I also told her that if I could do anything to help her, I would do it cheerfully; that I should probably be able to answer all the questions he would ask, and I would do it if she would show me how to make the raps. She said that, as Margaretta was absent, she wanted somebody to help her, and that if I would become a medium, she would explain it all to me. She said that when my cousin consulted the spirit, I must sit next to her, and touch her arm when the right letter was called. I did so, and was able to answer nearly all

the questions correctly. After I had helped her in this way a few times, she revealed to me the secret. The raps are produced with the toes. All the toes are used. After nearly a week's practice with Catharine showing me how, I could produce them perfectly myself. At first it was very hard work to do it. Catharine told me to warm my feet, or put them in warm water, and it would then be easier work to rap; she said that she sometimes had to warm her feet three or four times in the course of an evening. I found that heating my feet did enable me to rap a great deal easier.[7]

Kate also explained some other trade secrets. If the person who asked the questions also called the alphabet, then it was easy enough to answer correctly by watching the face and movements of the questioner (this technique is called muscle-reading and is used by professional thought-readers and fortune-tellers). As for making the raps sound in different places, 'all I should have to do to make the raps heard on the table would be to put my foot against the bottom of the table when I rapped; and that, when I wished to make the raps sound distant on the wall, I must make them louder and direct my own eyes earnestly to the spot where I wished them to be heard. She said, if I could put my foot against the bottom of the door, the raps would be heard at the top of the door.' According to Kate, it was Lizzie Fish who had first discovered how to make raps 'by playing with her toes against the foot-board when in bed'. Mrs Culver was also advised to have her little girl with her at the table whenever the spirits were consulted, and to tell everyone that she was the medium, 'for she said they would not suspect so young a child of any trick'.[8] If the three years of spirit-rapping had done nothing else, they had provided a crash course in worldly wisdom for Maggie and Katie Fox.

To return to 1848: that summer, under the direction of David Fox, the cellar of the Hydesville house was dug up and some bones and teeth discovered beneath it, belonging, so David asserted, to the pedlar whose spirit had first spoken to William Duesler. It should be added that no identification was found with these relics, nor any reason ever adduced for assigning them to the mysterious pedlar other than that a great many people wanted them to belong to him, and wanted the story to be true.

Why was this? Why were people – and, as time went on, these included people of the highest intellect and sophistication – so eager to accept, or impose, the so much less likely supernatural explanation? What, amid all this, was the state of mind of the people who, very soon, came to be known as 'mediums'? And (more mundane, but not least interesting) how did they obtain their effects?

These are some of the questions with which this book will be concerned.

The paradoxical corollary of that part of the American constitution which forbids the teaching of religion in public schools is that the United States is one of the most religious places on earth. It possesses a vehemence of religious feeling equalled today only by Islam and communism, but set apart from these by an extraordinary and characteristic individuality of expression.

That amazing multiplicity of sects and self-announced prophets today so marked on the west coast was paralleled, in the mid-nineteenth century, in the state of New York. If ever a society was inclined to accept and search out wonders, it was the so-called 'burned-over district' – 'burned-over', that is, by numberless religious revivals. It was the home of at least two prophets who founded and led successful new religions, complete with religious testaments: Mary Baker Eddy and Joseph Smith. It was a centre for social experiment. Elizabeth Cady Stanton produced her proclamation of women's rights from Seneca Falls, N.Y. Brook Farm, the Oneida Community, the Shaker settlements, were to be found in the same state.

These experiments were no more than a logical extension of the American ideal. If a man could engage in constructing a new country and a new society, why should he not equally devise his own form of religion? Experimental communities of all sorts – Fourierist phalansteries, Owenite co-operative settlements – went naturally together with home-grown prophets and miracles.

As might be expected, this combination produced on occasion some bizarre results. Perhaps the acme of strangeness was reached in the extraordinary story of the 'new motive power', by which a woman imparted energy to a machine. This was tenuously connected with spiritualism through John M. Spear, a Universalist clergyman and philanthropist (known as 'the Prisoners' Friend') who, in the wake of the Fox sisters' revelation, himself became a spirit medium, specializing in writing and 'impressions': he would be 'impressed' to go to a place to visit someone who needed healing.

Even in that society of rugged individualists, both John M. Spear and his 'new motive power' were regarded as somewhat extreme and eccentric; but I cite the story here as an example of the kind of thing that went on and was more or less accepted, if with reservations. On 29 June 1854, the *Boston New Era* published the following account:

1. It was announced to Mrs —, by spiritual intelligence, several months since, that she would become a mother in some new sense; that she would be 'the Mary of a new dispensation'.

2. Previously to this, Mrs — had for some time experienced certain sensations and agonies similar to those attendant upon gestation. Subsequently these indications gradually increased, until they at length became very marked and inexplicable, and presented some very singular characteristics. They were supposed, however, to be at least partially indicative of disease; but were not imagined to have the remotest connection with either the mechanism [the machine to contain the new power] at High Rock, or with the prophecy which has been alluded to. As the crisis approached, a variety of singular events . . . seemed to point to some unusual result. . . .

3. At length a request came, through the instrumentality of J. M. Spear, that on a certain day she would visit the tower at High Rock. No one in the flesh – herself least of all – had any conception of the object of this visit. When there, however (suitable preparations having been carefully made by superior direction, though their purpose was incomprehensible), she began to experience the peculiar and agonizing sensations of parturition, differing somewhat from the ordinary experience, inasmuch as the throes were *internal*, and of the *spirit* rather than of the physical nature, but nevertheless quite as uncontrollable, and not less severe than those pertaining to the latter. This extraordinary physical phenomenon continued for about the space of two hours. Its purpose and results were wholly incomprehensible to all but herself; but her own perceptions were clear and distinct that in these agonizing throes the most interior and refined elements of her spiritual being were imparted to, and absorbed by, the appropriate portions of the mechanism: its minerals having been made particularly receptive by previous chemical processes. . . .

4. The result of this phenomenon was, that indications of life or pulsations became apparent in the mechanism; first to her own keenly sensitive touch, and soon after to the eyes of all beholders. These pulsations continued to increase, under a process, which she was impelled to continue for some weeks, precisely analogous to that of nursing (for which preparation had previously been made in her own organization) until at times a very marked and surprising motion resulted.

The narrator of these experiences, presumably John M. Spear himself, concludes:

Neither Mrs — nor myself can profess to have, as yet, any definite conception as to what this 'new-born child', the so-called 'Electrical Motor', is to be. However 'enthusiastic' or 'extravagant' may be the expectations of others, we do not know that we yet at all comprehend the ultimate designs of the intelligences engaged in it. . . . But the incalculable benefits which have already accrued to us in the unfoldings of the interior principles of physical and human science . . . have overwhelmingly compensated us for all that it has cost us, whether in means or reputation.[9]

The only drawback of this new Motive Power (also known as the Physical Saviour, Heaven's Last Gift to Man, New Creation, the Great Spiritual Revelation of the Age, the Philosopher's Stone, the Art of all Arts, the Science of all Sciences – and so on) was that nobody could make up his mind *what it was for*. 'The new motor would not move to any purpose,' drily remarks one commentator. 'This was the only drawback in its great benefits to mankind.'

The combination, in this story, of religious naivety and the vocabulary of scientific progress is a significant one; it recurs constantly in the history of spiritualism. It is also a gothic mixture; and this was the age of the gothic, in literature as well as (if the preceding story is to be taken as in any way typical of its time) religion. The essence of the gothic is, of course, the blurring of the boundaries between life and death, and the American public did not need to rely solely on reports of fact or quasi-fact to feed its appetite for the wonderful, for publishing in newspapers up and down the east coast throughout the 1830s and 1840s was that master of the gothic *frisson*, Edgar Allan Poe.

Poe's was an imagination of the utmost creative and poetic originality. But no imagination, however powerful, is dissociated from the preoccupations of its time; and the source of many of Poe's most chilling effects is the notion of the extension of life beyond the usually fatal frontier – that moment when one is neither dead nor alive. It is a topic explored in many of his stories, and perhaps treated most directly in *The Facts in the Case of M. Valdemar*.

The storyteller in this tale is a mesmerist who suddenly realizes that despite all the experiments which have been made in his art, 'there had been a very remarkable and most unaccountable omission: no person had as yet been mesmerised *in articulo mortis*'. Meanwhile M. Valdemar is dying of phthisis, and promises to let the mesmerist know when his doctors tell him (as they have promised to do) that his last hours are upon him. He is mesmerised at the very point of death;

he is asleep, but the sleep is also a mesmeric trance in which he can reply to questions. Then, visibly, he dies.

> There was no longer the faintest sign of vitality in M. Valdemar; and concluding him to be dead, we were consigning him to the charge of the nurses, when a strong vibratory motion was observable in the tongue. This continued for perhaps a minute. At the expiration of this period, there issued from the distended and motionless jaws a voice – such as it would be madness in me to attempt describing. There were two particulars, nevertheless, which I thought then, and still think, might be fairly stated as characteristic of the intonation – as well adapted to convey some idea of its unearthly peculiarity. In the first place, the voice seemed to reach our ears – at least mine – from a vast distance, or from some deep cavern within the earth. In the second place it impressed me (I fear, indeed, that it will be impossible to make myself comprehended) as gelatinous or glutinous matters impress the sense of touch. . . . I had asked him, it will be remembered, if he still slept. He now said: 'Yes; – no; – *I have been sleeping* – and now – now – *I am dead.*'[10]

And in this state of suspended decease he remains for nearly seven months until, at the pleading of the corpse, he is released from his mesmeric trance and instantly collapses in putrefaction.

Mesmerism, the study and use of the hypnotic trance and its medical and psychological implications, was a science which had been developed chiefly in France by Antoine Mesmer and his disciples since the 1770s. Its power was widely ascribed to mysterious magnetic qualities, and it was also known as animal magnetism, under which name it became and remains anathema to Mary Baker Eddy and the Christian Scientists. It was a study of the greatest fascination to many medical men and scientists, but its use was never really considered respectable outside France. One reason for this was the lack of a tradition of clinical psychology in other countries; and in fact pioneering French studies of the trance state induced by this technique were later found to be of the greatest relevance to psychical research, itself often concerned with the varieties of self-induced trance.

Mesmerism could be of very great use and interest to medicine. One reason for its rejection by the 'respectable' medical profession of the day was the discovery of reliable anaesthetics – the most obvious use for the mesmeric trance had been in the operating theatre – but another was the conservatism of the medical profession, doubtless reinforced by the fact that mesmeric enthusiasts were inclined to extend their theorizing to include clairvoyance, phrenopathy, and other distressing and unscientific extremes.[11] It may be imagined that these constituted mesmerism's more popular forms, and it was largely these forms which were taken up in America.

There was never, in the United States, a respectable school of medical hypnotism. But this did not prevent people from setting themselves up as medical clairvoyants, magnetizing people, giving clairvoyant tests, prescribing for diseases and maybe doing some faith-healing. One such itinerant clairvoyant was Andrew Jackson Davis, the 'Poughkeepsie Seer'.

Davis had no formal education. His father was a shoemaker, and he himself was apprenticed in that trade. He got to know about animal magnetism when a series of lectures on the subject was given at Poughkeepsie in 1843. In December that year he was first put into a magnetic trance, and from then dates his career as a clairvoyant. The step from mesmeric clairvoyance to mystical dreams was not (as Swedenborg had already shown) a very large one. This step Andrew Jackson Davis now took. He began to give lectures on philosophy while in the trance state, and these were taken down by a couple of friends and later issued as a book, *The Principles of Nature, Her Divine Revelations, and A Voice to Mankind.* This dealt with world history and philosophy in the most general and wide-ranging way, and Davis cited his lack of education as further evidence for the miraculous nature of its composition. It came out in July 1847, and was a great and immediate success. It began, 'In the beginning the Univercœlum was one boundless, undefinable, and unimaginable ocean of Liquid Fire! The most vigorous and ambitious imagination is not capable of forming an adequate conception of the height and depth and length and breadth thereof' – and went on from there.

Davis was still less than twenty-one years old, which makes the production of such a work even more remarkable; but his protestations of ignorance were probably exaggerated. One man who met him then remarked that 'at that time Bohn's cheap translations of the classics abounded, and I perceived that Davis had got Plato by heart if not so well by head'.[12] Another acquaintance said that he 'loved books, especially controversial religious works, which he always preferred whenever he could borrow them and obtain leisure for their perusal'. Davis was attracted not only to the mystical and imaginative nature of these works but also to the philosophy standing behind many of them, which was often socialist and specifically, at that time, Fourierist. (Charles Fourier, the French egalitarian and utopian thinker, had flourished during the French Revolution, dying in 1837.)

This combination of a poetic and vigorous vision, apocalyptic themes, indignation at the unjust state of the world and desire for its betterment proved immensely popular. Davis acquired an enormous public following. And – which was to be of the greatest importance to the Fox sisters – Davis made a specific prophecy.

> It is a truth [he said] that spirits commune with one another while one is in the body and the other in the higher spheres – and this, too, when the person in the body is unconscious of the influx, and hence cannot be convinced of the fact; and this truth will ere long present itself in the form of a living demonstration, and the world will hail with delight the ushering in of that era when the interiors of men will be opened, and the spiritual communion will be established such as is now being enjoyed by the inhabitants of Mars, Jupiter and Saturn.[13]

In such a place and at such a time, it is hardly surprising that that perceptive and enterprising woman, Leah Fish, saw definite possibilities in the new-found talents of her sisters.

What exactly did she have in mind? One commentator states unequivocally that she had 'the project of founding a new religion'.[14] This is of course possible: it must sometimes have seemed as though new religions were being founded all over the United States every day. And doubtless there would be distinct advantages in being accepted as the revealed prophet of a new faith. But compared with other such prophets Mrs Fish was at something of a disadvantage. They, on the whole, enjoyed the advantage of believing in the faiths they preached. By contrast, all she and her sisters had were their 'phenomena'. Could they, by themselves, do the trick?

One feels in Leah nothing of the sophistication of her near contemporary Madame Blavatsky, founder of the Theosophical Society, who wrote of her own very similar, if more complex, activities in this field:

> What is one to do when, in order to rule men, you must deceive them, when, in order to catch them and make them pursue whatever it may be, it is necessary to promise and show them toys? Suppose my books and *The Theosophist* were a thousand times more interesting and serious, do you think that I would have anywhere to live and any degree of success unless behind all this there stood 'phenomena'? I should have achieved absolutely nothing, and would long ago have pegged out from hunger.[15]

But Madame Blavatsky had what Leah and her sisters did not: the confidence and magnetism to perpetrate barefaced fraud with great success and without for a moment pretending to herself that she was anything but fraudulent. The woman who could write, 'If you only knew what lions and eagles in all countries of the world have turned themselves into asses at my whistling and obediently clapped me in time with their large ears,' had seen more of the world than Rochester, N.Y. The Foxes were both more transparent and more equivocal. Leah 'tried hard to convince her younger sisters and her own child that there were really such things as spiritual communications, notwithstanding that all of those that were produced in their seances they knew to be perfectly false'.[16] And in her own accounts of those early days, Leah stuck to her story. She wrote:

> In the evening, my friend Jane Little and two or three other friends called in to spend an hour or two with us. We sang and I played on the piano; but even then, while the lamp was burning brightly, I felt the deep throbbing of the dull accompaniment of the invisibles, keeping time to the music as I played; but I did not wish to have my visitors know it, and the spirits seemed kind enough not to make themselves heard.[17]

The spirits were not often so discreet. When Leah, Kate and Lizzie arrived in Rochester, they took a new house which had never been lived in before, and so was presumably not haunted. But nevertheless, the day they moved in, they were greeted by the distressing sound of buckets of coagulated blood being poured onto the floor. Then, at night, Kate and Lizzie complained that they were being touched by cold spirit hands, and even their moving into the same bed as Leah, one on each side of her, could not prevent this. Meanwhile, the rapping continued. A Methodist minister visited the family with a view to exorcizing the annoyance, but failed to do so – upon which a group of Methodists and Christian Perfectionists took to calling round in the evenings and ranting and speaking in tongues, at which the spirits rapped louder and more boisterously than ever.

It soon became clear, however, that interest in mere disjointed rappings could not be indefinitely sustained. Leah now recalled the method of telling the alphabet which her brother had invented at Hydesville. This was introduced, and immediately the spirits began giving messages. Their fame spread. More and more people began calling on the Foxes (for the whole family had now moved from Hydesville to Rochester) to speak with the spirits and ask their advice. A certain George Willets, who had decided to move west with his family to Michigan, was advised against this and assured that, against all likelihood, if he stayed in Rochester he would be offered a job on the railroad. The spirits were most specific: 'Apply to William Wiley, Superintendent of the Auburn and Rochester Railroad, to-morrow at two o'clock, at his office, for a situation, and thee will have one before this week is out,' they said, adding that in the meantime, would it not be a good thing if Willets occupied himself with helping to organize the anti-slavery fair? And the prediction was fulfilled.[18]

Despite these wonders, it seemed for some time that the 'Rochester knockings', as they were now called, would remain a purely local miracle. For more than a year the spirits operated in relative peace. They acquired a few new tricks: they could sometimes move a table, even in broad daylight; and sitters might find themselves touched by a spirit hand, though that only happened in darkness, and observers noted that the ghostly hand possessed a wrist, and the ghost of a lady's dress as well. But it was not until 1849 that interest became really intense. In this year, Andrew Jackson Davis and his supporters discovered that their prophecy of imminent spirit communion seemed to have been fulfilled in Rochester, and various commentators began to take the sisters up. And not only the sisters; for many people were beginning to discover that they, too, could be practitioners. It became quite normal for people who had participated in spiritual conversations through the mediumship of the Fox sisters to discover that they, too, could produce raps and thus communicate with the next world. In Rochester and Auburn and nearby towns and villages, mysterious rappings began to manifest themselves in an increasing number of households.

The Fox household was now continually overrun with visitors. They arrived after breakfast and did not leave until midnight. Obviously, there was no possibility of continuing with music lessons. It is not clear exactly when it occurred to Leah that there might be money to be made out of the spirits. At any rate, she was careful not to be the first to suggest it publicly, but finally allowed herself to be persuaded to 'take compensation' for her sisters' services. How else, with all that was going on, was the family to live?

Everything did not go entirely smoothly. There were a great many people who did not believe in the spirits, and threatening mobs of these gathered from time to time outside the house, so that the girls did not like to go out alone. Clearly, something would have to be done. The phenomenon had grown beyond the point where it could be contained within the family.

It was also a watershed for Maggie and Kate. They were under great pressure from enthusiastic friends to give public demonstrations of their powers, and also to allow themselves to be publicly tested, thus giving the lie to doubters who alleged that the raps were not produced by spirits at all, but by the girls. This was also the course of action advocated by Leah. Whether or not it had been her original intention to found a new religion, it was by now amply apparent that a good deal was to be made, in one way and another, out of this situation – if only her sisters would co-operate. But nothing would be achieved by sitting at home and waiting for recognition. It was all very well being famous in Rochester, but Rochester was a small town.

But if Leah had wider ambitions, they could only be achieved through her sisters. And *they* were by no means sure that they wanted to be tied to the spirits for life. The whole thing had begun as a joke, but it was visibly running out of their control. They could still – just – back out. The 'spirits' could desert them and no one would be very much worse off. But once the spirits became public and official, then backing off would become proportionately more difficult, and the danger of discovery more real.

In November 1849, the conflict came to a head.

> The spirits [writes one of the girls' greatest supporters at this period] had long been urging the mediums to allow the utmost facilities for investigating this subject; but the aversion of the Fox family to the notoriety consequent upon such publicity was not easily overcome. . . . The spirits informed the family that they could not always strive with them; that such was the mediums' continual disobedience to the spirits' requests, that they must leave them. To this the mediums made no objection, but declared that nothing could please them more, and they hoped they would leave. Accordingly, while a few friends were present, . . . the spirits announced that in twenty minutes they would bid them farewell and discontinue their manifestations as they were unwilling longer to contend with such continued opposition. The friends conversed freely until the appointed time, when they spelled, 'We will now bid you all farewell.'[19]

Then they departed, and despite all entreaties, silence prevailed.

The scenes that went on in the Fox household during this period of silence may be imagined. Leah must have been furious beyond measure – more especially as she had to hold herself in check. She could not produce the manifestations herself; she could do nothing without her sisters' co-operation; she could not risk alienating them. The girls' resolve, however, did not last. We are not told whether they thought better of it themselves, or whether Leah was too much for them in the end. What is certain is that, even at this stage, saying goodbye to the spirits was no easy task. Every day friends called round wondering whether the lost spirits had returned, and Maggie and Kate 'soon began to realize their loss, and were affected even to tears when their friends called'.[20] There must certainly have been a considerable sense of anticlimax after the past year's excitements. Perhaps they realized, now, that life with the spirits promised to be a good deal more interesting than life without them. At any rate, after twelve days the spirits relented and returned 'in a perfect shower of raps'. Everyone was delighted; and plans were laid for the public demonstration.

The Corinthian Hall, the largest public hall in Rochester, was taken for the evening of 14 November. Leah and Maggie were to perform; perhaps it was thought that Kate was still too young to be subjected to such trials. The sisters would produce their rappings; then there would be a lecture which would recount the events of the past months, and which, while making no claims as to what the rappings *were*, would 'merely state, from well-proved facts, what they were *not*'. Then a committee of investigation would be appointed.

When the day came, four hundred people crowded into the hall. The *Rochester Democrat* was so sure that the fraud would be exposed and the rappings heard of no more that they had an article to that effect ready set up in type. However, they were to be disappointed. The committee also conducted their investigations in the Temperance Hall and in various private houses. Rappings were heard on the floor, on walls, on a door. Questions were asked of the spirits, and answered 'not altogether right, nor altogether wrong'. A member of the committee placed one hand on the ladies' feet and another on the floor, 'and though the feet were not moved there was a distinct jar on the floor'. (Kate later told Mrs Culver that they had arranged with a Dutch servant girl to rap under the floor from the cellar; she was to rap whenever she heard the sisters' voices calling the spirits.) Finally, the committee had to admit that although the sounds had undoubtedly been heard they could offer absolutely no explanation of how they had been produced. The sisters had co-operated with every test, and were willing to let themselves be examined by a committee of ladies, if this was desired. It was an anticlimax, and the public was not satisfied with it. There was nothing for it: more tests must be conducted. It was arranged that the same performance should be given, and the same procedure followed, on the two following evenings.

The second day's committee made no more progress than the first day's. Some of the gentlemen on it had formed theories about the raps being produced by ventriloquism, or by machinery of some sort; but they could find no evidence to support these ideas. By the third evening excitement was high. Far more people than before packed into the hall, and some of these were very hostile to the girls. The third committee, too, had its share of hostile members. A Mr Burtis declared that the girls would not have him on the committee, and was immediately voted onto it. He then promised that if he could not find out the fraud he would forfeit a new beaver hat. A Mr Kenyon declared that if he could not find out the trick, he would throw himself over the Genesee Falls, and he, too, was voted to the committee.

This time a group of ladies examined the sisters and their clothing to make sure that they had no lead balls sewn to the hems of their dresses, or any other such devices. None were found; and raps were heard even when they were standing on pillows with their skirts tied tight round their ankles with handkerchiefs. The gentlemen, too, heard raps, and a number of questions were answered more or less correctly by the spirits. No beaver hats were lost, and no one jumped over the Genesee Falls, but Mr Burtis and Mr Kenyon concurred with the rest. The girls, they declared, were genuine.

On hearing this, part of the audience began to stir up a riot. The ringleader, one Joe Bissel, left the hall and returned with his hands full of firecrackers, which he distributed to all takers to throw on the floor and create havoc. There was a general shouting and furore, speeches were made from the floor, and the police had to be called in. But, disappointed though some sections of the public might be, they had to admit that no fraud had been proved.[21]

'These young women will have to be pretty smart, if they deceive everybody,' the *Democrat* had said; and despite all the tests, there were still those who were not satisfied. A Professor Loomis opined that the noises were the result of a nearby dam vibrating (though he did not explain why in this case they should only occur in the vicinity of the sisters). A Dr Langworthy, who had been a member of the second committee, had second thoughts and attributed everything to mysterious objects hung on the girls' inexpressibles. If, he said, they had to perform before ladies and *sans culottes*, no raps would be forthcoming. But, of course, they had done just that, and the raps had been present nevertheless. A Dr Potts stood on the stage of the selfsame Corinthian Hall and cracked his toes, assuring his delighted audience that here lay the secret of the 'Rochester raps'. But whether or not he was right, it was too late. The bandwagon had begun to roll.

The Rochester demonstrations had attracted considerable publicity, and in particular had brought the Fox sisters to the attention of two very influential men who were to have a large effect on the subsequent spread of what came to be known as modern spiritualism. These were Judge John W. Edmonds, a respected member of the New York Court of Appeals, and Horace Greeley, the editor of the *New York Tribune*. Both these men were at a point in their lives when the prospect of messages from the next world held particular appeal: Judge Edmonds had just lost his wife, Mr Greeley, his son. So tempting was the promise of communication with these otherwise lost spirits that the ridicule of their compeers seemed a small price to pay for the potential consolation should communication prove possible. And, as was later to be proved countless times, what may seem satisfactory to a person in this frame of mind has everything to do with desire, and nothing to do with dispassion.

Judge Edmonds came upon the Fox sisters and their phenomena by chance. He happened to be paying a visit to his friend Chancellor Whittlesey in Rochester at the time of the Corinthian Hall demonstrations, at which Mr Whittlesey was a member of the second committee. The committee, as we have seen, was convinced; and so was Judge Edmonds. From that day forth he was a convinced spiritualist, and devoted the rest of his life to the advocacy of the spiritualist cause. This was to destroy his legal career and reputation (he eventually resigned from the court in 1853, in which year he published a book on spiritualism), but although he in some ways regretted this, it was a price he was prepared to pay. John Edmonds thus became the first of a select group particularly prized in spiritualist circles: men whose undoubted public reputation for intellect and judgement enabled them to be used as living proof that here was something that was no mere trivial fraud, as its detractors might suggest. How could it be, when such people as Judge Edmonds were prepared to swear by it? It is a question to which we shall return.

Greeley was alerted to the goings-on at Rochester by a letter sent to the *Tribune*. He thereupon commissioned his friend Charles Partridge to visit that city and see what was happening. Partridge reported that the stories were indeed true, and it was arranged that the Fox girls and their mother, and, of course, Mrs Fish, should visit New York under Greeley's auspices. Accordingly, in the spring of 1850, they arrived in the city where for the first time the general public was enabled to experience the mysterious rapping spirits in, so to speak, the flesh. There are a number of different accounts of what went on at these sessions, and comparison of them is revealing.

Here, for example, is the experience of a contributor to the *Spiritual Telegraph*, a paper which commenced publication in Boston in July

1850: 'The sisters have been directed by "the spirits" to visit New York,' it began, thus unwittingly elevating Greeley to the higher plane.

> They are now at Barnum's Hotel, with their mother, and two gentlemen who accompany them and attend to their business. . . . Their hours for receiving visitors are at 9 and 11 a.m. and 3 p.m. The sittings which I attended were conducted in the following manner: The sisters (Mrs Fish and the Misses Fox) are seated together upon a sofa. In front of them is a table, or rather two tables joined together, around which are seated from a dozen to forty or fifty visitors. The sitting is commenced, as I have stated, by silence, solemnity, and attention to the subject which has drawn them together. After a few minutes Mrs Fish, in a low subdued tone, and the eyes turned to the floor, says – 'Will the spirits converse with me?' After being present for some three or four hours, and hearing the responses given to a large number of persons, most of whom were skeptical when they came into the room, but who, on leaving it, were perfectly convinced and often over-whelmed with emotion, I embraced the moment offered me, and asked, 'Are there any spirits present who will respond to me?' – 'Yes.' – 'May I know who?' – 'Yes'. . . . Then I proceeded to write down the names of all my near relatives who have departed this life; and placing my pencil on each name, I asked, 'Is it this?' and in this way was given to understand it was the spirit of a beloved sister, whose hand I held in mine twenty-two years ago, when she left the body. Then followed other questions . . .
> Q: How old were you when you left this sphere?
> A: Twenty-nine. (This was true.)
> Q: What was your given name?
> A: Sally. (True.)
> Q: Where did you depart this life?
> A: Oxford, Mass. (True.)
> . . .I asked her numerous other questions, which left no room for me to doubt but that I was really conversing with the spirit of my dear departed sister. . . .
> . . .During one of the sittings . . . a gentleman present was noticed standing up writing while the responses were made by the spirits. All at once the responses ceased, and the alphabet was called for, when the following caution was spelled out: 'Tell that man to write no more fake answers!' It was whispered that the writer referred to was an editor of the *New York Picayune*. . . .[22]

Generally at these seances, when the spirits did not wish to answer any more questions, they spelt 'Done'; which disposed of some awkward moments.

Here we have perhaps the first instance of that circumstance which was henceforth to form so essential a feature of spirit intercourse:

unsympathetic presences at a seance would prevent the spirits from manifesting satisfactorily. It will be seen that the very circularity of this argument renders it quite unanswerable. It is thus of the greatest usefulness; and it was an argument which was early called into play by Mrs Fish herself. Thus, when a doubter asked whether he might leave the table during the seance so as to see the spirit bells ringing, the spirits said, 'What do you think we require you to sit close to the table for?' and Leah added, 'When spirits make these physical demon-strations, they are compelled to assume shapes that human eyes must not look upon.' Or, when a series of tests were carried out on the girls by a committee of doctors in Buffalo, N.Y., to see whether they made the noises by cracking their knee-joints (the doctors concluded that this was indeed how at least some of the raps were made), Leah said: 'It is true that when our feet were placed on cushions stuffed with shavings, and resting on our heels, there were no sounds heard, and that sounds were heard when our feet were resting on the floor; and it is just as true that if our friendly spirits retired when they witnessed such harsh proceedings on the part of their persecutors, it was not in our power to detain them'.[23]

Certainly the spirits failed to convince the correspondent for *Holden's Dollar Magazine*, who also visited Barnum's Hotel that summer. He confessed to 'no faith in them before we went and less, if possible, when we came away'; and yet it is clear from his description of what occurred that, to the person inclined to believe, the proceed-ings would have seemed no less miraculous than they did to the *Spiri-tual Telegraph*. It was all a question of what you chose to notice, or not to notice. He wrote:

> After all was ready, the usual question was put by Mrs Fish, Will the spirits reply to this gentleman? A few faint knockings were heard in reply, which seemed to us under the floor near one end of the sofa, and there they continued from first to last. His questions were then asked. . . . The answers were generally correct, a few were not at first, but after stating the questions in various ways as suggested by Mrs Fish, correct answers were at last obtained and a final assent was given that all the questions were answered correctly, without regard to the fact that a few had been answered several times wrong, and correct answers obtained by repeating the ques-tions in various forms.
>
> A person in the room wished to put some questions to the spirit of John C. Calhoun, and Mrs Fish asked if the spirit would reply to the gentleman? on which a louder and more rapid knocking commenced than before. Mrs Fish explained this by saying that the force and rapidity of the knockings

indicated the character of the individual; if he was decided and energetic, the knockings would be loud and strong, and the knockings of infants were always feeble. The spirit of J.C.Calhoun was then asked if it was in favour of the immediate abolition of slavery throughout the United States? to which loud knocks in the affirmative were given. After some further questioning another person wished to ask some questions, to which the spirit assented; and it was then asked if it was in favour of the abolition of slavery according to a *gradually progressive serial law of labor* which the questioner then had in his mind, (the gentleman we suppose to be an Associationist or Fourierite from the tone of his question) which was answered by knocks in the affirmative loudly. Now to our mind here was plainly a contradiction of the spirit against itself; but we said nothing.[24]

Certainly the spirits seemed to display an endearing naivety at times quite surprising in view of their eminence when in the body. One observer remarked that the spirit of Benjamin Franklin used remarkably poor grammar, and when complaints were voiced Miss Fox left the table in a huff exclaiming, 'You know I never understood grammar'! On another occasion, when the spirits had failed to understand a question and had returned no answer even after it had been put to them three times, one of the girls explained, 'Why, I don't understand your question.' It was then put more simply, and the spirits were enabled to reply.[25]

There was also a certain vulgar earthiness about the seances at Barnum's. The whole performance, reported *Holden's*, was commenced and carried through in a most natural and matter-of-fact way, and seemed to be to the parties interested as commonplace an occurrence as eating their dinner: 'While the spiritual revelations were still in progress Mrs Fox came in from a walk with a handkerchief full of peanuts and distributed them among her daughters' who ate them 'with a relish which showed that they did not undervalue the good things of this world, even when attending to the revealings of spirits from another'. The performance ended by the spirits, at Mrs Fish's request, knocking the rhythm of *Hail Columbia*, very distinctly, while she hummed the air.

Critics might carp; but those who wished to believe that the rappings really did represent communications from the spirits of the dead were not to be put off. The season in New York was an immense success, both commercially and in point of spreading the word. Horace Greeley, in an open letter published in the *Tribune* just after the sisters had left, endorsed their honesty and the wholly convincing nature of the manifestations. The number of people who, after participating in a seance, were discovering mediumistic talents in themselves, was increasing exponentially. So was the number of publications devoted to the subject. Andrew Jackson Davis kept up a perfect flood of tracts and pamphlets, quite apart from his immensely successful books. The erstwhile editor of his *Univercoelum*, S.B.Brittan, started a monthly journal, the *Shekinah*, as early as 1850; by 1852 this had been joined by the *Spiritual Telegraph*, the *Spiritual Messenger*, the *New Era*, a Missouri journal called *Light from the Spirit World*, and any number of spiritual books, pamphlets and ramblings, including such titles as *The Spiritual Pilgrimage of Thomas Paine*, received through the mediumship of the Rev C.Hammond, of Rochester; *Elements of Spiritual Philosophy*, by the Rev R.P.Ambler, of Springfield, Mass.; *The Clairvoyant Family Physician*, by Mrs Tuttle; *Messages from the Superior State*, by the Rev John M.Spear – and a host of other titles.

When Kate, Maggie and their mother and sister returned to Rochester from New York, they were no longer left with any possibility of choice as to how their lives should be spent from then on. The spirits had taken over. The house was besieged by eager seekers after spiritual truth. An excellent living – far more than they could hope for in any other way – was to be made by charging a dollar a head for participation in their spirit circles. They were surrounded by enthusiastic supporters; and they resigned themselves, not too unwillingly, to their fate.

It was perhaps not such a bad fate, at that; but there were drawbacks. The sisters were now public figures, and every public figure becomes the focus for unwelcome attentions of some sort. Thus, on a visit to Troy, N.Y., Maggie was the victim of what seemed a concerted attempt to kidnap or murder her by a gang of Irishmen, described variously as large, stout and drunken. When Mrs Fish set off to succour her sister and took a seat in the Troy railroad car, a 'large, animal-looking Irishman' came up to her and wanted to know where she was going. When she arrived at Troy the train was greeted by a hostile mob, the telegraph operator having betrayed his trust and told them she was expected. The sisters escaped alive, just. . . . This was, after all, country where accusations of witchcraft were not unknown.

We have already seen that the Buffalo doctors came uncomfortably close to divining the source of the rappings. At first, they confessed, they found themselves puzzled by the loudness of the sounds and the different directions from which they appeared to emanate. 'Close observation, however, of the countenances and deportment of the two females, led to the conviction that the production of the sounds involved a voluntary effort by the younger sister of the two. . . . The elder sister

... was apparently the managing partner, conducting the spiritual communications, while the former, it was clear, was the performer, i.e. the one that produced the knockings.'[26] The doctors noted that both sisters wore long, adult dresses: 'The principal rapper ought to be attended by a train-bearer,' was one opinion.[27]

The doctors attributed the sounds to cracking of the knee-joints, a near guess. They also divined the technique for making the sounds seem to come from nearer or farther off, as described by Kate to Mrs Culver. And they observed the very considerable effect exercised on people's perception of what was going on by their expectation of what would happen – in other words, people saw and heard what they wanted to see and hear.

In this as in so much else the Fox sisters set the pattern for much that followed. There are those who spend their time promoting events such as the Rochester knockings; there are those who spend theirs exposing such things as frauds. Then as now, there can have been few occupations as unsatisfactory as the latter. It is like punching a feather pillow: an indentation is made, but soon refills, and the whole soft, spongy mass continues as before. Not only did the Buffalo doctors fail to shake the faith of believers but, as one historian of spiritualism puts it, they 'only threw a publicity over the subject of the rappings, which resulted in a perfect torrent of investigation, and filled the public prints with reports of seances whose highly favorable and often astounding character – witnessed by many of the most distinguished citizens of Buffalo – culminated in the conversion of more investigators to the belief in Spiritualism than had been known in the space of so short a time in any other city.'[28] The same writer characterized the doctors' report, which, though condescending, is notable for its clarity, as 'almost unrivalled for folly and psychological absurdity.'[29] This technique of dismissal rather than rebuttal has remained the favoured form of response to 'exposures' ever since. It is, of course, highly effective: by simply ignoring the argument it makes its continuation more or less impossible.

At any rate, the Buffalo investigation did not discernibly damage the sisters' career. Soon afterwards Leah moved to New York, where she opened rooms for public seances on 26th Street. Her mother and sisters moved with her, and Horace Greeley, perhaps feeling in some measure responsible for the imposition of this way of life on two such young girls, undertook responsibility for educating Kate, who was still only thirteen.

Greeley was eager to see that not only Kate, but Maggie, got a proper education, something for which there had been little time over the past couple of years. He felt that the girls might have made a human discovery of the first importance; and if this were the case, they ought to have a good education in order to be able to cope with the consequences of what they had discovered. Certainly, regardless of the genuineness or otherwise of the raps, they were going to have to face a life greatly different from anything they might have contemplated before. But Leah was adamant. There could be no question of taking Maggie, too, out of circulation. Without her, as the Buffalo doctors had rightly pointed out, there would be no knockings, and no show, and, more particularly, no income. So Maggie went on rapping, in New York and on trips to different cities which had not yet heard the spirits. It was on one such trip, to Philadelphia, where the sessions were held in the 'bridal parlor' of Webb's Union Hotel on Arch Street, that Maggie met Dr Kane.

Dr Elisha Kent Kane was quite a figure in Philadelphia in the early 1850s. The son of a wealthy Philadelphia family, he was at this time in his late twenties, a sailor and a well-known Arctic explorer. In 1852, the year he met Maggie Fox, he was planning an expedition to try and find Sir John Franklin, who had failed to return from a Polar journey. Dr Kane was a slight, good-looking young man, with a head that seemed rather too large for his body. Of all the cities in the Union, Philadelphia was the most correct; and among the local families, the Kanes were of the most respectable. It might therefore seem a trifle strange that such people should demean themselves so far as to visit the 'bridal parlor' at Webb's Hotel, but as Maggie herself, writing some time later, put it: 'It is at all times easy to create a sensation in Philadelphia. The number of Quakers who live there, the social habits of the people, the absence of public amusements generally patronized, render the population – especially the higher and more educated part of it – particularly susceptible to any excitement stirring in the neighborhood of their quiet city.'[30] The Foxes therefore (Maggie had come this time with her mother, leaving Leah and Kate in New York) created a considerable stir, and their rooms were crowded with all the best people of the city.

There is something of a puzzle about Maggie's age at this time (it was December 1852). She herself asserts that she was then only thirteen; but others had already given her age as thirteen at the time of the first knockings at Hydesville, in 1848. Certainly an age of fifteen or sixteen would seem a great deal more probable in view of what followed – which was that young Dr Kane, coming one morning to see the mysterious rapping spirits for himself, fell in love at first sight with pretty Miss Fox. Before long he was besieging the ladies with a flurry of notes in the most correct possible style:

My Dear Madam [Dr Kane to Mrs Fox]:
    The day is so beautiful that I will call with Mrs Patterson, at half past two, in hopes of persuading Miss Margaret to take the vacant place in her carriage.
    Tell Miss Maggie to dress warmly.
    Faithfully your ob't servant,
    E.K.Kane.[31]

And before long the celebrated explorer was swearing the most ardent love and devotion to the young medium.

No one was more aware than he of the incongruity of the situation. In the normal way of things, it was inconceivable that a member of Philadelphia society would even meet, let alone consider, a girl from the New York backwoods. But one attribute of mediumship, as the Foxes had already found and as many more ladies of equally humble background were to find in the future, was that it broke through social barriers like no other career. Leah, her marriage to Mr Fish left far behind her, was already being courted by a wealthy banker, Mr Underhill. Kate was to end up marrying a respectable English barrister. So why not an explorer for Maggie?

The difference was that, unlike those other dazzled gentlemen, Dr Kane was never taken in by the rappings. He never made any secret of this. Maggie's strange career had been the means of their meeting, but in every other respect he thought it wholly deplorable. He referred to her 'melancholy' way of life; and if he did not say in so many words that she earned her living by fraud, he reminded her that other people often hinted as much. Would she be willing to give it all up for him, to acquire some education, to put her present life behind her? 'When you are thus changed, Maggie, I shall be proud to make you my wife.' Perhaps somewhat to Dr Kane's surprise, it seems that Maggie, although not averse to this view of the future, was not as enraptured as he was, or as he thought she should be. Never, throughout the several years of their correspondence, did he lose his sense of the great honour he was doing her.

At the time they met, Dr Kane was intended for a suitable and wealthy girl. He assured Maggie that since their meeting *that* was at an end; but he seemed nevertheless curiously unwilling to acknowledge his new love in public. 'I was unwilling to call upon you tonight for fear of talk', he wrote once, and another time, 'I will return if possible;

if not, good-bye. When this party leave, raise both window-curtains.'
(This was passed to her on a slip of paper in the guise of a question for
the spirits to answer at a seance.) Certainly he seemed to assume that
Maggie would stomach any amount of patronizing. 'Maggie, dear, you
have many traits which lift you above your calling,' he wrote her not
long after their first meeting.

> You are refined and lovable; and, with a different education, would have
> been innocent and artless; but you are not worthy of a permanent regard
> from me. You could never lift yourself up to my thoughts and my objects; I
> could never bring myself down to yours. . . . Maggie, darling, don't care for
> me any more. I love you too well to wish it, and you know now that I really
> am sold to different destinies; for just as you have your wearisome round of
> daily money-making, I have my own sad vanities to pursue. I am as devoted
> to my calling as you, poor child, can be to yours. Remember, then, as a sort
> of dream, that Doctor Kane of the Arctic Seas loved Maggie Fox of the
> Spirit Rappings.

And then almost immediately afterwards, he was full of love again,
and begging for a lock of Maggie's hair and reproaching her for her
coolness.

As time went on it became clear that his was no passing fancy. Dr
Kane started seriously to try and persuade Maggie to change her way
of life, which he found so distasteful. He hated the publicity of her life.
'It haunts me to see you perched over a twopenny song with "Margaretta" in great big print underneath', he wrote once. And not only
her image but, in a way, her person was public property. 'Maggie
Dearest: I am mad, angry, disgusted, at the hogs who have kept me
from you on this my last day,' he wrote at the end of a visit he paid to
New York while Maggie was at Leah's house on 26th Street. 'What a
life to lead – at the call of any fool who chooses to pay a dollar and
command your time.' And, in a revealing outburst: 'You know I am
nervous about the "rappings". I believe the only thing I ever was
afraid of was, this confounded thing being found out. I would not know
it myself for ten thousand dollars.'

As to Maggie's own feelings at this time, since few of her letters were
preserved, it is hard to know quite what they were. She could hardly
have failed to be dazzled by her conquest. Dr Kane was not only
eminently eligible; he was a noted figure, well known and highly
respected. But what he was asking her to abandon was her living – the
only life she knew – and her family. She knew that if she did quit her
'rappings', she would seriously harm her mother and sisters. She must
have felt very equivocal about her lover's scorn for what was, after all,

her way of life. As for his attitude to her family, while he was always
the soul of courtesy with Mrs Fox, and seems to have been very fond of
Kate, he made no secret of his dislike of Leah. For, it need hardly be
said, Mrs Fish was to the last degree averse to Dr Kane's courtship of
her sister. Not only was he trying to dissuade Maggie from playing her
part in the family business, but he was also trying to turn her against
Leah. 'Be careful not to mention me to the Tigress', he said once, and
another time, hopefully, 'I told my friend Mr — that you are all not
very cordial and will perhaps not stay very long in Twenty-sixth street.
He wrote to me today saying that Mrs Fish "really surprised him". He
is half inclined to believe. Oh, Maggie, 'tis a damned shame! Take
care of yourself. God bless you!' And he signed himself, disarmingly,
'Preacher'.

What was more, he was thus working his will on Maggie just as the
highest circles in the land seemed to be opening to them. Mrs Pierce,
the President's wife, whose son had just been killed in a railroad
accident, had invited them to Washington to give her a demonstration
of the rappings. And here was Dr Kane writing, 'Don't rap for Mrs
Pierce. Remember your promise to me. . . . No rapping for Mrs Pierce,
or evermore for anyone. I, dear Mag, am your best, your truest, your
only friend.'

Did Maggie believe this? She still addressed him as 'My dear Dr
Kane' and ended her letters, 'Ever most truly yours'. As for the con-
tents of these letters, they must have made Dr Kane's respectable
Philadelphia blood run cold. They are artless, and full of horrors.
From Washington she wrote:

> This afternoon I went out to do some shopping, and lost my way. I grew so
> frightened that I was obliged to ask a lady to show me the way home. When
> I entered the room I cried aloud; and looking up I saw General Hamilton,
> who asked me what was the matter. I told him I had lost my way, and that I
> did not like Washington at all. He laughed heartily, and insisted upon it
> that no young lady could ever lose her way in Washington unless she had
> some '*affaire du coeur*'. I did not deny the charge. Doctor, there is a rumor –
> so the General tells me – that you and I are to be married before you go to
> the Arctic. Last evening I saw a large company of officers. I believe they
> took me for the 'spirit', for they looked at me so incessantly that I nearly
> fainted; and I heard one gentleman ask his friend sitting next to him
> 'whether Miss Fox did not attend the ball'. His friend did not know; when
> he very coolly asked me, 'whether I was not at the ball given by Mrs B —,' I
> told him I was not there. He said if it was not myself it must certainly have
> been an apparition. He was a Frenchman.

But – *was* Dr Kane in fact planning to marry Miss Fox? Well, maybe he was; but, not immediately. No; while he was away in the Arctic she should wait for him, not at 26th Street, under the pernicious influence of Leah, but staying in the country in a respectable family he knew well, where she would at last gain the education necessary for the future Mrs Kane. 'No more Waddys, no more Greeleys, no more wiseacre scientific asses and pop-eyed committees of investigation! No more sympa- thizing evenings with your one true friend, nor dinners, and drives to quaint country inns!! Yes, dear darling, you must give up all these, and draw upon your self-denial and energies to sustain you; but then what a return!' Maggie was to live with a Scots family whose daughter was to be her governess, after which she would enter an academy in Albany and spend her vacations with Mrs Turner, a friend of the Kanes. Meanwhile he urged her, 'Do have neat neck and arm linen, and believe always and everywhere in the confiding love of Ly.'

It may be imagined that Leah did not like this plan. She did every- thing she could to prevent it, abused Dr Kane, forbade him her house, and assured him that if it were in her power he and Maggie should never meet again. A distraught 'Ly', facing the prospect of leaving for the frozen north without being able to say goodbye to his sweetheart, urged her to remember that Leah was not her legal guardian: that was her mother, who had always been his friend, but who, like the rest of the family, quailed before her eldest daughter. But finally it was settled: Maggie was to be educated, and her lover set off for the Arctic, clutching her portrait and leaving her a charming remembrance of the kind of conversation which must often have taken place between them:

> Dialogue between the sentimental PREACHER and practical MAGGIE:
> PREACHER: Dearest, may thy life be gilded as the sunset sky!
> MAGGIE: I really think I'd like a 'sassage'; hand me one, dear Ly.
> PREACHER: May thy thoughts be free from passion as an infant's dream!
> MAGGIE: There's a pin against your Maggie – catch it or I'll scream!
> PREACHER: Maggie, I have watched the feelings welling in thy breast.
> MAGGIE: Confound this frock! It always slips, and leaves me half undressed.
> PREACHER: I've often longed to make life's stream a fountain clear and bright.
> MAGGIE: How can I fix my hair, dear Ly, if you stand in the light? . . .

Dr Kane sailed for the Arctic in July 1853. He did not return until October 1855. And during this interval, as anyone might have predic- ted, Maggie's light-hearted attitude to her 'Ly' underwent a sea-change. Now that she no longer had the distractions and excitements of the life he so disapproved of, but was being properly educated according to his instructions; now, above all, that he was no longer constantly present, to be kept in proportion, but was only a delightful and glamorous memory, constantly revived by every detail of her present life – fond expectancy naturally filled her heart. The Kane family, though, were to prove a major obstacle. Not that they had ever met her. Somehow Elisha had never got around to introducing his sweetheart to his family circle. His reason, at the very beginning, was that they were moving house, so that it was not convenient. He would drive around town with Maggie perched beside him; would take her out to dinner at country inns where he introduced her as 'the future Mrs Kane'; he introduced her to some of his intimate friends and his brother John – though, somehow, his references to her meetings with John are always a little nervous. And, inevitably, the arrangements he made for her before his departure meant that a great many people were aware that he had a tender regard for her welfare. She was left in the care of his aunt, and his friend Mr Grinnell was deputed to keep an eye on her. But still there was no escaping the fact that she never had met his parents; and since it is inconceivable that they were unaware of what was going on, one can only conclude that it was they who declined this honour. Nevertheless, to their chagrin, as the time came when their son was due to return from his expedition, statements and speculations appeared in a great many newspapers to the effect that Dr Kane was engaged to Miss Fox, one of the spirit-rapping sisters, and would marry her on his return.

One day in October 1855, Maggie, who was staying with a friend in New York, heard that Elisha's ship was approaching, and would arrive the very next day; and sure enough, next day, as it sailed up the Bay of New York, she could hear the guns fire a greeting. The girl's excitement may be imagined. What should she do? Her friend insisted she should stay quietly at home and try to calm down. All that day they waited for the doorbell to ring; but by midnight it was clear that Dr Kane would not come. Next day Maggie could bear the suspense no longer, but went out for a walk. While she was out a caller did come; all her friend would say was that it was not Dr Kane. In fact it was a Kane family friend, asking for the return of all Elisha's letters. Mrs Walters, Maggie's friend, indignantly refused to give them to him, and when Maggie returned said nothing to her about this request. Still Dr Kane did not come; and when, finally and belatedly, he arrived at nine the next morning, Maggie indignantly refused to see him. He persisted; finally she came down; and soon they were in each other's arms, kissing and crying. Then Elisha said what he had come to say. His parents violently opposed any thought of his marrying Maggie; it was they who had prevented his seeing her until now; and he wanted Maggie to sign a paper which he could give to his mother, acknowledging that they had never had any intention of getting married, and had no such intention now.

Maggie signed the paper, in despair. Her idyll was at an end; and the violent controversy which now arose in the press with regard to the matter can have done little to comfort her. One paper said they were engaged, one said they were not; the Kane family inserted a notice in the Philadelphia papers denying that any such engagement existed, or ever had existed; and although kind Horace Greeley asked, in a *Tribune* editorial, 'What right has the public to know anything about an "engagement" or non-engagement between these young people? Whether they have been, are, may be, are not, or will be "engaged", can be nobody's business but their own . . .'[32] – the press, as always, did not allow fine feelings to come between it and news, and Maggie and Dr Kane were news.

Meanwhile, Dr Kane was in no mood to give up either Maggie or melodrama. He brought back the paper she had signed; he had been unable to bring himself to give it to his mother. So would he, after all, marry her? Certainly he was not relinquishing his proprietorship of her way of life. Towards the end of December he was still urging her to keep out of spirit circles: 'I can't bear to think of you sitting in the dark squeezing other people's hands.' And, unbelievably, shortly after: 'Maggie, be careful of Lish! Sometimes I am tempted to give up friends, name, position, honor – all for you, Maggie!' The poor girl might have been forgiven for wondering what, if anything, had been achieved over the past three years.

Others might wonder quite what it was about Maggie Fox that the Kane family found so supremely undesirable. After all, they had never actually met the girl; and those of Elisha's friends who had, concurred in finding her charming. There was, of course, the question of social standing, which the Kanes had and Maggie had not. But, after all, this was America, not the Austrian court. There were perhaps two reasons for the Kanes' reaction, quite apart from the distaste any quiet and respectable Victorian family might feel at seeing itself allied to so notorious a phenomenon as a spirit-rapping Fox sister.

One of these was theological. It was quite true that the spiritualist hypothesis – that the rappings (and, as time went on, other manifestations, such as table-turning and tipping) were communications from the dead – had been eagerly adopted and promulgated by many adherents of various Christian sects. But there were others who could not believe in this – in which case, the girls could be seen as perpetrating the grossest blasphemy. Calvinists hated it because the implication was that divine grace was enjoyed by everyone, elect or not. 'A miserable debauchee like Poe, who lived without the thought of a Redeemer, dies; and straightway, through a "medium" announces himself to be in glory,' thundered *Blackwood's Edinburgh Magazine*.[33] Others saw the rappings as originating with the devil, or with his near associates. Such topics were live and serious subjects for debate. The *Banner of Light*, a spiritualist newspaper which had been started in Boston, organized a series of four debates, on consecutive evenings, between a leading local Methodist clergyman and a spiritualist. The hall was filled on all four evenings, and the standard of argument was very high: the debates were later printed as a pamphlet.

But if the spiritualist connection might be undesirable theologically, there can be little doubt that it was the sexual behaviour of the spiritualists which gave rise to the greatest scandals at this time. The spiritualists were very much associated with those sections of society interested in social experiment, which often included sexual experiment, or free love, to use the faintly titillating phraseology of the time. Moreover, spiritualists so inclined now found, and, as we shall see, would continue to find, that the spirits offered them unequalled opportunities for sexual indulgence. This did not stop at sitting in the dark squeezing other people's hands. Doubtless plenty of this went on, but it was the solace of timid souls. But, as Judge Edmonds put it, 'In many cases . . . Spiritualists are deeply impressed with a want of congeniality between themselves, and their wives, or husbands, and they very often receive directions from the spirits that it is their duty to sever these uncongenial ties, and seek other affinities, more in harmony with their own spirits.'

It was a course followed by Edmonds himself, and also by John Spear, whom we have already encountered in connection with the new motive power. A contemporary describes him at this time, 'over fifty years of age, many years a clergyman of high moral standing. . . . He has now been nine years a medium.' (This was written in 1858.) 'His family is broken up, and the wife, to whom he was a most worthy husband, is forsaken; he is travelling with his paramour who acts as his scribe . . . and, last Fall, bore to him what they call a spiritual baby – but of sufficient materiality to counterbalance nine pounds.' Spear himself was quoted as saying, 'Cursed be the marriage constitution;

cursed be the relation of husband and wife; cursed be all who would sustain a legal marriage. What if there are a few tears shed, or a few hearts broken, they only go to build up a great principle, and all truths have their martyrs.'[34]

The same writer (who had, as might be guessed, his own personal axe to grind) went on to name thirteen other well-known spiritualists whose marriages had broken up as a result of their new enthusiasm, including the Hon Warren Chase, who recommended his 'free love' association on Long Island as an interesting home for spiritualists. He went on:

> I commenced writing this work with the full determination to publish the names of all mediums, as far as I could ascertain, who had broken off their marital relations. But . . . I find this startling fact (viz.), we have more than four hundred public mediums and spiritual lecturers in the northern States. At least three hundred of them have married. Nearly one-half of these have absolved [sic] their conjugal relations; a large proportion of the remainder are living in the most discordant relations, having abandoned the bed of their partner; many cohabiting with their 'affinities' by mutual consent of husband and wife; and a still greater number living in promiscuous concubinage. . . . And when we see John W. Edmonds visiting and holding private circles with Kate Hastings, the most notorious wanton in New York, it clearly shows how little virtue is respected, and how great a leveller, not upwards, but downwards, is Spiritualism.[35]

In the face of such tales, the unwillingness of the Kanes to have their beloved son marry Maggie becomes more understandable.

They tried to stop the marriage; but did they succeed? Like so much else in the Foxes' story, this, too, is full of ambiguities. For a while, after his return and his subsequent caddish behaviour, Maggie refused to have anything to do with Dr Kane. But by the spring of 1856 they were reconciled, and as fond as ever. Elisha was now working very hard on the book of his Arctic adventures – so hard, indeed, that his health, which had never been very robust, was quite broken by the effort. His plan was to sail for England in the autumn, to see Lady Franklin, whose husband he had gone to find, leaving his book with the publishers. As the summer wore on, the relations between the lovers clearly became more passionate. He was a man of principle, or so he kept saying. He had already avoided marrying Maggie before his last journey, excusing himself by saying she was not yet ready for him. Well, she had done all he asked; and however other spiritualists might behave, she was a respectable girl – of that, there seems no doubt. If he had had the slightest backbone, he would have married her and taken

her to England with him as his wife, but he had already shown that
backbone, in the last resort, was just what he did not have. He could
not stand up to his mother. On the other hand, he really did love
Maggie. So, inevitably, there was a compromise. Shortly before his
departure, Dr Kane and Maggie Fox went through a form of marriage, exchanging rings in the presence of a friend; thereafter they
looked on one another as man and wife.

Elaborate preparations were made for the journey. Kane was by
now very ill, and evidently doubted whether he would return from
the voyage. He spoke several times to Maggie and Mrs Fox about his
will, telling the mother that he had left a legacy to 'that dear child'.
In fact, even in the business of making a will he could not face the
wrath of his mother, though presumably she would not be seeing it
until he died – perhaps this showed some belief in spiritualism after
all! Maggie was not mentioned in the will; the legacy he spoke of was
left in a 'secret trust' to one of his brothers. Before he left he gave
Maggie an envelope. If she found herself in distress she must send it
to him; when he received that envelope he would set out instantly,
whatever he happened to be doing, and come back to her.

Finally he left, indecisive to the last. 'Tell me, Maggie, shall I go
or stay?' he cried to her as he set off for the last time; a question
which, since obviously she would have preferred him to stay with her,
did not require an answer. He left, and she did not see him again.
The voyage to England seriously undermined his health; and it was
decided, on his return, to send him directly to the West Indies. Her
last letter to him makes sad reading.

My dear Dr Kane:
  How are you? Why have you not written? Or, if you were too ill to
write, why have you not given Morton orders to do so? Had you attended
to this it would have made me much happier. I always thought you were
very wise; but, indeed, my powers of wisdom would have far surpassed
yours.
  I know not whether this will find you alive or not: only think how very
cruel it is in you to leave me to all manner of awful imaginings! I read the
newspaper articles, of course; but what reliance can I place on what they
say! One day they say that you are rapidly recovering, and perhaps the next
morning the old *Tribune* will say, – 'Dr Kane is dangerously ill, and it is
feared he will not live to return to his home again.' Oh, dear, I am so
unhappy! Mr Grinnell has returned, and I am sometimes tempted to ask
Dr Bayard to take me to his house, and see if he could give any satisfactory
news concerning your health. But there it is; I have been so very unkind to
the poor fellow in sending so abruptly for my letters, that I would not dare

go to him. Did the Consul hand you my letters? Are you Dr Kane or not? Really, I begin to doubt that I have ever known Dr Kane!

I am very well but wretchedly unhappy. Katie sends much love. From yours truly,

Margaret Fox.

P.S. – Do write at once, or get Morton to write.

But on his arrival at Havana, Dr Kane died.

Maggie, in all her dealings with Elisha Kane, seems much the more genuine and straightforward of the two. His behaviour, by comparison with hers, though affectionate, is always marred by his ultimate uncertainty, and his family were absolutely determined to avoid any obligation. At first they refused to pay Maggie anything at all from Elisha's estate. They denied that she had been married to him, and declared she had no rights at all over anything that was his. She was not at his funeral; and when, a short time later, a biography of him was published[36] – for his adventures had made him famous, and his book sold many thousands of copies – Maggie was not mentioned in it.

What could she do? The one thing she did have from him was his correspondence – the many love-letters he had sent her. The family knew this and were doing their utmost to deprive her of them. They had already tried once, and failed; and now they threatened to take them from her by process of law. Maggie therefore determined to have copies of the letters made, and to write a memoir which would incorporate them. This volume finally went to the press in 1862. The Kanes' reaction to this may be imagined. At the same time, Maggie was bringing a suit in the Philadelphia Orphans' Court for a share of her husband's estate – hoping, presumably, to prove her status by the letters. There was nothing for it but to try to compromise. It was agreed that one of Elisha's brothers would pay her an annuity equal to the interest on the money left her, in quarterly instalments. He would also pay her two thousand dollars down, to repay the expenses she had incurred. In return, she would discontinue her suit for dower and would seal up all the letters and copies, together with the MS of the memoir, and hand them to a trustee, who would be bound to prevent her access to them, and who would surrender them to the Kane family at her death. The brother, in his turn, executed another bond, guaranteeing to pay the moneys as stipulated; if he should fail to pay any quarterly instalment, Maggie was permitted to reclaim her letters and papers.

It was not long before the agreement was violated. The brother refused to pay her more than a thousand dollars, and demanded to be released from the other half of his bond. This Maggie refused to do, and began to sue him for it; but the suit was expensive, and dragged on. Meanwhile the quarterly annuity payments were missed from time to time, so that these, too, had to be solicited by a lawyer; and eventually the brother informed her that he would not pay the annuity at all unless she dropped altogether the suit for the remaining thousand dollars. This was the last straw. These payments were, after all, hers by right and agreement: why should she have to beg them as a favour? So she went to the trustee and reclaimed her letters, and published them, together with her memoir. But, like Dr Kane himself, they did her little good in the end.

How far it had all come from Hydesville now! By the time Maggie was entertaining Mrs Pierce, ex-Governor Tallmadge of Wisconsin, General Waddy Thompson, the one-time Ambassador to Mexico, and other Washington luminaries, to raps and table-tippings in 1853, many thousands of others were communicating with the dead by similar means. On 17 April 1854, Senator James Shields of Illinois presented a petition signed by fifteen thousand of his constituents, all of them spiritualists, demanding that Congress finance an official commission which would investigate the apparent attempt on the part of beings from another world to communicate with this one. Whatever the senators themselves might or might not believe – and many of them, despite attending the seances, were unconvinced: 'This is all humbug, but it's worth a dollar,' declared one drunken but not unrepresentative legislator, gazing into the eyes of Katie Fox[37] – they could not ignore the convictions of such a large body of voters.

The debate on the petition was marked by a certain amount of waggery:

MR WELLER: What does the Senator propose to do with the petition?
MR PETTITT: Let it be referred to three thousand clergymen. (Laughter)
MR SHIELDS: I present the petition.
MR SUMNER: To what committee is it to be referred?
MR WELLER: I suggest that it be referred to the Committee on Foreign Relations. (Laughter)
MR SHIELDS: I am willing to agree to the reference.
MR WELLER: It may be that we have to enter into foreign relations with these spirits. (Laughter) . . .
MR SHIELDS: This is an important subject and should not be sneered away in this manner. (Loud laughter) I was willing to agree to the motion of the Senator from California, but I do not wish the petition to go to the

Committee on Foreign Relations unless the chairman of that committee is perfectly satisfied that he can do the subject justice. (Laughter) I had thought of proposing to refer the matter to the committee on post offices and post roads, because there may be a possibility of establishing a spiritual telegraph between the material and the spiritual world. (Laughter)[38]

But despite the laughter and the corny jokes, the spiritualists were not to be so lightly disposed of. By the time the twentieth anniversary of the Rochester Rappings came round, it was estimated that there were eleven million believers in America alone.[39] The numbers increased; but the forms remained remarkably constant. The methods of 'communication' established during the first few years continue in use, many of them virtually unchanged, to this very day. In this characteristic some of them might truthfully be described as cultural fossils, since the forms were dictated so very much by the particular time and place from which they sprang.

Take, for instance, the popularity of Indian spirit guides. It was very early on established that a medium communicated with the spirits not always, or indeed often, directly, but through the good offices of a 'control' or 'spirit guide', a friendly denizen of the next world who would, so to speak, perform the necessary introductions, and lead the different communicating spirits to the right place. It might be imagined that each medium would find his or her own spirit guide. But in fact there was remarkably little individual initiative shown in this matter. We shall see that the pirate John King and his daughter Katie acted as guides to innumerable mediums. And, from the very first, among the most popular of all spirit guides were the departed souls of American Indians. Time and again we meet them, Raging Bull, White Feather, Pink Cloud, Feda, Pocha and the rest of their tribe, officiating at seances not only in their native continent but in the most unlikely parts of Europe and Asia. A book of advice to mediums was dismissive of these Indians. 'Never prostitute yourself, or the cause you serve, by stooping to personate a dead Indian, or the majority of the more intelligent spiritualists will promptly brand you as a fraud,' it advised;[40] but the author showed too much faith in the discernment of most spiritualists.

One possibility is that these guides developed from the Indian spirits who used to visit the Shakers. The Shakers, one of the visionary religious and socially experimental sects who so eagerly took up spiritualism from the first, had experienced spirit manifestations through rappings, movings of furniture, visions, trances, clairaudience and clairvoyance since the time of their foundation at the beginning of the nineteenth century, but they also communed more directly with the spirits, who would knock on the door while a Shaker meeting was in progress and ask permission to enter. The spirits would then troop in and take possession of the Shakers' bodies. Then there would be shouting, whooping and wild dancing, and the Shakers would talk 'Indian' amongst themselves, dance 'Indian' dances, and consider themselves possessed by the spirits of red men. This was presumably no more than a variant on the well-known ecstatic phenomenon of 'speaking in tongues'; the 'tongues' in this case being attributed to the Indians because, at this time, upstate New York and its surroundings were Indian territory, the various tribes speaking their own languages, unknown and certainly outlandish to Shaker ears. So the tradition of possession by Indian spirits was well established among the Shakers, many of whom later took up spiritualism; this tradition then spread to spiritualists quite unconnected with its origins. (Indian spirit guides are still not unknown in spiritualist circles.)

Spirit drawing of an Indian spirit guide

We have seen that, in taking apparently disembodied rappings and movements of furniture, especially tables, to be communications from the spirit world, the Hydesville group and their followers were part of a very long tradition, mystical and magical. But in the middle of the nineteenth century the rappings, considered as spirit communications, were satisfactory from another, almost converse, point of view. For – extreme sects apart – this was not a mystical age. It was, rather, the age of scientific progress. Science was concerned with the tangible, religion with the intangible. The two often seemed irreconcilable, and Darwin, with the publication of the *Origin of Species* in 1859, was to make them even more so: a metaphysical milestone which had, as we shall see, an enormous effect upon the later development of spiritualism.

But here at least was something: a religious fact. Thus, the Rev Thomas Wentworth Higginson, a well-known clergyman, speaking in New York in 1858, said: 'The progress of our age is remarkable for the quality of its facts. From the discovery by Galileo of the pressure of the atmosphere, how far have we advanced! What a step to steam from the brute muscle of the horse! Then the imponderables – electricity, magnetism and their combinations and applications; then the discovery of a human power akin to this – a spiritual electricity – the power of man over man, of soul over soul.'[41] A fact – and what a fact! 'I suppose that there is no fact so absolutely momentous to the human soul as the personal conviction of immortality,' said Mr Higginson, and gave it as his opinion that all the suffering there ever was upon earth stemmed more from doubts upon this score than from any other cause. And now – no more doubts: it was proved!

Was it? Well, perhaps; some, more obdurate, or perhaps merely perverse, were not convinced. But certainly where people did accept the new fact, their view of life and death was profoundly altered, and their actions and reactions altered accordingly. Parties would be held to celebrate a loved one's leaving the body and attaining the shining life of the soul; for would one not now be able to stay in touch through the new spiritual telegraph? In a more bizarre development, Benjamin Pierce, son of the President, who, it will be remembered, had died in a railroad crash, was married years after his death to one Katie Eaton, who had died at the age of only three weeks, to the accompaniment of great rejoicings at the Eaton home at Fort Leavenworth, Kansas.

Calvinists railed at this general assumption of glorious immortality for all, but there were many, in this centre of Calvinism, who were only too glad to get rid of the fear of damnation it engendered. As a spirit speaking through the mouth of Judge Edmonds put it, 'Fear of God is a terrible fear. The soul shrinks within itself in contemplating the jealousy of an omnipotent God. Every nerve thrills with unutterable anguish at this anger, and many have wished that God had never existed, or had never caused them to exist.'[42] Edmonds enlarged on this theme, speaking this time as himself. Authority, he said, had been the curse of the religious world for two thousand years. One great good which spiritualism had accomplished was to destroy all faith in prescription and authority, and throw men back on their own investigations.[43]

Certainly spiritualism rendered heaven utterly democratic and accessible to all in a way which appealed to the American view of things. And this accessibility extended to far more than free entry to heaven. In virtually all other forms of religion contact with the deity is maintained through a select priesthood, usually male, which is either born or lengthily trained to the job. And now anyone who wanted might personally contact the next world! The very triviality of what were accepted as spirit communications had a good deal to do with the popular nature of this new priesthood. The actual phenomena presented at seances were rarely impressive in themselves. Their effect lay in what they were supposed to represent. But when it came to the simple mechanics of spreading the faith, then this triviality became a distinct advantage. Rappings, table-tiltings and the rest might or might not be the work of discarnate spirits, but the fact was that they were phenomena within the power of anybody to produce. Whether so many would have been capable of anything much deeper or more complex is another question. Thomas Wentworth Higginson, defending the new cult against popular criticisms, said, 'They say that the utterances through mediums are poor and weak. How should they be otherwise? The answers are as good as the questions.'[44] And the questioner this time might well be giving the answers next.

So Hydesville was left far behind. And Maggie, Kate and Leah – were they, too, left behind? As might have been expected, the erstwhile Mrs Fish had done far the best of the three. Whatever spiritualism might or might not have done for her sisters, she had drawn nothing but profit from it. By the end of the 1850s Leah had divorced Mr Fish and was married to Mr Daniel Underhill, a wealthy New York banker. She had a fine house on 37th Street which she opened for spiritualist receptions on one evening of each week. Although everyone who attended the very earliest demonstrations had agreed that Maggie and Kate produced the actual phenomena, and Leah merely stage-managed their show, she had now acquired for herself the reputation of being the best and most powerful medium of her day, and the privilege of being invited to her seances was highly prized. Among her regular guests were Horace Greeley, James Fenimore Cooper, Robert Dale Owen, Washington Irving, Henry Longfellow, James Greenleaf Whittier – the cream of the spiritualist cream.

Maggie and Kate were not so successful. As Maggie had found, it was not so easy to jump the classes if the other party was not a believer. She was broken by the Kane episode, and never really recovered from it. She went on giving her spiritualist demonstrations: for whatever 'Lish' might have wished for her, he had so left matters that she had to go on making her living in the only way she knew. Maggie went down in the world as Leah went up: 'The best test, rapping and physical medium I ever met, as well as one of the kindest and most noble-hearted of women,'[45] was the opinion of one who only met her after her incarnation as Mrs Underhill. Leah soon disowned her sister altogether.

As for Kate, after the closing of Leah's 26th Street establishment, she found employment with a Mr Horace H. Day, a wealthy spiritualist who owned a large India rubber works. He had taken the lease of a building situated in the heart of New York's business district, at 553 Broadway. From this house Mr Day published and sold a paper, *The Christian Spiritualist*. Other books and pamphlets relating to the subject were also sold there. The upper floors were occupied by the printers, and in the large back drawing-room sat Kate Fox, who was engaged at a salary of twelve hundred dollars a year to sit free for the public every morning. There she spent every day, 'poor, patient Kate Fox, in the midst of a captious, grumbling crowd of investigators, repeating hour after hour the letters of the alphabet, whilst the no less *poor, patient* Spirits rapped out names, ages and dates to suit all comers'.[46]

2
Mr Sludge and Other Mediums

By 1850 – only two years after the Hydesville happenings – it was estimated that there were a hundred mediums in New York City, and fifty or sixty 'private circles' in Philadelphia.[1] A decade later, believers could be numbered in their millions. 'My naburs is mourn harf crazy on the new fangled idear about Sperrets,' wrote 'Artemus Ward' (Charles Farrar Browne).

> Sperretoul Sircles is held nitely & 4 or 5 long hared fellers has settled here and gone into the sperret bizniss excloosively. A atemt was made to git Mrs A. Ward to embark into the Sperret bizniss, but the atemt faled. 1 of the long hared fellers told her she was an ethereal creeter and wood make a sweet mejium, whareupon she attact him with a mop handle & drove him out of the house.[2]

In displaying this firmness of character, Mrs Ward was unusual. Most people were only too eager to explore the suggestion that they might have mediumistic gifts. At their most trivial, as we have seen, these were simply the expression of a popular craze – though nonetheless seemingly mysterious. For instance, the diarist George Templeton Strong, a stalwart of New York society, records that on 7 March 1853, he and his wife went to 'the Lydigs Saturday night. Met William Schermerhorn and wife there, and *moved tables*. Miss Maggie is a "medium". Her table answers questions by the alphabet. . . . Very queer indeed; no deliberate mystification, unquestionably. Could the effects have been produced by the unconscious muscular effort of any person assisting? Hardly.'[3] In fact, that was exactly what did produce such effects, as Michael Faraday had just demonstrated, and as the French scientist Chevreul had shown twenty years earlier in relation to the 'magic pendulum'. But, as anyone will know who has taken part in similar sessions, that does not make the end result any less extraordinary to experience.

Whether or not Miss Maggie Lydig was a 'medium', it was quickly recognized that, for simple table-tipping or even rapping, it was sufficient to assemble almost any group of people, whether or not they contained anyone with an accredited gift. *The Spiritualist*, a weekly magazine published in England in the 1870s, carried every week a set of instructions for those eager to find out more: 'Inquirers into Spiritualism should begin by forming spirit circles in their own homes, with no Spiritualist or professional medium present. Should no results be obtained on the first occasion, try again with other sitters. One or more persons possessing medial powers without knowing it are to be found in nearly every household.' More specific helpful hints were given. The room should be comfortable, but cool rather than warm. People who did not like each other should not sit in the same circle. Powerful physical mediums (i.e. those who could produce physical effects such as moving furniture, etc.) were likely to be 'of an impulsive, affectionate and genial nature', a description few would be likely to reject if applied to themselves. The first indication of spirit presence would probably be a cool wind playing over the hands of the participants. . . .

Thus anyone could get started in spiritualism. But in fact it was unlikely that one would do so if one had had no previous personal experience of the phenomena. Spiritualism, and especially mediumship, was like a contagious infection, now running in epidemic form. Thus, almost as soon as the Fox girls began to display their powers, Kate was sent to stay with friends in Auburn, N.Y.; and within a very short time various Auburn ladies began to exhibit very similar propensities. One, for example, was able to prophesy. She said she was going to fall ill at a certain time – and she did; she dreamt that a fire was about to break out, woke up – and, lo, a candle had fallen over, and was just setting fire to the bed curtains. 'It came upon them like the small-pox, and the land was spotted with mediums before the wise and prudent had had time to lodge the first half-dozen in a madhouse,' wrote the English mathematician Augustus de Morgan, himself an early and unexpected convert to the faith.[4]

The reader who looks through the enormous pile of books and pamphlets in which people give accounts of their mediumship, or describe the mediumship of others, will find that the most interesting question of all is rarely even broached. We know what these people did; but what did they really think?

Elisha Kent Kane was sure he knew the answer to such questions. Mediums, he believed, were all cynics. In 1853 he wrote to Kate Fox:

I saw a young man, with a fine forehead and expressive face, but a countenance deeply tinged with melancholy, seize the hand of this medium. . . . He
seized her hand and begged her to answer a question which I could not
hear. Instantly she rapped, and his face assumed a positive agony; the
rapping continued, his pain increased; I leaned forward, feeling an utter
detestation of the woman who could inflict such torment. . . . Now, Katy,
although you and Maggie never go so far as this, yet circumstances must
occur where you have to lacerate the feelings of other people. . . . You do
things now which you would never have dreamed of doing years ago; and
there will come a time when you will be worse than Mrs Fish, a hardened
woman, gathering around you victims of a delusion.

But was the seance always a conscious fraud? Often, of course, it
was – although this is not always as easy to carry off convincingly as
might be imagined. For example, Kate and Maggie Fox were
effectively destroyed by years of carrying through a deception against
the grain of their natures. Mrs Fish was able to survive, not only
because she was much tougher than her sisters, but because she was
much clearer-headed. She had summed up the situation from the
start; they never really came to terms with it. Once again one can draw
a parallel between Leah Fish and Madame Blavatsky. Both were
under no illusions about what it was they were doing, though H.P.B.
possessed a charm which always seems to have eluded Mrs Fish.

Madame Blavatsky founded the Theosophical Society in New York
in 1881. It was an amalgam of eastern esotericism and spiritualism;
she had, until that date, been active as a spiritualist medium. The
disarming thing about her is that she saw theosophy as a vast and
delightful joke which she played at the world's expense – and if,
incidentally, she was enabled to get rich, or at least to live a very
decent sort of life – well, why not? No one else was much the poorer for
it. 'If personal sensibilities can be trusted, she is a genuine being, with
a vigorous nature intellectual as well as emotional, and a real desire for
the good of mankind,' wrote Henry Sidgwick of her not long before she
was unmasked in her fraudulence by the Society for Psychical
Research, of which he was a founder-member and leading light: thus
demonstrating the variable trustworthiness of human sensibilities. He
went on:

This impression is all the more noteworthy as she is externally unattractive
– with her flounces full of cigarette ashes – and not prepossessing in
manner. Certainly we like her, both Nora [Mrs Sidgwick] and I. If she is a
humbug, she is a consummate one: as her remarks have the air not only of
spontaneity and randomness but sometimes of an amusing indiscretion.

Thus in the midst of an account of the Mahatmas in Tibet, intended to give us an elevated view of these personages, she blurted out her candid impression that the chief Mahatma of all was the most utter dried-up old mummy she ever saw.[5]

Mrs Fish was never in the same class as this. (Henry Sidgwick was so unimpressed by the one Fox sister he met, Kate, that he remarked she must 'for the present drop . . . out of my "case for Spiritualism"': a curious remark considering that she had for a while been almost the only case *for* it.) But what the two did have in common was the perceived end of their effort. They both saw in spiritualism and its offshoots the means of making a good life for themselves, and of acquiring a satisfying power over other people at the same time. Once this was clear, the rest followed.

And there were a great many other people who, once the path was opened up, perceived and pursued the same opportunities. For women especially, there were not at this period so many ways of making a decent living – particularly if (like the Fox sisters themselves) they were uneducated. Thus we find the mother of the 'Magnetic Girl' writing a pathetic letter to the *Spiritual Magazine*, a London publication:

> I had hoped that this power in my daughter would have been the means of aiding, and honestly too, in the support of our family, for my husband is at times scarcely able to work for asthma; but the effect of the misrepresentations in *All the Year Round* has been to deprive us of that aid willingly given by Charlotte. I am thankful, however, that . . . some enquiries have been made, and the phenomena have been witnessed, both here and in their own houses, by some parties of ladies and gentlemen, to whom, if need be, I may refer. All the phenomena witnessed through my daughter, are perhaps more satisfactory to parties at their own residences, but we should be glad to satisfy enquirers into those phenomena which relate to the irons, at our own abode, in the afternoon of Wednesdays and Saturdays; the other afternoons my daughter attends school.[6]

No explanation is given of the function of the mysterious irons.

Different operators had different techniques for producing raps and other 'phenomena'. Quite a cottage industry arose preparing special equipment for them, including, for example, telescopic reaching rods by which objects might be mysteriously moved around the (darkened) room – tambourines were especially prone to fly in this manner; luminous paint for the preparation of ghostly materializations; specially prepared shoes, which might have a rigid, heavy toecap, and out of which the medium could slide his or her foot backwards, thus giving those who were supposed to be 'controlling' the feet the impression that they were still doing so. Other shoes might be built to produce raps. This was evidently the case at one seance where the 'media', both male, having arrived at the house, insisted that they must be last going upstairs to the seance room, despite the fact that it was considered most indecorous for a gentleman to climb a staircase behind a lady. But they were not to be moved on a mere point of manners, being determined that nobody should get a glimpse of their shoes. These particular 'media' put on a most artistic performance, ending with the words, 'We are going off', followed by diminishing rapping indicating that the spirits were going away.[7]

PRIVATE SITTINGS IN THE DARK.

The physical phenomena, so called, presented relatively little difficulty (at least at first; as time went on they became much more complicated). More demanding were what very soon came to be known as 'tests', where the medium told the sitter about various relatives and acquaintances, living and (especially) dead. Once again, there were a number of recognized methods in use. Some were very down-to-earth. When a medium visited a new town, he was advised to visit the local cemetery and make a note of names, dates and any other information to be obtained from the tombstones. He might also consult the 'Blue Book' for the area, a compilation circulated among mediums listing, for an increasing number of places, the names of leading spiritualists likely to attend seances, with descriptions, family histories and details (deceased spouses, children, parents, etc.) and other information likely to be of use. After the medium had left town he would add his portion of new information to this useful manual.

Other methods involved the use of elementary psychology. One popular trick was the reading of messages written on sheets of paper which were folded up tightly, placed in a basket, and brought up to the medium, who 'read' them by holding them, still folded, to his forehead; he then confirmed the contents. Generally this trick was managed by the technique known as 'one ahead': the first message 'read' is acknowledged by a plant in the audience, the medium then opens the paper to confirm it, and is thus able to read what is really written there – which is duly read out as the next message. A combination of this trick with the use of acquired information could be most effective.

If the history of the widow Jones – who sits opposite – appears in your diary . . . you may be quite sure that her ballot will contain the name of her deceased husband; therefore, when she is called upon to write, you will not be obliged to change her ballot, or even to touch it, but may boldly invite the most skeptical person present to place the closed ballot on your forehead, when, as he pronounces the letters of the alphabet, you can correctly spell out the name. This piece of strategy will throw the skeptic completely off his guard, after which he will freely testify, with every other member of the circle, that you read all the ballots without taking them into your hands.[8]

There were many similar devices. For instance, if you got someone to write down a list of six names, one under the other, of which one was to be that of a dead relative, the medium then to indicate the correct name: the writer would almost certainly hesitate over five out of the six names. . . . And so on. Some methods necessitated the use of sleight of hand. One observer saw a medium tell a sceptical and uncooperative sitter what his (the sitter's) name was and what the worry was that was on his mind and that had driven him to a medium, by overawing him, holding his eyes, tapping his chest, palming a letter which was in his breast pocket, doing a trick during which he read the letter, replacing the letter and then using the information in it.

Such were the techniques used by the highly professional fraternity of fraudulent mediums who soon grew and multiplied. It will be seen that these persons, whatever one's opinion of them might be, certainly gave value for money; and, moreover, worked hard for that money. And it may be remarked that most of the really proficient conjuring was done by men; women tended more to tamer manifestations and vague pronouncements, aided by 'fishing' – hazarding a likely guess and following the sitter's reactions. The Fox sisters certainly used this technique. Any too definite statement of course carried the risk that it might be seen to be definitely untrue. When Dr Livingstone was missing in Africa, and was presumed to be dead, a well-known London medium, Mrs Marshall, received a visit from his spirit who told her and her sitter how he had been killed by natives and eaten. The sitter, Signor Damiani, made a note of this and put the paper in an envelope, to be opened when Dr Livingstone's fate should be known. 'But we all know [now] that Livingstone was not killed at all, and that the spirit was simply lying.'[9] Damiani does not seem to have entertained the notion that the liar might have been Mrs Marshall.

Clearly no one could carry out such elaborate trickery, with all the attendant preparations, who did not know exactly what he was up to. These effects depended on the medium's being totally in control of what was going on; and if he was thus in control, then it was obvious that there was no room in the act for any quantity so imponderable as a spirit. Such shows might be excellent value, taken as the performances of itinerant illusionists; but when they purported to be spiritual revelations they were both fraudulent and cynical in the highest degree.

People inimical to the new sub-religious epidemic – such as the philosopher Ralph Waldo Emerson, who, according to Moncure Conway, called spiritualism 'this rat-hole revelation', and many others, their objections founded on both religious and moral grounds – were of course only too ready to attribute these low motives, and the accompanying low cunning, to all mediums. But to make such a generalization was as simplistic as to believe that all mediums were genuinely in touch with spirits. For while it was undoubtedly true that a great many mediums – among them the most effective and convincing – were cynical opportunists, it was equally true that a great many others believed in the reality of what was happening to them as fervently as any of their sitters.

Moncure Conway, the Virginian divine and radical thinker who became the leading light of London's humanists in the 1880s and 1890s, gives an extraordinary picture of a training-school for mediums which he visited in Whitechapel. Conway would have like to believe – he had been deeply distressed by the death of a child – but could not stomach what the spiritualists had to offer. 'In a large, dingy room about twenty men and women sat at an uncovered table fifteen feet long,' he wrote.

> All except myself were 'mediums', and the object of their meeting was that the spirits might develop their powers further, each in his or her specialty. There were writing, rapping, pantomimic and musical mediums. . . . One of the pantomimic mediums (who described one's deceased friend by imitating his manner) began gesticulating before me, clearing his throat, and turning his head to one side. I could not recall any who did that, but said I would think it over.

Presently they became noisy; there were loud raps around the table; some talked to the spirits that rapped, some uttered their inspirations; they all talked at once. The word 'bedlam' arose in my mind but swiftly resolved itself into its original 'Bethlehem', for it was in the Eastern region that I had read of things like the wild scenes before me. I did not need any Peter to tell me that these people under their Whitechapel Pentecost were not 'drunken', but realized the kind of frenzy that overtook possession of those early disciples who really believed that a dead human being had returned to life. . . . Grotesque features vanished under the thought that if I should believe – really, and without any trace of doubt – that a deceased person had spoken to me, I also would be frantic, and my life revolutionized. [Conway added:] How often in the Royal Society building had I seen the great men of science displaying by their lenses the miracles of nature! But how petty would all their wonders appear if one of those frantic mediums could utter a single word proved to have come from another world![10]

But how did these people get to the point where they were assembled in this strange gathering? How did they know they were mediums? What did it *feel* like?

Not surprisingly, convincing accounts of these things are hard to find. Clearly these people had been through some kind of mystical crisis. Such things are hard to describe to others; and these were not often particularly articulate people. There are, of course, any number of passages where mediums *purport* to describe how they came to be the special people they are. Leah Fish, even, said that the Fox family had always been inclined to the 'mediumistic vein, that her mother's family had had the gift of second sight, foretelling events and seeing phantom funerals, etc.' – and the words mean as little to us as they did to her. Leah's great friend Emma Hardinge Britten, one of the most famous mediums on either side of the Atlantic and a prolific writer on the subject, carries equally little conviction:

The Spiritual gifts that are normal to mediumistic individuals from birth may change and alter during earth life, but never wholly depart, and as this was happily my own case, and I was 'born a witch', as some of my public opponents have politely informed the world, I have experienced many changes, though no actual loss of mediumistic enfoldment. . . . Looking back upon my own earliest recollections, I fancy that I was never young, joyous or happy, like other children; my delight was to steal away alone and seek the solitude of woods and fields, but above all to wander in churchyards, cathedral cloisters and old monastic ruins. Here strange sounds would ring in my ears, sometimes in the form of exquisite music, sometimes in voices uttering dim prophecies of future events, especially

coming misfortunes. At times forms of rare beauty or appalling ugliness
flitted across my path. . . .[11]

The hallmark is that of what was expected, not of what was
experienced.

What genuinely happened to people is at once more trivial and more
dramatic. Here, for example, is a woman who, in 1853, suddenly found
herself the source of 'rappings'. She was induced to join a circle,

> and the table we surrounded soon began to oscillate rapidly. My right arm
> was seized with a convulsive tremor, and though then in a 'positive condi-
> tion' it refused obedience to my will. . . . A pencil and paper were lying on
> the table. *The pencil came into my hand*: my fingers were clenched on it! An
> unseen iron grasp compressed the tendons of my arm: my hand was flung
> violently forward on the paper, and I wrote *meaning* sentences, without any
> intention, or knowing what they were to be. . . . The medium . . . said that
> my hand rested on a cloud, while my guardian-spirit – my father – dictated
> to me.[12]

The lapse into medium-speak at the end throws the real experience
into sharp focus. The experience sounds perhaps less spiritual than
hysterical; but the boundary between mysticism and hysteria is notoriously ill-defined.

The next writer found that, while sitting in church, he felt his will
more and more detached from the parts of his body – hands, knees – so
that he felt he would be quite unable to move them should he try to do
so. The hymn which ended the service always snapped him out of this
condition.

> In proportion as the will became passive, the activity of my imagination
> was increased, and I experienced a new and strange delight in watching the
> play of fantasies which appeared to come and go independently of myself.
> There was still a dim consciousness of outward things mingled with my
> condition; I was not beyond the recall of my senses. But one day I remem-
> ber, as I sat motionless as a statue, having ceased any longer to attempt to
> control my dead limbs, more than usually passive, a white shining mist
> gradually stole around me; my eyes finally ceased to take cognisance of
> objects; a low, musical humming sounded in my ears, and those creatures
> of the imagination which had hitherto crossed my brain as *thoughts* now
> spoke to me as audible voices.[13]

Not long after this he visited the Fox sisters, who were then in their
early days in New York, and was much impressed by them. When
circles were formed in his home town – as they were in just about every

town in the northern United States – he became a medium. And a believing medium he remained for ten years, despite some things that puzzled him: 'The spirits of our deceased relatives and friends announced themselves, and generally gave a correct account of their earthly lives. I must confess, however, that, whenever we attempted to pry into the future, we usually received answers as ambiguous as those of Grecian oracles.' This man finally left spiritualist circles when he realized that he and his group were being used by the leading male participant to conduct a 'spiritual affinity' with a girl member, and that the man was just about to leave his unfortunate wife on the girl's account. He refused to allow himself and his powers to be used as an excuse for what he saw as disgusting and immoral behaviour; but nevertheless, he could, even long afterwards, see no other explanation than the spiritual for the state that overtook him on these occasions.

Such abdications of muscular and intellectual control were a very usual prelude to mediumship. But it took an unusually detached and analytical intelligence to work out what was happening and its relationship to anything that might follow: the kind of intelligence not usually to be found twined in the meshes of trance mediumship. We do, however, have at least one such analysis: that of the English engineer J.W.Dunne, famous for his book *An Experiment with Time*. This, his best-known work, first published in 1927, is an account of a series of prophetic dreams which he experienced, but gives little indication of the background of the writer. However, just before he died, Dunne wrote an autobiographical account of himself and his mystical experiences called '*Intrusions*' (the intrusions being those of other-worldly intelligences trying to communicate with this world). In it he discloses a background of spiritualistic dabblings which are quite unrevealed in the earlier work. As a young man in South Africa, Dunne himself became a medium. He witnessed scenes which recall those described by Moncure Conway, and was himself adept at automatic writing – until one day he realized that he knew *what the end of the sentence he was writing was to be*. In that moment he realized that the intelligence which guided his hand was none other than his own, albeit a submerged facet of it.

Practically all intelligent spiritualists are fully aware that those early stages of apparent 'mediumship' which are observable in a considerable percentage of beginners are merely examples of self-deception [he wrote, perhaps a trifle optimistically]. They put up with them, however, on the score that these things may be the necessary preludes to performances more sincere. That I doubted. To my mind the self-deception would become merely more and more profound, more and more unnoticed by the victim, until it would become almost impossible for any real intruding intelligence to get a genuine message through that egotistical crust. I had good grounds for that belief. . . . I had experimented with myself freely. . . . From the initial 'goose-flesh' shudderings (started, I found, by any sudden expectation that one was about to be influenced by some mysterious agency) to the adaptation of the vocal chords to the *expected* impulse to speak, was a remarkably easy step; and I could realize clearly that any ensuing speech would be as much one's own composition as the script in automatic writing. . . . To give imagination that much rein might lead to self-hypnotism – sham, self-induced trance, in which one's continued self-deception would be *completely* beyond one's power of recognition, and become a source of intellectual danger to all credulous listeners.[14]

This description – perhaps the coolest analysis of its kind ever written – should be borne in mind throughout what follows.

The mediums multiplied. But they did not, on the whole, develop. The stationary quality, which has been such a salient characteristic of all investigations and research in this field, set in early with the very phenomena which were the subject of the interest. There were rappings, there were table-tiltings, there were messages using the alphabet, there was a certain amount of speaking in tongues, but such things could not hold people's interest for ever. And yet, what more could be done? Certainly it seemed unlikely that the Fox girls would be the source of any more innovations. Their ingenuity was taxed to the limit in the maintenance of the *status quo*, and their energies entirely occupied with spreading the faith as it stood.

However, within two years of the Hydesville happenings, powers of mediumship manifested themselves in a young man who was to become perhaps the most famous name in spiritualism. This was Daniel Dunglas Home, who in 1850 was seventeen, and living with his aunt in Greeneville, Connecticut.

A great deal is known about the life of D. D. Home. He himself wrote various autobiographical volumes; his second wife wrote a book about him; at least three other biographies have been published, to say nothing of numerous short sketches; he figures in many of the memoirs and volumes of correspondence of the time; and, lastly, there have been detailed examinations of various individual aspects and exploits of his career. Yet he remains a mysterious and shadowy figure. It is as if he were the protagonist of a badly written novel whose author has not thought about those aspects of the character not immediately involved in the action. Partly this may be a result of conscious policy.

Home was a magician, and the magician's stock-in-trade is mystery. Certainly he was more adept at preserving the aura of magic than anyone who preceded him, or any of his successors. D.D.Home performed astonishing feats. He floated in the air, he elongated his body, he raised heavy tables without touching them, he depressed spring balances, also without touching them – and he was never exposed in fraud. Many people since have offered explanations of how he might have achieved his effects, but the fact remains that nobody ever caught him at it at the time. He seemed, to his contemporaries, hardly human. On hearing of Home's marriage, Elizabeth Barrett Browning, a firm believer in the genuineness of the manifestations, wrote to her sister, 'Certainly her taste must be extraordinary. . . . Think of the conjugal furniture floating about the room at night, Henrietta.'[15]

A spirit woodcut of D.D.Home

Even when describing himself, Home preserves an unbreakably two-dimensional façade. Giving an account of himself to the London Dialectical Society, which was conducting an investigation into spiritualism, Home said: 'I am . . . extremely nervous and suffer much from ill-health. I am Scotch, and second sight was early developed in me. I am not imaginative; I am sceptical, and doubt things that take place in my own presence. I try to forget all about these things, for the mind would become partly diseased if it were suffered to dwell on them. I

therefore go to the theatre and to concerts for change of attention.'[16] It
is a presented front that we see; and the question with Home is
whether, by that stage, there was actually anything behind it, whether
he was more than his façade. (It was then 1871, and he had been an
active medium for more than twenty years.) It is a question which
immediately throws doubt on his genuineness. People are of a piece; if
one aspect of them is worrying, then it is hard not to distrust the whole
of them. And there were certainly plenty of people who distrusted
Home. He was a man who inspired violent feelings. People were either
his devoted partisans or his sworn enemies. It was a circumstance
which (as we shall see) was not without its uses from a technical point
of view.

Daniel Dunglas Home was born in Edinburgh. His family (upon
this he was later very insistent) was descended from a by-blow of the
Earls of Home, but they were poor; and at the age of nine, Dan was
sent to live with his aunt, his mother's sister, in America. The rest of
the family followed some years later, but Dan remained with his aunt.
In his autobiography, Home insists that he had had 'spiritual' and
'second sight' experiences from a very early age, foreseeing the death of
a schoolfriend at the age of twelve and communicating with his spirit
afterwards. What is certain is that in 1850, at the age of seventeen, he,
in company with increasing numbers of others, found that he could
produce raps, move tables, and generally converse with the other
world in the fashionable manner. These manifestations shocked his
aunt, who was a pious Christian. Perhaps she was especially put off by
the rather unctuous religiosity of manner with which Home tended to
accompany his performances. (He was particularly fond of the notion
of happy deathbeds, and recounts one peculiarly nauseating tale of a
young boy who knew, because Home had told him, that the end was at
hand, and who, when this news was 'broken' to him by the doctor,
said: 'Little does he imagine that I have already decided who my
bearers are to be.'[17]) At any rate, she told him that these performances
must cease, or he would have to leave her house. They did not cease;
and he left.

But his fame was beginning to spead. If the Fox sisters were able to
keep themselves by their spiritual talents, why should not he? Indeed
he could, and did, and quickly established his mode of doing so, which
was different from theirs. Neither then nor ever did D.D.Home take
money for his professional services. Instead, he accepted hospitality.
He was, as someone remarked, the proverbial 'man who came to
dinner' – and usually stayed the night. It is an important distinction;

for it very much affected the psychological atmosphere in which the performances were viewed – and psychology, in this field, is all-important.

Such a setting could, of course, be seen as a more difficult one in which to operate. This was how the naturalist Alfred Russel Wallace, a devout and devoted spiritualist, saw it. He wrote: 'When we consider that Home's seances almost always took place in private houses at which he was a guest, and with people absolutely above suspicion of collusion with an imposter, . . . it will be admitted that no feat of legerdemain will explain what occurred.'[18] But another view could also be taken. If you pay to see an exhibition, your view of what is on offer is quite different from what it would be if a guest in your house were kindly giving the same performance as a favour. The first is an impersonal situation, in which any findings reflect only on the performer; in the second, if the performance, having purported to be genuine, turns out to be a fake, then not only is the performer a charlatan, but the host is a dupe. At any rate, Dan was able to keep himself, more or less, in this way for the next couple of years, and his reputation as a wonder-worker grew apace. Then he discovered that he had consumption. He had the typical consumptive's physique, tall and thin; and he was told that, unless he left the harsh climate of New England, he would not live long. He therefore decided to take ship for Europe, hoping not only for better health, but also, we may fairly assume, for a wider field in which to exercise his talents.

It had not taken long for the news of the new spiritual telegraph to cross the Atlantic. 'My attention had been drawn to the phenomena now known as spiritualism in the year 1853,' wrote a correspondent in the *Spiritual Magazine*. This person had read Judge Edmonds and Dr George Dexter's volume, *Spiritualism*, and 'I thought these knockings, these table-turnings, these phenomena, if they can be produced in America, can they not also be brought about here?' Accordingly he had experimented with his family and found that, indeed, tables tilted as strongly in England as anywhere else. The family, however, got bored; but 'these results, scouted then, I recognize as spiritual phenomena – "true grit", now. They consisted in tables turned, tables upset, tables tilted, and by tilts, words and sentences spelt out amidst recriminations and mutual accusations of all present.'[19]

The new cult also arrived in person: the person of Mrs Hayden, an American medium who came over to London in 1853 and enjoyed a great success. She charged a guinea a head to perform her 'rappings' and various other wonders, and she made a number of illustrious converts. These included the veteran socialist, Robert Owen, and the brilliant mathematician and well-known sceptic Augustus de Morgan, Professor of Mathematics at University College, London, whose steadfast atheism had denied him a place at either Oxford or Cambridge. Owen was, of course, very much the type of person who had been attracted to spiritualism in America. He was only interested in communicating with spirits who supported his ideas for the general improvement of society, such as Jefferson, Benjamin Franklin (a perennial favourite with a great many people), Shelley, Channing, and the Duke of Kent, who had been a great patron of his. De Morgan was a more surprising conquest. It seems clear that it was his wife who first persuaded him to visit Mrs Hayden, where de Morgan was amazed and convinced by the manifestations, for which he could find no explanation other than a supernatural one. He was thus the first in a long line of mathematicians and scientists who could not believe that there might be a simple explanation for anything they could not make out.

On the whole, however, Mrs Hayden's success was only moderate. Her performance was not especially spectacular (she was later exposed in fraud) and a great many people were not convinced. A Swedenborgian, J.J.G.Wilkinson, wrote to his fellow-believer, Henry James, Sr, across the Atlantic in Boston:

> The only people who are actually contra are the stony materialists & the gassy philosophers: both of them hate this noise which the approaching spiritual world makes with its big toes. The pious Atheists too want Mrs Hayden and her coadjutor to be put in prison: she is, they say, blasphemous; and degrades the mighty dead by summoning them to her table; as if the meanest degradation were not infinitely superior to the annihilation to which Man has been consigned by Philosophers and Atheists.[20]

Some, however, saw degradations meaner than that. 'I have not the least belief in the awful unseen being available for evening parties at so much per night,' wrote Charles Dickens, adding: 'Although I shall be ready to receive enlightenment from any source, I must say I have very little hope of it from the spirits who express themselves through mediums; as I have never yet observed them to talk anything but nonsense.'[21] Dickens's horror had he known that his unfinished novel *Edwin Drood* would be completed by a lady medium in America after his death, does not bear thinking about. . . . Of this effort his son commented: 'I never myself saw this preposterous book, but I was told that it was a sad proof of how rapidly the faculties . . . deteriorate after death!'

Other authors were less obdurate. Mrs Catherine Crowe, who wrote the best-selling *Night Side of Nature*, an enormous compilation of ghost stories, was found 'in the street, clothed only in her chastity, a pocket-handkerchief, and a visiting-card. She had been informed, it appeared, by the spirits, that if she went in that trim she would be invisible.'[22] And the popular novelist Bulwer Lytton, by then Lord Lytton, was a staunch convert. Dickens, in an effort to shake him out of his belief, arranged a seance with a popular medium at which the other participants were Lytton, Wilkie and Charles Collins, and the renowned French conjurer Robert-Houdin. 'Everything the medium did was promptly outdone by Houdin, who really outspirited the spiritualist.'[23] Lytton, however, remained a believer. Dickens then found another reason for what he saw as his friend's delusions. Speaking this time about Home, he said: 'Bulwer, you see, is deaf, and he does not like to have it remarked; so Home would say, "Do you hear the raps?" And Bulwer would say, "Oh, yes, I hear them per-fect-ly."'[24]

If Robert Owen was typical of the kind of person attracted to spiritualism in America (where his son Robert Dale Owen was soon to become one of its most vociferous advocates), so Lord Lytton was an example of the kind of person a successful medium might hope to meet in Europe. For although it was widely taken up by all classes on both sides of the Atlantic, the maid being as likely to prove a 'medium' as the mistress, spiritualism became, in Europe, very fashionable indeed among the upper and moneyed classes. If its principal advocates in America were pioneers of social experiment in its wildest forms, those in Europe were drawn from precisely the opposite end of the social spectrum. And this was very much the clientele Daniel Dunglas Home had in mind when, in the spring of 1855, he sailed for England.

When D.D. Home arrived in England, he made for a hotel in Jermyn Street, in the heart of London, which was owned by a spiritualist named Cox. Here he was able to stay free of charge, Mr Cox presumably hoping that he was thus helping to spread the word, and that a stream of fashionable visitors would soon be crossing his threshold. In this he was not disappointed, for Home's first two clients were soon announced: the aged Lord Brougham and his friend, the Scottish natural scientist Sir David Brewster. Had Home only known it, he could not have picked a worse prospect on whom to begin than Brewster. For Sir David was the author of *Letters on Natural Magic*, a compendium dealing mainly with the physical explanation of many apparently extraordinary, wonderful and inexplicable facts, with a glance at conjuring and at various feats of strength. There was no-one in Britain less likely to be taken in by trickery. And indeed he was not taken in. Home produced his phenomena, which seem mainly to have consisted in rapping and in lifting the table. He offered to be searched, but the offer was declined by Brougham and Brewster. The two professed themselves satisfied with the exhibition, and left; and Home sat back to await the endorsement and valuable advertisement which he was sure would be forthcoming.

In this, however, he was disappointed. Brewster, although Home's friends averred that he had professed himself mystified, obdurately refused to give any written testimony to that effect. Cox wrote a furious letter to the *Morning Advertiser*, berating him for his treachery, to which Brewster answered,

> In reply to Mr Cox, I may take this opportunity to answer his request by telling him what I have seen, and what I think of it. At Mr Cox's house, Mr Home, Lord Brougham, and myself, sat down to a small table, Mr Home having previously requested us to examine, if there was any machinery about his person, an examination, however, which we declined to make. When all our hands were upon the table, noises were heard – rappings in abundance; and, finally, when we rose up, the table actually rose, as appeared to me, from the ground. This result I do not pretend to explain; but rather than believe that spirits made the noise, I will conjecture that the raps were produced by Mr Home's toes, . . . and rather than believe that spirits raised the table, I will conjecture that it was done by the agency of Mr Home's feet.

The Home camp quoted other remarks by Sir David, which (they said) showed that this was merely a dishonest evasion and a refusal to acknowledge his real feelings about the occasion. A Mr Benjamin Coleman, who had been completely convinced by Home, had subsequently met Brewster.

> I . . . asked him, 'Do you, Sir David, think these things were produced by trick?'
> 'No, certainly not,' was his reply.
> 'Is it delusion, think you?'
> 'No, that is out of the question.'
> 'Then what is it?'
> To which he replied, 'I don't know; but spirit is the last thing I will give in to.'[25]

All of which reactions may seem not only perfectly reasonable, but no more than might be expected from the author of *Natural Magic*.

By now, however, enough people had encountered and been dazzled by Home for Sir David Brewster's refusal to join their numbers to matter very little (though it continued to rankle throughout the medium's subsequent career). Continuing in his usual mode, Home left Cox's to go and stay with another believer, a wealthy solicitor named Rymer, who lived in Ealing. And here the most famous encounter of his early career took place. This was the seance attended by Robert and Elizabeth Browning. They were, in the summer of 1855, on one of their rare visits to England from Florence, where they lived. Elizabeth, who was exceedingly interested in spiritualism and inclined to believe, persuaded Robert to visit the Rymers with her. As a result of this seance, while she was even more convinced of the miraculous nature of spiritualism in general and Home in particular, he conceived the aversion – one could almost say loathing – for the whole subject, and Home above all, which eventually led him to write his famous poem 'Mr Sludge, "The Medium"', published in 1864. The events at this gathering are best described in Browning's own words.

At about 9 we were placed round a large table, as Mr Home directed – and the results were some noises, a vibration of the table, then an up-tilting of it in various ways, and then more noises, or raps, which were distinguished as the utterance of the family's usual visitor, the spirit of their child 'Wat' who died three years ago, aged twelve. They ceased presently, and we were informed that the circle was too large – it was lessened accordingly by the ejecting of five individuals pointed out by the spirit – and the business was resumed, those remaining being Mr Home, Mr Rymer, Mrs Rymer, ourselves, two lady-friends of the family, Miss Rymer, & Mr Wilkie Rymer (son & daughter of our Host.) We had the same vibration, & upraising the table – a table-cloth, a few ornaments, and a large lamp were on it – all hands were visible. I don't know at all how the thing was done. Then Mrs & Mr Rymer were touched by what they recognised as the spirit of their child, & next my wife: whose dress, near the waist, I saw slightly but distinctly uplifted in a manner I cannot account for – as if by some object inside – which could hardly have been introduced there without her becoming aware of it – this was repeated. The spirit then announced (by raps in answer to questions) that it would play on the accordion & show *myself* its hand, – all the raps seemed from or about the table – not the region outside us. The lamp was then extinguished, and all the light permitted came from the two windows thro' their muslin curtains – you could just distinguish any substance held up directly against them – not against the wall which divided them – but nothing of what was done *at the table*, – the night being

cloudy. A hand appeared from the edge of the table, opposite to my wife
& myself; it was withdrawn, reappeared & moved about, rose & sank – it
was clothed in white loose folds, like muslin, down to the table's edge –
from which it never was separated – then another hand, larger, appeared,
pushed a wreath, or pulled it, off the table, picked it from the ground,
brought it to my wife – who had left my side for the purpose of receiving
it, at Mr Home's desire, and had taken the chair by him – and put it on
her head – thence, at her request, it was carried, under the table, and
given to me. I was touched several times under the table on one knee and
the other – and on my hands alternately (a kind of soft & fleshy pat) but
not so as that I could myself touch the object. I desired leave to hold the
spirit-hand in mine, and was promised that favor – a promise not kept,
however. Then Mr Home took an accordion with one hand, held it below
the table, and sounds were produced and several tunes played – on it, I
suppose, – but how, it is difficult to imagine – (there was light in the room
for this experiment). . . . The lights being away, the first hand pulled a
small bell off the table, picked it from the floor & rang it. Another hand
was held up, which opened & shut the fingers, turning itself as if to be
seen. – I desired leave to touch it, but was refused (by the spirit). It was
clothed to the *base* – (for one can't say *elbow*, where form was not
distinguishable beneath the muslin-like drapery) and, like the other, kept
close to the table. These performances were repeated, several times –
always in the wide space between Mr Wilkie Rymer & Mr Home – never
in the open space of the room, tho' one hand crawled (as it were) up Mr
Home's shoulder, and, as I said, put the wreath on my wife, *how*, I was
unable to see – but *under* the table their action was freer, apparently. Mr
Home observed that he supposed the hand with the wreath was that of a
particular relation of my wife's – raps confirmed this opinion, the
alphabet was put in requisition to discover the *name* – . . . it was given
successively as William, Frank, Charles, Henry – misses all. Hereupon
Mr Home went into a trance, & began to address Mr Rymer, in the
character of his dead child – in a sort of whisper, at first, to represent a
child's voice, but with Mr Home's own inflexions, peculiarities, and
characteristic expressions – beginning 'Dear Papa, – is not God *good*, isn't
he *lovely*?' &c. As this continued, by degrees Mr Home's natural tones
were resumed, the talk affected the parents, as you might suppose.

Home then gave a sort of sermon, in the name of the spirits
collectively; and repeated various tricks, including tilting the table
without the lamp's moving. Mr Rymer remarked on the way in which
all the objects on the table were held by the spirits, at which
Browning responded that a silver pen was rolling around freely.
Could the spirits hold it still? he wanted to know; 'on which Miss
Rymer (who had gone into a trance also), replying as from the spirit,

said "Do not put that question! Have you not seen *enough*?" – and so all ended.'[26]

The Brownings reacted very differently to this display (which, incidentally, was a pretty fair catalogue of Home's usual repertoire, excluding only a few very special effects which he did not develop until several years later). 'For my own part I am confirmed in all my opinions,' wrote Elizabeth to her sister a few weeks later. 'To me it was wonderful and conclusive; and I believe that the medium present was no more *responsible* for the things said and done, than I myself was.'[27] But Robert was not impressed.

> On the whole I think the whole performance most clumsy, and unworthy anybody really setting up for a 'medium' [he wrote]. I, – the poorest of mechanicians, – can fancy such an obvious contrivance as a tube, fixed & flexible, under Mr H's loose clothes & sack-like *paletot* & inordinate sleeves [a reminder, here, of the Fox sisters' excessively long gowns] which should convey some half a dozen strings, & no more, to his breast – for instance, – and work the three fantoccini-hands, after these various fashions, – just as he did, and easily. There are probably fifty more ingenious methods at the service of every 'prestidigitateur'.[28]

These differences illustrate some factors which were clearly of the utmost importance to the success, not only of Home, but of every 'spirit-medium', but of which his manipulation reached the level of a particularly fine art. We shall encounter them time and again in his company. One was the use of atmosphere to play on subjective impressions. Thus, Elizabeth, willing and susceptible, saw Robert's 'fantoccini-hands' as

> of the largest human size, as white as snow, and very beautiful. It was as near to me as the hand I write with, and I saw it as distinctly. . . . These hands seemed to Robert and me to come from under the table, but Mr Lytton saw them rise out of the *wood of the table* – also he tells me . . . that he saw a spiritual (so called) arm, elongate itself as much as two yards across the table and then float away to the windows, where it disappeared. Robert and I did not touch the hands. Mr Lytton and Sir Edward both did.[29]

Thus Elizabeth not only sees a miracle where Robert saw none; but she takes the Lyttons' even more miraculous experiences – which she has not seen, and which sound as if they may have been somewhat magnified in the telling – and adds them to her own, factual experience.

The other significant factor is the way in which the private setting operated to Home's advantage. To a very large extent he was enabled, because of it, to exercise a control over his clientele, and their reactions to his performance, which would never be available to anyone operating in the overtly professional setting of the Fox sisters. Thus, even Robert Browning was obliged to control himself and behave politely in the face of what he considered blatant humbug. He remarked on

> the impossibility of a stranger taking the simplest measure for getting at the truth or falsehood of the 'manifestations' – it was a family-party, met for family-purposes, and one could no more presume to catch at the hands (for instance) of what they believed the spirit of their child, than one could have committed any other outrage on their feelings. I heard that somebody who had been there two days before, and had told Mr H. 'the hand is *yours*' – showed thereby his 'forgetting he was in a private house' – so *I* remembered it, you may be sure.'[30]

Normally, of course, Home would have been able to go further than this. He could simply have desired Robert Browning to leave the room, pleading, as he so often did – and as others have so often done since – that the presence of such a sceptic, with his unsympathetic vibrations, severely reduced the possibility of the manifestations occurring. We have seen that, if he ordered people from the table, like the supernumerary five who left at the start of the seance in question, they meekly left. He only needed to say that he could not operate, or rather the spirits could not, with such and such people present; there was no need to give his reasons, even. An amateur conjurer who, as an experiment, faked mediumship in the 1880s found that the occasional blank seance increased verisimilitude. And who knows why the unfortunate five had to go on this occasion? No explanation was given and none was called for. The famous poet could not be so easily disposed of, for he was accompanied by his wife; and she was a very desirable member of the seance circle. If he left, so, no doubt, would she. So he was suffered to stay, with the results we have seen.

Home and his supporters reacted to Browning's disparagements in much the same way as they had reacted to Brewster's. First of all, Home asserted that immediately after the seance Browning had confessed himself mystified; it was only later he had decided that the whole thing was a fraud. Then he put up the preposterous notion (preposterous to anyone who knew of Browning's devotion to his wife, and his respect for her talents – 'I am the clever person; my wife is the genius,' he would say) – that the poet was sulking because his wife, and not himself, had been crowned with a wreath by the spirit hands. Another assertion was that Browning was jealous of Home, because he had won over Elizabeth and nothing the poet could do could break the allegiance. Nothing else, we are told, could explain the peculiar venom of 'Mr Sludge'.

Punch's view of Elizabeth Barrett Browning being crowned with a wreath by D.D.Home or one of his spirits

Certainly this was the one subject on which that devoted couple ever positively quarrelled. After that evening Robert so hated any mention of Home or of spiritualism that Elizabeth had to warn her sisters never to mention the subject, even in letters. But it is not as if Elizabeth much liked Home personally. Quite apart from her barbed comment on the occasion of his marriage, she wrote, a year later, to her sister Henrietta: 'Everybody would be delighted to disbelieve in Home – but they can't. They hate him, and believe the facts.'[31] So the argument continued, and still continues, resolvable according to personal preference. The salient fact remains that on that summer evening Home made one of his most illustrious converts, and at the same time – and perhaps on that account – his most implacable enemy.

By now, however, Home was becoming too well-established for such sceptics as Browning or Dickens to affect his career. Increasingly, such disturbing influences were excluded from his seances – a fact recognized by Browning, who said, 'I should like to go again and propose to try a simple experiment or two, but fear that it is already out of my power – my wife having told one of the party that I was "unconvinced".'[32]

Instead, unruffled by over-critical observers, D.D.Home continued

his progress through Europe. He was a striking-looking young man –
though not quite as young as he liked to make himself out to be. In
1855 he was still telling people that he was 'only twenty' when, in fact,
he must have been at least twenty-two – a deliberate confusion of such
worldly details which recalls the similar mystifications of Maggie and
Kate Fox. Browning said that he looked much older than twenty, and
was always proclaiming that he had 'no strength at all' – presumably
so that no one should suspect him of lifting tables by main force.
Browning goes on:

> He . . . affects the manners, endearments and other peculiarities of a very
> little child indeed – speaking of Mr and Mrs Rymer as his 'Papa and
> Mama' & kissing the family abundantly – he professes timorousness, 'a
> love of love' – and is unpleasant enough in it all: being a well-grown young
> man, over the average height, and, I should say, of quite the ordinary
> bodily strength – his face is rather handsome & prepossessing, and indica-
> tive of intelligence.[33]

This insinuating and demonstrative manner, which Home retained
throughout his life, was certainly not in the restrained British style,
though it seems to have appealed well enough to his British devotees.
But, for the next few years, his life and career were not to be centred on
Britain, but spent in touring the continent of Europe – with extraordinary success. For he spent this time moving from ducal palace to
imperial court, bringing spiritualism to circles as far removed from
those surrounding such manifestations as the 'new motive power' as
could possibly be imagined. The whole thing was managed by introductions. In London, Home had got to know and impress some of the
'best' people. His next step was a logical one. He was suffering from
consumption, and England is far from enjoying the best climate for
sufferers from that affliction, then so generally fatal. What is needed is
somewhere warmer and drier. Italy has such a climate; and Italy, and
especially Florence, had also at that time a sizeable British colony,
including the Brownings, and also various other people whom he had
already met at the Rymers', such as Mrs Fanny Trollope and her son
Thomas. Armed with these acquaintances, and also with introductions from his London friends to theirs abroad, D.D. Home set out for
Europe. He began in Italy, where he conducted seances among the
expatriates and their Italian aristocratic friends along very much the
same lines as we have seen at the Rymers'. But in the social sphere,
there can be no doubt that he reached his apogee at the courts of
France and Russia.

Home reached Paris, armed once again with introductions, and very soon penetrated the circle of the Emperor and Empress themselves – Napoleon III and the lovely Eugénie. And having arrived, he quickly attained an intimacy and influence there which marked him out as a target for both flattery and resentment. No one else could amuse the Empress so divinely. Tables, in Paris, took on a new life. Eugénie's personal table was called 'Joséphine'; it had its own moods, sometimes playful, sometimes naughty; it was not always easy to understand. There were the usual other phenomena: bells rung from a distance, accordions played by unseen instrumentalists, taps and pats from spirit hands. One lady, having received such a spirit touch on the knee – the ghost actually squeezed her leg – was so alarmed that she could not sleep at night. Recounting this fright to a circle of friends, one of them, a certain M de Pierre, reassured her. 'Sleep in peace,' he said. 'I was the spirit; mine was the hand.'[34]

Another visitor to Paris at this time was the young Madame Blavatsky, then embarking on her peripatetic career. She had abandoned her husband, the aged and bald General Blavatsky, Vice-Governor of Erevan. Armenia had held no charms for the seventeen-year-old Helena Petrovna; she ran away, and at this time was living with – possibly married to – a Bulgarian opera-singer named Metrovitch, whom she had met while working in a circus – she did trick-riding – at Istanbul. She, too, had got to know the Empress – she had been commissioned to decorate her private apartments, or so she later said – and this may be how she met Home. At any rate, they recognized kindred spirits in each other, and it is generally admitted that Madame Blavatsky learned many of the tricks which she later used to such effect from the master sorcerer himself. Quite what light this throws on her teacher is a question I have not seen discussed, for, if it is true that Home was never exposed in fraud, it is equally true that Madame Blavatsky was, thoroughly and comprehensively. Home's interlude of glory at the French court was not, however, to be long-lived. In 1857, very suddenly and not all voluntarily, he left under a cloud.

The exact nature of the cloud is uncertain. The simplest explanation is that put about in America by *Harper's Weekly* – for D.D. Home remained an object of intense curiosity to the American press. This magazine ran a long description of a failed seance which, they said, had led to Home's exposure and disgrace. The scene was set, so the story went, for one of the medium's most spectacular *coups*. In a dimly lit room a crowd waited for Home to summon up the spirit of the dead. Who would be called? 'A faint whisper . . . thrilled through the room: "Let it be Socrates, the greatest of philosophers."' Since no one raised any objection or made any other suggestion, Home raised his arm, waved it towards the door and solemnly bade Socrates appear. The crowd watched, fascinated, as the door slowly opened and a figure entered, enveloped in floating drapery rather like a shroud; but with the unmistakable bald head, white beard and broken nose of Socrates himself. . . .

The spirit disappeared, and the crowd, now as excited as can be imagined, called for another manifestation. Home modestly havered. He was not sure whether he had the strength to summon up another such spirit the same evening. . . . But the audience insisted, and the same voice as before suggested that Frederick the Great be called for. Unwillingly Home agreed. Silence fell. The door began to open – and in the dim light, the magician was seen to be even paler than usual. He called aloud for Frederick the Great, King of Prussia, to appear before him. Once again a white-draped figure entered, but once again the head was instantly recognizable as that of the spirit in question; it was even wearing Frederick's unmistakable little cocked hat.

This time, however, the spirit did not go away. Home got angry. 'Enough, enough, begone, depart,' he adjured it in a hoarse whisper. But it would do no such thing, even when commanded to leave once more. Then, with a supreme effort, the medium roused himself. 'I have been made the dupe of some mystification!' he declared, and stepped up to the figure, which until then had entirely retained its composure. Suddenly it could contain itself no longer, and burst out laughing. 'What! Don't you know me?' it asked, and thereupon revealed itself as one Nadaud, an old enemy of Home's. 'And here is my friend Socrates, otherwise Marshal Baraguey d'Hilliers, ready to appear again whenever you choose; and close at hand is my comrade, Eugène Guinot in life, and Alcibiades in death, waiting to be summoned after me, as he most assuredly would have been, had I been able to follow up the joke.'[35] Utterly mortified, Home could do no more than leave the French capital as quickly and quietly as he could. This story the medium indignantly denied. He had, he said, been in Italy at the time. But the fact remains that he did leave Paris very abruptly; if this was not the reason, then what was it?

Clearly the departure was unwilling. It was the result of pressure of one sort or another from Home's enemies, who were worried that he was exercising altogether too much influence, and that not of a very desirable sort, over the imperial circle. They were looking for a lever with which to dislodge him, and they found one.

It has been suggested[36] that the reason was that Home had been accused, rightly or wrongly, of homosexual practices. The surrounding details are not very clear. One story goes that, the charge having been brought and substantiated, the medium was hustled off to prison at Mazas, near Lyons, where the police, when they questioned him, were so appalled at the stories he was able to tell and was quite prepared to back up about goings-on at court, that they simply thought it best to hustle him out of the country as fast and quietly as possible. There had, it was rumoured, been an enormous homosexual scandal at court not many years before, and the last thing anyone wanted was any sort of repetition of this.

Was this true? Certainly it fits well with some of the glimpses we get into Home's relations with some of the young men who participated in his circles – and whose testimony was later to be of the greatest importance in establishing his reputation for posterity. Time and again in accounts of episodes with the medium, it is remarked that, since it was late by the time the evening's events were over, the medium was invited to stay the night, or himself invited a member of the seance circle to stay the night, the night then being spent in the same room and often in the same bed. These nights were (as we shall see) frequently pervaded by an extraordinary atmosphere of overheated sexuality – an atmosphere not without its professional uses for Home.

Nothing so intimate as (for example) Lord Adare's diaries of these nights exists in relation to Home's time in Paris, but we do know that he was rumoured to be having an affair with a young man named Ernest Baroche who used to go and stay with him in his apartment so that he 'might be able to observe some of the more startling and spontaneous phenomena', as his mother put it in her diary, adding that what Ernest saw only confirmed him in his belief that Home was an accomplished charlatan, but that he possessed in a high degree powers of magnetism and a sort of fascination.[37]

What kind of thing went on during these sessions? Elizabeth Barrett Browning gives an account of one such which took place at about this time – not, of course, with her; even the latitude allowed to spirit mediums did not extend to their spending the night, unchaperoned, with respectable ladies, even in the interests of other-worldly communications. The night in question was spent with the Brownings' American friend James Jackson Jarves, a rich dilettante who took an interest in spirit doings. 'A four-posted bed was carried into the middle of the room – shadowy figures stood by the pillow, or lay down across the feet of those about to sleep – nothing threatening,

everything kind; but at best [concludes Mrs Browning] extremely
disturbing.'[38]

Disturbing such events undoubtedly must have been; but – were
they real? And if not, how were they engineered? And how did Home's
subjects come to be convinced by them? On at least one such occasion,
it seems likely that an accomplice was brought into the act. This was
none other than Kate Fox herself, now Mrs Jencken, married to a
London barrister who was an ardent believer, and living in some
comfort in south London, near the Crystal Palace.

The subject on this occasion was a Scottish aristocrat, the Master of
Lindsay. The seance took place about ten years after the events in
Paris. In the course of these years Home had visited Russia, where he
had been taken up by the Tsar himself, and had married the daughter of
one of the inner court circle. The marriage seems to have been a happy
one. The young couple set up home in London, and had a son; but the
idyll was broken when Mrs Home in her turn contracted consumption,
and died of it. Home and his son remained in London, where (his wife's
estate being contested by members of her family) he found himself
very short of money. The continuing success of his mediumistic career
therefore took on ever more importance; and it was at this time that
Home began seemingly to produce miracles such as had not been
witnessed before, and were certainly not to be witnessed again.

Lord Lindsay was quite a frequent visitor to the Jenckens' house,
and Home often conducted the seances there. It would seem more
natural than not to conclude that he found in Kate Jencken a willing
and experienced helper. Certainly the seances seem to have been
satisfyingly filled with wonders, the furniture moving and levitating at
will, mysterious lights flashing on and off, knocks in abundance in all
corners of the room. It was at one of these seances that Home performed one of his most particular special effects, when he elongated
himself. According to Lindsay, he elongated eleven inches.

> I measured him standing up against the wall, and marked the place; not
> being satisfied with that, I put him in the middle of the room and placed a
> candle in front of him, so as to throw a shadow on the wall, which I also
> marked. When he awoke I measured him again in his natural size, both
> directly and by the shadow, and the results were equal. I can swear that he
> was not off the ground or standing on tiptoe, as I had full view of his feet,
> and moreover, a gentleman present had one of his feet placed over Home's
> insteps, one hand on his shoulder, and the other on his side where the false
> ribs come near the hip-bone.[39]

An interesting point that should be noticed here is that evidently everyone knew that Home was going to elongate himself; measuring equipment was conveniently to hand. This implanting of expectation was, as we shall see, an important part of his technique.

On this particular night the seance had gone on very late, and Lindsay missed the last train back to central London. He was offered, and accepted, a shakedown in the medium's room.

> I was just going to sleep, when I was roused by feeling my pillow slipping from under my head; and I could also feel, what seemed to be a fist, or hand, under it, which was pulling it away; soon after it ceased. Then I saw at the foot of my sofa, a female figure standing *en profile* to me. I asked Home if he saw anything, and he answered, 'a woman, looking at me.' Our beds were at right angles to one another, and about twelve feet apart. I saw the features perfectly, and impressed them upon my memory. She seemed to be dressed in a long wrap, going down from the shoulders, and not gathered in at the waist. Home then said, 'it is my wife; she often comes to me.' And then she seemed to fade away.

Mysterious lights then flickered through the room, disappeared, and the parties went to sleep. 'Next morning, before I went to London, I was looking at some photographs, and I recognised the face I had seen in the room upstairs overnight. I asked Mrs Jencken who it was, and she said it was Home's wife.'[40] The photographs are the give-away. Why should anyone look at photographs at breakfast-time unless they were deliberately put in his way? And why should anyone bring out the photographs at that time of day unless with a particular purpose: to confirm that the previous night's ghost really had been the person it purported to be?

From Home's point of view, the advantages of these late-night operations are obvious. No one is more suggestible, less certain of what really is or is not going on, than when caught between sleep and waking in the early hours. The recipient of the impressions may well wonder whether it was not all a dream. But when it is confirmed, next morning, that it was not a dream – that the experiences were shared, and really happened – then faith in the wonder-worker will be immeasurably strengthened. And the inclination to accept other wonders as real, even if they take place in broad daylight, will be that much greater.

Lindsay was not the only viewer of Home's nocturnal miracles at this period. His friend Lord Adare, heir to the Irish earldom of Dunraven, had become very intimate with the medium, and seems often to have spent the night with him. And if Lindsay's experiences were strange enough, they were nothing to Adare's. It has been truly pointed out that the tales of Edgar Allan Poe are essentially pre-Freudian. They are bald accounts of fantasies, naked of analysis and with no consideration of what they may reveal about the author, such as it would be literally impossible to produce today. One might make much the same observation about the diaries kept by young Lord Adare and published in 1869 under the title *Experiences in Spiritualism with D.D.Home*. The notion that anyone might countenance the publication of such a document today, even in the service of research, and even for limited circulation, is almost unthinkable. But the possible implications and reverberations of his account do not seem to have struck Adare or his father, Lord Dunraven, who arranged the publication of the diaries. Evidently, it was a more innocent age. As a result we are left with a detailed account of how Home gained complete ascendancy over the young man and came utterly to dominate his mind.

Home met Adare, whose interests were mainly sporting, and certainly not intellectual, at Malvern. The two men struck up a friendship which soon developed into considerable intimacy. Adare was plainly fascinated by the glamorous Home, and content to follow where he might lead. Inevitably, Home soon came to stay with Adare. His visits were frequent, and when they took place Home would often share Adare's room. It may be imagined, then, that a great many of Home's more extraordinary manifestations, as witnessed by Adare, took place late at night when the two were both in bed. These manifestations featured two principal personalities: Adare's mother, then recently dead, and the actress Adah Menken, whom the two had visited the previous year in Paris, and who had, at the time of these events, just died. The extraordinary atmosphere in which these things took place is further enhanced by the equally extraordinary matter-of-factness with which Adare recounted the happenings. Here, for example, is his account of one such nocturnal seance – No. 31 :

The other night, having been unwell for some days, I went to bed very uncomfortable and agueish; I could not get warm. Home's bed was rocked about, and he said, 'I do not know who you are, but unless there is some object in it, I wish you would leave off rocking my bed, for it makes me dizzy.' The bed left off shaking and a spirit spelt out 'Adah'. She said, 'I am here and seek to do you good; can you imagine my inexpressible joy, your angel mother has taken my hand in hers.' Home went into a trance, got out of bed, wrapped a fur rug round his middle, then warmed his hands at the fire, and commenced shampooing me over my chest, stomach, legs and feet. He then took off my fur rug, warmed it at the fire, and put in on again, and made passes over my head, retreating as he did so to the further side of the room. He then got into bed and awoke. I fell asleep soon and slept soundly.[41]

Clearly, Home had both both Lindsay and Adare into a state where they would literally believe anything he told them. It seems, then, less than coincidental that these should have been the principal witnesses to what is generally recognized as the outstanding feat of his career: the levitation at Ashley House.

This was seance No. 41 in the sequence, and it followed two seances at which those present had been Home, Adare and the Master of Lindsay. It is interesting, in view of the importance attached to them by spiritualists, to look not just at the events of 16 December 1868, but at the sequence leading up to them.

The event which was to cause such a furore was a levitation beside which all other levitations pale into insignificance. On 16 December, or so it is reported, D.D. Home floated out of one third-storey window and in at the adjacent one, into the room where Adare, Lindsay, and another friend of theirs, Captain Wynne, were sitting. Then (according to the story) he offered to demonstrate how it had been done, took Lord Adare into the next room, floated out of the window once again and hovered horizontally, returning feet first into the room.

This was not the first time Home had levitated himself miraculously before this audience. Indeed, he had done so, if less spectacularly, on the previous occasion they had met. At seance No. 40, with Adare and Lindsay present, a conversation was held between two spirits, both speaking through Home's mouth. There had been some play with a glass of brandy, and Adare had questioned Home on the capacity of spirits to hold their drink. (Home averred that a spirit could certainly drink a glass of beer and retain it for a certain length of time, but not for long: 'It must have been spilled outside. If the doors and windows had been shut, so that he could not carry it out of the room, it must have fallen upon the floor.') Then there were some abortive experiments with a chair; and finally the spirits began to discuss whether or not to lift Home up into the air. As was Home's invariable habit, the idea was well implanted first.

He [the spirit] then began talking about lifting him (Home) up, and after speaking for some time in a low tone, apparently suggesting different ways, he said, 'Well, then, I will lift him on to the table and sling him right off into the air.' 'Oh, yes,' said the other, 'and perhaps break his leg, that will never do.' They then arranged that he was to try by lifting him first on to the back of my chair. Accordingly, in about a minute, Home was lifted up

on to the back of my chair. 'Now,' he said, 'take hold of Dan's feet.' I took
both his feet in my hands, and away he went up into the air so high that I
was obliged to let go his feet; he was carried along the wall, brushing past
the pictures, to the opposite side of the room; he then called me over to him.
I took his hand and felt him alight upon the floor; he sat down upon the
sofa and laughed, saying, 'That was very badly done, you knocked Dan up
against the pictures.'[42]

Then, and only then, it is revealed that this performance had taken
place in the darkness: 'Home got up, opened the door, pulled up the
blind and made the room much lighter'; a detail of the utmost
importance.

The next seance was to be far more spectacular. There were this
time three participants; but it is noteworthy that all the important
testimony for what took place is provided by either Adare or Lindsay –
Captain Wynne, the third witness, being less satisfactory from Home's
point of view.

The room was once more dark. Adare says, 'There was no light in
the room; but the light from the window was sufficient to enable us to
distinguish each other, and to see the different articles of furniture.'
The manifestations began at once. 'Immediately on sitting down we
had physical manifestations and messages, chiefly from Adah
Menken. Lindsay saw two spirits on the sofa, and others in different
places.'[43] Then Charlie Wynne was drawn into the spirit circle; a
spirit was summoned especially for him; he admitted to recognizing it.
Home said, 'Then he will sit down beside you.' A chair was then drawn
up beside Wynne, who said he could feel that there was someone there,
although he could see nothing. The conversation with this spirit continued for quite some time, presumably to make sure that Wynne
would be sure to be in a suitably receptive state of mind. 'Poor fellow,'
says Home at one point, 'he seems to want to speak about something
that has been lost.' 'Is it about some missing papers?' asks Wynne, to
which Home eagerly assents. Not long after this the spirit leaves: 'He
is rather abrupt in his manner, is he not? He does not brook much
delay,' Home remarks.[44]

Now the time has come to move on to the next stage in the proceedings. Adare says, 'Home then got up and walked about the room. He
was both elongated and raised in the air. He spoke in a whisper, as
though the spirits were arranging something. He then said to us, "Do
not be afraid, and on no account leave your places;" and he went out
into the passage.'[45]

The process of implanting the suggestion now took place. Either

Home tiptoed back into the room or a spirit spoke for him; for Lindsay now heard a voice whisper in his ear: 'He will go out of one window and in at another.'[46] Alarmed, Lindsay said, 'Oh! good heavens! I know what he is going to do; it is too fearful.' Lindsay's alarm was perhaps compounded by his estimate of the distance of the windows from the ground. It will be remembered that the seance room was on the third storey, and Lindsay estimated this as being eighty-five feet from the ground – as Harry Houdini put it, when considering this tale: '*Tall stories* appear to have been a specialty of these remarkably observant gentlemen.'[47] Adare asked, 'What is it?' and Lindsay replied, 'I cannot tell you, it is too horrible! Adah says that I must tell you; he is going out of the window in the other room, and coming in at this window.' They then heard Home go into the next room, heard the window thrown up, 'and presently Home appeared standing upright outside our window; he opened the window and walked in quite coolly. "Ah," he said, "You were good this time",' referring to our having sat still and not wished to prevent him. He sat down and laughed.

> CHARLIE: What are you laughing at?
> HOME: We are thinking that if a policeman had been passing, and had looked up and seen a man turning round and round along the wall in the air he would have been much astonished.[48]

Home then took Adare into the next room to show him how he passed out of the window.

It will be remarked that these reports are both detailed and circumstantial; and if the events they describe are luridly improbable, the tone is matter-of-fact throughout. And indeed it may be said that it is this series of seances, with its spectacular culmination, which provides one of the two principal supports for Home's continuing reputation as a miracle-worker – the other being the series of experiments which he was soon to conduct with the famous scientist William Crookes. Here (it is argued) are sober, reliable witnesses describing events in which they severally participated. Why should we not believe them?

The Home levitation has, naturally enough, given rise to endless discussion; and in the end, any verdict on what actually happened can be dictated by nothing more definite than opinion and inclination. Certainly anyone asserting that he doesn't believe the accounts of Adare and Lindsay – which is to say, that he doesn't believe the noble lords actually did see what they patently believed they saw – must justify the assertion. If they didn't see *that*, then what did they see? And how did Home make them believe so substantially in a miracle that didn't take place?

The basis for the inclination not to believe their tales is succinctly stated by Frank Podmore, the most thorough and pains-taking historian psychical research ever had. 'It is easier to find the explanation of the marvel in a fallacy of memory than in a fallacy of sense,' he says, and quotes the famous French psychologist Pierre Janet. 'I want to ask your advice,' said a patient to Professor Janet. 'How can I distinguish between memory and a dream?'[49] It is a distinction which, as we have seen, Home's preliminary 'softening-up' process, with its bemused nocturnal wonderments, did its very best to blur. It has often been said that Home was an expert in the arts of suggestion and mesmerism, and that he was able effectively to hypnotize his subjects into seeing and believing what he wanted them to see and believe.

This may or may not be so; we are as unable to prove the case one way or the other as we are to prove that he actually floated out of the window at Ashley Place. But we are able to look at a number of material aids and processes which certainly would have helped the illusion solidly along. Let us, for example, consider the first levitation: the one which took place in the presence of Adare and Lindsay alone. This is just one of many such performances which Home put on. Sometimes he would offer to write on the ceiling, to prove that he had really been up there. Charles Dickens's son Henry recalls that when the Dickens family rented a house in Hyde Park Place owned by one of Home's enthusiastic followers, they noticed a large stain on the ceiling of the drawing-room – rather a high room – 'which my father remarked was obviously the mark of the medium's greasy head as he floated up to the ceiling on one of his manifestations'.[50]

Various magicians have in fact described in some detail how such an illusion might be achieved. Here, for instance, is Henry Ridgely Evans, writing in *Hours with the Ghosts*:

When the lights are extinguished the medium – who, by the way, must be a clever ventriloquist – removes his boots and places them on his hands. 'I am rising, I am rising, pay no attention,' he remarks, as he goes about the apartment, where the sitters are grouped in a circle about him, and he lightly touches the heads of various persons. A shadowy form is dimly seen and the smell of boot leather becomes apparent to the olfactory senses of many present. People jump quickly to conclusions in such matters and argue that where the feet of the medium are, his body must surely be – namely, floating in the air. The illusion is further enhanced by the performers' ventriloquial powers. 'I am rising! I am rising! I am touching the ceiling!' he exclaims, imitating the sound of a voice high up. When the lights are turned up, the medium is seen (this time with his boots on his feet) standing on tip-toe, as if just descended from the ceiling.[51]

Any writing can be done with a piece of black chalk on the end of an extending rod.

It may be thought that such a description is fanciful, and that no one could be so crudely taken in. But in fact Joseph Rinn, one of that band of professional and amateur magicians who so delighted (and continue to delight) in exposing fraudulent mediums, performed precisely this illusion, with a few embellishments, on stage in New York, working with a 'committee' who were blindfolded, while the audience could see everything that was happening. The committee believed that Rinn levitated.[52]

A contemporary sceptic, writing in 1876, says of the second levitation: 'A whole party of believers affirm that they saw Mr Home float out of one window and in at another, while a single honest sceptic declares that Mr Home was sitting in his chair all the time.'[53] This is presumably a reference to Captain Wynne. It is perhaps an extreme view; it seems more likely, if the Ashley Place levitation was a trick, that Home would have helped the illusion along more than that – for instance, by leaving the room, opening the window audibly, perhaps tiptoeing back in the dark and letting himself out of the window of the seance room, standing on the ledge and re-entering with panache; all of which is entirely feasible. The private demonstration to Adare of how it was done might have been worked by hypnotic suggestion. But certainly – as yet another analyst of this episode has pointed out[54] – the witnesses were in, to put it mildly, a receptive enough mood that evening. After the levitation, the seance went on.

> Lindsay and Charlie saw tongues or jets of flame proceeding from Home's head. We then all distinctly heard, as it were, a bird flying round the room, whistling and chirping, but saw nothing, except Lindsay, who perceived an indistinct form resembling a bird. There then came a sound as of a great wind rushing through the room, we also felt the wind strongly; the moaning rushing sound was the most weird thing I ever heard. Home then got up, being in a trance, and spoke something in a language that none of us understood; it may have been nonsense, but it sounded like a sentence in a foreign tongue.[55]

And certainly Home went to great lengths to make sure everyone knew just what was supposed to have happened. He had described what the policeman would have seen, had he happened to look up; and 'when Home awoke, he was much agitated; he said he felt as if he had gone through some fearful peril, and that he had a most horrible desire to throw himself out of the window.'[56]

We shall never know what happened that evening at Ashley Place. Either Home was a sorcerer in the most classical and fantastic mould; or he was one of the most skilled illusionists never to perform before a paying public.

3
Scientists and Spirits

I confess I rather despair of any popular religion of a philosophic character; and I sometimes find myself wondering whether there can be any popular religion raised on the ruins of the old Christianity without the presence of that element which in the past has presided over the origin of all religions, namely, a belief in new physical facts and possibilities. Abstract considerations about the soul and the reality of a moral order will not do in a year what the glimpse into a world of new phenomenal possibilities enveloping those of the present life, afforded by an extension of our insight into the order of nature, would do in an instant. Are the much despised 'Spiritualism' and the 'Society for Psychical Research' to be the chosen instruments for a new era of faith? It would surely be strange if they were; but if they are not, I see no other agency that can do the work. – WILLIAM JAMES, 1884.

After the series of seances whose high point was the Ashley House levitation, Lord Adare took little further active interest in spiritualism. He explained why in the introduction to his book about Home:

> The simple reason is that having satisfied myself that the facts were not due to trickery or fraud, I found that I made little progress after a certain point. Phenomena were all of the same character . . . designed apparently to prove that some force or forces other than physical, as we understand it, could be made to operate upon inanimate objects. I had no inclination to investigate the nature of these forces.

Adare, it seems, was not of an inquiring turn of mind. Enough, for him, that the existence of such forces as were, apparently, at Home's command was proved to his satisfaction. But for others both the question of proof and the question of just what it was that was being proved were matters worthy of the closest attention. Chief among these was William (later Sir William) Crookes, the chemist.

Crookes, although still only in his thirties, had already attained a considerable scientific eminence, mainly as a result of his discovery of the element thallium, for which he had been elected to the Royal Society. He was a man of the widest abilities and interests, and in the course of his reading had come across Adare's book of his experiences with Home. This fired his curiosity, and he decided that he would like to conduct some experiments with Home. He first contacted Home very soon after Adare's account was circulated, in July 1869, and by July of 1870 was ready to commit to print his views on the subject of spiritualistic researches. That month he published an article called 'Spiritualism Viewed by the Light of Modern Science', the first of four articles on spiritualism which he was to print in the *Quarterly Journal of Science*, of which he was then editor and proprietor. The most famous passage in this article sets out with admirable clarity the nature of the problem:

> The spiritualist tells of manifestations of power, which would be equivalent of many thousands of 'foot-pounds,' taking place without known agency. The man of science, believing firmly in the conservation of force and that it is never produced without a corresponding exhaustion of something to replace it, asks for some such exhibitions of power to be manifested in his laboratory, where he can weigh, measure, and submit it to proper tests.

In a note to this passage, Crookes adds:

> In justice to my subject, I must state that, on repeating these views to some of the leading 'spiritualists' and most trustworthy 'mediums' in England, they express perfect confidence in the success of the inquiry, if honestly carried out in the spirit here exemplified; and they have offered to assist me to the utmost of their ability, by placing their peculiar powers at my disposal.[1]

At the time this article was written, Crookes had already begun his researches into the subject. Home, we may imagine, was more than happy to co-operate. After the series of seances in London with Adare and his friends, the medium had journeyed to St Petersburg, hoping to clear up the dispute regarding the estate of his wife, and while there had got engaged to yet another Russian lady, the sister of Boutlerow, Professor of Chemistry at Petersburg University, and a friend of Crookes. Collaboration with the English scientist in his experiments would therefore help Home to establish himself more firmly in the

Leah, Kate and Margaret Fox and Elisha Kent Kane

Florence Cook, 1874

'Katie King' with an unidentified gentleman, possibly Dr Gully. This is probably one of the photographs taken by William Crookes.

Bien-Boa, the ghost who convinced Richet

Schrenck-Notzing and Richet

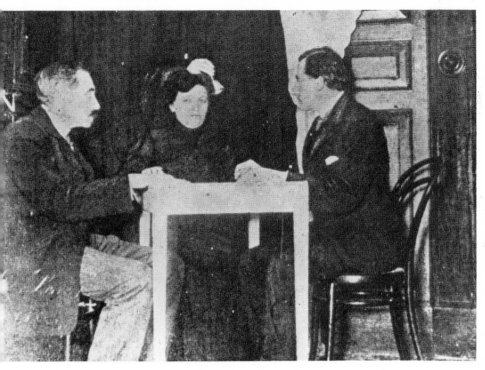

apia with Richet (*left*) and an unidentified man, possibly in the south of France
894 since Eusapia looks younger here than in any other extant photograph. A
d above her head rings a bell; it seems to be coming from the curtains of the
net. Notice the table, with its convenient dimensions for lifting by a variety of
ns.

e Bisson, Mrs Feilding and Mlle Eva

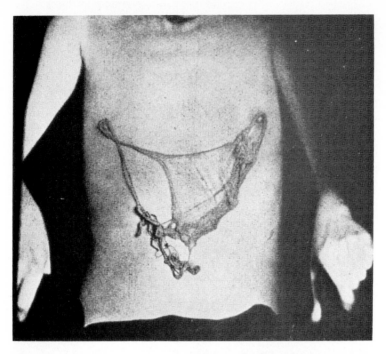

Mme Bisson's photograph of 'ectoplasm' emerging from Eva C's bosom

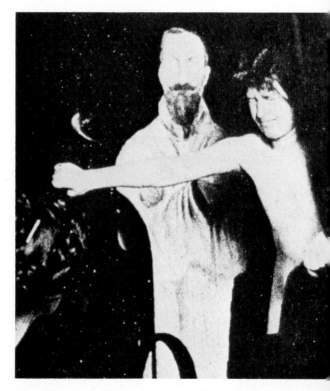

Mme Bisson's flashlight photograph of 23 February 1913, the fi
photograph of an entire phantom, together with nude medium

enck-Notzing's photograph of Eva C materializing the head of a phantom,
ember 1912, and (*inset*) the portrait of the the actress Monna Delza published
emina, April 1912

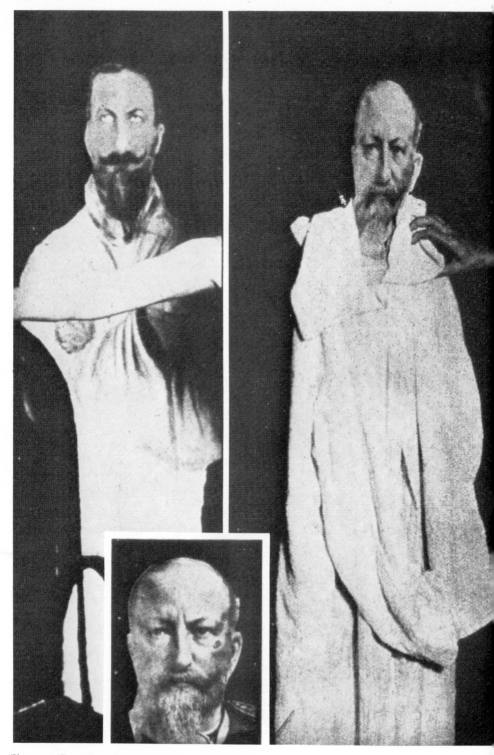

Phantom 'Dormica' photographed by Schrenck-Notzing in February 1913 (*left*) with (*inset*) the portrait of the King of Bulgaria published in *Le Miroir*. On the right the portrait has been given a white mantle to resemble a phantom.

good graces of his prospective in-laws, as well as giving him an even stronger foothold in London; for to impress a hard-headed scientist like Crookes would be a greater achievement than to amaze a posse of young bloods about town.

In both these objectives, Home succeeded admirably. Crookes was soon writing of him in the warmest terms to Professor Boutlerow. 'As far as Mr Home's character is concerned, I thoroughly believe in his uprightness and honour; I consider him incapable of practising deception or meanness,' he said, adding, 'I think . . . that Mr Home's social position would be improved were he to be married. His many friends are now somewhat embarrassed to know how they can make a fitting acknowledgement to him for the charms of his company, and his readiness to place his mediumship at their disposal for seances. We can do so little in the way of return, except ask him to dinner, and this only adds to the obligations we are under.'[2] Evidently Home's lifestyle had changed little over the past ten years.

As may be gathered from the terms in which this letter was written, Crookes and Home were by now good friends; and Crookes had conducted a number of experimental seances at which the power of the medium was tested. The first of Crookes's experimental reports appeared in the *Quarterly Journal of Science* for 1 July 1871. It was entitled 'Experimental Investigation of a New Force', and was taken from notes of a seance which had been held on 31 May the same year. The participants at this seance had been Crookes and his wife; Dr Huggins, an astronomer, and, like Crookes, an FRS; Serjeant Cox, an enthusiastic spiritualist; Crookes's daughter; a Mrs Humphrey; Crookes's laboratory assistant, Gimingham; and, of course, Home.

The phenomena at the start of the seance were very reminiscent of the sort of thing Home had been doing for years. First, several of those present felt a cold air over their hands, though the room was warm. (Readers may remember J.W.Dunne's description of the goose-flesh felt before expected phenomena.) Then there were raps, or, as Crookes liked to term them, 'percussive sounds'. The table moved slightly; people felt their feet and legs being touched under it. An accordion was locked in a cage and placed under the table; although Home apparently neither did nor could touch it, it moved, played some notes, and, some time later, a simple tune. 'This,' wrote Crookes, 'was considered by those present to be a crucial experiment, as such a result could only have been produced by the various keys of the instrument being acted upon in harmonious succession.' A little later there was more play with the accordion, accompanied at one point by Crookes reading aloud extracts from Lord Dunraven's introduction to his son's (Adare's) account of his *Experiences in Spiritualism with D.D.Home*. At one point an electric current was passed round the cage; the accordion sounded and moved about. When Crookes remarked that this seemed to help, the spirits replied (by raps): 'We can see it, but it does not aid us.' Not long after this the accordion played, appropriately enough, *Home Sweet Home*. It may be noted in passing that this was regularly performed by Home's accordion – this trick being one of his most popular; its other favourite tune was *The Last Rose of Summer*.

There were some spirit messages at this seance, even though it was supposedly convened for the purposes of strict scientific investigation only. When Serjeant Cox referred to an incident which had occurred at a seance with Home a few evenings before, at which Cox had been put in touch with a dead daughter named Florence, the spirits immediately assured him, 'I will do it again, you dear old Chinchilla.'[3] This exchange was omitted from the *Quarterly Journal of Science* account of the seance. All these may be described as fairly routine wonders. (It is generally assumed by magicians that the mysterious accordion music would have been produced either by another accordion playing nearby – which, in the circumstances, seems unlikely: this was not Home's home ground but Crookes's, and Home had no obvious accomplice there – or by a concealed musical box which the medium could activate, which would certainly explain the repetition, time after time, of the same two tunes.)

However, the experiment to which Crookes drew most attention took place at the end of the seance. Before the start of the evening's proceedings, Crookes had fitted up a spring balance apparatus. This consisted of a long mahogany board, one end of which rested on a table, while the other end was supported on a spring balance, fastened to a strong tripod stand. Crookes wrote:

> Mr Home placed the tips of his fingers lightly on the extreme end of the mahogany board which was resting on the support, whilst Dr A.B. [Dr Huggins] and myself sat, one on each side of it, watching for any effect which might be produced. Almost immediately the pointer of the balance was seen to descend. After a few seconds it rose again. This movement was repeated several times, as if by successive waves of the psychic force. The end of the board was observed to oscillate slowly up and down during the experiment.
>
> Mr Home now, of his own accord, took a small hand-bell and a little card match-box, which happened to be near, and placed one under each hand, to satisfy us, as he said, that he was not producing the downward pressure.

The very slow oscillation of the spring balance became more marked, and Dr A.B., watching the index, said that he saw it descend to six and a half pounds. The normal weight of the board as so suspended being three pounds, the additional downward pull was therefore three and a half pounds. On looking immediately afterwards at the automatic register, we saw that the index had at one time descended as low as nine pounds, showing a maximum pull of six pounds.[4]

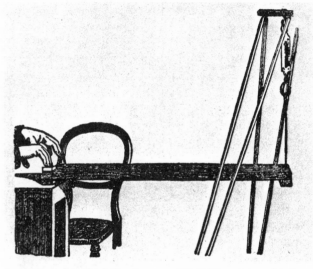

Apparatus with which Crookes tested D.D. Home's 'psychic force'

Did this experiment demonstrate the existence of a hitherto unknown force? Crookes believed it did, and so did Serjeant Cox, who after the seance wrote to Crookes: 'The results appear to me conclusively to establish the important fact, that there is a force proceeding from the nerve-system capable of imparting motion and weight to solid bodies within the sphere of its influence.' Carried away, perhaps, by the novel scientific atmosphere, he added,

I noticed that the force was exhibited in tremulous pulsations, and not in the form of steady continuous pressure, the indicator rising and falling incessantly throughout the experiment. This fact seems to me of great significance, as tending to confirm the opinion that assigns its source to the nerve organisation, and it goes far to establish Dr Richardson's important discovery of a nerve atmosphere of various intensity enveloping the human structure.[5]

Huggins, however, was much less ready to commit himself. When he received his proof copy of Crookes's article, he wrote:

Your proof appears to me to contain a correct statement of what took place at your house. My position at the table did not permit me to be a witness to the withdrawal of Mr Home's hand from the accordion, but such was stated to be the case at the time by yourself and by the person sitting on the other side of Mr Home.

The experiments appear to me to show the importance of further investigation, but I wish it to be understood that I express no opinion as to the cause of the phenomena which took place.[6]

(It may be remarked here that such effects as those with the board and the balance may be achieved by surreptitiously looping a hair or a length of black cotton around the board. This is easily disposed of afterwards, and invisible, especially if – as in this case – unlooked for.)

Crookes sent a substantially unaltered version of this paper to the Royal Society for publication, but to his chagrin, they did not accept it. This was humiliating; but despite this rebuff, and the hostility of many of his scientific colleagues to his spiritualist activities (ranging from dismay on the part of his friends to ridicule and innuendo from those less friendly), he was not deterred. Another article on experiments with Home was published in the October issue of the *Quarterly Journal of Science*, and the fourth and last, a summary of his 'inquiry into the phenomena called spiritual' during the years 1870–3, in the issue for January 1874.

In this last article Crookes gave a classified list of the phenomena he had encountered in the course of his investigations:

1. Movement of heavy bodies with contact, but without mechanical exertion.
2. Percussive and other allied sounds.
3. Alteration of the weight of bodies.
4. Movement of heavy substances when at a distance from the medium.
5. Rising of tables and chairs off the ground, without contact with any person.
6. Levitation of human beings.
7. Movement of various small articles without contact with any person.
8. Luminous appearances.
9. Appearance of hands, either self-luminous or visible by ordinary light.
10. Direct writing.
11. Phantom forms and faces.
12. Special instances which seem to point to the agency of an exterior intelligence.
13. Miscellaneous occurrences of a complex character.

This is indeed a pretty exhaustive list of phenomena, and includes almost everything that anyone, before or since, had produced or was to produce.

In the course of his article, Crookes made a definite distinction between seances taking place at the medium's home, and therefore to a greater or lesser extent under conditions dictated by the medium, not the experimenter, and those which he was able to organize on his own premises. He wrote:

> To gratify curiosity is one thing; to carry on systematic research is another. I am seeking the truth continually. On a few occasions, indeed, I have been allowed to apply tests and impose conditions; but only once or twice have I been permitted to carry off the priestess from her shrine, and in my own house, surrounded by my own friends, to enjoy opportunities of testing the phenomena I had witnessed elsewhere under less conclusive conditions.[7]

There are some definite conclusions to be drawn from the tone and content of these articles. First, it is assumed that although the subject-matter may seem eccentric by scientific standards, Crookes approached his experiments with mediums in just the same way as he would approach any other scientific experiment: dispassionately and methodically. And second, the only seances which provided material for his articles – the only ones he considered scientifically worthwhile – were those which were conducted at his own house and strictly under conditions dictated by him, not the medium, be it Home or Kate Fox (who, by 1871, was occupying a lot of his time). And, granted that these had indeed been the conditions of experiment, Crookes's indignation with those who sought to belittle this work purely on account of its subject-matter would seem to have been quite justified.

Thus he wrote to his old friend and collaborator John Spiller:

> I ask myself: Can this be my old friend who has worked with me in unfolding the mysteries of photography; who has helped me to track out and give to the world a new element; and who now thinks that the anonymous scribble of an ignorant penny-a-liner [Spiller had sent him a cutting from the *Daily News*] will induce me to *sift* my evidence before accepting phenomena as facts!
>
> Good heavens! one of us must have strangely altered before advice like that could pass between us. Have I ever shown haste in forming an opinion? Have I ever admitted a new fact in science on insufficient testimony?[8]

And in reply to a highly destructive article published in the *Quarterly Review*, entitled 'Some Recent Converts to Spiritualism', and written by Professor W.B.Carpenter, he demanded: 'Now, let me ask what authority has the reviewer for designating me a recent convert to spiritualism? Nothing that I have ever written can justify such an unfounded assumption.'9

This is more than a mere quibble. It is a matter of some moment; for enormous importance was attached to Crookes's evidence. His endorsement lent the weight of scientific discovery to what had hitherto been dismissed as superstition and gullibility. If the world accepted Crookes's authority for other scientific discoveries, why should it not do so for this one, too? This is why those concerned with what was soon to be termed psychical research, and what is more often known today as ESP or 'psi' or 'the paranormal', attached and still attach such immense importance to the endorsement of well-known scientists.

Now, what particular qualification have such persons for pronouncing on such things – more, say, than priests, or conjurers, or ordinary intelligent interested observers? The answer, of course, is that they are trained investigators, and are trained, also, to record minutely and accurately what they observe. But there is an important rider to this. The observation must be dispassionate. If a person is extremely anxious to prove something, desperately wants it to be true, then his evidence – if he subsequently finds that the thing is true – must be looked at with great care. Scientists themselves are well aware of this – perhaps none better. If the evidence proving a particular thesis seems to be too perfect it is usually regarded with great suspicion. And stories of scientists who have been totally discredited because they were caught nudging the evidence to prove a particular pet theory are not at all uncommon. More than one brilliant career has been quite destroyed in this way. Even if the scientist's past work is beyond suspicion, even if the contentious theory turns out in the end to be true, there is no salvaging lost credibility.

Bearing this in mind, it is of no little interest to observe that Crookes's unequivocal declarations of objectivity and non-involvement, beyond an understandable fascination with the subject, were quite untrue. He had for the past several years ardently wished to believe in spiritualism. One of the great griefs of his life had been the death of his beloved younger brother Philip in 1867, at the age of only twenty-one, when he was engineer on a cable-laying expedition in Havana. Ever since then he had made strenuous and (he felt) successful efforts to contact Phil by means of spiritual seances. The subject was constantly in his mind, and at the time of the experiments with Home, he entertained no dearer wish than to prove, systematically and scientifically, the truth of the spiritualists' claims.

There is, then, a considerable discrepancy between what Crookes allowed to appear in public print about his involvement with spiritualism, and what was actually the case. This was undoubtedly the result of conscious policy. Crookes was aware, none better, of the importance of seeming objective. Credibility was inseparable from objectivity. Thus the young Henry Sidgwick, later to be President of the fledgling Society for Psychical Research, wrote to his mother in 1874:

> No-one who has not read Crookes's articles in the *Quarterly Journal of Science*, or some similar statement, has any idea of the weight of the evidence in favour of the phenomena. As a friend of mine (who is a disbeliever) says: 'There are only three alternatives – Crookes is either affirming a tissue of purposeless lies, or a monomaniac, or the phenomena are true,' and we seem to be driven to one of these conclusions. And then there is the startling fact that while all this is going on Crookes is exhibiting before the Royal Society experiments of novel and great interest on the motive force of heat. Altogether I am surprised that the thing is not attracting more attention.[10]

Of these three conclusions, Sidgwick plumped, provisionally, for the third – supported by the authority of Crookes's scientific reputation in other fields; the disbelieving friend was inclined, despite everything, to think the whole thing was lies, but, for the same reason, found this hard to credit; whereas the real truth of the matter, as nearly as any of these three alternatives came to approaching it, lay, as we have seen, in the second: that Crookes was a monomaniac. It was the very notion he was doing his utmost – and successfully – to conceal.

For the cool, scientific tone of his *Quarterly Journal of Science* articles is very far removed from the undisguised enthusiasm of his private reports of seances he has attended. Thus on 12 April 1871, he wrote a most excited letter to Huggins – his partner in objectivity, as far as the *Quarterly Journal of Science* was concerned – about a seance the previous night with Home and two other well-known mediums, Herne and Williams (both of whom were later caught in trickery). Among other revealing remarks he says:

> You know that it is universally agreed upon by spiritualists that the phenomena are better in darkness than in light, but Home always refuses to sit in the dark, as he says it is not so satisfactory to those present. On this occasion, however, we induced him to join our dark seance as the phenomena with Herne and Williams are not strong in the light.

This is certainly a far cry from his stated strong preference for conducting seances on his own ground and under strictly controlled conditions.

Later in the letter he makes another revealing statement. He says:

> I feel it is impossible to describe to you all the striking things that took place, or to convey the intense feeling of genuineness and reality which they caused in our minds, but I want you to come and attend at another seance which is appointed for next Tuesday week . . . when Home has promised to come, and we are going to try and get the same party and if possible the same conditions. You must, however, prepare for the chance of a failure. Home was in wonderful power last night, but he is the most uncertain of mediums, and it is quite as likely that the next time absolutely nothing will take place.[11]

If this is a fair description – and why should it not be? – of Crookes's expectations of, and relationship with, D.D.Home during his seances, then it is of some importance. For it shows that, whatever impression to the contrary he may have liked to give, it was not Crookes but Home who was really in control of conditions at those seances. That is to say, Home would only perform when the conditions – whatever these might have been – were right for him to do so. This may have been a question of atmosphere and sympathy – or of being able to distract his watchers at the crucial moment.

And certainly Crookes's notes on these seances, published in 1889, give a very different impression of them from the highly selective articles which he had published so many years earlier. Of course, it is natural for notes to be much fuller than any articles drawn from them; but in this case the question of what is included and what omitted makes a crucial difference to the final effect. As one commentator put it:

> Everyone who reads the . . . accounts of 1871 will be under the impression that the . . . experiments were made at a few seances where everything went on quite smoothly. Men of science are superintending everything; there are no intervals, no hindrances, no unsuccessful experiments, no suspicious movements on Home's part; his psychic force is acting exactly as if it were not proceeding from a man, but from a well-arranged machine.[12]

But, we learn, this was by no means the case. There were a great many seances that were not reported, because nothing of particular interest happened at them; and many moments which went undescribed even during the seances which were the subject of the *Quarterly Journal* articles. These include instances in which the gas was raised or lowered, at the medium's instigation; when Crookes and the other experimenters remained sitting at the table, at Home's request, while the latter was free to move about; when sometimes he ordered them to keep their hands on the table, and they obeyed, and so on. Such things are of course not at all unusual in the average seance; but they do rather destroy confidence in what have been described as the 'alpha and omega of the scientific evidence in the question of mediumistic phenomena'.[13]

This curious dichotomy between what was really at the base of curiosity about spiritual phenomena, and what people were prepared publicly to admit to, was by no means confined to William Crookes. On the contrary, it was common to almost all the scientists and intellectuals who took such an interest in these things at this period, and indeed still persists today. For although it may be considered perfectly respectable to look into the phenomena in a spirit of scientific detachment, people perhaps recognize (as Crookes certainly did) that a quasi-religious involvement undermines any pretence at detachment – just as no one expects the Vatican's report on the Turin shroud to be objective. Moreover, spiritualism was certainly never in any way intellectually respectable; it could only be seen to gain intellectual respectability as a branch of scientific inquiry.

When the Society for Psychical Research came to be established, many spiritualists saw it, with its unremittingly intellectual and rigorous approach to testing its subjects, as generally inimical rather than friendly to spiritualism. In 1885, three years after its foundation, *Light*, then the leading English spiritualist journal, said of it: 'The real *mot d'ordre* of the Psychical Society may be summed up in the well-known phrase, "spirit is the last thing I will give in to", a position which involves some of the most wanton assumptions possible.'[14] But in fact the impulse which led to the establishment of the SPR was un-doubtedly a religious one. Its founder members all approached the subject in the first place through an interest in spiritualism. The publication of Darwin's *Origin of Species* destroyed, for those who accepted it, the fundamentalist conception of the Creation and substituted an essential randomness which many found deeply upset-ting. In common with many others at this time, Henry Sidgwick, the product (like both Gurney and Myers, his co-founders) of a religious household, was racked by religious doubts. It was not only the doubts which were worrying but the very fact, in that obsessively religious time, of doubting at all. From 1860 on, Sidgwick dabbled increasingly in spiritualism. After his first seance he wrote: 'I intend to have as absolute proof as possible whether the whole thing be imposture or not';[15] and it is clear that, from the first, his whole interest was directed at obtaining, if he could, some tangible proof – acceptable scientifically, just as Darwin was acceptable scientifically – of immortality. Certainly this was always F.W.H.Myers's main objective.

In 1867 Sidgwick wrote, after reading Lecky's *History of Rationalism*:

> With the perverseness that sometimes characterises me I took up the subject from the opposite point of view to Lecky, and determined to investigate the evidence for mediaeval miracles, as he insists it is not an investigation of this evidence. . . . The results have, I confess, astonished myself. I keep silence at present even from good words, but I foresee that I shall have to entirely alter my whole view of the universe and admit the 'miraculous', as we call it, as a permanent element in common history and experience. You know my 'Spiritualist' ghost-seeing tendencies. These will link on, and the origins of all religions find themselves explained.[16]

Thirteen years later, in 1880, he put it even more strongly: 'The dilemma is clear and certain to me. *Either* one must believe in ghosts, modern miracles, etc., *or* there can be no ground for giving credence to the Gospel story.'[17] Thus the SPR was from the first involved in a quest for a peculiarly nineteenth-century grail: positive and intellectually acceptable proof of immortality cleared of any association with fraud or humbug. Spiritualism seemed to offer a path to this goal; it was therefore hard to resist, even though humbug, fraud and triviality were associated with a good deal of spiritualism.

As an intellectual pursuit, though, Sidgwick found psychical research, on account of its lack of development and the trivial nature of most of the phenomena, very unsatisfying. In 1884 he noted: '. . . though I think Psychical Research profoundly important to mankind, whereas sound views on the evolution of political ideas are a luxury easily dispensed with, I am ashamed to find how much more interested I am in the latter than in the former.'[18] But if Sidgwick, a political scientist, could not get up any real intellectual interest in the psychical phenomena he had set out to investigate, the same was not true of a great many natural scientists. For these, the question of spiritualism was intimately entangled with one of the burning arguments of the moment.

The theory of natural selection propounded by Charles Darwin in the *Origin of Species*, published in 1859, with its ideas of evolution through random variation and competition for survival, was of course not the only view then in circulation of how species had arrived at their present state. It was in competition, for instance, with the account of events given in Genesis – the set of ideas now known as Creationism. And it was also competing with Lamarckism – the theory of evolution through the inheritance of acquired characteristics propounded by Jean-Baptiste de Lamarck. For many people – including many who did not think of themselves as being profoundly religious, but who had inherited a pattern of religious thought which had, almost unconsciously, become part of their outlook on life – Darwinism was profoundly disturbing in its implications. It was not that they wanted to adhere to the fundamentalist view that the Bible was the literal truth, but the notion of randomness which was so essential a part of the theory of natural selection seemed to preclude any possibility of there being a God. Darwinism meant that there was no grand plan, no pattern, no thought behind the universe. As an indignant defender of the old order put it in an anonymous pamphlet, 'Tyndall says, "Depend upon it, if a chemist, by bringing the proper materials together in a retort or crucible, could make a baby, he would do it." Doubtless he would, and eat it too, if he could only make it savoury enough. Why not? what are life and death to a physical-force philosopher? Simply the starting and stopping of a bit of mechanism.'[19]

Darwin himself, and also Alfred Russel Wallace, who had arrived independently at the theory of natural selection and whose name was associated with Darwin's in those Linnaean Society papers which preceded the publication of the *Origin of Species*, were as worried as anyone by the distressing religious implications of their own theory. And for Wallace, there was an additional difficulty: this lay in the size and complexity of the human brain, whose capacities were so much greater than the uses to which it was put, and so infinitely greater than those of any animal brain. He was absolutely unable to see this as a product of natural selection. This great leap seemed to him quite irreconcilable with the gradual, many-stepped process of evolution through natural selection. In the event he came up with a solution to this difficulty which horrified many evolutionists. Quite simply he put that part of man represented by his brain into an entirely different category from his body or from any other species on earth. These had all evolved through the millennia; but man's brain was a direct gift of God, and thus exempt from theory and randomness. So Wallace, the strictest of evolutionists, was able, though only by crude dissociation, to mesh his scientific and his religious views and incidentally to adopt, in their minutest and most literal detail, the wilder extremes of spiritualism.

The supporters of Lamarck had no such philosophical difficulties to contend with. Lamarckism was not random. It implied a constant upward progression of the natural order, as species passed on those

improvements and adaptations they had acquired during their life-
times. One of the most obvious anomalies of this view of things hinged
on its apparently excessive optimism. Why should it always be progress that was implied, why were the only characteristics that were
passed on the good and helpful ones? The explanation given was the
very opposite of what Herbert Spencer was soon to call Darwin's
'survival of the fittest'. It was that there existed a great directing life
force imposing its pattern on the universe.

Supporters of this theory were known as vitalists. They were not
necessarily religious. Lamarck himself was not, nor was the intellectual and scientific tradition from which he sprang, that of Diderot and
Goethe. And some of the best-known adherents of vitalism were
distinctly anti-religious, notably Samuel Butler and, later, George
Bernard Shaw (both, however, utopians). But clearly, although
vitalism did not imply a religious view, it was easy for any vitalist who
felt so inclined to see God's workings in the transcendent life force, and
to view the heritability of those characteristics acquired by the thinking, feeling, learning side of the organism as proof of the existence of
that distinctly non-corporeal entity which some people liked to call
the soul.

A nicely paradoxical philosophical situation thus occurred when
Wallace tried to convert Samuel Butler, the leading Lamarckist of the
day, to spiritualism. He failed absolutely. Butler had not spent the
whole of his adult life shaking off the chains of religion only to have
them reimposed as a consequence of his scientific outlook! So he, who
could from a philosophical point of view so easily have reconciled
religion – though perhaps not spiritualism – with his biological views,
utterly rebuffed poor proselytizing Wallace, for whom the reconcili-
ation involved such intellectual agonies. When Wallace sent Butler a
copy of his pamphlet *Miracles and Modern Spiritualism*, Butler

wrote me three letters in a week, chiefly to explain that the whole subject
bored him. In the second letter Butler wrote: 'Granted that wonderful
spirit-forms have been seen and touched and then disappeared, and that
there has been no delusion, no trickery. Well; *I don't care.* I get along quite
nicely as I am. I don't want them to meddle with me. I had a very dear
friend once, whom I believed to be dying, and so did she. We discussed the
question whether she could communicate with me after death. 'Promise', I
said very solemnly, 'that if you find there are means of visiting me here on
earth – that if you *can* send a message to me – *you will never avail yourself of the
means, nor let me hear from you when you are once departed.*' Unfortunately she
recovered, and never forgave me. If she had died, she would have come back

if she could; of that I am certain by her subsequent behaviour to me. I believe my instinct was perfectly right; and I will go further: if ever a spirit-form takes to coming near me, I shall not be content with trying to grasp it, but, in the interest of science, *I will shoot it.*'[20]

Had he done so, this might have given rise to an exceptionally interesting legal case.

It may be thought that these particular controversies, embedded as they were in the age which gave rise to them, died with Queen Victoria, and that, as time went on, other, more 'modern' arguments took their place; much as 'psi', ESP, UFOs, and Uri Geller have replaced levitation, ectoplasm, spirit materializations and mediums in the vocabulary of today's psychical researchers. Nothing, as it happens, could be further from the truth. The philosophic and scientific positions of leading enthusiasts in this field remained and remain founded upon the same preoccupations as concerned Darwin's contemporaries.

Certainly vitalism is the link between many of the leading scientific and philosophical intellects who have been and are connected with psychical research since the foundation of the SPR and until the present day. These include such diverse names as Henri Bergson, proponent of the *élan vital*; C.G.Jung, with his 'collective unconscious'; Hans Driesch, biologist turned philosopher, and the leading theoretical proponent of vitalism (like Bergson, he was for a time President of the SPR; today Sir Alister Hardy, who proposes the idea of a 'group mind' or 'psychic blueprint' among some lower animals; and, perhaps the best-known and most highly respected of today's theorists of 'psi', Arthur Koestler – who is also an enthusiastic Lamarckist.

Naturally, everyone is entitled to adduce whatever arguments he wishes in order to support his particular theories and philosophies. Such arguments may or may not be rebutted, but what is essential, if there is to be any possibility of logical argument, is to be quite clear from what basis the argument is being conducted. In particular, it is important to know whether that argument is a scientific or a religious (or quasi-religious) one. For the criteria are absolutely distinct. In science the criteria generally accepted are those stated by Popper: 'Bold ideas, unjustified anticipations, and speculative thought are our only means of interpreting nature. . . . And we must hazard them to win our prize. Those among us who are unwilling to expose their ideas to the hazard of refutation do not take part in the game.'[21] Indeed, the scientist adhering to Popperian standards must be quite ruthless with his darling theories: 'Using all weapons of our logical, mathematical and technical armoury, we try to prove that our anticipations were false.'[22] The scientist, then, must be prepared, however unwillingly, to sacrifice his theory. And, above all, there is no place in the scientific world for what Camus called 'the leap into the absurd', or the emotion accompanying it. Belief is based only on proof: to demand belief without proof, or in the hope of proof, is to demand an act of faith. Psychical researchers, like Crookes himself, have been well aware of the necessity of distancing scientific inquiry from religious attitudes – and in particular, psychical research from spiritualism – if it is to stand any chance of acceptance as science. Thus Hans Driesch, the distinguished vitalist, said:

> The attitude of 'official' science to psychical research is still one that will in the future appear quite irresponsible. People constantly confuse psychical research with spiritualism, and they do not appreciate the fact that the former name is descriptive of a specific field of *investigation*, whereas the latter is that of one particular *hypothesis*, the truth or falseness of which does not in the least affect the results of the investigations on which it is based.[23]

The difficulty is that time and again the issue is confused: writings which purport to be objectively and scientifically based turn out to be founded upon a religious rather than a scientific standpoint. William Crookes may have been among the first to perpetrate this sort of confusion, but he was certainly not the last.

Take, for example, J.W.Dunne, author of *An Experiment with Time*, who has already been briefly mentioned. In this book, Dunne explicitly based his theory upon the possibilities of the new space-time continuum offered by the Einsteinian view of the universe. And speaking of the views available to the thinker 'towards the end of the last century' (i.e., the nineteenth century) he said:

> Supposing, now, that a man of that time had experienced a series of dreams similar to those narrated in the earlier part of this book; he would have discovered something flatly opposed to the conventional view of Time. And that view was sacrosanct: the whole supposedly unassailable structure of physics bore witness to its accuracy. In these circumstances, our hypothetical dreamer would have been compelled to take refuge in Mysticism.[24]

Who, reading this passage, could possibly imagine that Dunne himself first approached the whole series of experiences which culminated in the series of dreams discussed in his most famous book through mysticism and spiritualism? Certainly no inkling of this was offered to readers of the *Experiment with Time*. But in his autobiographical book '*Intrusions*' this is made quite clear.

> Between the ages of twelve and thirteen I experienced on three or four occasions the curious thing which is called, I understand, 'ecstasy'.
>
> I can remember only the last of those adventures. . . . The cause, that time, was a garden viewed from my bedroom window on a still and silent night. As I stared at it, there came upon me an overwhelming awareness that everywhere, just behind the scene, lay a reality too wonderful, joyous and exciting for words – a reality which was making itself more and more apparent – a reality on the very point of breaking through – a reality which I should *remember* then as, 'of course', having always been there. Then, as I waited eagerly, I began to sense through the growing transparency a multitude smiling at me and pleased with my delight. The feeling grew until the joy was almost unbearable; and then it faded away, and the scene strengthened into impenetrable solidity. But I was left happy.[25]

It may reasonably be argued that such experiences, though undeniably important in forming the person who was later to report his 'experiment with Time', were not essential to the understanding of the latter. But in *Intrusions*, Dunne makes it quite clear that he deliberately omitted any spiritualist or mystical aspects of the very dreams he was discussing:

> In *An Experiment with Time* I wrote: 'The dream had been a peculiar one (in ways which have nothing to do with this book) and the net result of it all was that I lit a match to see whether the watch had really stopped.'
>
> Curiously enough, nobody has ever asked me what were those undescribed 'ways' in which that dream had been peculiar.
>
> This is what happened: In the dream, at the end of it, I was looking down at the stopped watch lying in my hands. At that moment I became aware of a growing din made by an immense multitude of voices. They were all shouting at me – shouting in the wildest excitement – but there was no unison in what they cried, and the clamour was a veritable babel. Then, as the visual part of the dream began to fade, someone said, 'That will do!', and the babel ceased for an instant. 'Now, then!' he cried, and all the multitude shouted in unison, '*Look! . . . Look! . . . Look! . . . Look! . . . Look!!*'
>
> And I awoke with the memory of those voices almost ringing in my ears. Naturally, I struck a match and looked.[26]

Of course, the experience in itself is interesting, but what is perhaps even more interesting is that Dunne was not prepared to reveal it when he first published the dream. Presumably he thought that such an emphasis would detract from the serious scientific approach which he so assiduously sought throughout his book, and in which light he was determined to have it received and discussed. He may or may not have been right. What seems to me undeniable is that he would have revealed a perspective on his experiences quite different from anything which was allowed to permeate the deliberately impersonal tone of *An Experiment with Time* – and which would have given, as it happened, a much more accurate picture of the experience in its entirety. Such an approach can hardly be called objective or scientific.

Dunne, not surprisingly, was a vitalist: he saw a refusal to believe in the Universal Mind as an act of blind solipsism. Another adherent of this belief was the man who more than anyone else put the investigation of what he liked to call 'parascience' on a respectable footing, Dr Joseph Banks Rhine. Rhine began his academic career as a Harvard biologist. While at Harvard he encountered the great psychologist William McDougall, the successor in the Harvard chair of William James and Hugo Muensterberg. McDougall was a leading member of the American Society for Psychical Research, which had been started by William James, following the establishment of the British SPR McDougall was a keen follower of the tradition of interest in these matters which James had begun. And when, subsequently, McDougall moved to Duke University, Rhine followed him there, eventually to set up the Parapsychology Laboratory which made him famous.

It was Rhine's adherence to vitalism that first brought him into the field of parapsychology. He says, in clearly autobiographical vein: 'For the young American biologist during the first quarter of this century to have attempted to build a successful career on a vitalistic theory of life, one that held that there was a distinctive life factor over and above the forces and substances that belonged in the world of matter, would have been professional suicide.' Of the biological circles of the time he adds: 'They naturally found the physical aspects of nature more easily caught by instruments and measured by mathematics. . . . Any hypothesis that dragged in the nonphysical: that is, any vitalistic hypothesis – would be downright subversive to the prevailing scientific philosophy.'[27] So, reasonably enough, Rhine went off and established his own laboratory, quite separate from biology or the accepted forms of experimental psychology, to pursue his own line of enquiry. But was this enquiry a purely scientific one? There are passages in *The New World of the Mind* from which one can only conclude that, whatever its reputation for balance and objectivity, it was not balanced and objective, but was rather motivated by the most extreme ideology. For Rhine, parascience was quite inseparable from religion.

In his discussion of the implications and further development of his work, Rhine first suggests that there should be a study of the effects of prayer. He proposes to co-opt God as an experimental partner: 'There is a belief . . . that a divine personal agency exists to which prayer is directed. The co-operation of this agency itself could in all sincerity and propriety quite well be included in the research plan. In fact, the older world religions were supposedly founded with the aid of miracles, that is, co-operative demonstrations by divine agencies.' And not only the older religions: to this list he might well have added Christian Science and Spiritualism.

Rhine is undaunted by the difficulties such an endeavour might be thought to present. 'This leads to the question which most devout religious minds consider the greatest one of all: Is there a universal mind or divine agency? . . . If such a universal personality exists, those who believe the hypothesis a reasonable one can perfectly well, with proper thought and ingenuity, design a research programme that would establish its presence and operation.' Does this mean that the tangible proof of the existence of God is, *pace* Driesch and all those others who battle to get this accepted as a science among other sciences, the real end and aim of all research into the supernormal? Rhine is in no doubt that this is indeed the case. He sees this, moreover, as the great undeveloped weapon in the cold war.

'Most thinking people know that blind faith in dogmatic revelationistic religion cannot counter the claims and promises of communism,' he asserts, and continues hopefully: 'It may force a realization of the need to push research on the spiritual armament against communism to its logical scientific limits. . . . Think of all the good man-hours of prayer spent through all the centuries by all the billions around the globe, with no-one throughout these ages taking the obviously sensible precaution of checking up!'[28]

Motivation and the conduct of experimental work are of course two quite separate things. The former *may* affect the latter, but it will not necessarily – and probably should not – do so. In fact Rhine was very much alive to the possibility that his work might be discredited if it were found that the results had been fudged, and there is little doubt that he himself was absolutely scrupulous. Unfortunately he did not get interesting results. (By contrast, the English mathematician

S.G.Soal got some remarkable results in card and number guessing, but it has since emerged that when he was not being duped, he was himself fudging the figures. Because Soal was a mathematician of repute, this went unsuspected for many years, and was not finally verified until after his death.)

What motivation clearly does affect is the way in which results are perceived. A typical response is that of Brian Inglis, in his recent book *Natural and Supernatural*. For Inglis, the mildest scepticism seems to be unacceptable. For instance, he talks about 'members of the Society for Psychical Research, some of whom were notoriously more interested in exposing fraud than in obtaining positive results'.[29] Or, talking about Richard Hodgson and his investigation, on behalf of the SPR, of Madame Blavatsky: 'Hodgson had studied under Sidgwick, and had been a member of the Cambridge psychical research society; the trip to India was consolatory, and in view of his inexperience, he might have been expected to be cautious. His report, however, describing a system of fraud worked by Madame Blavatsky, bluntly pronounced that "none of the phenomena were genuine".'[30] In fact Hodgson's report was a thoroughly painstaking piece of work which has never been seriously questioned, least of all by Madame Blavatsky herself.

The attitude expected of responsible investigators in this field is thus made quite clear. Fraud is a possibility they should be rather unwilling to accept, even when, as in the case of Madame Blavatsky, it is thrust under their noses. It is hardly the scientist's approach, any more than is the frequently reiterated cry (particularly plaintive among the early spiritualists, but still very far from unknown) that just because someone has been caught cheating once does not mean that all his or her other, possibly genuine, productions should be discredited. If this is really to be the case, then parascience is unique among sciences: for in all other scientific fields, to be caught out just once in fraud is to be instantly discredited. And yet Inglis concludes by talking about 'the long and often bitter struggle to obtain scientific recognition and acceptance; the campaign which is still in progress today'.[31]

The importance of clear thinking in this field, and more particularly of sorting out the basis from which one is conducting one's argument, is perhaps shown most clearly in Inglis's discussion of the contribution of scientists to this enquiry. He particularly cites the evidence of Crookes, who was an outstandingly successful and respected research-er in a great many scientific fields and who later (in 1913) became President of the Royal Society; and that of Charles Richet, one of the leaders of psychical research in France, a biologist who was eventually awarded the Nobel Prize for his work on allergic reactions. Is it to be suggested, asks Inglis (in this, as in much else, representative of a great many enthusiasts in this field) that these eminent men were somehow unhinged – in this respect at least? But if that were so, how could they possibly have achieved what they did in other fields? Or are we to suggest that in this field alone they were not scientific in their approach?

The answer to this question would seem, precisely, to be – yes! The premises were indeed different in this one field. And if this is realized, then much that was puzzling falls into place.

4
The Ghost-Grabbers

If, now, I am asked where all this is to end; what is to come of it in case familiar converse with visitants from a higher life shall continue to be permitted here; I reply that it is not our affair. We have to deal, for the present, with facts, not with the results from facts. – ROBERT DALE OWEN, January 1875

As the 'physical phenomena' of mediumship developed in scope, it was clear where, ultimately, they were tending. What, after all, distinguished spiritualism from any itinerant conjuring-show or display of parlour magic? – Why, it was about *spirits*; and after they had shown what they could do, it was obvious that the next step must be for them to show themselves. The first 'full-form materialization' of which we hear seems to have taken place as early as 1860, at a seance held by Robert Dale Owen, with the ineffable Mrs Leah Underhill (lately Fish) as medium. Owen reported that in the course of this seance a veiled and luminous female figure appeared and walked about the room. It may be imagined that such a fashion, once begun, could not but become the rage. It was not long before spirit figures were to be encountered at seances all over America.

This new and (if it were veritable and not fraudulent) astonishing phenomenon was greeted by devotees with the usual matter-of-factness, that tone of voice which creates such a strange effect in conjunction with the subject-matter under discussion. Thus a popular handbook for aspiring mediums headed its fifth chapter 'Materialization' and began:

This phase of mediumship usually develops from some more simple form. Probably every physical medium has potential materializing power, but few seem capable of supplying it in a sufficient quantity for the building up

of complete forms. . . . As materializations are built up by discarnate entities who have a knowledge of the work, it is wise for the would-be materializing medium to pay attention to the advice of the guides. This kind of
mediumship does not develop very rapidly, and those who have the power
will need patience to sit for some time, even though nothing happens. It
must be borne in mind that a lot of preparation is needed on the inner
planes before the manifestations take place. [The author added rather
disconsolately:] In the early days of the Spiritualist movement people
seemed more ready to wait.[1]

The form of materializing seances seems to have been more or less
established very early on. The company would sit in the dim half-dark
surrounding the medium's 'cabinet' from which, in time, the materialization would emerge. Time would pass. Hymns would be sung. 'In
the Sweet By-and-By', 'There Are Angels Hovering Around' and
'Beulah-land' seem to have been considered especially appropriate.
Then 'there is a mysterious gleam of something white before the dark
curtain behind which the medium has gone in her trance; the music
pauses, and the more susceptible lean forward and draw long intense
breaths. The white gleam becomes a veiled woman who advances into
the room; and I feel my next neighbor tremble, and see the big drops of
sweat start out on his forehead, and the woman on the other side leans
heavily against my shoulder.' The spirit form, like her dematerialized
cousins, would then generally pick out one or more members of the
audience with whom to communicate in particular; and at the end of
the performance 'she retreats to the curtain and "dematerializes"
directly in front of it. . . . The form appears to grow gracefully shorter
and fainter until it becomes a mere glimmer and melts away, leaving
nothing but a rapidly disappearing puddle of white muslin against the
opening in the curtains.'[2]
    There can be no doubt that such performances, whether fraudulent
or not, were extremely effective. Most people found the mere notion
of communication with a lost relative emotional enough, even
though the means were primitive and the communications rudimen-
tary. For such people, the experience of actually meeting these
hitherto lost souls in what might be described as the flesh could be
moving almost beyond bearing. And there can be no doubt that many
people really did recognize their lost loved ones in such 'materializations'. Dr H.H.Furness, a member of the Seybert commission appointed by the University of Pennsylvania, in memory of a wealthy
spiritualist benefactor, to investigate spiritualism, was particularly
astonished by this. He had, in the course of his enquiries, attended

twenty or thirty materializing seances, and himself remained unconvinced. 'I have never seen anything which, in the smallest degree, has
led me to suppose that a Spirit can be, as it is termed, materialized,' he
wrote. 'It is superfluous to add that I never recognized a materialized
Spirit; in only two instances have any Spirits professed to be members
of my family, and in one of those two instances, as it happened, that
member was alive and in robust health, and in the other a Spirit
claimed a fictitious relationship, that of niece.' Nevertheless, he had to
admit that others were undoubtedly convinced, though he could not
for the life of him work out how or why.

> It is, I confess, a very puzzling problem . . . to account for the faith, un-
> doubtedly genuine, which Spiritualists have in the personal reappearance
> of their departed friends. Again and again have I asked those who have
> returned, from an interview with a Spirit at the Cabinet, to their seats
> beside me, whether or not they had recognized their friends beyond a
> peradventure, and have always received an affirmative reply, sometimes
> strongly affirmative. I was once taken to the Cabinet by a woman and
> introduced to the Shade of her dead husband. When we resumed our seats,
> I could not help asking her: 'Are you sure you recognized him?' Where-
> upon she instantly retorted, with much indignation, 'Do you mean to imply
> that I don't *know* my *husband*?' Again, at another seance, a woman, a visitor,
> led from the Cabinet to me a Materialized Spirit, whom she introduced to
> me as 'her daughter, her dear, darling daughter,' while nothing could be
> clearer to me than the features of the Medium in every line and lineament.
> Again and again, men have led round the circles the Materialized Spirits of
> their wives, and introduced them to each visitor in turn; fathers have taken
> round their daughters, and I have seen widows sob in the arms of their dead
> husbands. Testimony, such as this, staggers me. Have I been smitten with
> color-blindness? Before me, as far as I can detect, stands the very Medium
> herself, in shape, size, form, and feature true to a line, and yet, one after
> another, honest men and women at my side, within ten minutes of each
> other, assert that she is the absolute counterpart of their nearest and
> dearest friends, nay, that she *is* that friend.[3]

Even for the unconvinced, such displays could hold substantial
attractions. When well produced they must, even if fraudulent, have
been very pretty. Recipes were circulated among mediums for producing the desirable diaphanous and luminous effect when
impersonating a ghost in this way. A typical one required twenty-one
yards of the finest white silk veiling, two yards wide and very gauzy.
This was carefully prepared: the fabric was first washed carefully in
seven waters, and while it was damp, worked thoroughly and rapidly
through a solution of 1 jar 'Balmain's Luminous Paint', half a pint of

Demar varnish, one pint odourless benzine, and 50 drops lavender oil. This was then to be tacked to a large wall space and left to dry for three days. It was then washed with naphtha soap until all the odour was gone and the fabric was perfectly soft and pliable. Only silk, it was emphasized, would retain the paint through this washing. Then, when the fabric was exposed to light, it would shine for a long time in the dark and appear as soft, luminous vapour – just the thing for a well-turned-out spirit. (The gentleman who revealed this recipe disclosed that he used this apparel for the impersonation of 'Cleopatra and other queens'.) The skirt could be made of ordinary white silk painted with a design of leaves, vines, etc., in undiluted luminous paint – this would appear much brighter than the gauze. Undiluted paint was also used for the crown and any beads and jewels. As for the face, it would only be visible when a dim luminous mask was worn; or the gauze could cling to it.[4]

The only other thing a medium needed to practise was his or her technique for appearing or disappearing. The trick of melting gradually into the floor has already been mentioned; and certainly the most effective method for producing the spirit was to have it materialize in the same gradual manner. Dr Furness was very enthusiastic about this method.

A minute spot of white, no larger than a dollar, is first noticed on the floor; this gradually increases in size, until there is a filmy, gauzy mass which rises fold on fold like a fountain, and then, when it is about a foot and a half high, out of it rises a Spirit to her full height, and either swiftly glides to greet a loved one in the circle, or as swiftly retires to the Cabinet. It is really beautiful, and its charm is not diminished by a knowledge of the simplicity of the process, which, as I have sat more than once when the Cabinet was almost in profile, I soon detected. The room is very dark, the outline of the black muslin Cabinet can only with difficulty be distinguished even to one sitting within six feet of it; a fold of black cloth, perhaps five feet long and four feet wide, is thrown from the Cabinet forward into the room, one end is held within the Cabinet at about two or three feet above the floor, and from under the opposite edge, where it rests on the floor, some white tulle is slowly protruded, a very little at first, but gradually more and more is thrust out, until there is enough there to permit the Spirit, who has crept out from the Cabinet under the black cloth and has been busy pushing out the white tulle, to get her head and shoulders well within the mass, when she rises swiftly and gracefully, and the dark cloth is drawn back into the Cabinet. I always want to applaud it; it is charming.[5]

But being a gentleman, Dr Furness restrained himself, just as he restrained himself from rushing to the spirit's assistance when her filmy robe caught on a nail and she was stuck on her knees. 'I shall never forget the half-comic, half-appealing glance as her eyes looked up into mine, when she was only partially-materialized. . . . It was very hard not to spring to her assistance, but such gallantry would have been excessively ill-timed.'

Dematerialization was less complicated. The easiest way was for the spirit to retreat slowly into the cabinet, and, once there, gradually to enfold herself in the black curtains, starting from the top. Collapsing into nothingness could be achieved by merely holding out the draperies on a stick, with no body inside: the spirit could first retreat into the cabinet, then immediately reappear, and magically dematerialize.

In all instances of materialization, it will be seen that the cabinet was an essential accessory. This was first introduced by the Davenport Brothers, a well-known travelling act of illusionists presenting themselves as spirit mediums, who allowed themselves to be securely tied by the audience and then performed all sorts of feats inside their closed cabinet – playing musical instruments, waving their arms about, etc. – appearing, when the doors were reopened, securely tied exactly as they had begun. (They had perfected the art of so holding themselves, when they were tied, that they ensured enough leeway to be able to slip a wrist. It is in fact very hard for an amateur to tie an experienced performer so securely that it is really impossible to slip the bonds. The person who brought this art to perfection was of course Houdini, of whom we shall hear more later, and to whom Ira Davenport confessed his secrets just before his death.) Naturally, it was not long before other mediums saw how useful a cabinet could be, and in a short time the cabinet, whether it was an elaborately constructed piece of carpentry or (more usually) just a curtain strung up across the corner of a room, became a standard piece of equipment at all spiritual seances.

Clearly the production of fraudulent 'full-form materializations' (and whether there were any other sort is a separate question, which will be discussed later) required the skilful exploitation of various different techniques if it was to be at all effective. It is therefore not surprising to find that the skills in question were handed on from medium to favoured medium, a chain of instruction which can be traced across the Atlantic.

We have seen that this fashion began in America, and was soon extremely widespread there, so much so that by the time of the University of Pennsylvania's *Seybert Report*, including Dr Furness's observations just quoted, in 1871, it was regarded as a commonplace of the medium's repertoire. However, we do not hear of it in England – let alone anywhere else in Europe – before this date, when it would seem to have been introduced to British spiritualists by three American mediums, Kate Fox and Mr and Mrs Nelson Holmes.

Kate Fox is of course already familiar, and had no doubt been acquainted with the detail of 'materializations' since Leah had begun experimenting with them. She had begun to produce her own ghosts in New York, when she gave a series of sittings to a rich widower, Mr Livermore, and was able to invoke a figure in whom he recognized his dead wife. She also specialized in spirits from outside the family circle, notably Benjamin Franklin, who even in his wholly discarnate form had always been a popular visitor to seances. Her materializing exploits after her arrival in England are less well-documented, although, as we have already seen, the ghost of the late Mrs D.D.Home appeared in her house. The spirits, it seemed, found her propinquity particularly comfortable. She even recorded that her baby son, Ferdie, inherited the gift: a 'spirit form' had lifted him from where he was lying and held him out to her, or so she recorded; as one commentator put it, the first instance of a baby being carried by spirits.[6]

Of more immediate interest to us, however, is Mr Holmes, who, with his wife, set up a highly successful mediumistic practice in the early 1870s in a house in Old Quebec Street, just behind Marble Arch. Among the highlights of the Holmes's seances was the materialization of John King, alias, or so he claimed, the famous pirate Sir Henry Morgan. The Holmeses were already familiar figures in American spiritualism, as was John King. King was by far the most frequently produced male ghost, just as his daughter Katie was the most generally known female. There seems no real reason why they, in particular, should have been so prone to reincarnation. Perhaps it was just that, once having begun, they had acquired a taste for it. Again, maybe mediums preferred to produce a tried and generally accepted figure rather than attempt a chancy individual flight of imagination. A Dr Eliott Coues suggested that 'he was condemned for his atrocities to serve earthbound for a term of years, and to present himself at materializing seances on call'. Maybe. Dr Coues went on:

Any medium who personates this ghost puts on a heavy black horse-hair beard and a white bed sheet and talks in sepulchral chest-tones. John is as standard and sure-enough a ghost as ever appeared before the public. Most of the leading mediums, both in Europe and America, keep him in stock. I have often seen the old fellow in New York, Philadelphia, and Washington

through more mediums than I can remember the name of. Our late
Minister to Portugal, Mr J.O'Sullivan, has a photograph of him at full-
length, floating in space, holding up a peculiar globe of light shaped like a
glass decanter. This trustworthy likeness was taken in Europe, and I think
Russia, but I am not sure on that point.[7]

Mr and Mrs Holmes were intimately familiar with both members of
the King family. 'King' materializations were their specialty in their
native Philadelphia, where the ghost was generally not John, but
Katie. This materialization, or series of materializations, was successful while it lasted, but it did not last long; for that Katie was revealed
to be a young lady living nearby – an exposure which received considerable publicity, embarrassing not only the Holmeses but also
Madame Blavatsky, who happened to be lodging with them at the
time. H.P.B., as might be expected, had little time for such a milk-
and-water creation as Katie King, but herself preferred to identify
with the swashbuckling John, whose signature and comments adorned
many of her letters. After this fiasco Madame Blavatsky moved to New
York, where she went on to found the Theosophical Society. Where the
Holmeses went is not stated; for Philadelphia had been their refuge
when John King, Katie's father, had incurred the wrath of Mrs Guppy
– after which London was too hot to hold either the Holmeses or this
particular incarnation of Mr King.

Mrs Guppy was a leading figure of the London spiritualist scene at
this time. She was at once grotesque, comical and more than somewhat
sinister, the kind of person who confirms that, even in his wilder flights
of imagination and what one might take to be exaggeration, Charles
Dickens never strayed far over the edge in his characterizations. Mrs
Guppy, then Miss Nichol, had begun her spiritualistic career in the
mid-1860s as a protégée of Alfred Russel Wallace. At that time her
main mediumistic feats were raps and *apports* – flowers and, later,
vegetables, which would, on request, drop from nowhere on to the
table and the sitters. Wallace was so impressed that he begged various
scientific friends to come and witness Miss Nichol's marvels. Many
declined; one who accepted was the physicist John Tyndall, who was
not, however, won over. Raps were duly produced. 'They were, in fact,
very varied in tone – some mere ticks, others loud slaps or thumps. But
to all this he paid no attention. He joked with Miss Nichol, who was
always ready for fun, and after the raps had gone on some time, he
remarked, "We know all about the raps. Show us something else. I
thought I should see something remarkable." But nothing else came.'[8]
On one remarkable occasion Miss Nichol, by then Mrs Guppy, was

herself apported, appearing amid considerable commotion upon the table during a seance being held in Lamb's Conduit Street. She swore, and members of her family confirmed, that but a moment since she had been sitting at the table of her own home in Highbury, doing the household accounts: she had just inscribed the word 'onions' when she was suddenly snatched away and whizzed through the air the two or more miles to central London. Considerable publicity was accorded to this event, which was the more remarkable in that Mrs Guppy was enormously fat.

Mrs Guppy's size might preclude the possibility of her being lighter than air, but in other respects she seems to have found it no disadvantage. Her hugely voluminous skirts might be used to great effect. It was widely suspected that this was how many *apports* arrived unseen in previously inspected rooms; and it was not only *apports* that the petticoats concealed. On at least one occasion an observer (Mrs Sidgwick's sister) saw them provide welcome refuge for a materialization called Abdullah, whence he was able, some time later, to re-emerge.[9]

Mrs Guppy had prided herself upon being the first medium in England to produce materialization phenomena. By 1872 she had perfected the Punch and Judy cabinet, a completely light-tight compartment in which the medium might close him or herself and there accumulate sufficient 'power' to construct a materialized figure, which could then be scrutinized by the assembled company, and although such displays were, as we have seen, by no means unknown elsewhere, Mrs Guppy seems to have assumed a definitely proprietary attitude to the whole London materialization scene, from then on.

It was not that she would not stand any competition: just that she wanted to control its nature and personnel. Mrs Guppy had her own protégés. These included the young mediums Herne and Williams who practised in partnership at Lamb's Conduit Street, and on to whose table she had herself materialized. In time, they began to produce their own 'full-form' spirits, John King himself making regular appearances at Lamb's Conduit Street. To this, Mrs Guppy had no objection whatever. She did not, however, like uncontrolled competition. And unlike most mediums, who preferred to co-operate among themselves and certainly hesitated before exposing a rival – a proceeding, after all, which might well rebound in the most embarrassing way – Mrs Guppy had no compunction about trying to destroy her rivals in the most determined and vindictive manner.

The first objects of her attention were the Holmeses. Any medium knew perfectly well how most effectively to destroy the phenomena at a seance. At a dark seance, this was the simplest thing in the world: one need only strike a light at the wrong moment. And on 27 February 1873, that was what happened at the Holmeses'.

Various accounts are extant of the happenings on this occasion. The most thorough collection is an assemblage of 'depositions' collected and published by Samuel Guppy, the elderly spiritualist who had married Miss Nichol. The agent of destruction was not, however, Mrs Guppy herself, but another medium called James Clark. Here is what took place, as recounted by a lady who was present:

> I went to the seance of Mrs Holmes on Thursday, 27th February. They placed the visitors in different seats. I turned round and saw Mr J.C. there. I sat by him. Some lady who had never been there before asked me to sit by her. Some gentleman in a velvet coat whispered to Mrs H., and then they sent some little boy who they said was there every day to sit between us. Then Mrs Holmes was tied by a gentleman, and the lights were put out – previously the holding hands being particularly insisted on. Then the guitar and tambourine were carried about the room touching several persons. When the light was struck, Mrs Holmes's hands were still tied. Before striking the light, the Spirit's order was waited for. Lights being again extinguished, there was an awful noise of guitar, tambourine, and people saying they were touched, in the midst of which J.C. struck a very bright light (a Bryant and May patent safety), which revealed Mrs Holmes dancing about the room like a fay, with the guitar in her hand (of course, free from all ties). She immediately threw down the guitar and rushed back to her seat, from which she was about six feet distant, and placed herself as though in a trance, and commenced speaking in a cracked voice: 'O, de blackguard, de blackguard, to break de conditions by striking a light – turn de blackguard out,' when Mr — said, 'Make him stay here till the seance is over, and then we will pitch him out of the window.' I did not see what Mr Holmes was doing when the light was struck, as my eyes were fixed on Mrs Holmes. Mr Holmes then locked the door; then Mr — went up to Mr J.C. and tried to persuade him to sit the seance out, and said that if he did not sit the seance out, he would expose him before the company present. Mr J.C. said to the effect, 'You can expose what you please – I defy you.' Then a gentleman got up and said that he had seen quite sufficient, and that he objected to see any one kept in the room against his will, and that he would not stay. Then they hesitated a little, and Mr Holmes unlocked the door, and Mr Edwin Ellis and Mr J.C. went out. After the gentlemen were gone, Mrs Holmes, in a cracked voice, said, 'De two blackguards haze been sent here by de squaw Guppy, dey were sent here to detect something, and I thought I would humour them, and I got up to go and take his matches away, but only got as far as de middie of de room.'[10]

(It will be noticed that Mrs Holmes's control was the inevitable Red Indian, a distinctively recognizable spirit voice in an emergency.)

Clearly, the Holmeses had been expecting something of the sort – they certainly seem to have been in no doubt about where the source of the trouble was. What had happened was that they were involved, to their misfortune, in what came to be known as the 'Guppy plot'. And at this time the Holmeses were not Mrs Guppy's only, or even her main, target. This was Miss Florence Cook, then a young and beautiful girl (she was still only sixteen), who was to become the most famous materializing medium of them all.

Miss Cook lived with her family in Hackney, now a run-down outpost of London's East End, but at that time a respectable suburb with rows of substantial houses. It was also a flourishing centre of spiritualism. The Dalston Association of Enquirers into Spiritualism was established in 1870, and held weekly seances for members, and open meetings to which strangers were admitted, once a month. The secretary of this organization, Mr Thomas Blyton, was to remain one of Florence's firmest supporters; a council member, Mrs Amelia Corner, was within a few years to become her mother-in-law. Certainly Florence Cook was the most celebrated spiritualist ever to emerge from the Association.

From the first, Florence specialized in materializations. At the beginning, however, these extended only to the spirit's face. 'Face manifestations' were given twice weekly at the Cook home in Hackney. No charge was made; this allowed Miss Cook to demonstrate a convincingly disinterested and uncommercial motivation. She was not in it for the money, at any rate. What *was* she in it for, then? The answers to that question might, as we have seen, be manifold; among them one might cite (apart from the ungovernable need to share her extraordinary powers with a wider public) the knowledge that excellent connections, otherwise quite unattainable for a young lady of dubious background from Hackney, were to be made through spiritualism, and the irresistible need, at sixteen, to have a bit of fun. . . .

Florence's shows were very much a family party. They were held in the Cooks' semi-basement breakfast-room. This possessed a conveniently large cupboard, which served as the 'cabinet'. In it was placed a Windsor chair; an aperture was cut in the upper part of the cupboard door, through which the 'spirit faces' might be seen. At the beginning of the seance Florence, who was small, dark and very pretty, and always rather elaborately dressed and coiffed, entered the cupboard and sat down on the chair. A length of cord was placed upon her lap, and the cupboard door shut. The company was then encouraged to sing hymns, a very usual practice at seances. Believers held that it encouraged the right sort of atmosphere to develop; sceptics thought it was a convenient cover for any suspicious noises which might otherwise be heard from inside the cabinet. At any rate, after some time the cupboard door was reopened and Florence was displayed tied round the neck, waist and wrists to the back of her chair. The knots were duly inspected and sealed by the company, and the cupboard door shut once more. Shortly after that, there appeared in the aperture 'a face which looked utterly unspiritual and precisely like that of the medium, only with some white drapery thrown over the head'. This observer, Maurice Davies, remarked that 'the aperture was just the height that would have allowed Miss Cook to stand on the chair and peep out. I do not say she did; I am only calculating the height. The face remained some minutes in strong light; then descended. We opened the cupboard, and found the little lady tied as before with the seals unbroken. Spiritual, or material, it was clever.'[11]

There were a certain number of variations available in the 'spirit faces'. Another version was black, once again surrounded by white drapery, and certainly not at all like the medium. Was this face a mask? Davies observed that 'the drapery ran right round the face, and cut it off at a straight line on the lower part. This gave the idea of a mask. I am not saying it was a mask. I am only throwing out a hint that, if the "spirits" wish to convince people they should let the neck be well seen.'[12]

Were those really the countenances of ghosts? There was certainly no question in the mind of Maurice Davies (and it should be remarked that he was by no means hostile to spiritualism; quite the contrary) that if Miss Cook could only slip her bonds, there was nothing to prevent her standing on the chair and making faces through the aperture. And as it appears that she tied herself up, there seems little reason why she should not so have arranged things that she could untie herself with a minimum of trouble. But the Dalston spiritualists, and a number of others, were ready to be convinced; the only question being – what next? Where should she go from here? And to that, there could only be one answer. So far, she had materialized spirit faces. Now, it remained only to add the bodies for the illusion to be perfect and complete. Which was where Mrs Guppy came in.

Full-form materializations were by 1873, the year Florence Cook began to make her mark upon the spiritualist scene, becoming increasingly fashionable in London spirit circles. John King could be met and shaken by the hand any Saturday night at Lamb's Conduit Street, *chez* Messrs Herne and Williams, thus giving excellent proof of the solidly material nature of the forms, or at least the hands, built up by spirits. The same gentleman might be met with at the Holmeses' in Old Quebec Street. Florence Cook did not have to look far to find a suitable ghost for herself. She would, of course, materialize John's daughter Katie King.

It was not long before the new spirit was all the rage. Florence still gave seances at home in Hackney; but her activities were no longer confined to that unfashionable quarter. There were a great many wealthy and well-connected spiritualists in London now only too eager to make her acquaintance. However, it was at home in Hackney that Florence, or Katie, or both (if indeed they were not one and the same) met her, or their, come-uppance.

The procedure was very much the same as that of almost all such 'materializing' seances. The medium was sat, in quiet and privacy, behind the curtains of her cabinet, to get together the forces with which she would produce the spirit. In the room outside the curtain, the audience waited. There were certain rules, unwritten but strictly imposed, which always applied. It was taken for granted that no one must ever try to touch the spirit, certainly not without its consent. This, it was generally known, would result in death or serious injury to the medium, out of whose bodily essences the spiritual substance was so laboriously produced. It was also strictly forbidden to peek behind the curtain while the process of producing the spirit was going on. Audiences must wait passively and accept what they were given, if indeed they were given anything at all.

It will thus be seen that the two simplest and most obvious ways of testing whether or not the spirit was a true ghost, or whether it was not rather the medium, or an accomplice, dressed up to look like a ghost, were ruled out of court. Cynics might say that it was for this very reason that these rules were imposed. Mediums retorted that, if people did not care for the rules, there would be no more spirits produced, and there would be an end to it. Of course, not everybody was so tractable. Ghosts were grabbed from time to time, on either side of the Atlantic, without any apparent mortal injury to the medium. And this, on that day in December 1873, was what happened to Florence, or rather, to Katie King.

The arrangement at the Cook household had now somewhat progressed from the rather primitive conditions in which the 'face manifestations' had been produced in the basement. The seances now took place in the first-floor drawing-room, which was conveniently divided by folding doors. The room on one side of the doors acted as cabinet, while the audience sat on the other side and waited for the spirit. On the occasion in question, the gentleman who broke the rules was a Mr Volckman. Florence was duly bound (with tape round the waist) and enclosed in her cabinet. In the fullness of time Katie King, draped in white, appeared. As was her habit, she offered her hand to all the sitters, and even made light conversation with them. For forty minutes the spirit entertained the sitters. At this point she gave her hand to Volckman. He, suspicious that it was Florence, not Katie, whom he was holding, would not let go her hand, and told her why; after which he put his arm round her waist. At this point the light was put out and Florence's fiancé, Edward Elgie Corner, rushed to her aid, assisted by a Mr Tapp, another of the sitters. After a struggle, during which the spirit scratched Mr Volckman's nose and even pulled out some of his whiskers, she was rescued from his grasp and hustled to join her medium in the cabinet, where, after an interval of five minutes, Florence was found, dishevelled and distressed but with the tape round her waist as it had been in the beginning. One might have thought that this would be enough, and that the last had been seen, if not of Florence Cook, at least of Katie King. But nothing could be further from the truth. As it turned out, this was just the beginning of Katie's splendid career.

There were in the 1870s two main weekly spiritualist publications in London. One, *The Medium and Daybreak*, was edited by John Burns, a radical who was very much in the mould of many American spiritualists. The other, *The Spiritualist*, was edited by a Mr W.H. Harrison, a partisan of Florence's. In this dispute, the *Medium* took Volckman's part, *The Spiritualist*, Florence's. *The Spiritualist*, on 12 December 1873, three days after the incident in question, published an article headed 'Gross Outrage at a Spirit Circle', which, although it could not deny some of the more suspicious features involved (e.g., the five minutes which had elapsed between Katie's being hustled back into the cabinet and Florence's being revealed there, duly taped to her chair) was – as the title would suggest – sympathetic to Florence and furious with Volckman. In reply to this, Volckman wrote a letter which *The Spiritualist* would not publish, and which he therefore sent to *The Medium*:

Sir: In the report which appears in your journal of a seance lately held at Mr Cook's, I am accused of seizing the ghost, thereby breaking the conditions by which the members of the circle were bound.

In reply I have to state that having for forty minutes carefully observed and scrutinized the face, features, gestures, size, style and peculiarities of utterance of the so-called spirit, the conviction irresistibly forced itself upon me that *no ghost*, but the medium, Miss Florence Cook herself, was before the circle. I perceived also an occasional tip-toeing by the young lady as if to alter her stature, and was much struck by the utter puerility of her remarks throughout the seance. I am confirmed in my conviction, as above stated, by the facts that the *struggling* ghost had to be *forcibly* extracted from my grasp, and afterwards to be 'aided' into her cabinet by a Justice of the Peace. I may add that no third parties had any knowledge of my invitation to, or presence at, the seance in question.[13]

This last sentence was perhaps an acknowledgement of the fact that all was not, or was alleged not, to be as simple as it might seem on the surface. Mr Volckman was an experienced investigator of spiritualist phenomena, having been a member of the committee which looked into the matter for the London Dialectical Society in 1871. But he was not (or so Florence's friends alleged) as impartial in this particular matter as his credentials might lead people to suppose. For (it was alleged) he was a special friend of Mrs Guppy – which must have been true, since, some years later, after the death of her then husband, the good-natured Sam, he married her. And it was common knowledge that Mrs Guppy wanted nothing more than to destroy Miss Cook, whom she perceived as a threat to her ascendancy over the London spiritualist scene – and of whom, being herself notoriously fat and ungainly she was, one may imagine, consumingly jealous.

These presumptions are borne out by comments in at least two contemporary documents. The first is from the private notebooks of the editor of *Light*, Stainton Moses. Moses is referring to the occasion already described when 'Mr J.C.', otherwise James Clark, struck his highly inopportune match at Mrs Holmes's seance. Moses was present on that occasion, and afterwards commented:

> . . .J.C. . . . sat in the centre of the circle holding the match which he had struck and looking with a fixed gaze before him. He said 'I think that is satisfactory.' His face was the most unnatural one I ever saw – the face of a maniac, or of one under possession by an evil spirit. . . . Mr Holmes told him to leave the room asking him, 'Who told him to strike a match'. He said 'I told myself' . . .J.C. is a dangerous and unscrupulous person, instigated, as I believe, by Mrs Guppy to molest Mrs Holmes. Mrs G. is now engaged in an attempt to bedaub the character of Miss Cook and Mrs Holmes. She is a jealous woman, and will stick at nothing. J.C. is her unscrupulous tool.[14]

And a little more than three years later, when he was safely back in

Philadelphia, Nelson Holmes wrote a letter about the whole Guppy–Holmes–Cook affair to D.D. Home, who was then in London:

> In January 1873, Mrs Guppy called at our residence, 16 Old Quebec Street,
> London, W., and endeavoured to enlist our co-operation in a plot whereby
> a certain Mr Clark, Mr Henderson and one Vlockman [sic] were to be hired
> to attend a seance at Miss Cook's, and, watching their opportunity, at a
> favourable moment, while the manifestations were in progress *to throw vitrol*
> [sic] *in the face of the spirit*, hoping thereby to destroy for ever the handsome
> features of Miss Florrie Cook, and thus at one fell stroke to effectually
> remove from further use a medium who, Mrs Guppy claimed, had and was
> taking all her, Mrs Guppy's, friends away from her and upon whose
> patronage Mrs G. had long depended. [Clearly, there was no doubt in Mrs
> Guppy's mind that Florence and Katie were one and the same.]
>   While reciting this horrible scheme to us, she seemed fairly possessed by
> a legion of fiends, and her rage at Miss Cook and 'her doll face', as she
> termed it, was fearful to behold.[15]

Holmes goes on to say that he immediately took steps to warn Florence
and her friends of what was afoot, and gave Mr Guppy a stern talking-
to – at which a promise was extracted that the affair should go no
further. This, says Holmes, was the reason for Mrs Guppy then
turning her rage upon the Holmeses. Meanwhile, Florence took her
precautions. It was rumoured that Volckman tried vainly for nine
months to gain admission to one of Florence's seances before he finally
bribed his way in with a present of jewellery.

Nevertheless, whatever the motive, there was no denying that the
ghost, when seized, seemed to have manifested decidedly unghostly
characteristics. Could a spirit, no matter what the provocation, have
scratched the nose and pulled out the whiskers of its molester? But
spiritualists seemed less perturbed by these inconsistencies than by
the breach of seance manners involved. *The Spiritualist* had, by 6 February, received (or so it said) only one letter in favour of Volckman,
and even this castigated him for breaking the rules and pointed out
that if Miss Cook wanted to neutralize any bad effect created, all she
had to do was to 'send . . . him an invitation to come and shake hands
with her in such a manner as would assure him of her ghostly state'.
The editor commented that none of the other sitters at the seance ever
wanted to meet Volckman again, 'and instead of desiring to convert
him, would prefer that he remain outside the movement. When testimony is wanted, that of old and tried leaders of the spiritual movement, is of infinitely more value than Mr Volckman's. Assuming a
medium to be powerful enough to get manifestations in the face of the

most unfavourable conditions, they do well to withhold them from persons who make seances scenes of violence and outrage.'[16] And although John Burns complained in *The Medium* that 'the absurd limitations imposed at the circle in question reduced the seance to the level of an exhibition, with a desire to force matters to a foregone conclusion',[17] it was pointed out that exactly the same limitations were in force at the 'face seances' held in the rooms over Mr Burns's bookshop.

Everyone agreed, however, that the thing could not be altogether dismissed. People's faith had been shaken, even if not hopelessly undermined. The real question, though, was whether, at the same time that Katie was promenading around the seance room, Florence remained in the cabinet. This question was raised in several letters to *The Spiritualist*, far the most significant of which was written by William Crookes. It was couched in his usual reasonable terms:

Amongst all the arguments brought forward on either side touching the phenomena of Miss Cook's mediumship, I see very few facts stated in such a way as to lead an unprejudiced reader, provided he can trust the judgment and veracity of the narrator, to say, 'Here, at last, is absolute proof.' I see plenty of strong assertion, much unintentional exaggeration, endless conjecture and supposition, no little insinuation of fraud, and some amount of vulgar buffoonery; but no-one has come forward with a positive assertion, based upon the evidence of his own senses, to the effect that, when the form which calls itself Katie is visible in the room, the body of Miss Cook is either actually in the cabinet, or is not there.

It appears to me that the whole question narrows itself into this small compass. Let either of the above alternatives be proved to be a fact, and all the other collateral questions may be dismissed. But the proof must be absolute, and not based upon inferential reasoning, or assumed upon the supposed integrity of seals, knots and sewing, for I have reason to know that the power at work in these phenomena, like love, 'laughs at locksmiths'.

Crookes then went on to describe a seance, featuring Katie, which he had attended a few days after the 'outrage', and at which he had heard the medium moaning in the cabinet while the ghost was out in the room. Did this constitute the evidence he was after? Clearly, despite his earlier stern words, he was inclined to accord the benefit of the doubt. 'I admit that the figure was startlingly life-like and real, and, as far as I could see, in the somewhat dim light, the features resembled those of Miss Cook; but still the positive evidence of one of my own senses that the moan came from Miss Cook in the cabinet, whilst the figure was outside, is too strong to be upset by a mere inference to the contrary, however well supported.'

Crookes now decided to invite Florence, as he had invited Home, to be tested in the stricter conditions of his own house. He reported:

Miss Cook is now devoting herself exclusively to a series of private seances with me and one or two friends. The seances will probably extend over some months, and I am promised that every desirable test will be given to me. The seances have not been going on many weeks, but enough has taken place to thoroughly convince me of the perfect truth and honesty of Miss Cook, and to give me every reason to expect that the promises so freely made to me by 'Katie' will be kept.[18]

There were a number of reasons why William Crookes must have been delighted to encounter a new subject for experiment in the field of 'psychic force'. The Home experiments had come to an end in 1871. Home had then left England for Russia, and on his return, his health had deteriorated so that he was no longer available for Crookes's work. His place, for a while, had been taken by Kate Fox, who presented herself to Crookes in 1871 armed with an introductory letter from her New York patron Mr Livermore, or rather, from his deceased wife, Bella, presumably written by herself.

There is a record of the sessions with Kate in Crookes's index of outgoing letters (reproduced by his biographer). This is, as one might expect, rather cryptic; but, for anyone acquainted with the story, the tale it has to tell is clear enough. The strain of life as a spirit medium, with all the responsibility entailed by her status as one of the founders of the movement, was proving too much for Kate; and by the time she arrived in England, she was succumbing to alcoholism and hysteria. A few of the entries from Crookes's 'index' tell the story only too clearly:

1871.
Nov. 24, Fox, K., 'Dear Wm Guard Katie.' Bella Livermore.
Nov. 24, Fox, K., Sick, will I call?
Nov. 24, Fox, K., Promise to Varley [Cromwell Varley, FRS., one of Crookes's scientific friends who shared his interest in spiritualism] after 'sickness'.

1872.
Jan.   Fox, K., Draft of letter for me to send to Mr L[ivermore] (not sent).
Feb. 8,   Fox, K., Summons for cab (cost me 7/6).
Feb.   Fox, K., Penitent letter after I brought her home.
Feb.   Fox, K., 'Can't come.' Engagement.
Feb.   Fox, K., 'Can't come.' Not well (German). . . .
April 4, Fox, K., Account at Bowler's (statement).
April 13, Fox, K., About my threatened letter to Mr. Livermore. . . .[19]

In September of that year, Mr Jencken proposed marriage to Kate. The sessions with Crookes thereafter tailed off; and finally came to an end in 1873 in what sounds like a burst of acrimony:

1873.
May 25, Fox, K., Abusing Livermore. Our invitation.
May   Fox, K., Nellie's [Mrs Crookes] answer to the above.
May 28, Fox, K. Preparations for coming . . . Penitent.
June 13, Fox, K., Lies about telegram of June 10.
June 22, Fox, K., Wants money (to Mrs H.).
July   Fox, K., Can't come. Boil. Note to Jencken.
July 24, Fox, K., Boil. My receiving Livermore. Threats.

And after three more entries, the Fox listings cease.

Clearly, after the consummate skills of Home, Kate Fox, even without her inconvenient lapses into incapacity, must have been something of an anticlimax. The only description of these seances with Crookes is in letters from Francis Galton, who interested himself in spiritualism and attended some of the seances, to Charles Darwin. It seems that nothing to compare with Home's marvellous tricks took place. Kate was held, or 'controlled', hand and foot; but all she needed to do was free a foot (no very difficult task) to produce her phenomena, which consisted (of course) of raps, and also of writing produced under the table. Galton says:

> I had hold in one of my hands of *both* the hands of Miss F's companion who also rested both her feet on my instep, and Crookes had equally firm possession of Miss F. Yet paper was sent skimming in the dark about the room and after the word 'Listen' was rapped out the pencil was heard (in the complete darkness) to be writing at a furious rate under the table, between Crookes and his wife and when that was over and we were told (rapped) to light up, the paper was written over – all the side of a bit of *marked* note paper (marked for the occasion and therefore known to be blank when we began) with very respectable platitudes – rather above the level of Martin Tupper's compositions and signed 'Benjamin Franklin'! The absurdity on the one hand and the extraordinary character of the thing on the other, quite staggers me.[20]

Mrs Sidgwick, one of whose very first experiences in spiritualism was a similar sitting with Kate Fox two years later, reports, 'It impressed me a good deal, though even at the time – in those early days of our investigation, when our experience was less than it is now – we thought that Mrs Jencken might have written the word with her foot, and the writing is just of the quality which can be so written without much difficulty.'[21]

In fact Kate Fox seems to have been a notably clumsy operator, and 'fished' for information from her sitters in the most obvious manner (or so Mrs Sidgwick tells us). Crookes's biographer, Fournier d'Albe, turns this to her advantage, spiritualistically speaking. Remarking on Kate's tendency towards alcoholism, he remarks: 'It is well known that most good conjurers are almost of necessity total abstainers, so that the above statement [about her alcoholism] tends to support the spiritualist version of the Fox episode.'[22] This might, however, seem a rather disingenuous interpretation.

After these rather disillusioning experiences, it may be imagined that Crookes turned eagerly to the possibilities offered by Florence Cook. In every way, they were more alluring. The production of actual, freely moving spirits was surely the ultimate, the peak, in spiritualist experience. To be able to look closely into such phenomena must be the only matter of any interest left to one who had been able to work so closely with Home, who in every other way so far outdid any other medium then practising. And on the personal level, who would not prefer to work with pretty, obliging little Florence rather than the distraught and unreliable Kate Fox?

It may be stated at once that William Crookes was not disappointed in the sanguine expectations of Florence and Katie with which he had begun his tests. The seances at which Katie King appeared were held either at Hackney or else at Crookes's house in Mornington Road. The atmosphere on these occasions may best be conveyed by Crookes himself:

I pass on to a seance held last night at Hackney. Katie never appeared to greater perfection, and for nearly two hours she walked about the room conversing familiarly with those present. On several occasions she took my arm when walking, and the impression conveyed to my mind that it was a living woman by my side, instead of a visitor from the other world, was so strong that the temptation to repeat a certain celebrated experiment became almost irresistible. Feeling, however, that if I had not a spirit, I had at all events a *lady* close to me, I asked permission to clasp her in my arms, so as to be able to verify the interesting observations which a bold experimentalist has recently somewhat verbosely recorded. Permission was graciously given, and I accordingly did – well, as any gentleman would do under the circumstances.

Mr Volckman will be pleased to know that I can corroborate his statement that the 'ghost' (not 'struggling', however) was as material a being as

Miss Cook herself. But the sequel shows how wrong it is for an experimentalist, however accurate his observations may be, to venture to draw an important conclusion from an insufficient amount of evidence.

Katie now said she thought she should be able this time to show herself and Miss Cook together. I was to turn the gas out, and then come with my phosphorus lamp into the room now used as a cabinet. This I did, having previously asked a friend, who was skilful at shorthand, to take down any statement I might make when in the cabinet, knowing the importance attaching to first impressions, and not wishing to leave more to memory than necessary. His notes are now before me.

I went cautiously into the room, it being dark, and felt about for Miss Cook. I found her crouching on the floor. Kneeling down, I let air into the lamp, and by its light I saw the young lady, dressed in black velvet, as she had been in the early part of the evening, and to all appearance perfectly senseless. She did not move when I took her hand and held the light close to her face, but continued quietly breathing.

Raising the lamp, I looked around and saw Katie standing close behind Miss Cook. She was robed in flowing white drapery, as we had seen her previously during the seance. Holding one of Miss Cook's hands in mine, and still kneeling, I passed the lamp up and down, so as to illuminate Katie's whole figure, and satisfy myself thoroughly that I was really looking at the veritable Katie whom I had clasped in my arms a few minutes before, and not the phantom of a disordered brain. She did not speak, but moved her head and smiled in recognition. Three separate times did I carefully examine Miss Cook crouching before me, to be sure that the hand I held was that of a living woman, and three separate times did I turn the lamp to Katie and examine her with steadfast scrutiny, until I had no doubt whatever of her objective reality. At last Miss Cook moved slightly, and Katie instantly motioned me to go away. I went to another part of the cabinet and then ceased to see Katie, but did not leave the room till Miss Cook woke up, and two of the visitors came in with a light.[23]

Not only did Crookes thus fulfil the original object of his exercise and see Katie King and her medium together at one and the same time – so proving that Katie was not merely Florence dressed in a white sheet; he actually photographed them together. (These photographs, sadly, seem to have been destroyed by Crookes later, although several photographs both of Florence Cook and of Katie King do exist.) The only slight drawback to the photographs, according to his description of them, is that the medium's face was never actually visible, since photography involved the use of strong electric light, and she muffled her head in a shawl to prevent this light falling on her face. 'We did not on these occasions actually see the face of the medium because of the shawl, but we saw her hands and feet; we saw her move uneasily under the influence of the intense light, and we heard her moan occasionally. I have one photograph of the two together, but Katie is seated in front of Miss Cook's head.'[24]

Cynics might wonder whether this really did prove anything at all. If Florence's face was not visible, then what was to prove that this was not merely an accomplice lying there? And if (as Crookes asserted) the ghost was actually taller than Florence – he ascertained this by super-imposing separate photos of the two of them standing in the same places; and various people affirmed that Katie had long, luxuriant light brown hair, while Florence's was short and dark – then what was to stop an accomplice from performing as the ghost?

This was certainly the impression received by another participant at one of the Hackney seances, Maurice Davies, who had witnessed and described her earlier 'face seances'. Of the later occasion he wrote:

The Professor [Crookes] acted all the time as Master of the Ceremonies, retaining his place at the aperture; and I fear, from the very first, exciting suspicion by his marked attentions, not to the medium, but to the ghost. When it did come it was arrayed according to orthodox ghost fashion, in loose white garments, and I must confess with no resemblance to Miss C. We were at the same time shown the recumbent form of the pillowed medium, and there certainly was something blue, which might have been Miss C., or only her gown going to the wash. By-and-by, however, with 'lights down', a bottle of phosphorized oil was produced, and by this weird and uncanny radiance one or two privileged individuals were led by the 'ghost' into the back bedroom, and allowed to put their hands on the entranced form of the medium. I was not of the 'elect', but I talked with those who were, and their opinion was that the 'ghost' was a much stouter, bigger woman than the medium; and I must confess that certain unhallowed ideas of the bedroom door and the adjacent kitchen stairs connected themselves in my mind with recollections of a brawny servant girl who used to sit sentry over the cupboard in the breakfast room. Where was she?[25]

It was a pertinent question, and unless it could be answered satis-factorily, of course nothing was proved. For Florence Cook was not the only 'materializing medium' able at this time to display both spirit and medium simultaneously. For example, this was also done by Charles Williams, whom we have already met as one of the Herne and Williams partnership, when he materialized Katie's father John King. At a seance on 16 December 1873, John King, after several attempts during which 'the light, notwithstanding the spirit's efforts, became so dim, that we could see no more than a dark something in the medium's place', was able to show Prince Sayn-Wittgenstein (but nobody else) 'Mr Williams asleep in his seat, while John King stood over him lighting up his figure with his lamp'.[26] But Williams has not gone down in history as having been able to produce genuine ghosts; rather, he is known as a famous fraud, and Prince Wittgenstein as a famous gull. It may be added that Florence Cook knew both Herne and Williams very well, having given joint sittings with them both early in her career.

Why, then, does any doubt remain about Florence Cook and her 'Katie'? What was there to differentiate her exploits from those of Charles Williams? After all, Volckman, whatever his motives, had shown up something that looked very like a fraud; and many years later, when Florence had long abandoned 'Katie King' and was materializing a spirit called 'Marie', Sir George Sitwell inflicted much the same indignity upon this spirit as Volckman had upon her ghostly predecessor. He grabbed; announced that he felt corsets beneath the spiritual draperies; and, after a struggle, the spirit was hurried away by a sympathizer, Florence reappearing in her cabinet, dishevelled, after a 'short interval' had elapsed. Florence's partisans assert that the claims of these persons to have unmasked a fraud should be regarded with just as much caution as the claims of others – including Florence – to have perpetrated a miracle. Given that the explanation of any such set of circumstances is likelier to be fraudulent than miraculous, one may agree or disagree with this approach. But even were one inclined, in this case, to prefer the miraculous to the fraudulent alternative, there is still more to explain away. For 'Katie King' did not always appear alone. On 4 April 1874, *The Spiritualist* published a letter from Crookes stating that 'Miss Cook's "Katie" has been walking about in my laboratory along with Miss Showers' "Florence" with their arms entwined schoolgirl fashion, and in a strong light.'

At the time when Florence Cook and 'Katie King' were becoming famous, another young lady, Miss Mary Rosina Showers, was producing yet another celebrated materialization by the name of 'Florence Maple'. (The reader must make an effort to disentangle the numerous Florences and Kates frequenting the spiritualist scene at this time.) Miss Showers, too, was among the mediums tested by William Crookes in his experiments. However, unlike Florence Cook, Rosina Showers was unmasked by mistake – and by a well-wisher.

The fiasco occurred while she was giving a materializing seance at the house of Serjeant Cox, the lawyer who had collaborated with Crookes on the Home experiments. Just as it was an unwritten rule that no spirit must be grabbed unawares, though it might consent to shake hands and even offer to cut off pieces of spirit veiling or spirit hair as souvenirs, so there was another important condition: there must be no peeking into the 'cabinet' while the medium was gathering her, or his, forces for the coming materialization. Unfortunately Miss Cox, the learned Serjeant's daughter, was not aware of this rule. On this occasion Miss Showers was proposing to materialize only the face of 'Florence Maple', and after a while the cabinet curtains parted, and the spirit's face duly appeared in the opening, coiffed in white, her eyes turned piously to heaven. The company filed past to look more closely. Nobody touched the curtains until it came to the turn of Miss Cox, who, unaware of the gaffe she was committing, drew them aside to reveal the very substantial body of Miss Showers standing on a chair and vainly clutching the curtains together. The spirit face was revealed to be undeniably attached to this body, and in the course of the struggle the white headgear was displaced, revealing the medium's copious locks beneath.

Even this however, was not the end of Miss Showers or 'Florence Maple'. Serjeant Cox, though obliged to admit that the two, at least on this occasion, seemed to have been one and the same, would not admit that any conscious fraud had taken place. Miss Showers, he insisted, was in a state of 'unconscious somnambulism' at the time.[27] Such intellectual contortions were by no means unique to the learned Serjeant. They formed part of the faith-preserving armoury of many a believer. Pre-eminent in this line was Alfred Russel Wallace.

This distinguished biologist performed many such mental gymnastics in his time, but perhaps none more spectacular than when he, in his turn, was trying to explain away a grabbed spirit which had, once again, turned out only too solidly fleshy. On this occasion the spirit of a little Indian girl named 'Pocha' materialized at a seance in Peterborough (it will be seen that the Redskins had now penetrated far into the English provinces) had turned out to be the medium, a Miss Wood, on her knees, with her dress off and draped in muslin. *Light* published this news 'with deep regret', and it elicited an extraordinary reply from Wallace.

He declared, first, that binding or tying the medium was not a satisfactory 'test' because 'it is known to all investigators that mediums can be loosened from any bonds or from clothing, and re-introduced into them, and that the medium's body can be *transfigured*. . . . The elongations of Mr Home, and the American medium (Mrs —) whose body was found to be absent from the cabinet in which her clothes remained, while forms of men, women and children successively came out, will occur to the memory of all acquainted with Spiritual literature.'

He went on to reiterate the old argument that mediums can only work under favourable conditions, when 'forms can be produced apart from the medium; when conditions are less favourable they can only be produced by releasing and transfiguring the medium; and the latter is in many cases only one degree less marvellous than the former'. But, unfortunately, if any of these 'transfigured' forms were seized at the wrong moment, the wrong impression would be got. 'But we may go further than this, and maintain on substantial grounds the extreme probability that if a form is seized which is really distinct from the medium, yet the result may be that the form and the medium will be forcibly brought together, and a false impression created that the form *was* the medium.' Wallace added:

> So far as I can remember, every medium for materialization, however perfectly their powers may have been tested, however good their character, has been subjected to accusations of fraud on somewhat similar grounds to Miss Wood. The fact that whenever a form has been seized it has been found, *after a struggle of some moments' duration*, to merge into the medium, lends additional support to the view here advanced, since on the mere doctrine of chances there ought to have been by this time, at least, one genuine form seized if such a capture is possible.[28]

Against sophistry such as this, who can argue? Yet the fact that Wallace, one of the finest minds of his age, was an unquestioning supporter of spiritualism and its phenomena, has been cited by spiritualists, then and ever since, as a reason why such phenomena as these 'materializations' cannot be dismissed out of hand.

Which brings us back to Florrie Cook and William Crookes. How is it that Miss Cook, though seized more than once (in a state of unconscious somnambulism or otherwise) pretending to be a spirit; though acting in conjunction with such a recognized fraud as Rosina Showers (who later confessed to her fraudulence); though producing (if the photographs are to be believed) a ghost so thoroughly unghostly looking as Katie King – who, whether or not she closely resembled Florence, certainly looked more like a Victorian young lady with a handkerchief pinned over her hair than anything else – nevertheless remains the one possible argument still cited for the production of 'full-form materializations'?

The answer, of course, lies in the identity of her sponsor. William Crookes, that celebrated man, like Wallace one of the leading scientists of his day, swore by her. And if he was not in a position to know, who was? Was not he privy to all the secrets of the cabinet? Did he not set up complex electrical tests to make sure that Florence could not move from her place while Katie King walked about in the next room, and did he not assure everyone that these had been foolproof, and satisfactorily carried out? Why, then, should he be doubted?

We have already, in the last chapter, discussed some of the reasons why; and these are undoubtedly the explanation for the contorted reasoning of Wallace, as quoted above. Where faith rules, logic flies out of the window. But they are not the explanation for the curious behaviour of William Crookes vis-à-vis Florence Cook. The story of Florence Cook and William Crookes, the Medium and the Scientist, has given rise to considerable controversy. Two books (*The Spiritualists*, by Trevor Hall, and *The Critics' Dilemma*, by E.J.Dingwall) and a book-length article in the *Proceedings* of the Society for Psychical Research ('William Crookes and the Physical Phenomena of Mediumship', by R.G.Medhurst and K.M.Goldney) have been published on the subject, to say nothing of many shorter pieces.

Briefly, the argument centres on the question: are we to believe Crookes's declarations about Florence Cook and Katie King? Was the production of spirits a skill particular to some Victorian mediums, in the same way that since the advent of Uri Geller people have claimed to bend pieces of metal in sealed containers? Or was Crookes lying, and if so, why? Hall and Dingwall contend that he was lying, and that the reason was that he was Florence's lover. The 'materializing' seances were an excuse for assignations, and the relationship gave Florence a hold over Crookes which would ensure that he never betrayed her, but helped, and would continue to help, her career. There are very good grounds for believing this argument. It is soundly based on evidence; it explains all the facts; and it feels right.

Certainly descriptions of the seances, both by Crookes himself and by other spectators, indicate that the scientist hardly took a detached view of the proceedings. 'The effusive Professor', wrote Maurice Davies, 'has "gone in" for the Double with a pertinacity altogether opposed to the calm judicial examination of his brother learned in the law, and with prejudice scarcely becoming an FRS.'[29] And Crookes's own description of Katie certainly bears out this judgement:

Photography is inadequate to depict the perfect beauty of Katie's face, as words are powerless to describe her charms of manner. Photography may, indeed, give a map of her countenance; but how can it reproduce the brilliant purity of her complexion, or the ever-varying expression of her most mobile features, now overshadowed with sadness when relating some of the bitter experiences of her past life, now smiling with all the innocence of happy girlhood when she had collected my children round her, and was amusing them by recounting anecdotes of her adventures in India?

Round her she made an atmosphere of life;
The very air seemed lighter from her eyes,
They were so soft and beautiful, and rife
With all we can imagine of the skies;
Her overpowering presence made you feel
It would not be idolatry to kneel.[30]

If Crookes and Miss Cook were using the seances to cover their assignations, this was not the first or the last time this convenient aspect of 'full-form materializations' had been noted and acted upon. (Readers will not be surprised to hear that Mrs Guppy was rumoured to set up 'seances' for the sole purpose of assignations.) A report of a materialization seance in America in 1868 laid great emphasis on the physical gratification to be gained from such spiritual intercourse:

The spirit beckons to some one; and a series of enquiries by the various members of the audience, 'Is it me?' 'Is it me?' presently shows that a young man is wanted who goes forward nearly to the curtain and is whispered to, embraced, and very audibly kissed; and the spirit then goes back behind the curtain, but reappears again for a moment to exchange some more kisses. Then a similar performance is gone through with another sitter, a young woman, who is so excited that she nearly faints away, the kissing being very animated and prolonged again. . . . Then comes a short delay, and a figure in man's clothes emerges from the cabinet and seats himself affectionately in the lap of a young woman and kisses her warmly.[31]

And very recently Dr Elisabeth Kubler-Ross was using sexual intercourse with alleged materialized spirits as part of her therapy for people trying to come to terms with death.[32]

So far all is of course mere supposition; but rather more solid evidence for the theory that Crookes was Florrie's lover can also be cited. A man who met her many years later, when she was in her late thirties (but still exceedingly attractive), told two separate witnesses that one day, with no ulterior motive, she told him that she had been William Crookes's mistress.

She used to keep a light burning at night in the bed-room, and told me that she did so because she had so often impersonated spirits and pretended these manifestations at seances that she became afraid that possibly there might have been such things, which might have a spite against her for her deceptions, and she had consequently a dislike of being in the dark. She told me that she had done all this in collusion with William Crookes (I am not sure whether he had at that time been knighted) and that she had been for some time his mistress; and that the materialization and assumption of earthly life by 'Katie King' (who was herself) was just a device by which she had been able to live in Crookes's house, under his wife's nose, without exciting too much suspicion. For the same reason, she said, she had been over to Paris with Crookes on several occasions.[33]

Why – one might reasonably ask – should such evidence as this be discounted? No real reasons are given by the opponents of the love-affair theory, other than a general unwillingness to attribute anything so sordid to the protagonists. Yet clearly Florence was not the soul of chastity – why, otherwise, was she indulging in casual affairs with young men when she was a married woman? For it seems clear that the gentleman who relayed her confession was her lover: he provided too much circumstantial evidence for that to be in doubt.

As for Crookes, we know that he was a devoted husband, and that at the time of Florence's 'materializations', Mrs Crookes was pregnant. Would such a man (we are asked) deceive his wife at such a time? To this there can be no answer except to say that if he did, he would not have been the first man ever to have done so. Indeed, there are (if one wants to continue this argument) convincing reasons why he might be more likely to take a mistress at this time. It is clear that Crookes liked sex, and women; and not all women feel very sexy during the later stages of pregnancy. Sexual frustration and the presence of a pretty, willing young girl would be a potent combination. Why should we assume that he resisted temptation when the consequences of believing in his chastity are so much harder to credit? Can we really believe that Florence really did, despite everything she said later and all evidence to the contrary, produce real ghosts?

Crookes was certainly partial to the company of spiritual young ladies. As well as Florence, he conducted his experiments with Rosina Showers and with Annie Eva Fay, a well-known American performer who took great pains never actually to say that she possessed mediumistic powers – she merely left her audience to make what deductions they wished from her show. (She was a highly successful and popular artiste, and continued in vaudeville until the mid-1920s.)

And although he went to great pains never publicly to give his critics any rope with which to belabour him further about his excursions into spiritualism and psychic force – 'I have nothing to retract,' he said of these researches twenty-five years later, when he was President of the British Association for the Advancement of Sciences; 'I only regret a certain crudity in those early expositions which, no doubt justly, militated against their acceptance by the scientific world' – there is no doubt that he knew Miss Showers, at any rate, was a fraud. We know this because he conducted a correspondence about it with D.D.Home.

As for Miss Showers, the facts are simply enough [he wrote in a letter dated from Mornington Road, Nov. 3rd, 1875]. She confessed to Mrs Fay that her manifestations were all a trick, and very properly Mrs Fay told me. I thereupon employed Mrs Fay, as I should employ a detective to unearth a fraud, and by her assistance got a complete confession in Miss S.'s hand-writing. I have since had several interviews with Miss S. and have induced her to give up these tricks, I promising not to bring about a public exposure but only to warn my private friends. Do not therefore say anything about this.

This discretion was not without its cost in trouble and reputation to Crookes, as he plaintively makes clear:

Mrs Showers found out I was meeting her daughter and fired up at it, putting the worst construction on it. I was bound by promise not to expose Miss S. to her mother, so I refused to explain. . . . But Miss S. had accomplices according to her account, and one of the gentlemen implicated has before now written very shameful things about me to Paris, so between the Mother and others I am getting the reputation of a Don Juan. My good and true wife knows everything about this and quite approves of my conduct, so I can well afford to let the matter blow over.[34]

It was at this point that Crookes dropped his spiritualistic researches, never to take them up again, although he accepted the Presidency of the Society for Psychical Research when it was offered him many years later, and, as we have seen, never recanted.

In another letter to Home, this time from Serjeant Cox, there is a description of what can only be Miss Showers's confession to Mrs Fay, referred to by Crookes. In it, she describes just how the 'materializations' are done:

She informs her friend that she comes to the seance prepared with a dress that is easily taken off with a little practice. She says it may be done in two or three minutes. She wears two shifts (probably for warmth). She brings a muslin veil of thin material (she gives its name, which I forget). *It is carried in her drawers!* It can be compressed into a small space, although when spread it covers the whole person. A pocket-handkerchief pinned round the head keeps back the hair. She states that she takes off all her clothes except the two shifts, and is covered by the veil. The gown is spread carefully upon the sofa over the pillows. In this array she comes out. She makes very merry with the spiritualists whom she thus gulls, and her language about them is anything but complimentary.

This explains the whole business. The question so often asked before was – where the robe could be carried? It could not be contained in the bosom or in a sleeve. Nobody seems to have thought of the drawers.[35]

It may be wondered why, in the face of such crude and obvious trickery, Crookes remained silent even where he was not circumscribed by the risk of possible scandal. (Of course, one cannot altogether discount the possibility that here, too, the 'Don Juan' rumour was not entirely without foundation.) Was he unwilling to lose face where he had previously committed himself so firmly? (If so, this is hardly the attitude of true science!) Did he, perhaps, think that any admission of error would throw doubt on all his researches? Or was he merely anxious not to probe too deeply in public into an area which was better left altogether shadowy, in so far as that was possible? 'As for Mr Crookes,' wrote Moncure Conway, 'he remains inexplicable. I last met this agreeable gentleman in a company at the Royal Institution, and Tyndall told me that when in conversation he had alluded to spiritism Mr Crookes was silent, and it seemed to give him so much pain that he concluded never to mention the subject to him again.'[36]

5
Why Ectoplasm?

Bear in mind, I am not a sceptic. It is my will to believe and if convincing evidence is brought forward I will be the first to acknowledge my mistake, but up to the present day nothing has crossed my path to make me think that the Great Almighty will allow emanations from a human body of such horrible, revolting, viscous substances as Baron Von Schrenck Notzing claims, hideous shapes, which, like 'genii from the bronze bottle,' ring bells, move handkerchiefs, wobble tables, and do other 'flap-doodle' stunts. – HARRY HOUDINI

The spiritualist world inhabited by William Crookes, Florrie Cook, Mrs Guppy and their contemporaries has a flavour very distinctly of its period. It is, in every possible way, what we now think of as Victorian. Its desire for new knowledge, its faith in science and progress, its fevered interest in new developments in religious or quasi-religious matters, all reflected the vital concerns of the age. Its sexuality, too, was a Victorian sexuality. The sense, in this context, of two parallel worlds, an overt and a covert, the hidden one unacknow-ledged by, and in some cases even unknown to, the denizens of 'respectable society', while nevertheless acting as mainspring and motivation for many of its actions and reactions, reflects that aspect of Victorian life seen at its most extreme in the person and writings of 'Walter', author of *My Secret Life*.[1]

By the turn of the century, however, things had changed. What might be termed the *dramatis personae* of spiritualism remained sub-stantially similar. There were the seance-holders, still spellbound by those 'phenomena' which had been introduced by the Fox sisters and their followers, phenomena which remained the stock-in-trade of most mediums. Then, ahead (so to speak) of this field was the vanguard of investigators, including many psychologists, philosophers and physical scientists. And, complementary to these, the more advanced mediums: those persons possessing, or claiming to possess, extraordinary and exceptional powers, worthy of the investigators' time and attention.

The atmosphere in which these people worked, however, was very different from what it had been when Crookes and Wallace led the investigative field, and D.D.Home and Florence Cook were in their heyday. It was – if one may put it this way – altogether less innocent. For, despite the undoubted deceptions of the Victorian spiritualist scene, it was pervaded by an essentially innocent vision. How else could the 'ghosts' produced by Florence Cook and Rosina Showers, robust flesh-and-blood Victorian young ladies that they so seemingly were, have deceived anyone for an instant? How else could the crude tricks of the professional mediums, including Maggie and Kate Fox, have taken in so many and rendered them fervent believers? Even the sexual aspect of it all – the unmentioned world into which spiritualist seances provided, for many, a gateway – seems to have been straightforward enough. Hands were held and squeezed, embraces exchanged with ghosts; a pretty young medium seduced a distinguished scientist. What could be more normal and natural? But with the onset of the twentieth century spiritualism abandoned these straightforward frameworks and motivations.

The first indication of how things might develop was Eusapia Paladino. Paladino, who was to dominate the spiritualist scene for twenty years, first appeared in the early 1870s, just when it seemed about to decline after the spectacular performances of Florence Cook and D.D.Home. She was brought to the attention of British spiritualists by way of a letter to *The Spiritualist* from a Signor Damiani, an Italian then living in England.

Damiani reported that an extraordinary medium had been discovered in Naples in the person of a young girl of about sixteen, called Sapia Padalino. She could do all the usual mediumistic tricks: produce sudden sounds, raise tables in the air, and the rest. But there was also a more sinister side to her, and this was to persist throughout her career, so that many of the comfortable bourgeois who constituted the main body of psychical investigators could never feel quite comfortable with her. Objects kept disappearing from the room where she sat, and not reappearing, to the chagrin of visitors. On one occasion she apported a dead rat, to the horror of the company which had, presumably, been expecting the more usual, and acceptable, flowers.

She came from a very poor family, from a village near Naples, and had been married very young to a travelling magician, but now she was in the city on her own, and some of the charitable ladies among her sitters thought they would help her to find a post as a servant. As a servant, however, Eusapia proved useless: furniture kept moving and china breaking in her presence. She therefore set up as a professional medium.

It was not long before Sapia Padalino, as she was still known, became a well-known figure in this world. She was taken up by an occultist, Ercole Chiaja, and kept before the eyes of the British public by Damiani: in 1873, Florence Cook, then developing her various powers as a medium, published a clairvoyant vision of her in *The Spiritualist*, the accuracy of which was confirmed from Naples by Damiani in the next issue. Florence commented disdainfully on Sapia's dirty dress and habits: 'She eats with her fingers. She is not a clean girl at all!' Florence saw an unpleasant male spirit following Sapia and controlling her. Damiani took this to be a literal description of a man following her, and commented sadly that he was indeed inclined to believe in the truth of this vision, 'for the poor girl has often been seen in company with individuals of a low standard' and added that, with the best of intentions, the spiritualists of Naples found themselves unable to help poor Sapia in this respect.[2]

This taint, or titillation, of slightly unsavoury sex was to persist throughout her long career. It was remarked upon with some distaste by Mrs Sidgwick, the principal of Newnham College, when, some years later, the Italian medium visited Cambridge in order to have her by then almost legendary powers tested by the SPR – a disastrous occasion when, lodged in the ultra-English sobriety of the Myers household and surrounded by disapproving intellectual Cambridge ladies, she was caught flagrantly cheating. But then, Eusapia always got on much better with gentlemen than with ladies: a circumstance which did her no harm at all, especially in her early years.

For in the mists which surround Eusapia's performances – which were repeatedly investigated, with the most contradictory results – one thing is quite clear: and that is that she relied heavily upon distracting her audience in order to achieve many of her effects. She became restless and moved her hands and feet about before the production of 'phenomena', so that it was impossible to know if they were satisfactorily 'controlled', or by whom. She dictated the conditions of the seance: the amount, if any, of the lighting, which was generally dim and red-shaded, though sometimes the seances took place in darkness, and sometimes (it was said) she produced some of her most remarkable effects, such as levitation, elongation of her body, and the production of a third arm from underneath her dress, in full light. When the famous Professor Lombroso of Turin (the inventor of criminology) was prevailed upon to observe her for the first time, in 1892, he was astonished by what he saw. He admitted that he was thoroughly confused by it all, and that he could no longer maintain the thoroughgoing scepticism which he had until then professed in the face of all spiritualist claims.

It was the conversion of Lombroso, who was the most famous scientist in Italy, which finally established Eusapia; and it is clear that he was as liable to her particular forms of distraction as the rest. Among these, her vivacity and overt sexuality were not the least negligible. They were remarked upon time and again. Eusapia made no bones about going to bed with her sitters if she happened to fancy them. The extent to which the relationship between medium and sitters was sexual is made clear in the comments of Lombroso and another professor, Schiaparelli, after some sessions which took place in 1893 in Milan. They gave it as their opinion that Paladino's phenomena were due to a redirection of fundamental sex-energy. They reported that her menstrual secretions increased at the start of her trances, that she had a particular zone of hyperaesthesia near her ovaries, and that when phenomena were about to occur they were sometimes accompanied by voluptuous erotic sensations followed by orgasm. Whatever may have been the conditions under which these facts were ascertained, it is hard to believe that they were either wholly detached or entirely scientific.

Be that as it may, Lombroso's imprimatur opened the intellectual doors of Europe to Eusapia. For by now, after a lull, and perhaps encouraged by the establishment, in England, of the Society for Psychical Research, the investigation of such phenomena was beginning to interest an increasing number of thinkers in various fields and countries. And even where the primary impulse was still recognized as a religious one – as with philosophers such as F.W.H.Myers, or psychologists such as William James – the prime importance of scientific reliability in investigation, and of the development of scientific method in this field, was unquestioned.

One of the leaders in this approach to the subject was Charles Richet. Richet was a distinguished French physiologist who went on to win a Nobel prize; but his interest in the study of the supernatural and its manifestations was at least as strong as his more orthodox specialism. From the first, Richet was particularly concerned to give his supernormal interests the kind of vocabulary and organization which would put them on an equal footing, in the public eye, with orthodox science. He established an Institute of Metapsychics in Paris; it was he who coined the word 'ectoplasm' to denote the substance from which mediums built up materializations of spirit forms. (It has been pointed out that while Richet, a biologist, used a neo-biological term for this substance, others coined terms more nearly approximating to their own particular professional interests. Thus William Crawford, an engineer, describing the same, or similar, phenomena, used the phrase 'psychical structures' and talked about 'cantilevers' and 'lines of force'; while William Crookes, a chemist and physicist, had talked of a 'psychic force' which, he felt, had obvious parallels with such natural forces as electricity.)

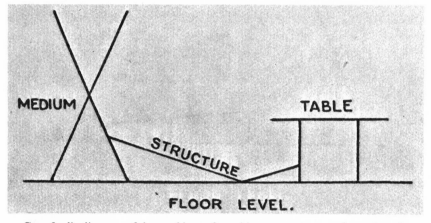

Crawford's diagram of the workings of psychic structures: note the engineer's-eye view of ectoplasm.

The connection between psychical research and the less accepted forms of orthodox science was soon very strongly established. Thus it was accepted that readers of the *Annals of Psychical Science*, published monthly in France in the early years of this century, would be interested in progress reports on Professor Blondlot's famous – soon to be infamous – 'N-rays', whose existence, together with clear and visible proof of the same, was sworn to by half a dozen of France's leading scientists, but which were soon shown never to have existed at all, but to have been visible only to those who already believed in them. Some might say that the parallels with psychical research were altogether too close for comfort.

And yet, in that astonishing period, when Röntgen was discovering X-rays and the Curies were discovering radioactivity – both of them inexplicable and indeed strictly unbelievable in terms of the then orthodox physics – why should not one thing as well as another be believable and possible? Exactly the same argument is of course used today with regard to the relations between 'parascience' and the more extraordinary discoveries of modern physics; and just as some distinguished physicists today interest themselves in 'parascience', so the Curies then, together with many of their colleagues, took part in experiments conducted by Richet at his Institut de Métapsychique – many of them involving Eusapia.

For if Lombroso had been the first scientist to put Eusapia on the map, Richet soon took her over. In 1894, the year after Lombroso's Milan sessions, Richet invited her to his country cottage in the south of France, on the Île Roubaud, near Hyères. Here a gathering of distinguished investigators was to test Eusapia at leisure, in the most relaxed atmosphere that could be devised. What exactly took place at the Île Roubaud? It is, of course, impossible to be quite sure. No photographs were taken, no instruments were used to record effects; all we have is the reports of the witnesses. These were a very distinguished group. They included the physicist Oliver Lodge, F.W.H.Myers, the Polish Professor Ochorowicz, and of course Richet himself. And they reported some quite extraordinary happenings.

These – if we can believe the observers, a question to which we shall return – consisted of phenomena of much the same sort as had been reported by spiritualists for the past forty years or more, but much more clear-cut and definite than the vague jugglings and misty veiled forms which had become a commonplace of the seance-room. Eusapia's hands and feet were carefully controlled throughout. Nevertheless, tables rose from the ground in full view of the company, and even moved about; a large melon, weighing about fifteen pounds, was moved from a chair behind Eusapia to the table around which the observers were sitting; Oliver Lodge, while holding both Eusapia's hands, felt himself pushed and pinched on his head, his back and his knees, and, on another occasion, had his hand grasped by another hand whose thumb and nails he could clearly feel. Window curtains five feet away from Eusapia billowed out towards her though there was no wind. A note-taker outside the seance-room heard the key being turned in the lock inside the room, and heard blows on the door. And so on.

It should be noted that these tricks, or phenomena, were, in various forms, part of Eusapia's regular stock-in-trade, and she was at different times – though not on these occasions – caught cheating while producing them. The explanation usually given was that, owing to her lax moral tone in all departments, she would certainly take any opportunity for cheating allowed her, since this was infinitely less effort than producing her effects supernaturally. This was the cause of the unsatisfactory happenings at Cambridge, when Myers, the Sidgwicks and the rest deliberately gave her such opportunities to see if she would take them. However, everybody seemed to agree that, in 1894 in the south of France, she did not cheat, and could not have done so. What, then, could have happened? There are two possible explanations. One, of course, was that Eusapia really did possess the powers claimed for her. The other is that, despite what they thought they saw and the control they thought they maintained, the distinguished observers were nevertheless, somehow, duped.

This would certainly have taken a considerable amount of skill. As has frequently been pointed out, they were all investigators very experienced in this field, and knew what to look out for. This was especially true of the Sidgwicks, who joined the party later, and were both highly sceptical with regard to 'physical phenomena'. But they were not present on the Île Roubaud, when some of the most extraordinary events took place. The house there was very small, no more than a cottage. Only Lodge, Myers, Professor Ochorowicz, and of course Richet and Eusapia could be accommodated. Lodge shared a big bed with Richet, Myers had a room to himself, Eusapia lived in a little turret room, and Ochorowicz slept in a sort of outhouse, a continuation of the verandah where they all ate, the dining-room having been converted into a seance-room for the duration. A seance was held every evening after dinner; Eusapia never appeared before the afternoon.

It seems, from Lodge's account, that the 'control' of Eusapia's hands was distinctly shaky during these seances in the intimacy of the island. Eusapia was very accomplished at the trick of making one hand serve for two – so that the people on either side of her were convinced that each was holding one of her hands, whereas really both were holding different parts of the same one. When taxed with this trick, Eusapia flew into a rage. 'Here am I taking all this trouble to show you these phenomena, and you don't even hold my hands so that I cannot do them normally; it is too bad!' she cried, in her Neapolitan Italian.[3] And, as was her habit, she equally flew into rages when methods of control other than those to which she was accustomed were suggested.

It was only up to a very clearly defined point that she would allow the conditions of the seance to be dictated by others.

Lodge reported that Eusapia's powers were very strong on the island. Manifestations usually began with hand-clutchings, very vigorous; once Lodge even felt a long hairy beard stroking him, as if a man was standing behind his chair. Eusapia told him this was the ubiquitous John King, who was at this time her main control. The raps on the table were so strong that they sounded quite dangerous, like blows struck with a mallet. Richet made them all grasp dynamometers before and after the sitting, so that the amount of energy consumed during the seance should be recorded. Eusapia's grip at the end was usually distinctly flabby, except for one evening when she cried out 'Oh, John, you're hurting!' 'and to our surprise we saw the needle going up, indicating a force far beyond what any of us could exert', reports Lodge, adding, 'This phenomenon is known to medical men, I believe, as an hysterical increase in strength noticed with some patients. It should be studied for what it is. Calling a thing hysterical is no explanation.'[4]

It was on the Île Roubaud that 'ectoplasm' made its first appearance. At the evening seances, Eusapia frequently produced a third arm, or 'pseudopod', which clutched, pushed, and performed other limb-like functions. Sometimes it seemed to emanate from her side, through her clothes; at other times, nothing was visible, but far-away objects were nevertheless moved. (Readers may remember the reaching-rods mentioned in an earlier chapter.) It appears that at these evening seances there was no light in the room; with a Mediterranean moon it would not be pitch-black, but, indoors, the light would never be other than very dim. (This was the same light used by Home for his more spectacular feats.) At any rate, Richet coined the word 'ectoplasm' for these protuberances. Lodge comments:

> As far as the physics of the movements were concerned, they were all produced, I believe, in accordance with the ordinary laws of matter. The ectoplasmic formation which operated was not normal; but its abnormality belongs to physiology or anatomy – it is something which biologists ought to study. It was something which Richet, as a physiologist, found repugnant and was very loth to admit, but the facts were too much for him. He often said, *'C'est absolument absurde, mais c'est vrai'* – or words to that effect.[5]

These sittings at the Île Roubaud, and later on the mainland at Richet's château near Toulon, when the party was joined by others, are generally regarded as the high point of Eusapia's career. When, on other occasions, her integrity was in doubt, or her powers seemed to be waning or insignificant, these were the sessions that were recalled, when she had performed extraordinary feats, unimpugned, before a body of respected and unimpeachable observers. And yet, it seems to me that what Lodge reveals about the attitudes of the observers, together with what we know of the seances held only the previous year with Lombroso in Milan, constitutes a very different picture from that popular among Eusapia's supporters – which is of miracles performed under strictly controlled conditions among hawk-eyed and impartial observers. To begin with, all the observers – on the Île Roubaud, at any rate – were clearly enthusiasts, very much disposed to believe in the medium if they possibly could.

Myers, after the Cambridge fiasco, later lost faith in Eusapia and would have nothing more to do with her, his extreme reaction on that occasion presumably being conditioned to some degree by his earlier unquestioning acceptance of her. He was at this time engaged on his great work *Human Personality and its Survival of Bodily Death*, and we have seen that his fundamental religious conviction and motivation was very strong, as strong as his desire to confirm the 'proof palpable' which Eusapia seemed to be offering.

Lodge, as is plain from his account, did not merely want to believe, he *did* believe, and assumed that explanations such as the 'ectoplasmic' one were the only possible truth. The possibility of allying this with the down-to-earth scientific commonsense and terminology to which he was accustomed in his professional life clearly afforded him much relief. Flights of mystical fancy were not for Lodge. In the British tradition – which he shared most notably with Sir Arthur Conan Doyle and the famous journalist W. T. Stead – he liked to keep notions of heaven as down-to-earth as he could.

As for Richet, the strength of his will to believe, and his disinclination to accept any unpalatably contrary indications, were perhaps to be shown at their clearest in the Villa Carmen business, ten years later.

Eusapia's career continued in a more or less desultory way until 1910, when a disastrous tour of America effectively destroyed her reputation. In all that time her repertoire had not changed, and more than one person, in the intervening period, received the strong impression that she was thoroughly bored with what she was doing, and physically worn out by it, but that this was the only way of making a living that she knew, and she had no choice but to continue with it. As far as psychical research was concerned, however, she had fulfilled her role

in 1894, when she convinced Charles Richet of the interest and importance of the 'physical phenomena'. For the next twenty years he was to
spend the best part of his time and energies investigating these things,
lending them a scientific weight and respectability unknown since
William Crookes had so abruptly ceased his own investigations in
1874.

It is an interesting fact that these investigations by Richet, and those
by his friend Schrenck-Notzing, have been relegated to oblivion by
today's historians of the paranormal. This is perhaps understandable.
All the investigations which we are about to examine had their
embarrassing aspects. Richet's Villa Carmen ghost was quickly
discredited, and it was perhaps felt that his observations and assertions
concerning it were best forgotten; while the activities of Schrenck with
regard to Eva C. are so extraordinary that it is perhaps felt they, too, are
better ignored, although photos of Eva and her ectoplasmic creations
are still sometimes to be found in collections of 'real ghost' pictures. Yet
there is no doubt that these investigations (together with those of Dr
William Crawford of Belfast, which share many of their characteristics)
were taken extremely seriously at the time by everyone interested in
such things.

There were various common features which characterized these investigations, and perhaps the most obvious is that they all gained
credibility and were given serious attention because of the calibre of the
scientists conducting them. As this is still a salient feature of psychical
research today, and as much highly dubious work continues to gain this
merit by association, it is worth taking a look at this situation.[6]

The importance attached by believers to scientific endorsement of
the phenomena has already been discussed. As an example of this
attitude's persistence, one need look no further than the foreword
written by Brian Inglis for a series of books published to commemorate
the centenary of the SPR in 1982. He writes:

> If evidence were lacking for 'parascience' – as it might now more embrac-
> ingly be described, because the emphasis of research has been shifting
> recently away from psychology to physics – it could be found in the composi-
> tion of the Society, from its earliest beginnings. . . . Among physicists have
> been Sir William Crookes, Sir John Joseph Thomson, Sir Oliver Lodge, Sir
> William Barrett and two Lord Rayleighs. . . . Among the philosophers:
> Sidgwick himself, Henri Bergson, Ferdinand Schiller, L.P.Jacks, Hans
> Driesch and C.D.Broad; among the psychologists: William James,
> William McDougall, Sigmund Freud, Walter Franklin Prince, Carl Jung
> and Gardner Murphy.

Inglis also cites Marie Curie, the astronomer Flammarion, Sir Alister Hardy, and others.[7]

It is clear from this that Inglis (and in this he is representative of a great many others) believes that the very fact of the connection of these people with psychical research, or parascience, proves that there is something in it. And it is equally clear that Richet, for one, believed the same thing. He constantly stressed the intellectual difficulty, for a scientist, of allowing himself to be convinced by the apparent absurdities of psychical research. In a typical passage he wrote:

> Assuredly we do not understand it. It is very absurd, if a truth can be absurd.
>
> . . . To ask a physiologist, a physicist, or a chemist to admit that a form that has a circulation of blood, warmth and muscles, that exhales carbonic acid, has weight, speaks, and thinks, can issue from a human body is to ask of him an intellectual effort that is really painful.
>
> Yes, it is absurd; but no matter – it is true.[8]

And why is it true? It is true because Richet thinks it is true.

> The alternative . . . is that the phenomena are genuine or that they are due to fraud. I am very well aware that they are extraordinary, even so monstrously extraordinary that at first sight the hypothesis of immeasurable, repeated, and continual fraud seems the more probable explanation. But is such fraud possible? I cannot think so. When I recall the precautions that all of us have taken, not once, but twenty, a hundred, or even a thousand times, it is inconceivable that we should have been deceived on all these occasions.[9]

Well, maybe; but the reader may feel that stranger things have happened.

The remarkable discrepancy between the overt, or admitted, reasons why people interested themselves in this field, and the genuine reasons why they did so, has already been discussed. It will become apparent that this discrepancy was no less great in the cases we are about to look at, although the underlying motivations were somewhat different. But Richet, in the passage just quoted, is talking about something else. He is saying, perfectly reasonably, that he is not a dupe. He knows what to look for and he knows how to look for it. If the world cannot trust people like him in this matter, whom can it trust?

The difficulty lies in the contrast between the world of the scientist – particularly the successful innovating scientist, of the genre of Crookes or Richet – and that of the fraudulent medium. (Clearly, we are only concerned with fraudulent mediums, because only they will try to perpetrate fraud and so need detecting.) The successful physical scientist has certain mental frameworks which very much affect the way in which he approaches new phenomena. He is used to the possibility that phenomena may be discovered which quite overturn the accepted ideas in any particular field; this is something that has happened from time to time in the various branches of science. But it does not happen very often – to put it mildly; and until it does happen, and is proved by the most stringent and repeated tests to have happened, he is used – as Richet pointed out – to working by certain accepted and immutable laws – for example, the law of gravity. That is to say, the scientist's world is essentially a logical one, in which one step logically succeeds another and any effect is preceded by a specific and discoverable cause. In this world he feels at home – which many, one could say most, people do not.

The world of the fraudulent medium, that is to say of a trickster trying to pass off his tricks as supernatural effects, is very different. Essentially he (or she) is an illusionist. What apparently took place is never what really took place. The medium, too, is master in his own particular world, but it is a world opposite in every respect to that of the scientist, for it is a world of deliberate disguise and concealment. In this world the scientist may consider himself pre-eminently suited to detect what is true and what is false, but is he? He is used to logic, and he is faced with the concealment of logic.

It is interesting that those magicians who have concerned themselves with this field have thought singularly little of the special investigative abilities of scientists. J.N.Maskelyne, who was instrumental in the exposure of Eusapia when she made her ill-fated visit to Cambridge in 1895, said in this context that he 'knew from experience that no class of men can be so readily deceived by simple trickery as scientists. Try as they may, they cannot bring their minds down to the level of the subject, and are as much at fault as though it were immeasurably above them.' When the anthropologist and psychical researcher Andrew Lang challenged him to reproduce certain of Eusapia's phenomena, he replied that 'though I could doubtless reproduce what [she] really did, the reproduction of what she was supposed to have done was quite another matter'.[10]

The successful scientist may not be skilled in the arts of the illusionist. His reputation as an investigator and theorist *may* render him a demon observer and ferreter-out of tricks and tricksters; it may equally make him unwilling to compromise this reputation, to the extent of admitting that he has been duped, especially if the dupery has been going on for a long time. And where the scientist becomes positively dangerous, and his activities inimical to the cause of truth, is where he himself acts fraudulently, where he brings his reputation for integrity and dispassion to the field of investigation, and then deliberately sets out, himself, to deceive. Of course, he finds it easy to do so should he so wish.

We have already seen that this has happened more than once in the field of psychical research[11], though I am in no way trying to suggest that Richet or any of his friends did anything of the sort. What seems clear, however, is that scientists, far from being, as they and many others feel, especially suited to this type of investigation, may, on the contrary, be quite the opposite.

The situation which Richet investigated at the Villa Carmen in Algiers, and that studied by Schrenck-Notzing with Eva C in Paris some years later, had other things in common besides the scientific standing and stance of the investigator. There was, for example, a certain triangularity of structure. In each case, while various peripheral participants came and went, there were three people seriously and permanently involved throughout the investigations: the medium, the investigator, and a person who might be termed the catalyst, or impresario, of the effects. At the Villa Carmen, this was Madame Noël, in Paris, Juliette Bisson. In both cases, the 'catalyst' had a very close relationship with the medium. In Algiers, the medium, Marthe Béraud, had been engaged to the Noëls' son, Maurice; he had died in the Congo in 1904, the year before Richet's investigation. In Paris, the medium, Eva Carrière, was living with Juliette Bisson more or less à deux: after her husband's death, Mme Bisson set up in an apartment with the medium, who had previously been lodged in her studio.

And, as it turned out, the medium was in both cases the same person. Eva C was the same Marthe Béraud who had been involved in the Villa Carmen episode. She had presumably thought it prudent, if she was to continue as a medium after the exposure of fraud in Algiers, to change her name. Richet, who was involved as an investigator in both cases, certainly knew this; but since he had staked his reputation on Marthe's genuineness, he was only too pleased to see her vindicate her powers as Eva.

The Algiers manifestations had in fact begun some years before either Richet or Marthe appeared on the scene (in 1905). General Noël had recently been sent out to command the Algiers garrison, and his wife, bored and friendless in this new town, decided to try a little table-turning. In due course, two distinct personalities 'got in touch'. One was a previous inhabitant of the house, an artillery officer, Commandant Branhauban; the other, an Indian brahmin, Bien Boa. Subsequently, both these entities were bodily materialized. Bien Boa, who was dressed in flowing white robes, later revealed that he had been a high priest at Golconda and had died about three hundred years earlier. At that time (1902–3) the Noëls were not yet living in the Villa Carmen. When they moved house, the artillery officer disappeared, and only Bien Boa survived the move.

It is fairly clear why only the noble Indian moved house with the Noëls. Branhauban was a typical soldier, representing everything that the romantic Madame Noël deplored about garrison life. His manners left much to be desired, and he was particularly fond of jokes in rather bad taste, especially jokes about women. Bien Boa, on the other hand, was everything that a lady could desire: his morals were irreproachable, his manners perfect, and yet he never lost an opportunity of proclaiming his undying love and affection for Madame Noël, the lovely Carmen. 'My beloved Carmencita, I love you, I love you,' he proclaimed on numerous occasions, kissing her face and hands – but never going any further; the very type of that platonic adoration of which a woman dreams. . . .

The procedure for these materializations, whether the medium was (as in the earlier seances) a friend of Madame Noël, or (as invariably later) Marthe Béraud, always took the same form. About half an hour before the appearance of the phantoms, the medium was 'magnetized' by Madame Noël, 'so that I can pass her my fluid'.[12] This, together with the fact that the phantom survived the change of medium and the constant quality of his appearance – he was very tall, about 6 feet 1 inch – indicated that it was to Madame Noël that he was attached, bodily (so to speak) as well as spiritually.

By the time Richet arrived, then, Bien Boa was well established and had been appearing regularly to the Noël circle for a number of years. It may be imagined that the death of the Noëls' son and the arrival in their circle of Marthe (the daughter of a fellow officer) and her sisters had considerably heightened the emotional tensions. In 1905, the year Richet conducted his investigations, the circle consisted of General and Madame Noël; Marthe, aged 19; her two sisters Paulette and Maia, aged respectively 14 and 16; M Gabriel Delanne, the editor of the *Annales de Science Psychique*, where Richet was to publish his findings, and who helped him with his apparatus and his camera; and a lady friend of Madame Noël. Generally all except Marthe were seated round the seance table, while she was behind the curtains of the cabinet. Occasionally with Marthe inside the cabinet were a young black servant-girl named Aischa and a person named Ninon whom Richet described as a 'chiromancer'. However, it seemed clear to him that almost all the credit for the production of the phenomena – that is to say, the materializations of Bien Boa – must go to Marthe. Richet, in this case, set himself a very straightforward task. His sole object, he decided, was to determine whether or not any deception was going on. He would make 'no attempt at a theory concerning these strange phenomena. It is a heavy enough task even to analyse their reality.'[13]

Before every sitting, then, he minutely examined the seance-room, a room separate from the house, built over a stable and coach-house. He lifted the chairs, looked behind the curtains and in the cabinet, examined every item of furniture. The windows were covered with canvas nailed to the wall. He satisfied himself that no one was hidden in the room or the cabinet, and that it was impossible for anyone to enter clandestinely. There were, he assured himself, no trapdoors in the room.

He next set out to demonstrate to himself and the world that Bien Boa was a real entity, and not a mere figment of anyone's imagination. Photographs were taken of the ghost using a magnesium flare. The creature they show is certainly peculiar enough. It is wearing a sort of white monk's habit, with the hood pulled up over its head; under the hood it wears a metal casque or helmet, the chinpiece of which hangs down below its black beard. The beard looks distinctly unreal. The figure under the all-enveloping robe seems singularly shapeless, but a large robe worn by a thin man might produce this effect. At any rate, there is unquestionably *something* there.

And the something, or somebody, was shown to breathe in the normal human way. Richet conducted an experiment where he required it to breathe through a tube into a bottle of baryta-water; the liquid immediately turned white, indicating that carbon dioxide had been breathed out by the ghost. Everybody studied the evidence, and having assured themselves that carbonic acid had really been produced, 'they became so enthusiastic that they broke out into applause, crying: "Bravo!"'[14] At this Bien Boa, who had disappeared behind the curtain, reappeared no fewer than three times, bowing his head and saluting to acknowledge the applause.

Here, then, was a real flesh-and-blood phantom. What was more, it was not Marthe in disguise, for she was always plainly visible in the dim light whenever Bien Boa appeared. What, or who, then, was it? As Richet put it, it had to be one of two things: 'either a phantom having the attributes of life; or . . . a living person playing the part of a phantom.' And as one of his critics put it, 'Whereas this affords conclusive evidence to Professor Richet's mind – as well as to mine – of the material nature of the spirit, it raises no doubt in his mind of the spiritual nature of the matter!'[15]

Richet's main justification for his conclusion, which seemed on the face of it somewhat rash, was another mode of appearance used by Bien Boa. This he found in every degree impressive and convincing.

I saw, without any movement whatever of the curtain, a white light . . . on the ground, outside the curtain, between the table and the curtain. I half rose in order to look over the table; I saw as it were a white luminous ball floating over the ground; then, rising straight upwards, very rapidly, as though issuing from a trap-door, appeared B.B. He appeared to me to be of no great height; he had a drapery and, I think, something like a caftan with a girdle at the waist. He was then placed between the table and the curtain, being born, so to speak, out of the flooring outside the curtain (which had not stirred). . . . At one moment he reels, as though about to fall, limping with one leg, which seems unable to support him (I give my own impression). Then he goes towards the opening of the curtains. Then, without, as far as I believe, opening the curtains, he suddenly sinks down, disappears into the ground, and at the same time a sound of clac, clac, is heard, like the noise of a body thrown to the ground.

Professor Richet (who had clearly not read Dr Furness's report on materializations for the Seybert Commission, quoted earlier) adds: 'It appears to me that this experiment is decisive.'[16] Bien Boa, then, was proved a ghost – at least to Richet's satisfaction; and this conclusion must have come as something of a relief to him because (quite apart from his own pleasure in such a finding) the alternative was unthinkable.

This alternative was, of course, that fraud was being practised; and there was only one person who could possibly be involved in that. 'The absolute honourableness, irreproachable and unquestionable, of Marthe B., the fiancée of Maurice Noël, the General's son, could never be called in question,' declared Richet. '. . . To suppose that Marthe, the daughter of an officer, and the fiancée of the General's son, should concert with a negress and a palmist to practise an odious deception on General and Mme. Noël for twelve months, is absurd.'[17] And there could be no question of such a fraud, if fraud it was, having been other than carefully planned and thought out. Nevertheless, Richet forced himself to think through the impossible. If Marthe was fraudulent, how did she work the trick? The only possibility, since there was no way in which anyone else could possibly enter the room, was that she herself dressed up as Bien Boa. But where would she hide his costume, to say nothing of the lay figure which would have to take her place while she was acting? It was impossible; she wore the very flimsiest and thinnest of chemisettes in the torrid heat of Algiers.

But, still contrary to all good sense, let us assume this also. Let us suppose that Marthe, whom we have never searched, nor bound, could bring in on her person all the apparatus necessary to serve for her disguisement, is it possible that she could have made use of them?
Now I answer boldly, No.[18]

Clearly, then, despite his protestations (frequent) that in this case he was acting with the detachment of a scholar, rather than with the reserve of a friend, Richet was determined that Bien Boa was real, and was unwilling to make any real effort to see whether he was not, either by subjecting Marthe to close scrutiny, or by tackling the phantom itself. If a deception was being practised, he was, if only by omission, as much a party to it as anyone. Which makes his final remark on the subject, in his report, even more unconvincing.

In spite of all the proofs which I have given, in spite of all that I have seen and touched, in spite of the photographs, conclusive as they are, I cannot yet resolve on admitting the fact of materialisation; it is too much to ask of a physiologist to expect him to accept, even after much experimentation, a fact so extraordinary and improbable, and I shall not yield so easily, even to evidence.[19]

Bien Boa was revealed as a fraud very soon after the publication of this account. On 23 February 1906 a lecture was announced on the subject of Bien Boa, which would give an exact explanation of the seances at the Villa Carmen. Large numbers of people flocked to the Université Populaire to hear Dr Z— expound on the subject.

It seemed, from what he said, that Bien Boa had, from the first, been a creation of some acquaintances of the Noëls. They had concocted letters, to be delivered in automatic writing, from Bien Boa and Branhauban. What had begun as a simple joke had very soon taken concrete form, in the person of one Areski, who had at one time been coachman to the Noëls, but who had since been dismissed from their service. It was clear that the mediums involved, including of course Marthe Béraud, must actively have connived at the trick. The fact that Marthe was visible at the same time as Bien Boa was clearly quite irrelevant –

though she had (said Dr Z) once played the part of his sister, Bergolia.
. . . The whole thing might have gone on indefinitely, to the satisfaction of all parties, had not Professor Richet come along and given it the
weight of scientific authority. This the jokers could not countenance,
and so they had confessed.

They supported their story with concrete evidence. Areski had been
caught *in flagrante* twice by M Delanne, Richet's friend and the editor
of the *Annals of Psychic Science* – once when blows were struck on a
communicating door, supposedly by an evil spirit, when the coachman
was found hiding in a nearby recess; once when hiding a piece of
muslin in the cabinet. Delanne had published his account of this. And,
besides, there was a confession from Marthe herself. General Noël had
written to Dr Z stating that Marthe's father had written to Richet:
there was (she said) a trapdoor in the seance-room by which Areski
had entered and left. All the phenomena witnessed by Richet and
Delanne had been fraudulently arranged.

What was Richet's reaction to this all too circumstantial account?
Did he turn his attention to more convincing, if not more compelling,
matters? He did not. Quite simply, he refused to countenance anything that Dr Z had said. Areski had never been into the seance-room,
with or without permission, at the same time as Richet. The mere idea,
even, was 'so impossible that I have difficulty in believing that any
person of common sense could be found capable of crediting it'.[20] As
for the confession of the original hoaxers, he knew nothing about that.
Moreover, he denied that Marthe had confessed anything, and denied
that there was a trapdoor in the seance-room, as she purportedly
alleged. This, he said, was confirmed by the architect who had designed the room in the first place.

This – and hence the reality of the Bien Boa phantom – remained
his position and that of M Delanne. Eight years later, when Marthe's
reappearance as Eva C was arousing yet more controversy in psychic
circles, Delanne said: 'What value can we place on the so-called
admissions of a very suggestible young girl, carried away by all the
excitement? How can they undermine our positive evidence?'[21]
Scientific detachment, it seemed, was capable of blinking.

The Villa Carmen episode is psychologically a very interesting one.
The deception was crude enough; but the motivation of the principals
was not without its subtleties. It need hardly be said that after Dr Z's
revelations Bien Boa disappeared, never to return. How Madame Noël
felt without the comfort of her manly admirer we do not know. After

receiving the letter of confession from Marthe's father, it seems unlikely that either she or the General could have gone on believing in their phantom. The mortification they must have felt at the treatment they had received at the hands of their friends and colleagues, and at the knowledge that the whole French community in Algiers knew of their gullibility and humiliation, hardly bears thinking about.

Perhaps worst of all was the knowledge that the person most closely concerned with the deception, at least for the past year, had been their son's fiancée, Marthe, who, but for his death, would have been their daughter-in-law. What kind of girl was this that they had nearly taken into their family? Callous, certainly. But was she also, maybe, a little mad? Were these the actions of a normal girl? Certainly, in assuming that the thought of such tricks could never cross the mind of a well-brought-up *jeune fille*, Richet was exhibiting an exceptional ignorance of the propensities of naughty girls. Colette, for example, would have had no difficulty in attributing such possibilities to a girl like Marthe; and the fact that her young sisters would almost certainly have had to be in on the joke, too, might have made it seem more rather than less possible that Marthe was up to no good.

But Marthe's later career makes it seem likely that something more than mere mischief lay at the bottom of her actions. Perhaps her experiences at the Villa Carmen gave her a taste for the special kinds of sensation available to her only in her capacity as a spirit medium. Certainly there can have been no question (as in the case of most of the professional mediums we have looked at) of cash rewards. But she was certainly the centre of attention; and there must, too, have been a satisfying sense of power.

Both these attractions held good in her later incarnation as Eva Carrière. But there is something pathological about Eva's career that is not apparent in Marthe's. The element of mischief has altogether gone, replaced by a neurotic compulsion. Marthe's tricks opened the door to something altogether more sinister. It was something which would doubtless have interested Richet's contemporaries Pierre Janet and Théodore Flournoy. Both these famous clinical psychologists interested themselves greatly in the phenomena of spiritualism and spirit mediums; and in this interest lies the key to a clear difference which is apparent between the European approach to such things and that more prevalent in Britain and the United States.

Quite simply, the feeling of underlying religious yearning is missing in Europe; and a genuine spirit of scientific enquiry seems to permeate the scene. This becomes clear if we contrast, for example, the reactions

of Charles Richet and of Alfred Russel Wallace when faced with debunkings which, against all the evidence, they refused to credit. On
the face of it, the two reactions are in fact very similar. But there is a
real difference between Wallace's desperate sophistical contortions
when trying to escape the consequences of the grabbing of Miss Wood,
and Richet's refusal to accept the fact that Bien Boa was a fake. The
former shows the desperation of obsession – and of obsession challenged; the latter is more a question of rock-like self-confidence.
Richet listed the objections to Bien Boa's genuineness:

    1. An individual dressed up in a white sheet can amuse himself by playing
the phantom on the stage.
    2. This individual may be General Noël's coachman.
    3. General Noël's coachman asserts that he has freely entered the seance
room with us, whereas that statement is an audacious lie.
    4. A doctor played a trick on Mme. Noël two years ago by teaching eleven
words of English to an individual who does not know English [and who was
thereby enabled to transmit a message from Branhauban].
    5. Mlle. Marthe B— is reported to have said that everything was done by
means of a trap door, whereas she has not said it, and there is no trap door.

He then went on to add: 'I confess, for my part, that in treating
seriously of these phenomena, their strangeness had, in spite of all
proofs, occasioned some doubts in my mind, and I have not neglected
to express them fully and forcibly. But now, in view of the poverty of
the objections which could be brought against them, many of those
doubts have disappeared.'[22]

It is the tone of voice of a politician at his most exasperatingly
patronizing; of a schoolmaster faced with a particularly dim class; of a
doctor explaining a patient to students. And indeed, in Europe at this
time, the study of phenomena such as these had become a recognized
branch of medicine. Specialists in clinical psychology such as Pierre
Janet in Paris and Théodore Flournoy in Geneva recognized that the
spiritualist scene offered rich case-study material. Flournoy's book *Des
Indes à la planète Mars*, about an extreme case of dissociated personality,
where a girl made up whole worlds, convincing in every detail, down to
a new Martian language complete with grammar, became and
remains a classic. The study of these phenomena therefore acquired a
genuine intellectual respectability in Europe which it never achieved
in Britain or the United States, and this, with the self-confidence it
brought with it, was naturally reflected in the attitudes of investigators.

Of course, Richet's attitude to Marthe Béraud and Bien Boa was very far from being clinical. But he was also a famous and brilliant physiologist; and, as we have seen, his studies in this field were dressed up with an elaborately scientistic vocabulary. As for Marthe's next investigator, the Freiherr von Schrenck-Notzing from Munich, he was a highly respected physician; and though, as will become apparent, his investigations of Marthe – who was by then no longer Marthe but Eva – were neither detached nor clinical, they might accurately be described as physical.

The spiritualistic career of Marthe Béraud was not allowed to lapse by her supporters, despite the untoward happenings which had brought its first phase to an untimely close. She did not, however, remain long in Algiers, but moved to Paris, where she changed her name to Eva Carrière. This was presumably to escape the unwelcome publicity which would always attach to the by now notorious name of Mlle Béraud.

We do not know what she did during the intervening years, but that she kept in touch with Gabriel Delanne of the *Annals of Psychic Science* is certain, because in 1908 he introduced her to Juliette Bisson. Mme Bisson was the wife of a well-known playwright, André Bisson. She was herself a sculptress. She had for some time interested herself in the phenomena of materialization, and had always hoped to be able to make some experiments in that direction. She was presented with the opportunity for which she had been hoping when M Delanne introduced her to Eva.

How much did Juliette know about Eva's past? She says nothing about the subject, and all that is said by Schrenck-Notzing (who was to duplicate the role of Richet in this triangle, while Juliette 'played' that of Mme Noël) is that 'In her family circle spiritualistic sittings were held with Eva C. four or five years before the beginning of the Paris experiments.'[23] In 1909, when this series of experiments began, Eva would have been about twenty-three. Over the years she and Juliette Bisson became increasingly intimate. By 1910 she began coming to the seances alone (we are not told who accompanied her previously). In November of that year, she moved into Juliette's studio, which was separate from the family apartment. In January 1912, following the death of M Bisson, his widow took a new apartment and Eva moved in to live with her, sharing her life in every detail.

Like Mme Noël at the Villa Carmen, Juliette Bisson began every seance by hypnotizing Eva. Schrenck-Notzing, who began his observations of these seances as early as May 1909, noted, in his methodical way, that the medium was very weak-willed and passive in her character, which made her a particularly easy subject for hypnotization by anyone to whom she was attached, and she was very attached to Juliette; Schrenck compared their relationship with that of 'a faithful dog to its master'.[24]

Nothing could have been more rigidly scientific and less emotional than Schrenck-Notzing's approach to the investigation of mediumistic phenomena, and in particular those of Eva C. The first forty pages of his book *Phenomena of Materialisation* – and they are large pages, closely printed – are taken up with a discussion of this methodology, the formulation of which obviously afforded him the same kind of intellectual satisfaction as the application of scientific or quasi-scientific terminology to psychical investigations afforded Lodge or Richet.

Schrenck's intellectual position with regard to the phenomena was quite clear. He specifically rejected the spiritualistic thesis, which 'not only fails to explain the slightest detail of these occurrences, but . . . impedes and hinders in every way serious scientific investigation'.[25] Instead, he preferred the possibility of a force which could be contained within the ever-widening boundaries of modern physics, comparing mediumistic energy, 'as regards velocity of propagation, with light, and it appears to have polarity, for there are persons whose actions neutralise each other. . . . We have, therefore, the possibility of a science.'[26]

The specific instance of this propensity to mutual neutralization is interesting, since it refers to those savants who suffer from what Schrenck like to call 'mediophobia', the presence of whom at a seance is likely to inhibit the advent of anything worthwhile. In particular, he draws the attention to the danger of wrong thoughts in the case of a medium such as Eva, highly suggestible. If anyone at one of her seances thinks too hard and repeatedly about the possibility of fraud, then it is only too likely that the suggestion will be picked up by the medium, who will consequently feel impelled to try cheating. (This was perhaps what happened at the Villa Carmen, always supposing that we feel the evidence in that case contradicts the faith shown by Richet and Delanne.)

Eva had somewhat extended her repertoire since those days. Then, she had simply stage-managed the appearances of a phantom quite separate from herself – indeed, another person. But now her specialty was the production of emanations from various parts of her body. These, over the years, did – as we shall see – develop into actual recognizable ghosts (recognizable both as ghosts and, in some instances, as people), but at first they were merely excrescences of various sorts. 'The problem of control', wrote Schrenck, 'is therefore very simple. It has only to guard against the introduction or handing in of objects and their subsequent removal.'

This might seem straightforward enough. There were, however, certain difficulties inherent in it. There were certain orifices of the body where materials might be concealed which a young lady medium might feel most reluctant to offer up for inspection, even in the name of science. Schrenck had encountered mediums of this kind, and, while he felt their modesty was understandable, he considered that nevertheless this 'must finally lead to a negative attitude, even though the phenomena be genuine'. Readers will not be surprised to hear that Eusapia had offered no such resistance, and neither did Eva C.

The general form of the seances remained constant throughout the years. The cabinet where the medium sat, and within which she produced her phenomena, was generally a curtained-off partition in the main seance-room. It was curtained and lined with black stuff, and the chair on which the medium sat was also covered with the same black material. This was always thoroughly searched beforehand; as Schrenck wrote on one occasion, 'Wherever a hand could be introduced into the stuff this was done, but with no result.' Before the seance Eva undressed, and put on a garment consisting of a dancer's leotard, over which she wore a schoolgirl's black overall. This was sewn to the leotard at the waist, and the neck and sleeve openings were also sewn up. She was then subjected to what Schrenck calls 'a gynaecological examination'. Mme Bisson, watched by Schrenck, 'introduced her finger into the medium's vagina. She was also explored by Professor B. and the author through the garment, but with negative result.'[27] Schrenck was very solemn about this. He was deeply conscious that he might be accused of negligence in not examining Eva's bare body, but only feeling through the knitted leotard. But,

assuming that a female medium wished to use the vagina as a hiding-place for some closely-rolled packets, e.g. chiffon gauze, she would have to attach some kind of cord or ribbon to the packet beforehand, in order to be able to withdraw it. This cord would be detected during the exploration of the mouth of the vagina, and any finger introduced into the vagina would feel the foreign body. In the case of persons with a very wide vaginal entrance, it might be possible to withdraw the packet by means of the fingers, deeply inserted. But such a manipulation supposes that the genitals are not separated from the hand by any partition, even a knitted one, and that the person is in a standing or reclining position.[28]

And to withdraw packets hidden up the anus was even less of a practicable proposition, since the strength of the sphincter muscle holding them in place would necessitate their being attached to a strong cord, which would be easily detected.

After the examinations were all completed, Eva would take her place behind the curtain and the other members of the seance circle would seat themselves in the room outside. The light would be extinguished, and a dim red light lit. Schrenck usually had one or more cameras with magnesium flares set up in the room, ready to take photographs of any phenomena that might appear. Eva would be hypnotized, and sank into a trance. The cabinet curtains were then closed, and everyone settled down to wait. In the early seances, the old spiritualist custom was adhered to, and the sitters were urged to sing while they waited, with the less musical ones humming in time, but after a while this was discontinued, much to Schrenck's relief, and the waiting took place in desultory silence, punctuated by cries of *'Donnez! Donnez!'* to encourage the medium. They rarely waited for less than half an hour, and it was often two or three hours before the cabinet curtains parted and the 'phenomena' were displayed to view.

Not all mediums were as ready to undergo intimate examinations as Eva. One has only to look at the experiments of Dr William Crawford with the Goligher family in Belfast to see what comparative advantages Schrenck had. Crawford was making his investigations a little while after Schrenck. He was dealing with a family all claiming mediumistic powers. Within the family one specific medium, Kathleen Goligher, was able to materialize phenomena which Crawford, an engineer, liked to call 'psychic structures'. Like Schrenck, Crawford succeeded in photographing these 'structures' (which look, in the photographs, remarkably like pieces of muslin draped over rods), but Crawford went one step further than Schrenck: he tried to obtain tangible traces of the path taken by the material as it issued from the medium's body.

There seems to have been no question of Crawford, like Schrenck, making a thorough body search of the medium first. Whether the Golighers would have countenanced this we do not know, since clearly Crawford could never have brought himself to make such a suggestion, let alone carry out the search. The method he used for tracing the source of the 'structures' was to place powdered carmine somewhere in their known path and see where it spread to. (Powdered carmine was found to be the most satisfactory substance for this purpose.) He began, coyly, with the medium's shoes. Spoonfuls of carmine were placed inside the toecaps, and it was found that traces later extended up the leg to the top of the stockings – just above the knee. But Crawford was still worried.

> The question then arose as to whether there was a flow of plasma from the medium's body down the legs, as well as the flow from the feet upwards, or, indeed, whether the whole of the plasma did not come from the trunk of the medium, flow down the legs and then, in some peculiar manner and for some particular reason connected with the building up of the psychic structures, enter her shoes and fill up the space between stocking and leather. For, after all, it has to be remembered that our feet and legs are only pieces of apparatus to enable us to move about, analogous to the wheels of a cart, and that the great centres of nervous energy and reproductive activity are within the body proper.[29]

Accordingly, the medium, for the next experiment, donned white calico knickers under the supervision of Mrs Crawford. At the end of the seance, the knickers were inspected. It was found that there were broad carmine paths up to the top of the stockings and then up the inside legs of the knickers. 'Thus, as I had suspected for some considerable time, it was abundantly clear that plasma issued from and returned to the body of the medium by way of the trunk.' It clearly issued from, and returned to, what Crawford liked to call 'the join of the legs'. This experiment was repeated several times, using clean knickers each time (Crawford stressed this) and there could be no doubt about the result.

Crawford actually took photographs of these experiments and their results, but he did not show them to the medium immediately. 'In order to prevent subconscious action affecting the moulding of the plasma, I withheld the photographs from the medium until the present series was obtained. When I at length showed them to her she was vastly astonished and diffident about my publishing some of them.'[30] This can hardly surprise us. What is surprising, in Crawford's dry, mad little book, is the sudden intrusion of sexuality – repressed, somewhat perverted, but undoubtedly present.

It was present, too, in the Eva C. experiments – though not repressed. But neither was it straightforward, as the Victorian version of sex-and-spirits had been, or even as Eusapia had been. There was, however, a certain amount that Eva undoubtedly had in common with Eusapia. Sexually, after a time at least, she seems to have quite lost her inhibitions. At the end of a sitting she would sometimes undo her tights and demand a gynaecological examination even when no one considered it necessary. As time went on, she liked to leave the tights off, to facilitate the production of materials from between her legs. And she displayed definite sexual excitement during the production of the phenomena. Schrenck noted that 'In both Eusapia Paladino and in Eva C. the violent muscular action, combined with pain, groans, and gasps, reminds one of the labour of childbirth.'[31] These were presumably the same sounds which Lombroso and Schiaparelli had taken to denote orgasm.

Whether these were birth-pangs or orgasm, one thing is quite clear, and that is that Eva's sexuality, as expressed through her mediumistic trances, was directed not at Schrenck or at any of the other men present (although Schrenck noted, perhaps not without pique, that she had a quite exaggerated idea of her attraction for the opposite sex), but at Juliette Bisson. Time and again, Juliette reports extraordinary scenes that take place when only she and Eva are present. These scenes are quite simply suffused with sex. Take that which occurred on 10 September 1911, when the Bissons and Eva were staying at Saint-Jean-de-Luz. Eva had requested that Juliette hypnotize her, as she felt strange. Juliette did so; Eva retired behind the cabinet curtains, and some materializations – a couple of heads – were produced.

> Suddenly Eva requested me to undo the seams. She removed the clothes and sat naked in front of me. Then followed a series of remarkable phenomena.
>
> A large, flat, dark-grey patch appeared on her breast, white at the rims. It remained for some time, and then disappeared in the region of the navel. I clearly saw it being reabsorbed there.
>
> The curtains were then kept closed for several seconds, without my releasing her hands. A round patch again appeared on her skin at the opening of the curtains. It had the same kind of shape as the first, but was larger. To this was joined, in the left ovarial region, a large, black, ball-shaped structure, white in the middle and dark-grey at the rims. With the curtain open, I counted twenty-two seconds. Suddenly the material folded itself together at right angles to the axis of her body, and formed a broad band extending from hip to hip under the navel. This apparition then folded up and disappeared in the vagina.
>
> On my expressing a wish, the medium parted her thighs, and I saw that the material assumed a curious shape, resembling an orchid, decreased slowly and entered the vagina. During the whole process I held her hands. Eva then said, 'Wait, we will try to facilitate the passage.' She rose, mounted on the chair, and sat down on one of the arm-rests, her feet touching the seat. Before my eyes, and with the curtain open, a large spherical mass, about 8 inches in diameter, emerged from the vagina and quickly placed itself on her left thigh while she crossed her legs. I distinctly recognised in

the mass a still unfinished face, whose eyes looked at me. As I bent forward in order to see better, the head-like structure rose before my eyes, and suddenly vanished into the dark of the cabinet away from the medium, disappearing from my view.[32]

Faced with such descriptions, the reader can only sit back in amazement. What was actually going on it is almost impossible to imagine. Did this extraordinary pseudo-birth, or anything like it, really take place? Had Juliette hypnotized herself, as well as Eva? Was Eva the real hypnotist? Or were the two women in collaboration, jointly engaged in an elaborate joke at the expense of the distinguished doctor from Munich? There were certainly a great many people who thought that they were in collaboration, since this seemed to be the only explanation for some of Eva's effects. For of the reality of many of her productions, there can be no doubt. Schrenck, like Crawford, was an avid photographer, and published his photographs. Something was certainly there on many occasions. The question is, what was it? And how did it get there? Eva's phenomena were very varied, though the framework of the seance was not. It is noticeable that even in private with Mme Bisson she retired behind the cabinet curtains before producing her materializations. As to the form these took, that depended on what she felt capable of, and on what was expected. Both these factors tended in the same direction: that of increasing complication as time went on. Cynics argued that practice makes perfect, and that she grew increasingly adept at deception and concealment. Believers thought her powers gradually increased.

In the very earliest seances, there was something faintly reminiscent of Bien Boa. A white-clad, turbaned, beardless figure was briefly visible when the cabinet curtains were parted. But this rather hackneyed phantom did not persist, and Eva began to display something quite new. This was the production of formless masses of white or grey material which might emanate from her neck, ankle, hands, or, most often, her mouth, and hover around the medium. This might sometimes resemble veiling, sometimes a kind of luminous smoke; it was sometimes described as a 'flocculent mass'. It sometimes seemed very light, sometimes sticky. At first, Eva seemed very nervous when Schrenck suggested that he might take a sample of the substance for analysis; later she sometimes permitted this.

As time went on, this stuff began to assume recognizable forms. By 1911, limbs, hands and feet were beginning to make their appearance. If we are to believe the photographs, they have varying degrees of credibility. A foot – which could, if she were sufficiently agile, have been Eva's foot – appeared on 29 May 1911. It was an unmistakable, living, clutching foot, and when tested later, Eva showed that she could not raise her foot so high while still remaining in the upright position shown in the photograph. But an extra hand which appeared a couple of months later gives the appearance of a cut-out or an empty glove.

By October 1911, Eva was producing her first notional faces. These appeared draped over the back of her head, and looked like painted scarves. By December a face appeared which seemed to have acquired a certain substance. These faces, which were generally attached to the back of Eva's head, continued to appear.

Obviously, after the more mysterious aura of the unformed masses of 'ectoplasm', the faces were something of a disappointment. They were static; the production of a living, breathing, second head seemed (not surprisingly) to be beyond Eva's capabilities. And somehow the unremitting gravity of Schrenck's Teutonically exact commentary only emphasizes the gulf between the high-flown nature of his enquiry and the rather unconvincing nature of these phenomena.

Take his comments on the face which appeared on 7 January 1912. Judging by the photograph, this appears to be a painted profile, covered with veiling and attached to the back of Eva's head. This sitting had begun at 8.30 p.m. Nothing happened until 9.45, when Eva opened the cabinet curtain a little and announced that '*la petite Estelle*' wanted to show herself. Then she turned her head away, and the profiled face was visible attached to the back of her head. Schrenck comments (after describing the appearance of the face, including a crease, or crack, traversing the cheek, and an elaborate arrangement of luxuriant curls not visible in the photograph):

> The composition and arrangement of this head appear to be a remarkably artistic performance, quite apart from the question as to how it was done.
> The question now arises as to the origin of the hair. We see real black-looking hair in shiny strands, well dressed and arranged in curls. Does this hair belong to Eva's head, or is it a sort of materialised wig? My personal impression favours the simpler assumption, viz., that Eva's coiffure was opened out broadly, and used for decorating the picture, especially as the lowermost curl can be followed direct from the medium's hair. . . . That this extraordinarily artistic arrangement could be produced, in the dark, without a mirror, by some power as yet unknown, is in any case remarkable.[33]

Faces continued to appear. They progressed from profile to full-face, and sometimes now appeared attached to the cabinet curtain, not to Eva. And in August of 1912, a slight *crise* arose. One Dr A drew Schrenck's attention to a number of small holes, which it was agreed could only be pinholes, in the cabinet curtain – and in just those places where materializations had recently appeared. Schrenck mused for some time on this unsettling detail. 'It goes without saying that the use of pins for fixing the images would be a negative factor of considerable importance,' he conceded. It would have been easy enough for Eva to introduce a pin, since the combs and hairpins were not taken out of her hair before a seance. And 'If these images, in spite of our precautions, were introduced by fraudulent manipulations, the pin is quite a natural addition, and we might assume that Eva had secured and hidden the pin in the waking state with a fraudulent intention'. But Schrenck was not too perturbed by this thought. 'There is no trace of any evidence for such fraudulent preparations. The observations, extending over three and a half years, speak to the contrary. The conditions under which the sittings took place exclude the introduction of pictures and other objects.' And in any case (he went on), 'we are obliged to distinguish between the question of suspension or location, and the mediumistic creation itself. I observed, during a later sitting, that the medium was capable of producing a picture, but could not place it in a position favourable to the observer.'[34] The sittings went on, pins or no pins.

Whether Eva felt that she must clear herself from any taint of suspicion, it is impossible to know. At any rate, things now took a new turn. Had there been suspicions that she was hiding materials somehow about her person? She would confound them. For the first time Juliette Bisson, as well as Schrenck, started taking photographs of the seances; but these were seances at which only she was present with Eva, and the medium was nude throughout the sitting.

At these sittings, some very curious phenomena were produced. At one, what looks like a rather decayed spider's web was suspended from nipple to nipple across Eva's body. At another, a man's head appeared – or rather, what looked like the picture of a man's head cut out of paper. He was wearing pince-nez, had a large moustache and a very contemporary-looking tie, and was adorned with what looked like parallel folds in the paper of which (had this not been an ectoplasmic materialization) one would have thought he was made. Schrenck described this as 'an artistically successful male face with a lively expression'.

Finally, and climactically, on 23 February 1913, Eva, nude once again, her hair down round her shoulders, produced a full phantom.

He appeared behind Eva's chair in the cabinet, 'fully developed already at the first exposure'. Juliette at once took a flashlight photograph. 'In spite of the shock the figure, which moved freely without feet, ending at the lower hem of its cloak, remained where it was and allowed itself to be illuminated by Eva's electric torch six times in succession. . . . It disappeared without a trace in the direction of the back wall.'[35] This phantom, who was christened 'Dorsmica', continued to reappear throughout the first half of 1913. He had an elegant moustache and beard, and wore what looked like a white lab-coat over a shirt and tie. Like Eva's other materializations of persons, Dorsmica seemed distinctly two-dimensional. But Schrenck was undisturbed by this flat quality. He thought that this was only a transitional stage, on the part of the 'psychic individuality', towards the kind of figure which would more nearly resemble a living person, in the style of William Crookes's 'Katie King', who, as he pointed out, was in every respect indistinguishable from the real thing.

'Dorsmica' really marked the apogee of Eva C 's mediumistic career. After that, she had little time to think where to go next before scandal once again broke over her head.

I have already commented more than once on the flat quality of Eva C.'s 'materializations' of faces and figures. This could certainly not be ignored, not even, as we have seen, by Schrenck himself, who might perhaps more relevantly have contrasted them, in this respect, with Bien Boa than with the long-disappeared Katie King.

We have just seen his explanation for this curious anomaly. But others, too, had been equally struck by it, and they, too, were looking for explanations. And in January 1914, it looked as if an explanation had indeed been found. In a series of articles beginning that month in *The Psychic Magazine*, a Miss Barkley claimed to have identified a number of the images of heads produced by Eva. She began by pointing out that in one of Schrenck's photographs, taken by a camera placed above the cabinet – one of a series depicting a 'materialization' of a woman's head, taken from different angles – the words LE MIRO were clearly visible in a portion of the substance just above Eva's head. She therefore concluded that some of the pictures might have been taken from a popular paper called *Le Miroir*. And sure enough, when she looked, the originals of the phantoms were, one and all, to be found among the various celebrities who had recently been depicted in that paper, at a little less than life-size, in black and white autotype.

Miss Barkley elaborated her accusations in the *Neue Wiener*

Tageblatt, which had taken up the story. She said:

Miss Eva prepared the heads before every seance, and endeavoured to make them unrecognizable. A clean-shaven face was decorated with a beard. Grey hairs became black curls, a broad forehead was made into a narrow one. But in spite of all her endeavours she could not obliterate certain characteristic lines. . . . There is, first of all . . . M. Poincaré. The hair of the President of the Republic has been altered and blackened, and his face has been lengthened, but all the other characteristic lines of his face remained.[36]

Among the other ghosts Miss Barkley identified President Woodrow Wilson, Paul Deschanel, King Ferdinand of Bulgaria (the original of Dorsmica) and the celebrated actress Mona Delza.

Anyone who compares the two sets of photos can see that Miss Barkley had undoubtedly hit upon something. But what? Schrenck became very indignant at the idea that fraud must be the natural hypothesis. Quite apart from anything else, he asserted that the controls on Eva, during all the seances in question, had been so thorough and painstaking that she simply could not have smuggled the materials in. And anyway (he went on) differences in the quality of the photographs and the phenomena proved that the faces portrayed in the phenomena could not have been the photographs, slightly tampered with, as was alleged. Moreover, he obtained written depositions to this effect from three photographers, two French and one German, and from a German professor. (It may be said that these convinced the general public as little as Professor Richet's deposition from the architect of the Villa Carmen, to the effect that Bien Boa could not have entered through a trapdoor because there was no trapdoor, had done eight years earlier.)

But if the 'materializations' were not taken from the *Le Miroir* photographs, then how could they be explained? For at the end of the day, bluster as he would, not even Schrenck could deny the resemblances. In the event he came up with an explanation as amazing, in its own way, as Dr Crawford's 'psychic rods'. The various materialized phenomena, he said, were 'ephemeral, externalised precipitates of the medium's psychic impressions and reminiscences'. In support of this theory he recalled how often Eva had produced specific phenomena at the suggestion of Mme Bisson. Not only that, but she had produced a materialized image of M Bisson not long after his death, when he could be expected to be in everyone's thoughts, and a reproduction of the Mona Lisa when it had been stolen from the Louvre, and was generally talked about. These images Schrenck termed 'ideoplasts'.

He went on to hypothesize that Eva displayed a condition called hypermnesia, common among hysterics, which allowed abnormal sharpness of recall. As her memory was chiefly visual, this would take the form, in her case, of visual recall. And this might also be combined with cryptomnesia, recall of a memory image which had never entered the normal consciousness, common among hypnotized persons.

Now, supposing (which was more than possible) that Eva had happened to catch a glimpse, from time to time, of the front page of *Le Miroir*? What could be more likely than that she should produce an unconscious ideoplastic image of it – even including the letters LE MIRO? Such a possibility might also go far to explain some otherwise inexplicable phenomena produced by other mediums. 'Thus, in a sitting held by Richet with Linda Gazerra, an angel head, by Rubens, was apparently the model for an ideo-plastic reproduction.'[37] Professor Morselli (who had observed, with Lombroso, the sexually stimulating effects of table levitation on Eusapia) had also noticed this phenomenon, and had remarked that in the first instance such forms were apt to be developed in two dimensions only, thus showing a flat appearance. This, Schrenck felt, finally disposed of Miss Barkley. Certainly, as an example of psychic scientism in full flow, this virtuoso performance has rarely been surpassed.

We may believe Schrenck's rationalizings or we may not, but one problem still remains, and that is: if Eva cheated, how did she do it? For, on the face of it, Schrenck's precautions really were exhaustive. Nevertheless, there are various ways in which she could have accomplished her different feats, and it is probable that, like all good illusionists, she varied her technique.

The first possibility is that she produced many of her effects by regurgitation. It is quite possible, with practice, to induce oneself to vomit up the contents of the stomach at will. This was certainly the opinion of Houdini, the great magician and illusionist, who attended a number of seances with Eva and Mme Bisson in 1920. He specifically mentions the disgusting quality of some of her productions, quite reconcilable with having spent some hours in the stomach; and indeed this is apparent in many of Schrenck's photographs.

It may be argued – as Schrenck did argue – that by no means all the phenomena showed this mangling. But there are a number of materials which may be swallowed and regurgitated with little deleterious effect. They include chiffon gauze, from which the dressing has been removed in hot water, and gold-beater's skin, which does not crease and is unaffected by moisture; both of these materials may have faces painted or photographically reproduced on them; these are then cut out along their contours and swallowed. Other possible materials are rubber gloves or other objects cut out in the form of hands; shreds of animal mesentery; and catgut or balloons, which can then be inflated.

The advantage of regurgitation is of course that, search as they may, investigators will never find anything concealed on the body. It has disadvantages. If the medium is forced to drink coffee or other staining substances, then the stomach contents will also be stained – and Eva's audience always emphasized the snowy whiteness of her products. It may take a long time; but Eva was always allowed to take all the time she wanted. It may not be a silent process; but, as we have seen, a great positive point was made of the groans, grunts and moans involved in the process of 'mediumistic birth'. So it seems likely that regurgitation was indeed one of Eva's techniques, more especially as she was sometimes observed to bleed slightly from the mouth. But it certainly does not explain everything.

Houdini's other alternative was that Eva had a secret accomplice, and this, he believed, must have been Mme Bisson. It is certain that no trust can be put in those accounts of seances at which only Mme Bisson was present with Eva; and it is surely no coincidence that it was at these private sessions that many of the most sensational results were recorded. And it was not only Houdini who harboured this suspicion. It was shared by so many people that, at least in the early days, Juliette routinely allowed herself to be searched along with Eva (though not, presumably, in quite such detail). No one who was not at the seances can of course be certain about this, but Houdini's thinking in such matters is generally to be trusted.

Yet another possibility is that, in spite of all Schrenck's thoroughness, Eva did have secret hiding-places either on her person or inside the cabinet. One that has been suggested is her hair-comb, which was not removed; it would have been quite possible to hide packets inside its hollowed-out head. As for the cabinet, every medium had his or her favourite hiding-places there. We know that Houdini, for example, in his fake-medium tricks, used a hollow pole, one of those of which his own cabinet was constructed. He also used the seat of the chair on which he sat inside it. Schrenck made a point of searching the cabinet and the chair; but Eva was wily and increasingly experienced in such matters.

All this is clear enough, but still the question remains: what, in the end, did Schrenck-Notzing really believe? Certainly the conclusion of his long and detailed book is quite unambiguous. 'A careful examination of the objections and arguments brought forward by our opponents has shown their baselessness,' he wrote; and he allied himself with Professor Richet, who, after staunchly upholding the Villa Carmen experiments, wrote: 'Man is so made that he does not want to accept truth if it does not appear probable, and it is certainly not our fault if the metapsychic region shows so many improbabilities and contradictions.'[38]

That, of course, is so; yet one has to ask: where does open-mindedness stop and credulity begin? In the case of Richet, Schrenck-Notzing and Crawford, the answer must surely be: a good way this side of the 'phenomena' to which they so firmly attested. Looking at the photographic evidence they so proudly produce, one can only wonder.

There are various possible factors which, it seems to me, do not come into the case. For example, the savants did not have the motivation of Mme Noël or Mme Bisson to preserve the illusion. This motivation was in each case sexual: Mme Noël basked in Bien Boa's embraces; Juliette Bisson and Eva C. almost certainly had some sort of sexual relationship. And – as we have seen more than once already in the course of this book – people will defy any possible logic for a lover. But Eva, hysterical, rather plain, clearly uninterested in straightforward sex as she was, did not have the same kind of pull over her savants as Florence Cook or even Eusapia had exercised over theirs.

Then the religious factor, in these cases, really does not come into it. There is no hidden religious yearning behind Richet's or Schrenck's pronouncements, but their belief was none the less fervent for that. Despite all their protestations of scientific detachment, it was clear that Schrenck, Richet and Crawford would contemplate anything rather than renounce their belief in the truth of their hypotheses. In poor Crawford's case this was literally true. Houdini met him once in London and had a long talk with him, in the course of which Crawford showed him pictures of what he claimed to be ectoplasm, or psychic structures, issuing from different parts of Kathleen Goligher's body, which he said he was going to use in a forthcoming book. Houdini concluded that he was mad. This was denied by many, including Schrenck, who denounced one investigator, Fournier d'Albe, the biographer of William Crookes and a man with enormous interest in psychical phenomena, with entering his investigation 'with prejudice against the genuineness of the Goligher phenomena'. But d'Albe actually saw Kathleen raising a stool with her foot, and concluded, despite his faith in Dr Crawford, that the Golighers, those 'simple, honest folks, all turned out to be an alert, secretive, troublesome group of well-organized performers'.[39] They certainly refused d'Albe's request to submit to fresh investigations with a new investigator. Had they been so investigated, he confidently predicted that no psychic phenomena would be observed, nor would any evidence of fraud, as 'the members of the Circle are exceedingly wary, and the evidence of trickery which I obtained was gathered under conditions which they had not foreseen but which they will doubtless avoid in the future'.[40]

That was published after Crawford's death; for in 1920 he committed suicide. In a note written to the then editor of *Light*, he explained that his nervous collapse was entirely due to overwork. He wrote: 'My psychic work was all done before the collapse, and is the most perfect work I have done in my life. Everything connected with it is absolutely correct, and will bear any scrutiny. It was done when my brain was working perfectly, and it could not be responsible for what occurred.'[41] But perhaps what forced him to the point of suicide was the realization that this perfect world was about to be shattered.

It seems to me that in this tragic note we have the real clue to the behaviour of these apparently deranged savants. In an age of burgeoning scientific discovery, when the most unlikely sounding theories were being proposed and proved to be right, they thought that they, too, had made world-shattering discoveries. As the psychologist Joseph Jastrow put it, 'It was not Eva C. but Charles Richet who created ectoplasm. She but made the substance, which would have commanded slight interest; he made the theory which commanded the world's attention.'[42] It was an attention which he, like Schrenck-Notzing, like Crawford, was unwilling to forgo. And to forgo it in humiliation was, literally, unthinkable. But, despite all the trappings, the vocabulary, the association with such scientific innovators as the Curies and such would-be innovators as Blondlot (the inventor of N-rays) the science of 'metapsychics' suffered from one enormous defect. It is a defect which dates from the earliest such investigations and which has persisted until the present day.

It is summed up in the pronouncement of Richet, already quoted, that there would be 'no attempt at theory concerning these strange phenomena'. And if we compare this attitude with that of 'regular' scientists, the difference is immediately obvious. The one aspect of 'parascience' that has most worried its scientific and philosophical adherents is that it does not progress. It is static. Thus, in 1909, towards the end of his life, the great psychologist William James, whose interest and enthusiasm had contributed so much to psychical research's seal of intellectual respectability, sadly wrote: 'For twenty-five years I have been in touch with the literature of psychical research, and I have had acquaintance with numerous "researchers". I have spent a good many hours . . . in witnessing (or trying to witness) phenomena. Yet, theoretically, I am no "further" than I was at the beginning.'

Seventy years later, the philosopher Antony Flew found himself in exactly the same predicament: '. . . the research has indeed gone on. In all probability, its sum in the years between is as great [as] or greater than the total for all the years before. Yet it is hard to point to any respect in which the general situation is better now than it was then.' Indeed, so far is this from being the case that John Beloff, a past president of the SPR, wrote in 1973: 'To me . . . the records of the great sensitives of the past still offer the best assurance we have that psi is not just a mirage or an artifact.'[43] (Readers, considering the story so far, may perhaps feel that this is a somewhat broken reed on which to lean.)

In short, the great scientific effort in this field has been concentrated on the amassing of evidence. This, by its very nature, is elusive; and we have already seen that even such rigorous experimenters as William Crookes accepted that because of the peculiar nature of the force under investigation, it could never be assumed that any particular experiment could be exactly repeated. And there's the rub. For to achieve a theory, repeatability is essential. In order to test different hypotheses, one must be able to rely on achieving a certain result by a certain process.

This state of affairs was never more apparent, the contrast never more strongly marked, than when Richet was conducting his experiments at the Institut de Métapsychique. Among the group he assembled there to test Eusapia were the Curies, who had just been awarded the Nobel Prize for their discovery of radium, together with several other members of their laboratory. Let us, then, contrast the two sets of experiments: those of the Curies and those of Richet.

The discovery of radioactivity and the isolation of radium was a process compounded, principally, of immense meticulousness and hard, hard labour. It involved constant repetition of processes, testing of materials, infinite refining down. And, once radium had been isolated and a theory of radioactivity formulated, it did not rest there. Others were waiting to carry on the work the Curies had begun. What caused radioactivity? How could it be used? How harnessed? How created? The reverberations of those efforts in the Sorbonne laboratory are with us, inescapably, to this day.

In the experiments with Eusapia, by contrast, it was never even certain that anything would happen. At the most, a table might lift, an unexpected pat be felt on a shoulder, an inexplicable bell ring. And that was that. As Richet said, far from being able to theorize about these phenomena, 'it was a heavy enough task to analyse their reality.' But that was where the Curies began – with the reality.

And if one is unable to analyse, can this be science? For the possibility that something happened is not, by itself, in the end, interesting. Hence the tedium of many of the texts of 'parascience'. They are merely repetitions: of ghost stories supposed to have been experienced, of attempts at guessing numbers, of the different kinds of ectoplasm materialized by Eva C.

Houdini, in his book *Magician Among the Spirits*, heads one chapter: Why Ectoplasm? Perhaps that question can now be answered (a feat, incidentally, which, having posed the question, Houdini never attempts). Ectoplasm, and teleplasm, and ideoplasts, and psychic structures, psi, metapsychics and the rest are essential if the trappings and feel of science, at least, are to be bestowed on what is essentially a non-, or at the most a pre-scientific activity.

6
Magicians Among the Spirits

Who was the greatest medium-baiter of modern times? Undoubtedly
Houdini. Who was the greatest physical medium of modern times? There
are those who would be inclined to give the same answer. – SIR
ARTHUR CONAN DOYLE, *On the Edge of the Unknown*

If a scientist is not necessarily the best person to investigate the wonders of spiritualist phenomena, then who is? The answer is, someone
who can spot tricks because he knows what to look out for: in other
words, a professional illusionist. This has always been the illusionists'
opinion. Throughout the history of spiritualism the most dedicated
and determined seekers-out of mediumistic fraud have been magicians, professional and amateur. Set a thief to catch a thief, they
argued. They could, like so many of their brothers, have set up as
mediums – some, indeed, had done so at one point or another in their
careers. But they had chosen to fight on the side of the angels – the real
angels, that is. Fraudulent angels were ruthlessly exposed – as they
still are: the long tradition which began with J. N. Maskelyne is vigor-
ously maintained by modern magicians such as Milbourne Christopher and James (The Amazing) Randi. Their exposés are, as they
always have been, thorough, fascinating and seemingly unanswerable.
What is surprising, to the detached observer, is the tetchiness and
reluctance with which they have been received, not just by the victims
– which would be understandable – but by those who might be expected to be grateful, since otherwise they would have been duped: the
scientists, for example.
    The way in which this still goes on can be seen by looking at two
recent books. One, *Flim-Flam*, is by James Randi, an American magician who takes a special interest in exposing 'psychical' fraud. The

other, *Explaining the Unexplained*, is by two psychologists, Carl Sargent and the very well-known H.J.Eysenck. Among the frauds shown up by Randi is a Frenchman, Jean-Pierre Girard, who claims to bend metal in sealed containers by means of psychic force. And among the 'unexplained' miracles cited by Sargent and Eysenck – who certainly could, and certainly should, have read Randi's book – are the activities of this very same Girard. The is no question of agreeing or disagreeing with Randi: they simply do not mention him, but assume – and leave the unknowing reader to assume – that Girard is genuine and unchallenged. And where the question arises of someone working to expose fraud by similar methods whom they cannot ignore – for instance Richard Hodgson, a member of the Society for Psychical Research from its earliest days, a man well acquainted with conjurers' trickery and who, often with the aid of a friend who was himself a highly proficient magician, exposed many frauds – they simply resort to abuse. Hodgson was, they assert, obnoxious, belligerent, insensitive and vituperative, his only saving grace being that even he could not fault the great 'mental medium' Mrs Piper (whom we shall consider in a later chapter). It may be remembered that Hodgson also came under fire from Brian Inglis for his presumption, as a young man, in exposing the methods of Madame Blavatsky. Why this vituperation? And why this conspiracy of silence?

Once can only conclude that respectable scientists and intellectuals, having decided to adopt a particular *parti pris*, deeply resent their views being challenged by non-intellectuals, or at any rate, by non-intellectual methods. Even when they will acknowledge such evidence, they will try to minimize its impact by decrying the character and motivation of the debunker in question.

Perhaps nowhere have these curious attitudes been more in evidence than with regard to the activities in spiritualism of the most famous illusionist of all time – Harry Houdini. What must always be remembered about Houdini was that he *wanted to believe*. Only in this way can the violence of his later fury against the tricksters be understood. They were making a mockery of something he wanted, more than anything in the world, to be true.

Spiritualists and students of the paranormal are very keen on 'open-mindedness'. Their definition of this state, however, is sometimes odd. One recently defined it to me in the statement, 'I believe that strange things do happen'; and this is a pretty fair approximation to the accepted attitude. This was not Houdini's state of mind. Rather (in something approaching a good deal nearer to the dictionary definition of open-mindedness) he was *prepared* to believe that strange things happened. He *wanted* to believe it, even. But first, he had to be convinced: a more difficult task. In this genuinely open-minded attitude, he was not alone among magicians. J.N.Maskelyne, part of whose act at the Egyptian Hall in London consisted in defying mediums to baffle him by producing an effect he could not reproduce, surprised an interviewer from the *Pall Mall Gazette* by admitting that there was something in this line that even he believed in. That, as it happened, was table-turning. Once, with some friends, a heavy table had turned in a way they had not been able to repeat afterwards, however hard they tried; and Maskelyne could not see that Faraday's explanation (of unconscious muscular action) could at all account for that particular phenomenon. (However, whatever did cause the effect, there was one thing he was sure it was not – and that was spirits.)

Like many illusionists, Houdini had experience of mediumistic fraud from the inside. Early in his career, when he was still struggling unsuccessfully to establish himself, he took an engagement in Kansas with the 'California Concert Company'; and part of his act was to give a spiritualist seance as a special Sunday night attraction. The programme read:

ANNOUNCEMENT EXTRAORDINARY
GREAT TRIPLE BILL
at
THE OPERA HOUSE
SUNDAY, JANUARY 9, 1898
HOUDINI THE GREAT
will give a spiritual seance in the light

THE ONLY TIME A SEANCE IN PUBLIC EVER GIVEN
BY HOUDINI, EXCEPT IN LARGE CITIES AT HIGH PRICES
When conditions are favorable, tables float through the air and musical instruments playing sweetest music are seen floating through space; all the spirit hands are seen in full light. A committee of businessmen have kindly volunteered to act as an investigating committee, which will insure honesty of purpose.[1]

That, however, was before the death of the magician's beloved mother. After that event, the one aim of his life was to re-establish contact with her; and he never faked mediumship again.

By the time Houdini became a name to conjure with in spiritualist circles he was no longer a penniless unknown trying to scratch a living in any way he could. Where a few years earlier he had tried (and failed) to sell the secrets of his tricks for a few dollars, now an offer of tens of thousands could not have tempted him. He was the foremost practitioner of his art; the poor Hungarian rabbi's son was world-famous. And it was on one of his European tours – he was performing at the Brighton Hippodrome at the time – that he met Sir Arthur Conan Doyle. Conan Doyle was one of the leading spiritualists in Britain, indeed, in the world. He was as famous as Houdini, his name and fortune both having been made – somewhat to his chagrin, for he considered them the least of his achievements – by the Sherlock Holmes stories.

To the reader whose knowledge of Conan Doyle is limited to those stories, the contrast between the ingenious but always logical mind of Holmes – and, it might be assumed, of his creator – and the character of Conan Doyle the spiritualist is extraordinary. When it came to spiritualism, his credulity knew no bounds. As Houdini said,

> Sir Arthur believes implicitly in the mediums with whom he has convened and he knows positively, in his own mind, they are all genuine. Even if they are caught cheating he always has some sort of an alibi which excuses the medium and the deed. He insists that the Fox Sisters were genuine, even though both Margaret and Katie confessed to fraud. . . . He has often told me that Palladino and Home some day would be canonized for the great work they did in the interest of Spiritualism.[2]

Above all, Conan Doyle possessed the quality of open-mindedness as spiritualists understood it. He was eager to believe that strange things happened and often outraged at the suggestion that fraud might be involved.

This contrast between the author's two selves was no greater than that between Doyle and his friend Houdini. Doyle was very tall and patrician, the picture of the British gentleman of letters. Houdini was short and thick-set, very intelligent but quite uneducated. Each had unshakable confidence in himself and in the accuracy of his view of the world (and, in Doyle's case, the other world). Each had great respect and affection for the other. Spiritualism was the topic that fascinated them both; but it was a subject upon which (as may be imagined) they profoundly disagreed.

The essence of their disagreement may be summed up by considering Doyle's view of Houdini. Quite simply he was convinced that the magician had psychic powers, and that these explained his more extraordinary feats. When he appeared to walk through a wall, or escaped from a sealed coffin suspended in a tank of water, the thing was done – Doyle was convinced – by dematerialization. Houdini dematerialized from one place and reappeared in another. Houdini naturally denied this, but no matter how vehemently he protested that everything he did was done by pure trickery and mystification, Doyle would not believe him. 'I had an interesting talk to-day with Houdini about his wonderful powers,' he wrote. 'Very naturally he gives nothing away, for a trick explained loses its virtue. I am quite sure that if the Davenport Brothers had done their performance as if it were a conjuring trick, and never told the honest and unpopular truth that it was of psychic origin, they would have amassed a comfortable fortune and been far wiser from a worldly point of view – which, after all, is not the highest wisdom when the end of the story comes to be told.'[3] (The truth about the Davenport Brothers was in fact precisely the opposite of what Conan Doyle wrote here. They were skilled conjurers who passed off their performances as being of psychic origin, with enormous success until they were unmasked in Liverpool in 1868. Even then they continued to retain many devotees. It was they who first introduced the 'cabinet', which subsequently became an indispensable accessory for all spirit mediums.) Doyle was certainly not the first spiritualist to be convinced that conjurers were psychic, rather than that psychics were expert conjurers. Alfred Russel Wallace had held exactly the same views about Maskelyne, saying: 'If you think it is all juggling, point out exactly where the difference lies between it and mediumistic phenomena.' This, of course, was precisely the point the magicians were trying to make – except that they drew the opposite conclusion. Doyle and Houdini therefore had their differences, but they did not let these come between them. After their first meeting they corresponded, discussing spiritualistic questions. Then Doyle invited the Houdinis to his home in Sussex, beginning a friendship between the two families which, though unlikely, nevertheless flourished.

During and after the First World War there was, as might be imagined, a huge surge of interest in spiritualism. Literally millions of families had suffered the sudden loss of a husband, father or son, and anything which gave some hope that these loved relatives were not lost for ever was seized upon. Doyle was not one to let such an opportunity pass. With missionary zeal he devoted himself to the spiritualist cause; a mission which took him, along with his wife and three children, on two hugely successful lecture tours of America. It was during the first of these, in 1922, that the incident occurred which was to wreck the friendship of these two extraordinary men.

It all began in the mildest possible way. It was June, the weather was hot, and the Doyles decided to take a short holiday in Atlantic City. Would the Houdinis join them? 'The children would teach you to swim! and the change would do you good.' To which Houdini replied, 'Mrs Houdini joins me in thanking you for the invitation to come to Atlantic City. . . . If the kiddies want to teach me to swim I will be there, and in return will show them how to do one or two things that will make it very interesting.'[4]

So it came about that on the afternoon of 17 June 1922, Harry and Bessie Houdini were sitting on the beach at Atlantic City playing with the Doyle children, whose parents had gone off for a rest. Suddenly Sir Arthur reappeared, walking along the beach towards them. He said (or this is what Houdini said he said): 'Houdini, if agreeable, Lady Doyle will give you a special seance, as she has a feeling that she might have a message come through. At any rate, she is willing to try.'[5]

Who could this mysterious message be from? Bessie Houdini silently gave her husband a hint. Years before, they had done a thought-reading act together, and still had a system by which they could pass each other messages without anyone else being aware of it. The night before, Bessie signalled, she had been talking to Jean Doyle and had told her about Houdini's great love for his mother. It was therefore not such a great surprise as it might have been when Jean Doyle confirmed that it was indeed Houdini's mother whom she felt might be 'coming through'.

What happened at this seance? As to the bare facts, there is not much argument. Jean Doyle had not, at the beginning of her marriage, been a believer in spiritualism, but the urgency of her husband's belief had gradually brought her round, until she reached a point where she developed mediumistic powers. These, in her, manifested themselves through automatic writing. Picture, then, the hotel room at Atlantic City. All three of the participants seated round the table were deeply moved, and fervently hoped that this might, indeed, prove to be the real thing. Unknown to the Doyles, that day, 17 June, had been Houdini's mother's birthday; the fact that the spirit never once commented on this fact was to be one of the disillusioning factors of the experience for him. But at the beginning no such doubts crossed his mind. 'I excluded all worldly thoughts and gave my whole soul to the seance.'[6]

The proceedings began with a prayer. Then they waited. And their prayer was answered. Lady Doyle was soon 'seized by a spirit'. Her hands shook uncontrollably, she beat the table, and in a trembling voice called on the spirits to give her a message. The shaking grew more violent; Conan Doyle tried to calm her, but to no avail. Her right hand, which held a pencil, jerked in spasm. The forces, said Doyle, had never manifested themselves as strongly as this. Finally, uncertainly, the pencil began to move on the pad of paper. 'Do you believe in God?' she enquired of the spirit. Her hand beat the table three times; she said, 'Then I will make the sign of the Cross.' And she did so at the head of the pad. Doyle then asked who was there, and whether it was Houdini's mother? Once more, the hand struck the table three times. Then it began to write. The message ran:

Oh, my darling, thank God, thank God, at last I'm through – I've tried, oh so often – now I am happy. Why, of course, I want to talk to my boy – my own beloved boy – Friends, thank you, thank you, with all my heart for this.

You have answered the cry of my heart – and of his – God bless him – a thousand fold, for all his life for me – never had a mother such a son – tell him not to grieve, soon he'll get all the evidence he is anxious for – Yes, we know – tell him I want him to try to write in his own home. It will be far better so.

I will work with him – he is so, so dear to me – I am preparing so sweet a home for him which one day in God's good time he will come to – it is one of my great joys preparing for our future –

I am so happy in this life – it is so full and joyous – my only shadow has been that my beloved one hasn't known how often I have been with him all the while, all the while – here away from my heart's darling – combining my work thus in this life of mine.

It is so different over here, so much larger and bigger and more beautiful – so lofty – all sweetness around one – nothing that hurts and we see our beloved ones on earth – that is such a joy and comfort to us – Tell him I love him more than ever – the years only increase it – and his goodness fills my soul with gladness and thankfulness. Oh, just this, it is me. I want him only to know that – that – I have bridged the gulf – That is what I wanted, oh so much – Now I can rest in peace – How soon –

At this point Conan Doyle broke in and said that Houdini should ask some sort of question, to make sure that this really was his mother speaking from the 'other side'. But what sort of question? Jean Doyle did not think the spirit would answer direct questions, and Houdini, wanting to help as much as he could, did not want to ask anything which might embarrass the medium. Doyle proposed that he might ask: 'Can my mother read my mind?' Houdini, unable to think of anything better – since this ought to cover anything he might wish to ask – acquiescently thought of this question. At once, the writing began again:

I *always* read my beloved son's mind – his dear mind – there is so much I want to say to him – but – I am almost overwhelmed by the joy of talking to him once more – it is almost too much to get through – the joy of it – thank you, thank you, thank you, friend, with all my heart for what you have done for me this day – God bless you, too, Sir Arthur, for what you are doing for us – for us over here – who so need to get in touch with our beloved ones on the earth plane –

If only the world knew this great truth – how different – life would be for men and women – Go on, let nothing stop you – great will be your reward hereafter – Good-bye – I brought you, Sir Arthur, and my darling son together – I felt you were the one man who might help us to pierce the veil – and I was right – Bless him, bless him, I say from the depths of my soul – He fills my heart and later we shall be together – oh, so happy – a happiness awaits him that he has never dreamed of – tell him I am with him – just tell him that I'll soon make him know how close I am all the while – his eyes will soon be opened – Good-bye again – God's blessing be on you all – [7]

The pencil dropped from Lady Doyle's hand; the trance was over. Houdini now asked about the instruction that he should write in his own home. Could he, could anyone, do automatic writing? He took a pencil to see what, if anything, would come, and wrote the first thing that came into his mind – the name 'Powell'. 'It was', he wrote in a memorandum the next day, 'like an electric shock to Sir Arthur, for a friend of his by that name, the editor of the *Financial News*, of London, had died about a week previously.' This, wrote Doyle in his account of the seance, was

the most marvellous thing of all. . . . Dr Ellis Powell, my dear fighting partner in Spiritualism, had just died in England – worn out, I expect, by his own exertions, for he was a desperately hard worker in the cause. I was the man he was most likely to signal to, and here was his name coming through the hand of Houdini. 'Truly Saul is among the prophets,' said I. . . . He muttered something about knowing a man named Powell, down in Texas, though he failed to invent any reason why that particular man should come back at that particular moment. Then, gathering up the papers, he hurried from the room.[8]

The Powell incident was to be one of the points of disagreement between Houdini and Conan Doyle regarding this extraordinary seance. For, far from being unable to find any reason for this particular name having come to mind, Houdini, in his next day's memorandum, gives a perfectly good one. He and his wife had just been having a conversation about a fellow magician of that name, whose wife had fallen ill and who therefore proposed to take on a new young woman assistant. They had disagreed about this, Mrs Houdini thinking this

Reproduction of the first two pages of the "automatic message" written by Lady Doyle at the sitting which she gave for Houdini in an effort to communicate with his mother.

was not fair, and Houdini arguing that 'it is perfectly all right for a magician to have young blood in his act, when his wife cannot assist him'. Discussing the affair with his wife, they agreed that this must certainly be the explanation. As for Conan Doyle's friend, that must be put down to coincidence.

Doyle, however, was not having that. He wrote to Houdini: 'No, the Powell explanation won't do. Not only is he the man who would wish to get me, but in the evening, Mrs. M., the lady medium, got "There is a man here; he wants to say that he is sorry he had to speak so abruptly this afternoon."'9

'Powell', however, was not the only aspect of the seance about which Houdini differed from the Doyles. They were in no doubt that the spirit which had 'come through' really was Houdini's mother; he was equally sure that it was not. He had two main reasons for being so certain of this. One, noted in the margin of the memorandum he compiled the day after the seance, was that 'My sainted mother could not write English and spoke broken English'. How, then could she possibly have been the source of Jean Doyle's trance writings? And the second was that, being a devout Jewess, she would never have begun any message with the sign of the cross. Doyle, however, rejected these objections, too. He wrote:

Concerning your difficulty about your mother's language, there is really nothing in that. . . . any trance or half-trance medium might get the Hebrew through. I don't think a normal automatic writer ever would. It would always come as a rush of thought, which is translated in coming, or else as a message through the control of the medium. In your case, the great excitement assures me that it was direct. . . . By the way, Mr Bird told me that, in the very complete test given you by your mother, you found it incredible that she, a Jewish lady, should put a Cross at the top. The Cross is put by my wife above the first page of all she writes, as we guard against lower influences, and we find it protective.[10]

Nevertheless, Houdini still found himself quite unable to accept that this really had been a message from his mother; and Doyle was infuriated. 'I saw what you got and what the effect was upon you at the time,' he wrote. '. . . However, I don't propose to discuss the subject any more with you, for I consider that you have had your proofs and that the responsibility of accepting or rejecting is with you. And it is a very real responsibility. . . . I will, however, send you my little book on Hope, but that will be my last word on the subject.'[11]

Houdini and Conan Doyle tried to pretend to each other for a while that their friendship was not at an end, but it could not really be salvaged. The hurt had gone too deep, on both sides, for that. For the Doyles, Houdini was wilfully blind and appallingly ungrateful. For Houdini, a frightful mockery had been made of his deepest feelings – for there can be no doubt that his love for his mother was the dominant emotion of his life, beside which his great affection for his wife paled into a commonplace thing. It was all very well Doyle's suggesting that they confine their correspondence, in future, to other topics – it was a nice idea, but not a realistic one. For the one thing that had originally drawn them together was their common interest in spiritualism, and this remained the overriding interest of both their lives. What the Atlantic City seance showed was that a violent argument over a deeply felt issue is most unlikely to convert either party to the opposite point of view. Rather, as in this case, each of the combatants will be confirmed in his conviction that he is right and his opponent quite wrong; and as time goes on, they will move further and further apart.

The first thing that happens is that memories of the controversial event which sparked off the argument change as time passes. This, of course, is a commonplace of evidence. Charles Richet had commented on its importance for psychical research:

> Our own conviction – the conviction of men who have seen – ought properly to convince other people – but, by a curious inversion of roles, it is *their* conviction, the negative conviction of people who have *not* seen, and who ought not, one would think, to speak on the matter, which weakens and ultimately destroys our own conviction. This phenomenon occurred in my own case with such intensity that scarcely a fortnight after witnessing the experiments in Milan [with Eusapia], I had persuaded myself that there had been nothing but fraud and illusion. [He added] Certainty does not follow on demonstration: it follows on habit.[12]

But while Richet found that time eroded the certainty with which he had started out – and, he judged, rightly started out – Conan Doyle found the opposite. His certainty of his original interpretation hardened, and Houdini became, in his eyes, increasingly blameworthy. At first, for example, there seems to have been no question but that the original impetus for the seance had come from the Doyles, but in a later book Doyle wrote: 'The method in which Houdini tried to explain away, minimize and contort our attempt at consolation, which was given entirely at his own urgent request and against my wife's desire, has left a deplorable shadow in my mind which made some alteration in my feelings towards him.'[13]

As for Houdini, he dismissed completely any suggestion that Doyle might be capable of detecting fraud in this field.

> It was not a case of being deceived, but merely a case of religious mania, and of knowing, in his own mind, according to his powerful deductions, that he was in the presence of the Almighty. . . . He is good-natured, very bright, but a monomaniac on the subject of Spiritualism. Being uninitiated in the world of mystery, never having been taught the artifices of conjuring, it was the simplest thing in the world for anyone to gain his confidence to hoodwink him.[14]

The two therefore parted, Conan Doyle to continue promoting the Spiritualist cause – he told Houdini that he was going to donate the whole £25,000 which he had earned on his lecture tour to this end – and Houdini to expose, with greater and greater ferocity, any examples of fraudulent spirit mediumship which he might encounter. Inevitably, it was not long before they met again – this time, as adversaries.

Houdini was now at the height of his fame and virtuosity. He was performing such feats as jumping from one aeroplane to another in mid-air, being suspended from a skyscraper in a strait-jacket from which he had to escape within a given time, being buried six feet deep in a coffin for three-quarters of an hour – it seemed there was nothing in the realms of escapology, daring and endurance which he could not successfully undertake.

But he did not let spiritualism drop. While on tour he would make a point of exposing fake mediums, and, more systematically, he was appointed a member of a committee set up to look into the subject by the *Scientific American*. The magazine, capitalizing on the publicity surrounding Conan Doyle's lecture tours, was offering $2,500 to anyone who could produce a psychic photograph (i.e., a photograph including a spirit) under test conditions, and a further $2,500 to anyone who produced an 'objective psychic manifestation of physical character . . . of such sort that permanent instrumental record may be made of its occurrence'. The committee, which was set up in January 1923, consisted of Dr William McDougall, Professor of Psychology at Harvard; Daniel F.Comstock, a former member of the MIT faculty; Walter Franklin Prince, who ran the American SPR; Hereward Carrington, an experienced investigator of psychic phenomena; Malcolm Bird, an assistant editor of the *Scientific American*; and Houdini. Conan Doyle wrote:

> My dear Houdini: . . . I see that you are on the *Scientific American* Committee, but how can it be called an Impartial Committee when you have committed yourself to such statements as that some Spiritualists pass away before they realize how they have been deluded, etc.? You have every possible right to hold such an opinion, but you can't sit on an Impartial Committee afterwards. It becomes biased at once. What I wanted was five good clear-headed men who would stick to it without any prejudice at all – like the Dialectical Society of London, who unanimously endorsed the phenomena.[15]

Conan Doyle thus demonstrated once again the very curious interpretation of the adjective 'open-minded' to be met with among enthusiasts. Later, when the committee had tested several mediums without finding anything 'psychic' about any of them, Doyle commented: 'The Commission is, in my opinion, a farce, and has already killed itself.'

However, this equivocal state of affairs in the committee was not to last long. For late in 1923, the *Scientific American* received a letter from Dr LeRoy G. Crandon of Boston.

Dr Crandon was a wealthy physician, living in Beacon Hill, the very best part of Boston. He was at this time in his fifties. He was writing, not about himself, but on behalf of his young wife, Mina, who was still only twenty-six. Mina, he said, possessed remarkable psychic powers. She had demonstrated these before Geley and Richet in France, and had given a private seance for the Conan Doyles in London. It was at their urging that the Crandons had contacted the magazine. Mina would be very happy to demonstrate her powers for the *Scientific American* committee. The only thing was, there could be no question of their coming to New York because of his medical practice, but Dr Crandon would be very happy to pay the expenses of any investigators who came to Boston to test Mrs Crandon; he was even ready to put them up at his house. So the committee was launched on its most contentious investigation.

It was in fact not Mina but Dr Crandon who had first become interested in psychic matters. This had been in the previous year when he had read Crawford's book *The Psychic Structures of the Goligher Circle* and been profoundly impressed by it. Pretty, energetic Mina was amused by this new-found enthusiasm of her husband's. This was her second marriage; she had previously been married to an Earl P. Rand, who ran a small grocery store. She liked sports, had played in an orchestra, had worked as a secretary, had helped run a church social group – clearly, the idle life of a wealthy doctor's wife was not for her and she welcomed anything which might break the monotony. At her husband's urging she visited a clairvoyant, who told her she had strong latent mediumistic powers.

Nothing could have delighted her husband more than this news. He was now eager to put these powers to the test; and he was not disappointed. He read everything he could find about spiritualism and psychical research, and passed his new-found knowledge on to Mina. At the first seance they held, when some family friends were invited up to the top-floor room they had decided to devote to their researches, they sat round a table which had been built to the exact measurements of the Golighers' table. For a while nothing happened. Then, suddenly, the table began to move. It vibrated, danced, slid about the floor and balanced on two legs. Everyone was thunderstruck; and Mina was launched on a new career.

To Dr Crandon, his wife's powers seemed truly miraculous. Anything he read about, it seemed that she could do. They decided to contact the *Scientific American* Committee, and Malcolm Bird arrived for a preliminary investigation in November 1923. By then, Mina was able to do bugle-calls without a bugle and rattles without a chain. Flashes of light travelled across the dark seance-room. She could stop the clock merely by concentrating on it; she produced a two-dollar bill and a live pigeon. All this might sound like elementary conjuring, but there was more. She went into trance and spoke with the voice of her dead brother Walter, who had been killed in an accident on the railroad. His voice was gruff and deep-pitched, and he used language which would never have passed the lips of the demure Mina. Bird was impressed; it was, presumably, at his suggestion that Dr Crandon wrote to the magazine with his proposition for transplanting the committee to Boston. The proposition was accepted, and the committee – or most members of it – came. Since some of them were on the faculties of Harvard and MIT, they already lived nearby anyway. And they were impressed with what they saw.

An article was eventually prepared for the July 1924 issue of *Scientific American* detailing their investigations and strongly hinting that here, at last, was a potential taker for the offered prize. This was not the first article written by Bird in which the Crandons were mentioned. Readers were kept abreast of the committee's investigations – this was, after all, a selling line for a commercial magazine. Two pieces by Bird had already been published describing Mina's feats. The Crandons were not identified in these pieces, Mina simply being referred to as 'Margery'.

One member of the investigating committee who had not been present at these sessions was Houdini. He was on tour during the first half of 1924, and the first he heard of the Margery investigation was when he read reports of Bird's articles in the press. To say he was angry at this intelligence would be to understate the case. He was furious, and returned post-haste to New York where he demanded to know what Bird thought he was doing, preparing to confirm Margery's mediumship before the full committee had so much as had a chance to look at her? Bird replied: 'Our only idea was not to bother you with it unless, and until, it got to a stage where there seemed serious prospects that it was either genuine or a type of fraud which our other committeemen could not deal with. . . . Mr Munn [publisher of the *Scientific American*] feels that the case has taken a turn that makes it desirable for us to discuss it with you.'[16]

The July issue of the magazine was now out, making Houdini even more furious than before. He was sure, from what he read, that the committee was being taken in. However, there was still time to undo the damage. He would go to Boston at once, accompanied by Mr Munn. They would certainly not stay with the Crandons: he was shocked that Bird and Hereward Carrington had accepted the doctor's invitation. How could they possibly make an impartial investigation when they were guests of the party being investigated? Houdini and Munn booked into the Copley-Plaza Hotel, and prepared to see what transpired.

It seems clear that from the start Houdini was regarded rather as an interloper by the Crandons. Whereas they had actively courted the attention of the rest of the committee, it was Houdini's opinion that he had been deliberately kept away from this investigation. This may seem somewhat paranoid, but the Crandons were certainly biased against Houdini before they ever met. In May Dr Crandon had obtained an advance copy of Houdini's book *Magician Among the Spirits*, and reported to Conan Doyle – to whom he wrote weekly – that Houdini was 'not in any way held back by ability or intent to tell the truth'. And in addition he had used Doyle's private letters 'as bait and material all through the book, entirely disregarding the usual obligations of civilized society'. Not surprisingly, Margery was not at all eager to meet this incarnate devil. Walter burst out against him from time to time – sometimes even in verse – and Crandon told Doyle that they planned to 'crucify' Houdini and so prove Margery 'the most extraordinary mediumship in modern history'. But, however they might feel, the Crandons were obviously going to have to submit to a scrutiny from the magician. On the morning of 23 July, Crandon reported to Doyle that Margery was 'vomiting merrily' [*sic*] at the prospect of the evening's activities and 'general nastiness'. But there was no avoiding it.[17]

Before the seance, Houdini had made some preparations and knew what he was looking for. He was to sit on the medium's left. Consequently, all that day he had worn a tight bandage just below the knee of his right leg, which had thus become swollen and tender. During the seance he rolled his right trouser leg up above his knee, so that with his sensitized leg he might feel any movement or flexing of Margery's leg against his.

This preparation was especially directed at a manifestation which had hitherto baffled all the members of the committee. This involved an electric bell enclosed in a box, which would ring whenever a certain pressure was applied to the boards on top of the box. In previous seances, the bell had been rung repeatedly when the box had been placed on the floor in front of Margery, even though the sitters were sure that they had perfect control over her hands and her feet. The explanation she gave was that her dead brother Walter must have closed the circuit. He had not only rung the bell, but had used a code to answer questions with it.

On this particular evening the box was placed between Houdini's feet, with his right foot between it and Margery's left.

As the seance progressed I could distinctly feel her ankle slowly and spasmodically sliding as it pressed against mine while she gained space to raise her foot off the floor and touch the top of the box. To the ordinary sense of touch the contact would seem the same while this was being done. At times she would say: 'Just press hard against my ankle so you can see that my ankle is there,' and as she pressed I could feel her gain another half inch.[18]

When she had manoeuvred her leg round into a position where she could reach the bell, Houdini felt the tendons of her leg tighten whenever she touched the box. Then, when the ringing was finished, he could feel her leg slide back into its original position with her foot on the floor beside his own.

On Margery's right sat Bird, and beside him, Dr Crandon. Bird held Margery's right hand and the doctor's left hand in one of his, thus leaving his other hand free 'for exploring purposes'. Suddenly, Walter asked for an illuminated plaque to be placed on the lid of the box containing the bell, and Bird went to get it.

Then Walter, equally suddenly, called for 'control'. Margery immediately placed her right hand in Houdini's. Bird was asked to stand in the doorway; suddenly the cabinet, which stood behind Margery, was thrown over violently. She then gave Houdini her right foot, too, saying, 'You now have both hands and both feet.' Walter then

called, 'The megaphone is in the air. Have Houdini tell me where to throw it.' 'Toward me,' replied the magician, and it instantly fell at his feet. This 'manifestation', too, had taken place before, and, as Houdini said, 'It had converted all sceptics.'

It did not, however convert Houdini, who was again able to see how it had been done.

When Bird left the room it freed her right foot and hand. With her right hand she tilted the corner of the cabinet enough to get her free foot under it, then picking up the megaphone she placed it on her head, dunce-cap

fashion. Then she threw the cabinet over with her right foot. Then she simply jerked her head, causing the megaphone to fall at her feet. Of course with the megaphone on her head it was easy and simple to ask me or anyone else to hold both of her feet and also her hands, and still she could snap the megaphone off her head in any direction requested. [Houdini added] This is the 'slickest' ruse I have ever seen.[19]

Next afternoon Mr Munn and Houdini went up to the seance-room alone, and Houdini demonstrated the tricks himself.

Before the next seance, Houdini and Munn arranged a series of signals and procedures. This time Munn was on Houdini's left, the magician once more on Margery's left. When Houdini pushed Munn's hand under the table, they broke the chain, and Houdini had his left hand free to feel around. What he felt was Margery's head at the edge of the table, tilting it until the box with the bell fell to the floor. She did the sliding trick again, this time catching a stocking on Houdini's garter. 'Shall I expose her now?' Houdini whispered to Munn. The publisher shook his head, however, and the seance continued.

After the seance, the committee met, and Houdini told them what he had found. Should he expose her then and there, or should this wait until everyone had returned to New York? It was decided to wait, continue with the tests, and see if more evidence of fraud was forthcoming. Meanwhile not a word was to be said to the Crandons.

The committee was in general agreement on this line of procedure – except for Bird. He continued to insist that Margery was at least fifty per cent genuine, and he did not want her exposed just yet. When asked why not, since they had been quick enough to denounce other dubious mediums, he said only: 'We will do it different this time.' It turned out that he was staying on with the Crandons for the next three days, and during this time, as he later confessed to Munn, he told them just what Houdini had found and what the committee had decided. This was important, because it meant that Margery would now be on her guard.

Something else that concerned Houdini, and also Dr Prince of the ASPR, was that it was through Bird that the public had heard, and unless they were very careful, would continue to hear, about Margery. For although he had joined the committee as the impartial representative of the *Scientific American*, he was now clearly quite under Margery's spell. (Indeed, in the course of this investigation, he resigned from the magazine and began to work full-time on psychical research, his first publication in this field being a book, *Margery the Medium*.) They were able to get yet another laudatory article which he had prepared for the September issue of the magazine, stopped, and Houdini made Munn promise that it would not be Bird who wrote up any exposé.

Nevertheless, that summer the sceptics continued to be annoyed by such newspaper headlines as BOSTON MEDIUM BAFFLES EXPERTS or HOUDINI THE MAGICIAN STUMPED or BAFFLES SCIENTISTS WITH REVELATIONS, PSYCHIC POWER OF MARGERY ESTABLISHED BEYOND QUESTION. Far from having been destroyed by the discoveries of 23 and 24 July, Margery's reputation continued to blossom among the faithful and the curious.

There was now a state of virtual open warfare declared between

Houdini and the Crandons and their partisans. At the next set of seances, which took place a month later, all pretence of anything else was dropped. Houdini was determined to outwit Margery, and she was determined to make him look a fool. He arrived in Boston on 25 August 1924 with a special box he had designed in which she was to sit during the seance. This was large enough to contain a chair, had holes for her arms at each side, and a hinged sloping lid at the front which closed, leaving her head and neck sticking out of a hole in the top. It was in fact very like a pillory, and it allowed very little freedom of movement – none at all for the feet and hardly any for the hands and head. Bird was not to be present at these August seances.

The first official seance took place on that same evening, 25 August. Needless to say, the Crandons did not welcome the new box. They, or their supporters, believed that Margery accomplished many of her feats by means of a pseudopod – along the lines of that produced by Eusapia – which emanated from between her legs. When he saw the box, Crandon announced: 'The psychic does not refuse to sit in the cage made by Houdini for the committee; but she makes the reservation that she knows no precedent in psychic research where a medium has been so enclosed; and she believes that such a closed cage gives little or no regard for the theory and experience of the psychic structure or mediumism.' However, on the first occasion, the box did not hamper Margery too much, for the simple reason that the lid enclosing her head and shoulders was broken open by main force, so that (supposing she had resorted to fraud) she could have rung the bell, which was set on a table in front of her, with her head. Certainly the bell did ring, and certainly Margery would not agree that she had rung it herself. That, she said, had been Walter's doing, just as it had been Walter who had broken open the box.

Whether or not this was the case, Houdini was taking no chances for the next evening. The lid had been fastened to the back of the box only by two thin brass strips, easily snapped by the athletic Margery; these he now replaced with much heavier locks. The Crandons accepted these, and seemed willing to experiment with the box again. Houdini had caught them, during the afternoon, examining it together and making some measurements; after which they announced that they were happy with it as it stood; previously they had wanted the neck opening enlarged.

The next seance began with a drama. Bird burst in, and demanded to know why he was being excluded. Houdini said, 'I object to Mr Bird being in the seance room because he has betrayed the Committee and hindered their work. He has not kept to himself things told him in strictest confidence as he should as Secretary to the Committee.' Bird, furious, at first denied this; then, when it was clear that he had been found out, resigned from the Committee. He then left the room, and the seance got under way.

After it had begun, Houdini repeatedly reminded Dr Prince, who sat on Margery's right, that he should keep firm hold of her right hand and not let it go. Finally – as no doubt he had intended – the medium asked him sharply what he meant by saying this so often.

'Do you really want to know?' Houdini asked.

'Yes,' she replied.

'Well, I will tell you. In case you have smuggled anything in to the cabinet-box you can not now conceal it as both your hands are secured and as far as they are concerned you are helpless.'

She then asked if he wanted to search her, but he declined. Soon after this exchange the voice of Walter was heard: 'Houdini, you are very clever, but it won't work. I suppose it was an accident those things were left in the cabinet?'

'What was left in the cabinet?'

'Pure accident, was it? You were not here, but your assistant was.'

And Walter went on to state that there was a ruler in the cabinet-box under a pillow at the medium's feet, and that Houdini's assistant had put it there. He wound up with a furious outburst, and exclaimed, 'Houdini, you Goddamned sonofabitch, get the hell out of here and never come back! If you don't, I will!'[20]

Certainly a ruler – a folding one, which could be used under cover of darkness to ring bells and move objects from the neck-hole – was found inside the cabinet later. The question remained, who put it there? Houdini, of course, maintained that Margery had concealed it; the Crandons, equally insistently, affirmed that the culprit was Houdini's assistant. At the time, everybody denied all knowledge of this ruler. Many years later, however, the assistant confessed that it had, indeed, been his work: they wanted to make sure of discrediting Margery once and for all, he said.

Not surprisingly, relations between Houdini and the Crandons now deteriorated even further. Mrs Crandon was worried that Houdini was going to denounce her publicly from the stage of Keith's Theatre. If he did that, she said, some of her friends would come up and 'give you a good beating'. To which he replied: 'I am not going to misrepresent you, they are not coming on the stage, and I am not going to get a beating.' And she: 'Then it is your wits against mine.' To which he heartily agreed. She tried pleading: she had a twelve-year-old boy, she said, and she would not want him to grow up and read that his mother was a fraud. 'Then don't be a fraud,' said Houdini.

Certainly, in the eyes of the world, he had not yet proved her a fraud. There was a contretemps over a public seance Houdini was to give, in which he would replicate Margery's effects while controlled in the same way as she had been controlled; but in the argument over what effects took place under what conditions, and exactly who had promised to do what, where, and when, the performance got lost, a circumstance of which Dr Crandon made much. And although some of the committee had lost faith in Margery, this was certainly not true of all of them. In an interview with the *Boston Herald* in December of that year, Hereward Carrington called Houdini a 'pure publicist', and said he had no scientific experience in psychic investigations, but had had himself appointed a member of the committee purely because of the publicity it would bring him. 'The reason I didn't go to Boston when he held his sittings with "Margery" was that I knew he distrusted me and I knew that anything he could not explain he would bring to my presence there. Nearly all the other members of the committee veer toward a belief that there were psychic phenomena at the seances,' he said, adding that he had had several indignant letters from England about Houdini's stand.[21]

It is true that Margery had aroused great interest in England, not least from Conan Doyle, who was delighted to take up her cause and confront his old adversary once again. He invited the Crandons to give some seances in London the following February (the *New York Herald*'s headline ran: 'MARGERY' FEARS FOG MAY BLOCK LONDON SEANCES. MEDIUM WHO FAILED TO WIN $2,500 PRIZE NOT SURE DAMP AIR WILL AGREE WITH 'WALTER', HER CONTROL). These seances did not take place, but instead the SPR sent its research officer, E.J.Dingwall, over to Boston to make his own investigations on their behalf.

In taking up this case, Conan Doyle made it quite clear what battle it was that he was fighting. His aim was to discredit Houdini. He felt himself, he said, uniquely entitled to comment on the business, because it was as a result of his psychic lectures in America that the *Scientific American* Committee had been set up in the first place. However, he did not think much of any of its members, with the exceptions of Carrington and Bird, whom he characterized as honest and clear headed, but over cautious where psychic matters were concerned. Dr Prince's 'utility was seriously impaired by the fact that he was very deaf so that he could hardly check those direct voice phenomena which were an important feature of the case'. Hereward Carrington, though he had bravely defended Eusapia Paladino's mediumship against all detractors, 'could never be convinced of the bona fides of any American medium'. Professor McDougall was only inclined to credit negative evidence. As for Houdini, Conan Doyle announced himself amazed that a committee consisting of 'honourable gentlemen' should have permitted such an attack on the reputation of a lady, and allowed a man 'with entirely different standards to make this outrageous attack'.[22]

Conan Doyle's objections to Houdini were very simple. He was not 'one of us', either socially or in his attitude to psychical research. He was a bounder and a cad, by contrast with whom the Crandons comported themselves with altogether an excess of courtesy.

> Margery from the first behaved with exemplary generosity. She announced that if the prize of $2500 offered by the paper for any well-attested phenomenon was won, it would be handed over for psychic research. She paid in part the expenses of the members of the committee in coming to Boston, and entertained them while there. This was no small matter, when it is recorded that it took 90 sittings before these gentlemen could form an opinion as to whether the phenomena which were going on under their noses and under their own conditions were genuine or not. Finally, this self-sacrificing couple bore with exemplary patience all the irritations arising from the incursions of these fractious and unreasonable people, while even the gross insult which was inflicted upon them by one member of the committee did not prevent them from continuing the sittings. Personally, I think that they erred upon the side of virtue, and that from the moment Houdini uttered the word 'fraud' the committee should have been compelled either to disown him or cease their visits.[23]

Thus Conan Doyle; under whose aegis it was clear that the Crandons would have had an easier ride in England than had been their lot in Boston. Indeed, the sittings with Dingwall were a huge success. In them, Margery concentrated on something new – or new for her: the emanations or pseudopodia which had been supposedly ringing bells, throwing megaphones, knocking over cabinets, etc., were now made visible. Dingwall, later to become one of the most sceptical of psychical investigators, wrote eagerly to Schrenck-Notzing, the world authority on such matters:

> It is the most beautiful case of teleplasm and telekinesis with which I am acquainted. One is able to handle the teleplasm freely. The materialized hands are connected by an umbilical cord to the medium; they seize upon

objects and displace them. The teleplastic masses are visible and tangible upon the table, in good red light. I hold the hands of the medium, I know where her fingers are and I see them in good light. The control is irreproachable.[24]

Dingwall took a number of photographs of these teleplastic phenomena, whose general effect is curiously obscene. Houdini wrote to Harry Price, another investigator, asking, 'By the way, is there any truth in the report that Dingwall was observed making ectoplastic hands out of liver and lights, I presume for experimental purposes?'[25] Whatever the original provenance of the 'hands', their appearance certainly bears out this theory; and a year later, when William McDougall submitted the photographs for examination to some Harvard biologists, they all agreed that the alleged ectoplasm was animal lung tissue, sliced so as to present a crude resemblance to a hand.

Whatever the respective merits *in re* gentlemanliness of Houdini and his adversaries, some of the other members of the *Scientific American* Committee lost no time in making it quite clear where they now stood. Professor McDougall for one, whose respectability was beyond question, as were his intellectual standing and inclination to the spiritualistic cause, came out against Margery in a long article published in the *Boston Evening Transcript* for 18 February 1925.

He had hoped, he said, to conduct a few more sittings with Margery before arriving at a final verdict. But the publicity generated by the Conan Doyle/Houdini controversy, together with the fact that Bird was about to publish a book which would clearly be very favourable to Margery, had forced his hand. The previous week he and Dr Prince had written to the editor of *Scientific American* stating an opinion adverse to Margery's claims, and recommending that the offered prize should not be awarded in this case. Dr McDougall made it clear that, so far as the other members of the committee were concerned, the Houdini–Margery battle was a personal one. It had not, he said, affected their decision. (This high-minded assertion may be questioned in view of the fact that, prior to Houdini's arrival on the scene, the committee had seemed to be on the point of awarding Margery the prize.)

What worried him most, said McDougall, was the inconsistency of the phenomena and, in particular, the unconvincing nature of the recent ectoplasmic hands. McDougall had not been allowed to take part in those sittings at which the hand had been produced, and photographed by Dingwall, nor had he been able, at that time, to borrow or copy the photographs for further analysis. When, finally, he had been allowed to participate in an ectoplasmic sitting, nothing whatever had happened so long as he had 'controlled' Margery's right hand and Dingwall had hold of her left. Really remarkable phenomena – such as movement of the ectoplasmic hand – only seemed to take place when Dr Crandon sat on his wife's right. As for the hand's provenance, he wished to reply to a recent lecture in which Malcolm Bird

> took exception to the verdict rendered by the committee, approved 'Margery's ectoplasm', and said that the 'ectoplasm' 'issues from openings in the anatomy.' The last statement is correct. There is good evidence that 'ectoplasm' does issue, or did issue on some, and probably on all, occasions from one particular 'opening in the anatomy'. The more interesting question is – How did it come to be within 'the anatomy'? There was nothing to show that its position there and its extrusion from that place were achieved by other than normal means.[26]

Dr McDougall now approached the heart of the matter. Why had Margery done it? The problem was the more perplexing in that, clearly, the motive was never financial. The Crandons were rich; Margery was not a professional medium, like Eusapia. Her interest in the *Scientific American* prize was simply a question of status: she never had any intention of taking the money for herself.

McDougall's theory was that this was an extreme case of dual personality. 'Walter', he thought, was Margery's secondary personality, and had been the prime mover and agent in producing all her phenomena; she herself, in her persona of Mrs Crandon, was therefore really innocent of fraud. 'If that hypothesis is the correct one, then the case is one that falls within the field of abnormal psychology rather than in that of supernormal physical phenomena.'

This may, of course, have been the explanation. But does it explain Dr Crandon's participation in the affair? It seems almost certain that he was colluding with his wife in her frauds. And yet his outbursts of indignant high-mindedness carry the stamp of true belief. When, in that same month of February 1925, the *Journal of Abnormal and Social Psychology* offered a prize of $5,000 to 'anyone claiming to produce super-normal material phenomena who will demonstrate the actuality of the same under rigid laboratory conditions and by recognized scientific method, in full light . . .' and hoped that Margery would enter the contest, [27] he reacted with fury. It was the money offer which seemed most to annoy him. 'This seems to be an age which has lost interest in priceless things and is only enamored of things with a price,' he declared. He was himself prepared to offer

1) $10,000 for a full materialization of a spirit-form on the roof of the Copley-Plaza in bright sunlight at noon on any Tuesday.
2) $20,000 for the metamorphosis of a larva into a butterfly, without a cocoon, on the north wall of the public library on Dec. 15 1925, 10 minutes before midnight . . .

And in conclusion he insisted that psychical research could not be ignored but must 'be given a place in the world of holy fact'.[28]

Were they both, then, suffering from delusions? Was Dr Crandon afflicted by that condition we have already examined in regard to Crookes, Rhine and others, in which he confused the worlds of religious conviction and scientific objectivity? His use of the word 'holy' in this context perhaps leads to that conclusion. If this was the circumstance, then the *Journal of Abnormal and Social Psychology* had a more interesting case on its hands than it suspected, in which two sets of separate delusions, those of husband and wife, reinforced and complemented each other. Another possibility is that Margery was, throughout, wholly mischievous, playing a game from which – as in other instances we have examined – she could not, after a point, back out. But it is hard to believe that, in convincing others so completely, she did not, to some extent at least, convince herself.

Whatever the verdict of McDougall, Walter Prince and Houdini, they did not close the case. There were those, notably Malcom Bird and Conan Doyle, who continued to endorse Margery and her phenomena through thick and thin. 'The amazing part of the business', comments Doyle, 'was that the other members of the committee seemed to have been overawed by the masterful conjurer, and even changed their very capable secretary, Mr Malcolm Bird, at his request.'[29] But in one real sense the Margery case was a victory for Houdini and his fellow magicians. This was the last time that 'physical phenomena' were cited as evidence for the supernormal until the advent, fifty years later, of Uri Geller, when the whole battle – of cynical magicians versus believing scientists – started again on exactly the same terms as before.

7
Whisky and Cigars on the Other Side

He was the last person who would admit that he was dead, and would object to be spoken of as dead, for he is not dead but alive, more fully alive than ever. – REV. HERBERT STEAD, speaking at his brother W.T.Stead's memorial meeting, Queen's Hall, 26 June 1912

Sir Arthur Conan Doyle had many striking characteristics. He was gigantically tall and strong. He was a gifted story-teller. He was a man of strong opinions and considerable political influence. He possessed the enormous self-confidence which the successful self-made man often acquires. But perhaps the most extraordinary thing about him was the combination of all the attributes of worldly success with an almost childlike literalness and credulity of mind, manifested particularly in relation to spiritualism and its surrounding phenomena.

This combination of characteristics was not unique to Conan Doyle, although it perhaps took its most extreme form in him. It was shared most notably by two well-known contemporaries of his, the journalist W.T.Stead and the physicist Sir Oliver Lodge. All of them were as quintessentially British as they could be. About them all there was an absolute confidence and certainty of their rightness in the face of all opposition which was quite different both from the shrill fervour shown by the distinguished devotees of spiritualism in the early days in America and from the intellectual acrobatics of Richet, Schrenck and their colleagues in Europe.

Indeed, although Doyle, Stead and Lodge were all intellectually able – in Lodge's case, brilliant – there was nothing at all intellectual about their devotion to spiritualism. Whereas Richet and Schrenck, and also the supporters of the Society for Psychical Research, carefully distanced themselves from religion and presented their work as being of primarily scientific value, Doyle, Stead and Lodge were essentially religious in their spiritualism. This did not preclude both Lodge and Doyle's belonging to the Society, though in Doyle's case his rather lukewarm sympathy with its approach can be seen from the fact that whereas he never contributed more than his annual subscription to its coffers, he spent enormous amounts of money on other spiritualistic endeavours – for instance, donating a total of £4,250 to the journal *Light* between 1896 and 1898.[1]

As for Stead, he harboured a real antipathy towards the SPR In a speech to the Cosmos Club in 1909, he drew a graphic analogy of the barriers interposed by the Society against communications from Beyond. He pictured himself shipwrecked and drowning in the sea (the fate which did, as it happened, eventually overtake him: he went down with the *Titanic*).

> Suppose that instead of throwing a rope the rescuers should shout back 'Who are you? What is your name?' 'I am Stead! W.T.Stead! I am drowning here in the sea. Throw me the rope. Be quick!' But instead of throwing me the rope they continue to shout back, 'How do we know you are Stead? Where were you born? Tell us the name of your grandmother!' Well, that is pretty typical of the 'help' given by the S.P.R. to the friends who are trying to make us hear them from the Other Side![2]

For Stead, the question was always a religious one (it did not become primarily religious for the others until after the start of the Great War, in which each lost a son, and Doyle a brother). This was not surprising, for it would have been impossible for him to separate any of his great interests in life from his religion. Stead's father had been a Methodist minister, and religion was always the most tangible of living entities for him. He invariably referred to God as 'the Senior Partner', which puzzled more than one acquaintance who was not aware that he was in partnership with anybody. It is clear that the very solid religious perceptions afforded by spiritualism would be particularly attractive to one who could remark, 'I have gone doubles or quits on the Senior Partner all my days. He has never failed me, and I don't think he ever will.'

W.T.Stead was the great crusading journalist of his time; and, for Stead, a crusade was, literally, a crusade. He first became internationally famous in 1885 with the series of articles exposing child prostitution and white slavery entitled 'The Maiden Tribute of Modern Babylon'. He was at this time editor of the *Pall Mall Gazette*; and to say that his descriptions in that publication of how he had gone out and bought a thirteen-year-old girl from her mother, and subsequently taken her to Paris, caused a furore would be grossly to understate the case. Rioting crowds outside the *Gazette*'s offices fought for every last copy. Indignant clergymen denounced him for obscenity from their pulpits. Members of Parliament debated the question hotly; Stead's aim had been to get the law changed so that it would no longer be possible to do what he had done and remain within the law. There had been pressure for this reform for a long time, but the administration then in power was refusing to make time for this legislation. The uproar following Stead's articles meant that it could no longer be swept aside, and a Bill was hurriedly passed through Parliament.

The opponents of this legislation – of whom more than one was known to have availed himself of this particular form of pleasure in the past – were beside themselves with fury at this railroading. They gleefully pounced upon a loophole, not in the law, but in Stead's own personal position relative to the action he had taken while getting up the articles. It turned out that he had no written record of the mother's receipt of the five pounds he had paid for her daughter, while the father had been nowhere in evidence. When the story broke the mother swore she had let her girl go only to be a servant girl, and the father said – quite truthfully – that he had never consented to the deal. Stead and his helpers were therefore arrested on a charge of abduction. They were found guilty, to the delight of their opponents, and Stead was imprisoned for two months in Holloway Gaol. While in prison, Stead carried on a constant correspondence with his great crowd of well-wishers. To one of these he wrote: 'What the future will bring with it, I do not know, excepting that it will only bring triumph even in defeat if we are but sufficiently humble and willing to do His will.' And in a postscript referring to the most vociferous of his parliamentary opponents he added: 'Never mind Cavendish-Bentinck. He is a good Turk's Head, and why should we object to be reminded of the existence of the Evil One?'[3] Quite unequivocally he saw himself as the instrument of God in the constant fight against the devil.

While this is understandable in the case of a religious man fighting a moral issue such as juvenile prostitution, it was a conviction Stead brought to all his crusades, including the campaign to refit the British Navy and the one to send General Gordon to Khartoum. Both of these were successful, unlike Gordon's campaign once he had arrived in the Sudan, and Stead's attempts, later in his life, to get the Pope, the Tsar and the Sultan of Turkey to agree on a policy which would guarantee peace in Europe.

This enormous self-confidence and sense of personal mission – and

there are many other incidents in Stead's career which attest to his
certainty that he personally was capable of influencing world events,
and that such influence would *ipso facto* be positive – are very reminiscent of his fellow enthusiast for spiritualism, Conan Doyle. It is hard
to imagine anyone today who could enjoy such sublime self-certainty.
Indeed, it is hard to imagine any such person outside Victorian and
Edwardian Britain, the richest country in the world, the seat of
Empire, and possessed of a national self-confidence which was the
counterpart of that personal quality so evident in such men as Stead
and Conan Doyle.

In addition to all this, Stead had particular personal reasons for
supposing that he was especially favoured by the Senior Partner.
Throughout his life he had premonitions which forecast the turn of
events at important junctures in his career. The happenings they foresaw were highly improbable, but each of them came true exactly as
prophesied.

The first of these premonitions occurred in 1880, when he was
thirty-one years old. At that time he was editor of the *Northern Echo* at
Darlington, a most satisfactory situation where he had *carte blanche* to
do exactly what he chose with the paper – a freedom which had already
earned him a certain journalistic celebrity and which was unlikely to
be equalled in any other position that might arise. He had been born
near Darlington, he was happily settled there with his wife and children, he was his own master and there was no reason for him to consider
any change of situation. Nevertheless,

> On New Year's day, 1880, it was forcibly impressed upon my mind that I
> was to leave Darlington in the course of that year. I remember on the first of
> January meeting a journalistic *confrère* on my way from Darlington station
> to the *Northern Echo* office. After wishing him a Happy New Year, I said,
> 'This is the last New Year's Day I shall ever spend in Darlington. I shall
> leave the *Northern Echo* this year.' My friend looked at me in some amaze-
> ment, and said, 'And where are you going to?' 'To London,' I replied,
> 'because it is the only place which could tempt me from my present situ-
> ation . . .' 'But,' said my friend somewhat dubiously, 'what paper are you
> going to?' 'I have no idea in the world,' I said; 'neither do I know a single
> London paper which would offer me a position upon its staff, of any kind,
> let alone one on which I should have any liberty of utterance. I see no
> prospect of any opening anywhere, but I know for certain that before this
> year is out I shall be on the staff of a London paper.'

Despite this certainty, the prospect did not seem to be forthcoming.
The summer came, and with it the date when Stead had to renew his

contract of employment. There seemed no option but to sign on for another year at the *Northern Echo*, and this he did, although he was still certain that he would be leaving Darlington at least six months before the contract expired.

Just at that time, the *Pall Mall Gazette* changed its editor. Under its previous editor it had been a journal utterly antipathetic to everything Stead stood for, and the prospect of his landing up there could not have been more remote. The new editor, John Morley, was less unsympathetic. Several of the paper's staff had left, and to help him out of his fix, Stead, together with two other north-country editors, agreed to send him occasional contributions. The new contract had been signed in June. 'Midsummer had scarcely passed before Mr Thompson [the proprietor of the *Pall Mall Gazette*] came down to Darlington and offered me the assistant editorship. The proprietor of the *Northern Echo* kindly waived his right to my services.'[4]

His second premonition occurred three years later, and concerned his assumption of the editorship of the *Gazette*. It happened during a short holiday which he was taking with his wife on the Isle of Wight.

One morning, about noon, we were walking in the drizzling rain round St Catherine's Point. It was a miserable day, the ground slippery and the footpath here and there rather difficult to follow. Just as we were at about the ugliest part of our climb I felt distinctly, as it were, a voice within myself saying: 'You will have to look sharp and make ready, because by a certain date (which, as near as I can recollect, was 16th March of the next year), you will have sole charge of the *Pall Mall Gazette*.' I was just a little startled and rather awed, because, as Mr Morley was then in full command and there was no expectation on his part of abandoning the post, the inference which I immediately drew was that he was going to die. So firmly was this impressed upon my mind that for two hours I did not speak about it to my wife. We took shelter for a time from the rain, but afterwards, on going home, I spoke, not without reluctance, on the subject that filled me with sadness. . . .

'Nonsense,' said my wife, 'he is not going to die. He is going to get into Parliament; that is what is going to happen.'

'Well,' said I, 'that may be. Whether he dies or whether he gets into Parliament the one thing certain to me is that I shall have sole charge of the *Pall Mall Gazette* next year, and I am so convinced of this that when we return to London I shall make all my plans on the basis of that certainty.'

And so I did. I do not hedge and hesitate at burning my boats. As soon as I arrived at the *Pall Mall Gazette* office, I announced to Mr Thompson, Mr Morley, and to Mr Milner, who was then on the staff, that Mr Morley was going to be in Parliament by March 16th next. I need hardly say I did not mention my first sinister intimation. I told Mr Morley and the others exactly what had happened, namely, that I had received notice to be ready to take sole charge of the *Pall Mall Gazette* by March 16th next.

Morley and the others were not impressed by this announcement. Morley at that time had more or less given up any hope of getting into Parliament. But Stead did not forget. Some months later, when Morley was consulting him about some change in the terms of his engagement with the paper, he interrupted with the words, 'Excuse me, Mr Morley, when will this new arrangement come into effect?' 'In May, I think.' 'Then you need not trouble to discuss it with me,' said Stead. 'I shall have sole charge of the *Pall Mall Gazette* before that time. You will not be here then, you will be in Parliament.' And he would discuss the matter no further, despite Morley's very reasonable comment, 'And pray, do you mean to tell me that I am not to make a business arrangement with you because you have had a vision?' Morley could make what arrangements he liked; quite simply, they were of no interest to Stead.[5] A month later the MP for Newcastle upon Tyne died suddenly, and Morley was elected in his place on 24 February. From then on Stead was, as he had foreseen, in charge of the paper, though he was never officially appointed editor.

During his early years in London, although he attended a number of seances, Stead was not really a spiritualist. He was a very religious man, and his belief was of the most literal sort, but despite his premonitions, the question of what he later came to call 'Borderland' was not uppermost in his mind. He did, however, during this period, have a considerable influence on one aspect of spiritualism – theosophy. It was, perhaps, inevitable that Stead should meet Madame Blavatsky. He met everyone, and so did she. This particular meeting was arranged through an old friend, Madame Olga Novikoff, 'the MP for Russia', an energetic and intelligent woman who made it her business to forward her country's interests in England, where she had lived for many years. When Madame Blavatsky came to London, in 1888, the two Russians met and were charmed by each other. Both were great Russian patriots, despite the fact that they lived abroad. They were both women of outstanding intellect; and while the occult was Madame Blavatsky's livelihood, it also held a certain fascination for Madame Novikoff.

Madame Novikoff, having been captivated herself, began to urge Stead to come with her and meet Madame Blavatsky. Stead, however, was inclined to resist these blandishments. He was exceedingly busy. In the end the only thing that prevailed with him was that Madame

Blavatsky was Russian, and Stead always had a particularly soft spot for Russia. Along, finally, he went. 'I was delighted with, and at the same time somewhat repelled by, Madame Blavatsky,' he wrote later. 'Power was there, rude and massive, but she had the manners of a man, and a very unconventional man, rather than those of a lady. But we got on very well together, and Madame Blavatsky gave me her portrait, certifying that I might call myself what I pleased, but that she knew I was a good theosophist.'[6]

The Secret Doctrine, one of H.P.B's enormous tomes, was then about to be published. When it came out, she naturally sent a copy to her new friend Stead for review, but he, not surprisingly, blenched at the task. However, he thought it might appeal to Mrs Annie Besant, who had for some time been doing book reviews for him, and was, he knew, interested in seances and spiritualism. Stead was a great feminist, and was always happy to find work for an able woman. Annie Besant was enchanted with the book, and begged Stead to introduce her to its author. This he did with pleasure; and neither Mrs Besant nor Madame Blavatsky ever looked back. The one had found her final life's work, the other, her most able, devoted and reliable lieutenant. Annie Besant went on to take over the leadership of the theosophists when Madame Blavatsky died.

One reason Stead was a feminist was that he was extremely interested in women, and so exceedingly attractive to them. His sympathetic manner, combined with the steady gaze of his bright blue eyes, convinced more than one that he was in love with her; but so far as we know he actually allowed himself to fall in love with only two: his wife, and Olga Novikoff.

Mrs Stead was a childhood sweetheart. Undoubtedly Stead loved her, and undoubtedly he went on loving her with all the warmth of his generous nature. But it was not an ideal marriage. She was never able to enter into her husband's wild enthusiasms, but regarded them rather as trials to be put up with. He adored country life; she found it lonely and inconvenient. He was hopeless with money, inclined to scatter it on wild schemes and give it to anyone who seemed to need it; she, with six children to feed and clothe, was driven to scrimping and, in the end, to meanness and unreasonableness.

He met Olga Novikoff in 1877. The flamboyant, uninhibited Russian, whose passion for politics equalled his own, was clearly as great a contrast as could be imagined to his quiet, domestic wife. He fell headlong in love with her – he was always a headlong fellow – and she with him. They became lovers: the affair lasted for two years, during which time he experienced ecstasies of pleasure and agonies of remorse. Was this the peaceful home he had planned to set up, the Christian example for his children? His wife was miserable; he loved her and was deeply sorry for her. Finally he broke off sexual relations with Olga, though they remained close friends and collaborators: doubtless yet another of Stead's enthusiasms of which his wife bitterly disapproved. He returned to the bosom of his family, and remained there, taking especial pleasure in his children, but he was sexually deeply frustrated. He enjoyed sex and desired his wife ever more warmly as the years went by; while she grew less and less interested in it. He noted in his diary the rare occasions, as their marriage went on, when his wife made overtures to him. In 1889 he wrote: 'Only once this year has she had fierce, strong longing. I had been preparing myself for apparently endless abstinence when suddenly it came on her in my absence. I noticed the change when I returned. She told me and was very loving. How rare are such moments. How longingly I remember them. Ah, if she were always so!'[7]

Havelock Ellis, who knew him well, was of the opinion that Stead's phenomenal energy stemmed from his frustrated sexual urge. It seems plausible, though this was a construction Ellis might have been expected to put upon such a situation. At any rate, the sexual motive, or metaphor, was rarely hard to find in Stead's work. Take the extraordinary extended metaphor he employs to describe the relationship between the conscious and the unconscious personalities in his *Real Ghost Stories*:

> The conscious Personality . . . stands for the husband. It is vigorous, alert, active, positive . . . so intense is its consciousness that it ignores the very existence of its partner, excepting as a mere appendage and convenience to itself. Then there is the Unconscious Personality, which corresponds to a wife who keeps cupboard and storehouse, and the old stocking which treasures up the accumulated wealth of impressions acquired by the Conscious Personality, but who is never able to assert her right to anything, or to the use of sense or limb except when her lord and master is asleep or entranced. . . . There is nothing of sex in the ordinary material sense about the two personalities, but their union is so close as to suggest that the intrusion of the hypnotist is equivalent to an intrigue with a married woman.[8]

And just as he concerned himself deeply with the emancipation of women, so he concerned himself with the emancipation of aspects of that unconscious personality. As it turned out, this brought him into close contact, both conscious and otherwise, with large numbers of women admirers, a circumstance which rendered spiritualism especially attractive to him.

The woman most responsible for tipping Stead's faith over to spiritualism from literal, premonitory fundamentalism was a young American journalist, Julia Ames. Stead met Miss Ames only twice. The meetings took place in 1890: one at his office, Mowbray House in Norfolk Street, off the Strand, where he now edited his own monthly paper, the *Review of Reviews*; one at his house in Wimbledon, where they sat under the shade of the trees in his large and pleasant garden. These meetings formed one of the high points of Miss Ames's European tour. Stead, too, was very much taken with the young woman, and when, the next year, she died, wrote of her as 'a singularly beautiful character, of devoted Christian enthusiasm'.[9] And there, for the moment, the matter rested. It was, indeed, hard to see that it could do anything else. Stead later swore that, although he and Julia had discussed almost every topic imaginable, the word 'spiritualism' had not passed their lips. Be that as it may, he was at this time taking an increasing interest in the occult. At Christmas 1891, he published his volume of *Real Ghost Stories*, with its admonition

> 1. [That] the narratives printed in these pages had better not be read by any one of tender years, or morbid excitability, or of excessively nervous temperament.
> 2. That the latest students of the subject concur in the solemn warning addressed in the Sacred Writings to those who have dealings with familiar spirits, or who expose themselves to the horrible consequences of possession.
> 3. That as the latent possibilities of our complex personality are so imperfectly understood, all experimenting in hypnotism, spiritualism, etc., excepting in the most careful and reverent spirit by the most level-headed persons, had much better be avoided.[10]

Although this was his first incursion into the world of the 'Borderland', the characteristics which were so particularly to mark Stead and those other adherents of what one might term the 'practical British' school of spiritualism, Conan Doyle and Oliver Lodge, were at once apparent. The emphasis was, from the first, on concrete certainty and solid practicality.

At the start of the book, Stead puts his case for the existence of ghosts: 'There are at least as many persons who testify they have seen apparitions as there are men of science who have examined the microbe. . . . The evidence for the microbe may be conclusive, the evidence as to apparitions may be worthless; but in both cases it is a

case of testimony, not of personal experience.'[11] Thus ghosts and spiritualism are at once assimilated into modern life and thought; and no one
was more enthusiastic about the possibilities of modernity than Stead.
A little later in the book he develops this theme. He has, he says, recently
been in conversation with a lady who has developed the faculty of going
anywhere in her Thought Body.

> 'But,' said I, 'if you can be seen and touched you ought to be photographed!'
> 'I wish to be photographed, but no one can say as yet whether such thought
> bodies can be photographed. When next I make the experiment I want you to
> try. It would be very useful.'
> Useful indeed! It does not require very vivid imagination to see that if you
> can come and go to the uttermost parts of the world in your thought shape,
> such Thought Bodies will be indispensable henceforth on every enterprising
> newspaper. It would be a great saving in telegraphy.[12]

The next step was, naturally, to develop this faculty on a systematic
basis. As things turned out, Stead found it easier to let other people's
'thought bodies' come to him than to travel himself. It was in the
following year, 1892, that Stead developed the faculty of automatic
writing, or, as he liked to put it, of letting other people 'use his hand'.
Characteristically, his first attempt took place over lunch with a lady
friend at his favourite restaurant (Gatti's, in the Strand, where his
lunch consisted, invariably, of sole, macaroni cheese, and fruit). The
lady was herself a practised automatist, and was, that day, receiving
persistent messages from one Frederick, through her own hand,
imploring Stead to try and receive a message, through his, from a Mrs D.
Obediently, Stead took up a pencil and tried for some minutes to receive
the message, but failed. At Frederick's urging, he tried again for 'five
minutes more'. Still he met with no success. Automatic writing, he
concluded, was not for him. But Mrs D would not let him alone. Some
days later she reiterated her appeal, and he agreed to try again, adding,
'Well, I'll do it on this one condition, that if nothing comes of it you will
never ask me to do it again'.

'Doubtless', remarks the chronicler of these events, 'the Invisibles
knew the issues that trembled in the balance as the result of that
reluctant promise.' This time, at any rate, there was no failure. Slowly
and hesitantly Stead's hand began to move, and eventually indited a
message from a Mrs D which did seem to make sense. He was still not
fully convinced; but after several more attempts he acquired the habit
of allowing an hour before he began work each morning in which his
hand might be at the disposition of any discarnate entity who wanted to
communicate through the hand of a person still in the flesh.[13]

From the point of view of Stead's journalistic work, this practice very soon began to show results. One of his great innovations as a journalist was his use of the interview. This, of course, is an indispensable element of today's newspapers and magazines; but it was Stead who first realized that there is no better way of conveying the ideas, character and living personality of some newsworthy person than this. He had a phenomenal short-term memory, and would hardly ever take notes during the interview, writing it down verbatim as he remembered it immediately afterwards. His subjects unanimously agreed that his recall was near perfect. He was helped, in his interviewing technique, by his remarkable ability to enter, immediately and without offence, on an informal and equal footing with whoever he happened to be talking to. He had no hesitation about questioning and interrupting his subjects, be they duke, prince, cabinet minister or the Tsar of Russia, a habit which horrified their minions but which, as might be expected, achieved excellent results.

As any journalist knows, one of the more frustrating aspects of trying to arrange interviews is that the desired subject is sometimes unavailable or impossible to contact. Stead now realized that his new-found power might enable him to overcome this disadvantage. If he wanted to talk to somebody or get their opinion about something, and failed to reach them, he could now contact them by putting his hand at their disposal and thus conducting what he liked to term 'automatic interviews'. These might involve either the living or the dead – though in the case of the living, there was always the danger that they might not agree with his version of their thoughts. The Countess of Warwick, for example, known for her socialist sympathies and as the mistress of the Prince of Wales (soon to become King Edward VII), was a great friend of Stead's. She was not, however, in sympathy with his spiritualist leanings – she was, she felt, too practical a person to empathize much with spirits. Nevertheless, Stead insisted on conducting automatic interviews with her – which annoyed her more than somewhat. She wrote from Sicily to her 'Very Dear Friend', announcing that she had torn up two letters to him. 'I won't write you "automatically" nor must you to me. It is not a bit all right. Besides I want my letters to you to be me and yours to me, the same, and I won't write with your hand. It's all too stilted and forced.'[14] (It is worth adding that by no means all Stead's automatic interviewees reacted with indignation; many, especially ladies, agreed that that was what they had been thinking, or anyway, what they *would have thought*, at the time.)

As far as interviewing the dead went, however, there could clearly be no substitute for Stead's method. How else could he have got the views of Catherine the Great on the Russian Question, or W.E.Gladstone on the 1909 Budget? This latter interview took up several pages of the *Daily Chronicle*. The front-page headline read: AMAZING SPIRIT 'INTERVIEW.' THE LATE MR GLADSTONE ON THE BUDGET.[15] Mr Gladstone, as it happened, had not much of interest to say; but the news (to paraphrase Dr Johnson) lay in his saying it at all.

By the time the Gladstone interview appeared, Stead's arrangements for getting through to the 'other side' were no longer in the slightest degree haphazard. Julia Ames had got him organized. Julia 'came through' to Stead very early on in his spiritualistic career. From 1892 onwards she was his chief contact with the spirit world. These other-worldly encounters began through the agency of a great friend of hers, to whom she had appeared after her death. She had appeared, but she had not spoken; and the friend was very anxious to know if she had a message to convey. Stead offered to introduce her to a medium, but went on to say, 'My hand has recently begun to write, and if you do not object, I will ask Julia if she will use my hand.' The friend agreed, and next morning, Stead went about contacting Julia in characteristically straightforward fashion. He sat before his bedroom window, pencil in hand, and said: 'Now, Miss Ames, if you are about and care to use my hand, it is at your disposal if you have anything to say to Miss E.'[16] Julia duly came through, and gave a most satisfactory test. From then on she was the most frequent user of Stead's hand, and passed on many useful tips, such as that living friends as well as dead ones could use his hand, if they wanted to. He found this power varied from friend to friend, some being able, some willing, and some – like Lady Warwick – unwilling even though they seemed to him able. 'I must say, nothing surprised me more at first than the frankness with which friends, who I knew were sensitive and shrinking, modest and retiring, who would never tell me anything about their personal circumstances or about money matters, would tell me in the frankest possible way their difficulties and troubles without any reserve whatever,' he commented on this mode of communication. Julia explained that telepathic conversation was conducted with people's real selves, not with those crass approximations to be encountered in the body.[17]

Having established these interesting facts, Stead's next psychic venture was the creation of *Borderland*, a quarterly review of psychic matters. (Appropriately, his co-editor for *Borderland*, Miss Ada Freer, was one of the most frequent users of his hand in this convenient spiritual telegraph. He informed readers in the first issue that he often, and successfully, made appointments with her in this way when she was not accessible on the telephone.)

One of the principal features of this publication was the first appearance of the 'Letters from Julia', later to be published as a book – automatic communications received from Miss Ames through Stead's hand. These had a mixed reception. The Bishop of Nottingham wrote Stead that 'The intelligence which uses your hand, and of which you are not conscious, is no other than the Devil,' but Stead always thought that, after his death, he would be remembered principally as 'Julia's amanuensis'. (The turgid quality of these letters, however, especially by comparison with the lively and compelling nature of anything written by Stead himself in, so to speak, his own consciousness, ensured that this did not happen.) *Borderland* did not last – it folded in 1897 – but the letters from Julia continued to arrive.

For the next ten years Stead's main energies were focused upon politics and journalism. And then the event occurred which once more brought spiritualism to the forefront: the death of his eldest son, Willie.

The death of a child is always unbearable. Stead dealt with it, as Conan Doyle and Lodge were to deal with the same circumstance, by simply refusing to accept it. Two years after the event a lady in a lecture audience, puzzled by Stead's frequent references to his son in the present tense: 'Willie told me yesterday', 'Willie is going with me tomorrow' and so on, was moved tentatively to ask, 'Is your son *alive*, Mr Stead?', to which Stead replied, '*Alive?* Of course he is! He died just two years ago. He is more alive than ever!'[18]

Being Stead, his constant preoccupation now was that the world should be able to learn and profit by these experiences and this knowledge. But how? As ever, Julia had the answer. She had for many years – in fact, since 1894 – been urging Stead to establish a Bureau to which the general public would be able to come and get into contact with the Other Side through her good offices. Through Stead's hand, she now became increasingly insistent on this. There was, of course, nothing he would have liked better; but how was he to find the money to do it? Stead, though his income was considerable, was constantly out of funds. His wife, knowing that any money he had would undoubtedly be spent on one hopeless cause or another, made a pre-emptive strike on as much of his income as she could lay her hands on. He was at this time bailing out, to the tune of many thousands of pounds, a Russian princess, introduced to him by the Tsaritsa, who was in 'temporary difficulties' until her estates could be realized; on her behalf, Stead had got himself into the clutches of a moneylender. To start Julia's Bureau at least one thousand pounds a year would be needed. Where on earth – or in Heaven's name – was it to come from? Julia would only say, 'You have to get the money, and when it comes you will have no doubt about its being intended for my Bureau!' And a little later she elaborated: 'You will get the thousand pounds; you will hear of it before Christmas; and it will come from America.'

On Christmas Eve Stead went as usual to his office. There he found a message from William Randolph Hearst asking him to be a special correspondent for the Hearst papers, for five hundred pounds a year. Was this the awaited sign? Julia assured him that it was, and that he should ask for a thousand a year, which he would certainly get. He cabled Hearst to this effect, and settled down to wait, his heart full of assurance. No messsage came. By the middle of January 1909 he had still heard nothing. 'No word from New York yet,' he wrote to his secretary, 'but Julia says it will be all right.'

In the third week in January he went down to his country cottage to revise some proofs. There was still no news about the money. Then, on 19 January, a letter came from Hearst. Stead telegraphed his secretary, 'Sing Doxology. Julia's prophecy fulfilled.'[19]

Members of the public who wished to make use of the facilities of Julia's Bureau could by no means be certain that they would be accepted. Every applicant had first to fill in an application form, giving his or her name, the name of the spirit to be contacted and the relationship while on earth, and certifying that 'the deceased would desire such an opening-up of communications as earnestly as does the applicant'. The applicant further had to certify, 'I have read the pamphlet entitled "Julia's Bureau and Borderland Library" and also the first series of "Letters from Julia".' This form was submitted to the Director (Stead's daughter Estelle), who decided whether it should go any further. If she accepted it, it was passed on to a psychometrist (who specialized in knowing about people by handling objects which had belonged to them, or been in their possession), to Julia's Secretary No. 1 and to Julia's Secretary No. 2, both automatists. 'If, as very seldom happened, the automatists and the psychometrist differed as to how an application should be treated, appeal was made to Julia in Council, when her decision, received by a clairvoyant, was final.'[20]

If the application was now passed, the applicant had to fill in two more forms. One, Form H, detailed the tests that would be considered satisfactory evidence that communication with the 'beloved one' had been achieved. These might include personal particulars such as name, date of birth, age, sex, height, appearance; description of death; pet names; names of special places; details of incidents; characteristic turns of phrase. This form was enclosed in a sealed envelope. Form D informed the Bureau that Form H had been filled in, and that 'When I have received and annotated the reports of the three sensitives, I will forward this envelope with seal unbroken to the Bureau, together with the annotated reports.' When all the paperwork was complete, psychic activity began. If possible the applicant was asked to attend in person; if this was not possible, he or she had to send in some small article which had belonged to the friend or relative in question – if possible, three such articles, so that each sensitive could have one which had not been handled by the others. Each sitter was accompanied by a stenographer, and no sitter was allowed to make any personal payment to a medium – these were all paid by the Bureau.

It was hoped that, at the end of the process, applicants would carefully annotate the reports they received from each of the three sittings, and send these, together with their comments, for filing and possible publication. Unfortunately, a great many failed to do this. Perhaps they were exhausted by the paperwork they had already undertaken. Nevertheless, at the end of three months, during which more than a hundred cases had already been handled by the Bureau, Stead wrote that the result of the experience 'has been to confirm my conviction that it is perfectly possible to establish communications with those who sincerely love. . . .'[21] Nevertheless, Julia's Bureau was not without its worries on the financial side. Each case involved out-of-pocket expenses of two guineas, and Julia expressly forbade charging clients for her services, though they could, if they wished, make a donation. After four months poor Stead wrote,

> I confess that this reliance for the financing of the Bureau upon gratitude for services rendered seems to most persons on the earth plane somewhat unbusinesslike. So far the results have hardly justified the splendid confidence of Julia. But I am going on relying upon her assurance that the necessary funds will not fail to be provided when they are needed.[22]

In these circumstances the Gladstone interview must have provided some necessary financial relief, since it, too, was obtained through Julia's good offices. Perhaps she felt that the public good which might be served by general dissemination of the Grand Old Man's opinions of current political goings-on excused the otherwise undeniably commercial nature of this interview, which was made at the special request of the *Daily Chronicle*'s editor. The interview took place at a special Saturday morning session. Present were, incarnate: Psychic (clairvoyant), Psychic (automatist), Stenographer, and W.T.Stead, Hon Sec; and discarnate: Julia, W.Stead junior, Cardinal Manning and others, who eventually included Gladstone himself, expressing his unwillingness to return to the 'limited and melancholy arena of party politics'. (Nevertheless, he expressed himself at length on such questions as whether he would disband the House of Lords if it threw out the Budget: 'In my opinion the Upper Chamber will act most ill-advisedly if they reject this financial measure.')

Julia's Bureau lasted for only four years, not surviving Stead's own death in 1912. Had he, and it, survived, the experiences of Conan Doyle and Oliver Lodge seem to indicate that, over the course of the next decade, it would have done a roaring trade.

Stead went down with the *Titanic*. It was a journey which he had felt was to be of particular importance to him, though the nature of that importance was undefined. Three weeks after his death he appeared in his inner sanctuary in Mowbray House, where his daughter, his secretary and other devoted ladies were waiting. His face (so they said) shone out; and as it faded his voice rang through the room saying: 'All I told you is true!'

In the years preceding the outbreak of the First World War, the notion that Sir Oliver Lodge and Sir Arthur Conan Doyle might be associated with W.T.Stead in terms of their literal and credulous attitude to the existence of the after-world would have been extraordinary and on the whole repugnant to both those eminent knights. Especially would this have been true of Lodge. Even as late as 1916 he could write, 'I know that my own attempt to hold the balance . . . evenly, has resulted in my being thought by my scientific colleagues over-credulous; whereas I think that Russel Wallace and W.T.Stead really were over-credulous at times.'[23]

A convenient measure of these differing attitudes may be had in looking at the feelings of the three about the SPR. We have already seen Stead's scornful rejection of that learned body and all its works. In this attitude he never faltered. Doyle never rejected the Society to this extent; but he was not immensely enthusiastic about it, as he was about those whose attitudes to spiritualism were less particular and less acerbic. And Lodge was always very much associated with it, though he could see why some convinced spiritualists distrusted it. In the same letter, he wrote: 'In dealing with strangers, and especially with enemies, it seems necessary to over-emphasize every point of

weakness. At any rate, that is the conclusion to which the SPR
leaders must have come . . . and the fact is a sufficient explanation of
the attitude which so many in the spiritualist camp condemn. . . . I am
not at all sure that this attitude of the Society may not prove, in the
long run, wise.'[24]

Lodge first really became convinced about the possibility of the
survival of personality and the possibility of communication after
death with the visit to Britain in 1889 of the famous medium Mrs
Leonora Piper, and he was far from being the only one on whom she
had this convincing effect. Frank Podmore, perhaps the most abrasive
and certainly the most encyclopaedic commentator on the phenomena
of spiritualism, thought that she alone was responsible for the movement's resurrection from the doldrums of the end of the nineteenth
century to the relative popularity it began once more to enjoy in the
twentieth.

Certainly, at the time when Lodge met Mrs Piper, the fervour and
popular appeal of the mass movement which had taken off with such
phenomenal speed in the wake of the Fox sisters' revelations, and of
which such practitioners as D.D.Home and Florence Cook had been
so noteworthy a part, had very much died down. There remained, of
course, a hard core of enthusiasts, ranging from such emotional
literalists as Stead and Wallace at one end of the spectrum to the
hyper-acute philosophizing intellectuals of the SPR at the other.
But the desperate fervour of religious questioning which had followed
the publication of the *Origin of Species* was dying down; and the
equally desperate yearning to believe that the young men cut down in
the 1914–18 massacre were not really lost for ever had not yet arisen.
A populist such as Stead was a spiritualistic anomaly in his time,
whereas a decade later he would have found himself in the mainstream
of that belief. As it was, his religious views caused no little embarrassment to his many friends in high political and literary places.

They would have had altogether less trouble in accepting Lodge and
his enthusiasm for Mrs Piper. For, whether or not Podmore was right
in his assessment of her popular appeal, she had first of all been taken
up by those at the more intellectually powerful and respectable end of
the spiritualist spectrum, notably by that extraordinarily attractive
and brilliant individual William James.

Mrs Piper, unlike most other popular mediums of her time, never
produced any 'physical phenomena'. Her speciality was doing what
Stead's 'sensitives' in Julia's Bureau did. Through her 'controls'
people could contact dead friends and relatives; and, speaking

Crawford's photographs of some of the
phenomena which convinced him of the reality
of 'psychic structures'. These structures, used
for lifting a table, were, he said, the variety
used when great force was needed.

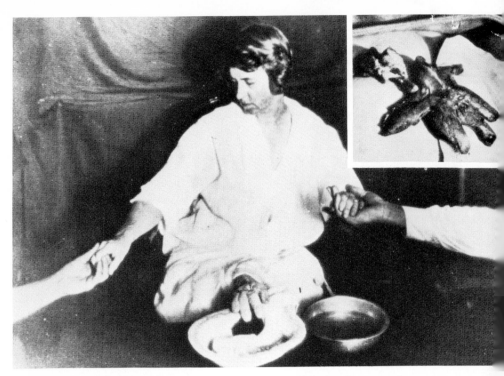

Margery and her 'ectoplasmic' hand with (*inset*) a close-up of the hand apparently emerging from Margery's navel

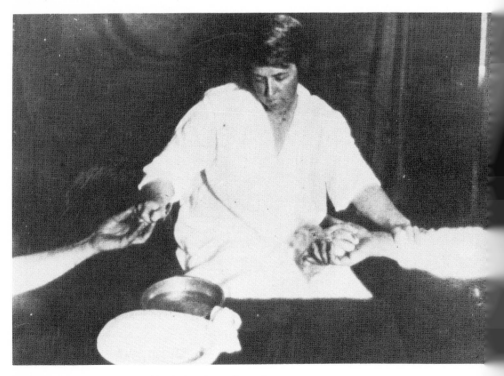

Margery's 'ectoplasmic' hand is shaken by an investigator.

...gery producing 'ectoplasm' from her nose; the gap in her clothes has ...umably been left for a pseudopod to emerge.

Richard Hodgson poses for a fake 'spirit'
photograph.

Madame Blavatsky

onan Doyle and Houdini

Two of the pictures which convinced Conan Doyle of the existence of fairies

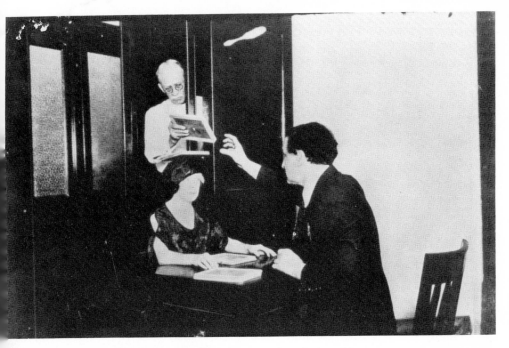

Houdini and Mrs Houdini demonstrate how slates may be substituted in a slate-writing trick.

Houdini, surrounded by 'spirits', two of whom can be recognized as Roosevelt and Abraham Lincoln

A yogi version of the 'levitation' act; the yogi's hand rests on a draped stick.

through these 'controls', she was able to enter, in a seemingly miraculous way, into people's lives, thoughts and family histories.

Mrs Piper had become a medium in 1883. The thing had happened in the usual way – by contagion. She had been suffering from a tumour and had gone to visit a medium who gave medical consultations, but who also specialized in developing latent mediumship in others. At her first sitting Mrs Piper felt very agitated and thought she was going to faint. On the next occasion, the medium put his hands on her forehead. Once more she was on the point of losing consciousness. She saw a flood of light, unrecognizable faces, and a hand which fluttered before her own face. She then passed out. When she came to, although she could remember nothing, she was told that a young Indian girl named, incredibly, Chlorine, had manifested through her and had given a remarkable proof of survival after death.

This, it will be admitted, was not a promising beginning. Nevertheless, her friends were very excited and immediately began to arrange sittings with her. Gradually, some strangers began to be admitted to this private circle, and her fame spread. At first, a great many controls manifested themselves. They included Mrs Siddons the actress, J.S. Bach, H.W. Longfellow the poet, Commodore Vanderbilt, and a young Italian girl named Loretta Pachini. There was also a Creole doctor named Phinuit, who gave medical consultations. As time went on, however, this multiplicity of controls disappeared and Dr Phinuit took over completely.

It was two years after this, in 1885, that William James was put into touch with Mrs Piper. To a member of the James family, nothing could be more natural than a concern with religion. William's father, Henry James senior, had been passionately concerned with religious matters and, as a Swedenborgian, had taken a keen interest in the early phenomena of spiritualism. This interest was carried forward by his son William, whose interest in psychology was always mingled with a fascination with religion and the reportedly supernatural. Naturally enough, his principal psychological alliances were with those European schools of psychology which shared this mix of interests, his great friend in this sphere being Dr Théodore Flournoy of Geneva (author of *Des Indes à la planète Mars*).

James's interest in the intellectually unfashionable topic of spiritualism stemmed from the combination of his strong interest in religion and desire for belief with his conviction that 'The great field for new discoveries ... is always the unclassified residuum' and that 'Anyone will renovate his science who will steadily look after the irregular phenomena.'[25] And among those residual irregularities, what could be more irregular, or more residual from a scientific point of view, than those generally lumped under the heading 'mystical'?

The trouble with such phenomena, however, was that they tended to be vague and unconfirmed: a mere question of affirmation. In James's view, the great virtue of the SPR was that it was a focus for people who would 'pay attention to facts of the sort dear to mystics, while reflecting upon them in academic-scientific ways'. For mere fuzzy speculation, thought James, was not enough. It was certainly not enough for him. 'It is a miserable thing for a question of truth to be confined to mere presumption and counter-presumption, with no decisive thunderbolt of fact to clear the baffling darkness.'[26]

For James, however, the thunderbolt had fallen. And it had fallen in the shape of Mrs Piper. Her capacity for telling him things about himself and his family amazed and puzzled him: her talents drew him like a magnet. Over the course of the next two years he sent as many of his friends and family – his own and his wife's – as he could persuade to visit her, quite secure in the certainty that she could not possibly know who these people were. Some years later he wrote:

> If you wish to upset the law that all crows are black, you must not seek to show that no crows are: it is enough if you prove one single crow to be white. My own white crow is Mrs Piper. In the trances of this medium, I cannot resist the conviction that knowledge appears which she has never gained by the ordinary waking use of her eyes and ears and wits. What the source of this knowledge may be I know not, and have not the glimmer of an explanatory suggestion to make; but from admitting the rest of such knowledge I can see no escape.[27]

For James, then, Mrs Piper provided that clinching proof of the existence of the supernormal, the scientifically inexplicable, for which he craved, and now she had been found, there must be nothing wanting in the thoroughness and rigour with which he examined her. His sister Alice groaned:

> I do pray to Heaven that the dreadful Mrs Piper won't be let loose upon my defenceless soul. I suppose the thing 'medium' has done more to degrade the spiritual conception than the grossest forms of materialism or idolatry: was ever anything transmitted but the pettiest, meanest, coarsest facts and details: anything rising above the squalid intestines of human affairs? And oh, the curious spongy minds that sop it up and lose all sense of taste and humour![28]

Despite this, and despite the boredom which many years of repeated experiments inspired in him, James never lost his faith in the reality of Mrs Piper's powers. He arranged for Richard Hodgson, the young Australian who had investigated Madame Blavatsky for the SPR, to come out to Boston, where he was to be the American branch's sole paid worker, almost the entirety of his assignment in this role being the continued investigation of Mrs Piper.

Hodgson devoted the rest of his working life to this investigation (he died suddenly of a heart attack while still in the prime of life, in 1906). He was not an easy man to deceive; he had already exposed not only Madame Blavatsky but also the tricks of the 'slate-writing' mediums who astonished so many people with their apparent miracles – miracles which were duplicated and even excelled by Hodgson and his magician friend Mr Davey, to the chagrin of both slate-writers and believers (who countered with the usual charges that Davey had, but would not admit to having, psychic powers). But Mrs Piper baffled him. From now on he took virtually sole charge of her, and all sittings with her were arranged by him and held under his auspices. It was Hodgson who arranged the trip to England during which Oliver Lodge met this extraordinary woman, and was in his turn dazzled by her.

The sittings were held at the end of 1889 and in the first months of 1890, and were reported by Lodge in great detail in the *Proceedings* of the Society for Psychical Research. The person controlling Mrs Piper during these sessions was Dr Phinuit.

There were a number of sessions, extending over many hours, and as might be expected a lot of what went on was worthless and was acknowledged as such by Lodge. But, amid all the rubbish, he identified a hard core of substance which he found quite inexplicable other than by supernatural means. There were two instances which made a particularly profound impression on him. First was one involving himself, when, starting from an old watch which had been in the family for many years, Mrs Piper identified his old Uncle Jerry, with whom Lodge had spent much time as a boy. She described escapades they had had together which Lodge had almost forgotten, Uncle Jerry's appearance, the manner of his death, and other details which – as Lodge pointed out – she could not possibly have known. The second one involved his friend Lund, who was chaplain of the Liverpool School for the Blind. Mrs Piper told him about the death, many years earlier, of a beloved younger sister, whom she named correctly; about a carpet recently burnt at his house; about the illness of his son; and various other such details.

Lodge was not necessarily convinced that these 'hits' represented any proof of the existence of discarnate spirits, but he thought that they did represent a proof of thought-transference; and other sitters from the SPR were equally convinced by their experiences. Was Mrs Piper, then, the one 'white crow' which should convince us all that something supernormal – let us leave aside the question of exactly what – was going on? If one read only Lodge's short accounts of these sessions, it would seem impossible to doubt it. Call it clairvoyance, call it thought-transference, call it the omniscience of the spirit-world – that something is at work could hardly be denied. But if – a much more laborious task – the verbatim reports published in the SPR *Proceedings* are studied, then light is shed on some methods used by Mrs Piper which are not supernormal in the least.

When first considering this matter, it is worth looking at some of the methods generally known to be used by professional fortune-tellers and 'thought-readers'. One person who made a thorough study of these things was a man named David Abbott. Abbott was one of that band of magicians who devoted themselves to exposing the methods of fraudulent 'mediums'. He lived in Omaha, Nebraska, and published his findings in the Chicago magazine *Open Court*, in the early years of this century – a time when Mrs Piper was still in full spate and high favour.

Abbott made a special study of a lady medium who was having a great success in the neighbourhood of Omaha, and whose work was along very much the same lines as that of Mrs Piper, except that she had been taken up, not by the intellectual élite of the day, but only by her ordinary fellow citizens. (However, as we have seen, the fact that someone is an eminent intellectual does not necessarily make him or her any more adroit in spotting trickery.) The first technique used by Abbott's lady medium was 'fishing'. She made her statements with a rising inflection so that they were really questions, which it was hard not to answer. Abbott commented: 'I saw how effective her system of "pumping" was; and I saw how most persons would have received much better results than I did, by talking more and making unguarded exclamations.'[29]

Anyone who has visited a fortune-teller or clairvoyant will recognize the situation; it is illustrated in this exchange between Lodge and Mrs Piper: 'After some preliminaries. Phin: "Have you anything to ask me?" O.L. (as instructed beforehand by F.W.H.M [yers]): "Can you tell me about my relations?" Phin: "I get your mother's influence. She's very near to you, a good mother to you." O.L. (stupidly indicating the fact of decease): "Yes, she was."'[30]

Most persons [continues Abbott] would have regarded this information as most wonderful and would have quickly forgotten the little failures she made. In fact, with most, she would not have carried her failures so far; for they would most naturally have stopped her when she was wrong, instead of allowing her to mislead herself, as I did. . . . The medium mentions many things and many subjects, and the sitter resists or overlooks the ones on the 'wrong track'; and while not intending to lead the medium, shows by encouragement when the medium is on the 'right track'. . . . She said that when she gave tests to any one, the stories they told afterward, continually grew, . . . so that when they came back to her, she could hardly recognize her own work.[31]

This is a phenomenon already met with often in the course of this book. To see how it can overtake even the most watchful – even the most sceptical – let us look at the account given of his meeting with Mrs Piper by Mr Lund, Lodge's friend from the School for the Blind. He begins:

With regard to my experiences with Mrs Piper, I do not feel that I saw enough to form data for any satisfactory conclusion. What impressed me most was the way in which she seemed to feel for information, rarely telling me anything of importance right off the reel, but carefully fishing, and then following up a lead. It seemed to me that when she got on a right tack, the nervous and uncontrollable movement of one's muscles gave her the signal that she was right and might steam ahead.

(It should be mentioned here – as it was rarely mentioned by Mrs Piper's sitters – that she held the sitter's hand during the seance, often against her forehead. Any experienced practitioner – and by this time Mrs Piper had been a medium for seven years – can learn this technique of 'muscle-reading'. It is the same technique by which a magician will 'lead' a member of the audience to an object which has been hidden in the room while he was outside. In reality, the magician does not lead, but is led by unconscious and uncontrollable signals which tell him when he is getting close on the trail.)

Mr Lund continues:

In some points she was entirely out of it. . . . In others . . . she made statements which singularly tallied with the truth – e.g. my son was ill, and my wife was going to see him. I found that at the very time given she left the house with a cloak on her arm, and brushed her dress in the way imitated by Mrs Piper. Still, I am bound to say, within earshot of Mrs Piper – before the sitting – I told Mrs Lodge of my son's illness in Manchester, and my wife's proposed visit to him, and Mrs Lodge addressed me by my name of Lund.

... But, without doubt, the feature of this sitting was the reference to my youngest sister, who died of diphtheria in my absence quite thirty years ago, and whose death was a heartaching sorrow of many years. Not only did she hit upon the name 'Maggie,' but even the pet name 'Margie,' which I had quite forgotten. However, the reason afterwards alleged for my absence at her death was quite wrong.[32]

From this account, it might be assumed that Mrs Piper jumped straight to the name 'Margie'. And this is certainly the impression that would be gained from Lodge's account of the incident. But this was not, in fact, the case. Here is what happened:

She (Mrs Piper) said I was away when my youngest sister passed out; not with her; a long way off. No chance to see her. She had blue eyes and brown hair – a very pretty girl. Pretty mouth and teeth; plenty of expression in them. She then tried to find the name and went through a long list; at last said it had 'ag' in the middle, and that's all she could find.... 'But it's your sister – Maggie – that's it – she says you are brother Tom – no, her name's Margie. Too bad you were not at home. It was one of the sorrows that followed Tom all his life. (Correct.) He'll never forget it.' I said, 'Ask her how it was I wasn't there?' She said: 'I'm getting weak now – au revoir.'

Previously, Mrs Piper had ascertained Lund's first name ('"Do you know Thomas?" "I'm Thomas," I replied') – and we already know that she knew his surname from before the sitting.[33]

It seems extraordinary that anyone should let such information drop in the medium's hearing, knowing that this was to be a test session. One explanation is that her sitters believed that once Mrs Piper had gone into trance and her 'control' – usually Dr Phinuit at this time – had taken over, her trance personality would not remember anything from her non-trance state. This assumption might explain all sorts of anomalies and careless slips which were allowed to occur – such as photographs being left about. Mrs Piper would be able to make use of such things but Phinuit would not. Quite apart from the doubtful validity of this assumption, it altogether begs the question of the nature of Mrs Piper's trance. Mr Lund said, 'I accepted the trance condition on Dr Lodge's authority; otherwise I should have felt bound to test it.'

But in addition to this, there is the question of the assumptions of this highly sophisticated and intellectual group of people with regard to the nature and intelligence of Mrs Piper herself. Her honesty and simplicity is often dwelt upon in descriptions: she was a simple housewife who found herself burdened with this strange power but whose real pleasure lay in domestic things, her home and children. This delightful woman was contrasted with the 'coarse, cunning' Dr Phinuit, who so frequently lapsed into bad language – a relation which of course brings very much to mind that of Margery and Walter. One might, perhaps, ask: how simple is simple? Is a university degree essential to the shrewd, or merely intelligent, conduct of life?

That William James did not make such mistakes may be assumed. He and Hodgson invariably introduced sitters to Mrs Piper under pseudonyms (a fact of which she was quite aware) and exercised the utmost care with regard to letting slip information unawares. They even had her watched when she was not with them, to make sure she did not get up to any professional medium's tricks. But about the series of sittings which originally convinced James that here was something extraordinary, a point may be made. Many of these sittings were with different members of his own and his wife's family. Even using pseudonyms, it seems unlikely that points of family resemblance should not have been noticed by an observant woman such as we may assume Mrs Piper to have been. This being so, she could have built on information already ascertained in a way that would undoubtedly have seemed most extraordinary and impressive.

And throughout the years, James remained impressed. Towards the end of his life, after Hodgson's death, when Mrs Piper appeared to be communicating, through her control 'Rector', with the spirit of R.H. (Richard Hodgson), he wrote: 'That a "will to personate" is a factor in the Piper phenomenon, I fully believe, and I believe with unshakable firmness that this will is able to draw on supernormal sources of information. It can "tap," possibly the sitter's memories, possibly those of distant human beings, possibly some cosmic reservoir in which the memories of earth are stored, whether in the shape of "spirits" or not.'[34] This led to interesting speculation as to whether Mrs Piper's were the only will involved in this process, or whether it was affected by other, extraneous 'wills to communicate', including that of Hodgson. The former instance would, in James's view, have been 'humbug pure and simple'; he himself inclined to the latter opinion. But, either way, the reality of Mrs Piper's powers was not, for him, in question.

The fact which for the moment concerns us, however, is the nature of Oliver Lodge's early interest in spiritualism and psychical research; and this was, on the whole, an intellectual and experimental one, very much aligned with the SPR, even if (as we have already seen in connection with the Eusapia experiments) his inclination was always to believe. This was the mainstream, received attitude. By contrast, Stead's eager, literal naivety was very much out on a limb.

In 1915, however, all that was to change.

The Lodges, in the Victorian tradition, had a very large family. By the time the Great War broke out in 1914, most of the boys were already too old for military service. But the youngest, Raymond, was only twenty-five, and at once volunteered. The Lodges were particularly attached to their youngest son, who was a youth of great ability – he was a mechanical engineer – and sweet temper. When he was killed, in September 1915, their grief was terrible. The knowledge that many others are in a similar predicament does little to ease particular pain. A few days after she had heard of Raymond's death, his mother scribbled a few lines on a piece of paper, which her husband picked up:

'*To ease the pain and to try to get in touch.*'

Raymond, darling, you have gone from our world, and oh, to ease the pain. I want to know if you are happy, and that you *yourself* are really talking to me and no sham.

No more letters from you, my own dear son, and I have loved them so. They are all there; we shall have them typed together into a sort of book.

Now we shall be parted until I join you there. I have not seen as much of you as I wanted on this earth, but I do love to think of the bits I have had of you, specially our journeys to and from Italy. I had you to myself then, and you were so dear.

I want to say, dear, how we recognize the glorious way in which you have done your duty, with a certain straight pressing on, never letting anyone see the effort, and with your fun and laughter playing round all the time, cheering and helping others. You know how your brothers and sisters feel your loss, and your poor father![35]

It will be seen that the Lodges already were, or believed themselves to be, in communication with their son on the 'other side'.

Raymond had had a few days' leave in July 1915, and had returned to the front on 20 July. This was the last time his family saw him. On 8 August there came the first indication that all might not be well. This was highly oblique, being a message communicated through Mrs Piper by 'Richard Hodgson' but coming from F.W.H.Myers. The sitter at the time was a Miss Robbins, and the sitting took place at Mrs Piper's house in New Hampshire. 'Hodgson' said:

Now, Lodge, while we are not here as of old, i.e. not quite, we are here enough to give and take messages. Myers says you take the part of the poet, and he will act as Faunus. FAUNUS.

Miss R: Faunus?

R.H.: Yes. Myers. *Protect*. He will understand. . . What have you to say, Lodge? Good work. Ask [Mrs] Verrall, she will also understand. Arthur says so. You got mixed (to Miss R.), but Myers is straight about Poet and Faunus.

This cryptic communication was sent to Lodge by Mrs Piper's daughter, Alta Piper. The references were to a prominent member of the SPR, well known to Mrs Piper (as were all the other persons referred to). The deceased Dr Verrall had been a classical scholar.

Lodge heard of this message from Miss Piper on 8 September (Raymond was killed on the fourteenth). Mrs Verrall immediately identified the reference as being to an Ode of Horace in which he describes his narrow escape from being killed by a falling tree; he ascribes this to the intervention of Faunus, protector of poets. What could this mean? Lodge points out that a falling tree is a frequently used symbol for death; it was to threaten, but Myers was, it seemed, offering protection. A week later, however, the blow had fallen and not been averted. A friend wrote: 'As bearing on your terrible loss, the meaning seems to be that the blow would fall but would not crush; it would be "lightened" by the assurance conveyed afresh to you by a special message from the still living Myers, that your boy still lives.'[36]

Given the circumstances, his beliefs and this apparent proof of spirit interest, it was of course the most natural thing in the world for Sir Oliver and Lady Lodge to try and probe further in this direction. The first of these attempts took place within a very few days of their receiving news of Raymond's death, on 17 September. On 25 September, Lady Lodge attended a sitting with the well-known medium Mrs Osborne Leonard, to whom she was introduced by some friends, Dr and Mrs Kennedy, who had also lost a son, Paul. On that occasion the table spelt out, by tilting, the message: TELL FATHER I HAVE MET SOME FRIENDS OF HIS. And on being asked for a name, the table said: MYERS.

Two days later, Lodge visited Mrs Leonard on his own account. The first thing Mrs Leonard did was to introduce Lodge to her 'control'. This was, banally enough, the inevitable young Indian girl, this time named Feda. It is clear that, for many of Lodge's friends, Feda presented a point of difficulty in the story. She spoke of herself coyly, always in the third person. She was, in fact, a typical hysterical secondary personality: naive, childish and unintelligent. Questioned about this by his old friend Arthur Hill, Lodge said: 'Concerning Feda, there is always the possibility that she, and her like, are secondary personalities. But at any rate she is a personality, and one whom my family feel friendly towards: I don't know that it much matters whether she is a secondary or a primary personality. I am inclined . . . to be guided by what they say on the other side about these things; they evidently treat these personalities as distinct people.'[37]

On this occasion – as invariably afterwards, which naturally accounts for Lodge's friendly feelings towards her – Feda came up with the goods. In theory, this sitting was anonymous, and Mrs Leonard did not know who Lodge was. But he was a well-known figure at that time, principal of Birmingham University; she knew he was a friend of the Kennedys, who might well have mentioned his name, or at any rate that of Lady Lodge; and she was well acquainted with many members of the Society for Psychical Research, of which Lodge had for years been a prominent member. At any rate, Feda soon said:

> There is someone here with a little difficulty; not fully built-up; youngish looking; form more like an outline; he has not completely learnt how to build up as yet. Is a young man, rather above the medium height, rather well built, not thick set or heavy, but well built. . . . He has not been over long. His hair is between colours. He is not easy to describe, because he is not building himself up so solid as some do. He has greyish eyes; hair brown, short at the sides; a fine-shaped head; eyebrows also brown, not much arched; nice-shaped nose, fairly straight, broader at the nostrils a little; a nice-shaped mouth, a good-sized mouth it is, but it does not look large because he holds the lips nicely together; chin not heavy; face oval. . . . Feda sees many hundreds of people, but they tell me this one has been brought quite lately. Yes, I have seen him before. Feda remembers a letter with him too. R, that is to do with him.[38]

The reader will doubtless decide how such a description might have been arrived at. It should be remembered that Mrs Leonard had by now met both Raymond's parents.

The sittings progressed, and there can be no doubt that both Sir Oliver and Lady Lodge found them a great comfort in their distress. At first, the rest of the family did not share their enthusiasm, but they came round, and soon Lodges of both generations were communicating with their dead son and brother through Mrs Leonard, through another well-known medium, Mr Vout Peters (who had been one of the sensitives employed by Julia's Bureau), and at home through table-tipping.

The picture built up of Raymond's life on the other side, or, as he preferred to put it, in Summerland, was extraordinarily substantial. Lodge himself had some doubts about publishing some of it, probably because he foresaw – correctly – that it would attract undue attention, both critical and naive. Here is part of this description:

> He says, my body's very similar to the one I had before. I pinch myself

sometimes to see if it's real, and it is, but it doesn't seem to hurt as much as when I pinched the flesh body. The internal organs don't seem constituted on the same lines as before. They can't be quite the same. But to all appearances, and outwardly, they are the same. . . . I knew a man who had lost an arm, but he has got another one. . . . After a while it got more and more complete, until he got a new one. (What about a limb lost in battle?) – Oh, if they have only just lost it, it makes no difference, it doesn't matter; they are quite all right when they get here. But I am told . . . that when anybody's blown to pieces, it takes some time for the spirit body to complete itself. . . . There are men here, and there are women here. I don't think that they stand to each other quite the same as they did on the earth plane, but they seem to have the same feeling for each other, with a different expression of it. There don't seem to be any children born here. People are sent into the physical body to have children on the earth plane. . . . He says he doesn't want to eat now. But he sees some who do; he says they have to be given something which has all the appearance of an earth food. People here try to provide everything that is wanted. A chap came over the other day, who would have a cigar. 'That's finished them,' he thought. He means he thought they would never be able to provide that. But there are laboratories over here, and they manufacture all sorts of things in them. Not like you do, out of solid matter, but out of essences, and ethers, and gases. It's not the same as on the earth plane, but they were able to manufacture what looked like a cigar. . . . When they first come they do want things. Some want meat, and some strong drink; they call it whisky sodas. Don't think I'm stretching it when I tell you they can manufacture even that. But when they have had one or two they don't seem to want it so much.[39]

When the collection of evidence for Raymond's survival was published in book form – which it was, under the title *Raymond*, in 1916 – this particular section, as Lodge had foreseen, was an obvious target for his detractors. It certainly seems a very crude view of the spiritual world. Yet there is no doubt that it corresponded to Lodge's own view of probable conditions there. In a letter to a friend written in November 1916, he said:

If people on the other side have 'things' at all, they will get used to them and things will feel to them much like 'things' feel to us. The way material things appear to us here must be a matter of habit and interpretation. It is hardly likely that things in themselves are like the impression which they make upon us – for instance, a blue colour, what is it in itself? I suppose it is something stimulated in us by a physical phenomenon, an ether tremor of certain frequency wholly disconnected from 'blue' or anything like it.[40]

Lodge did not publish such intimacies without some reluctance. It was a painful business, and in a way he was disinclined to do it; but he felt he was uniquely qualified to help the bereaved, especially those who had been bereaved by war in the same way as he had. And the book's success shows that he read the temper of the times quite correctly. It went through twelve impressions between 1916 and 1919, and a shortened version, *Raymond Revised*, was published in 1922. But, as may be imagined, it did not have an easy critical ride. A great many reviews were hostile or jocular. It was banned from the shelves of Aberdeen Public Library. Some clergymen thought the whole thing was a Satanic delusion: 'He and his agents often know the history of deceased lives, and so are often well able to personate deceased people and to reveal family or other secrets through various mediums, and possibly also by table-turning, etc.'[41]

Lodge himself was quite unworried by these objections. He rejected those of the clerics by taking refuge in his position as a scientist who must allow himself to be ruled only by evidence: 'I must claim that Science can pay no attention to ecclesiastical notice-boards.'[42] His testimony, he asserted, was in no way merely theoretical, it was based upon fact. When it came to the objections of intellectuals and rationalists, however, he took a quite different line. He contended that, throughout history, whenever science had discovered some new and hard-to-credit fact, it had invariably been accepted by 'simple-hearted folk' long before the intellectual establishment of the day had allowed that it might be true.[43]

In fact, generally speaking, the very reverse is true. Isaac Asimov, the famous science fiction writer, has made a study of these cases, and his rule of thumb ('Asimov's Corollary') is this: 'If a scientific heresy is ignored or denounced by the general public, there is a chance it may be right. If a scientific heresy is emotionally supported by the general public, it is almost certainly wrong.'[44] This, of course, is precisely counter to what the proponents of psi, from Lodge onwards, would have us believe, their claim invariably being that if only science would look seriously at these things, as the public would wish it to do, then it would realize. . . . But the public did not support Galileo. It did not – and a sizeable proportion of it still does not – support Darwin. The only exception Asimov can find is that of Jenner and his claim that vaccination could offer protection against smallpox, when, clearly, the public dearly wanted him to be right, and to hell with science.

The review which came closest to Lodge's view of things was probably that by Conan Doyle, published in *The Observer* on 25 November 1916. Here, said Doyle, was 'a new revelation of God's dealings with man which must modify some ill-defined and melancholy dogmas as to the events which follow the death of the body'. For Doyle, too, who lost both a son and a brother in the war, the year 1916 was that in which the true personal significance of spiritualism was borne in upon him, and the more literal, solid and tangible the revelation, the better.

For W.T.Stead, the whole question of the 'other side' had been one of blithe and secure acceptance. Nothing would have surprised him; and nothing would have interested him less than elaborate justifications of the type attempted by Lodge with his consideration of the reality of the concept 'blue'. For Lodge, on the other hand, to accept something of the sort without trying to justify it scientifically would have been impossible. And although a psychological imperative dictated his actions and reactions with regard to Raymond, he never pretended to Stead's facility for communing with any number of other spirits on the most intimate terms. (Stead never hesitated to commune with anybody, living or dead, on intimate terms.) Conan Doyle was yet a different case. By the time the war came he was getting on in years, rich, famous, secure and immensely self-confident. He was an influential figure in many fields outside literature. The hard times of his early attempts to set up in medical practice, the unsatisfactory nature of his first marriage, had both receded into the past. He adored his second wife, Jean; he loved his house in Sussex, and his way of life (he thought) could in no way be bettered. When, therefore, the great revelation came upon him, he saw himself in messianic terms. He had the message and the truth, and it was his duty to spread these far and wide. About the nature of that message he was as unabashed as his two compeers. Like them, his view of the afterlife was clear. Quite simply, England's green and pleasant land was transmuted to the higher sphere. What more could any spirit, British or foreign, desire?

Doyle had, by 1916, known Lodge for many years. They had met in 1902 in the anteroom at Buckingham Palace, waiting to be knighted: Lodge for his scientific distinction and services to academic life, Doyle for his literary fame. At that time Lodge was very much involved with the SPR and, specifically, with Richet's experiments; Doyle was a keen supporter of *Light*. (Stead had just been forced to close *Borderland*, for lack of funds and time, and was desultorily seeking around for the funds which would eventually enable him to open Julia's Bureau; meanwhile he was making the fullest possible use of his spiritual telegraph service.) But at this time neither Doyle nor Lodge shared Stead's religious view of spiritualistic proceedings.

For Doyle, the blinding revelation came in 1916; and when it came, there were no half measures. He embraced the religion of spiritualism in a way that, common enough in the nineteenth century, was extraordinary in the twentieth. His second wife, Jean, had at first discouraged this interest; but she was brought round by the death of her brother Malcolm at Mons in 1916. This was the battle at which soldiers reported seeing angelic hosts in the clouds. A story was put about at one time that the Germans had manufactured this illusion using a magic-lantern projector; but it seems more likely that this was a case of mass suggestion, swiftly circulating and irresistible, occasioned in the first instance by a short story, then recently published, in which such a vision was seen. At any rate, her brother's death in such circumstances effectively brought Jean round, and it was after this that she discovered her faculty for automatic writing, first manifested in the Doyle household by the children's governess, who had also lost three brothers in the war. The Doyle 'home circle', then, was an intense, emotional and highly motivated affair. Doyle was reassured in his work of spreading the word by his dead son Kingsley, who 'came through' congratulating him on the 'Christ-like message you are giving to the World'. W.T.Stead also, and most appropriately, communicated. He described Doyle's work as the 'Review of Divine Reviews' (a reference to his own magazine, the Review of Reviews) and told Doyle he had 'looked into the eyes of Christ with Cecil Rhodes by my side and he said tell Arthur that his work on Earth is holy and divine – that his Message is Mine'.[45] (Both Stead and Doyle had known Rhodes well; both were much in sympathy with his view of the Empire and its mission.)

Doyle spent a large part of the rest of his life in lecture tours, spreading the word in Britain and America. A map of the British Isles hung in his study thick with marks indicating the towns at which he had spoken. As for his American lecture tours, his success was extraordinary; only Oliver Lodge, on a similar mission, had come anywhere near it. In 1922 he filled the largest halls in Manhattan and Brooklyn to overflowing seven nights in succession; he estimated that there alone more than twenty-two thousand people had received his message. Such was the hunger of the bereaved generation which had endured 1914–18.

What these people wanted to hear had little to do with the painstaking inquiries preferred by the SPR. Their conviction, or their wish for it, was an unintellectual as that of their mentors, Doyle and (despite himself) Lodge. They wanted to know that there definitely was a life for their loved ones 'over there'; and they wanted to know what that life was like. It was no coincidence that this had been the part of Lodge's book which had attracted most attention.

Doyle had none of Lodge's self-conscious qualms about including such concrete and simplistic details in his addresses. His own passion for literal detail was, after all, one of the things which made him such a supreme story-teller. He told a press conference on the occasion of his first American tour that 'the conditions of the other world offered a boundless field for questions. Of course, the alcohol and cigars came up.' This was a reference to the passage from *Raymond* quoted above. Many of Lodge's readers and Doyle's audiences were teetotallers and non-smokers and were deeply shocked and distressed at the notion that such immoral habits might be tolerated in Heaven. Lodge, quibbling nicely, felt that what he was describing was not Heaven, but Paradise, where the rules would, he thought, be less strict. One person who would undoubtedly have joined Lodge in Paradise rather than the saints in Heaven any day was Mark Twain. In his *Letters from the Earth* he set out his puzzlement that anyone should want to go to Heaven, given the usual Christian description of what is on offer there. He said:

It has not a single feature in it that [man] actually values. It consists – utterly and entirely – of diversions which he cares next to nothing about, here on the earth, yet is quite sure he will like in heaven. . . . He has imagined a heaven, and has left entirely out of it one of the supremest of all his delights . . . sexual intercourse. . . . Exalting intellect above all things else in his world . . . this sincere adorer of intellect and prodigal rewarder of its mighty services here on the earth has invented a religion and a heaven which pay no compliments to intellect, offer it no distinctions, fling it no largess; in fact never even mentions it.[46]

(The Pope, however, has recently informed the world that men and women will retain their sex in heaven, though what use they may or may not make of it there he did not say.)

Conan Doyle was not to be drawn on the question of whisky and cigars.

I could only say that I had never personally heard any claim that such things existed. It has always seemed to me that one of the most startling passages in the New Testament is that in which Christ speaks of wine in the beyond. Possibly some unfermented drink was in His mind or possibly He only used the phrase as a synonym for making merry. . . . The usual information is that any nutrition is of a very light and delicate order, corresponding to the delicate etheric body which requires it. Then there was the question of marriage, and the old proposition of the much-married man and which wife he should have. As there is no sexual relation as we understand it, this problem is not very complex and is naturally decided by soul affinity.[47]

Golf, he thought, was likely to be played. In fact, Conan Doyle's Heaven was rather like Sussex, slightly watered down.

The outstanding feature of this spiritualist mass-movement of the early twentieth century was that, unlike that of seventy years before, the so-called 'physical phenomena' were nowhere in evidence. Where they had once been such an important element of popular appeal, they were now more a concern of such students of *arcana* as Richet, Schrenck-Notzing and Crawford. The millions of bereaved, whose desperate desire to contact their dead brought them in multitudes to the lectures of Doyle and Lodge and sold those gentlemen's books in tens of thousands, were not interested in ectoplasm. Nor was Lodge, and nor, in his time, was Stead.

Nor, or so he said, was Doyle. He wrote: 'The phenomena interest me very little, nor am I attracted much by the scientific side of the question. One might as well, it seems to me, be keenly interested in how the loaves and fishes fed the multitude but give no heed to the Sermon on the Mount.'[48] But despite these protestations, the fact is that, when it came to 'phenomena', Doyle was more eager and more credulous than almost anyone before or since in the history of spiritualism. We have already seen something of this characteristic in relation to the Margery affair. Not only was he eager to be taken in: his fury when fraud was shown up – for instance, by Houdini – knew no bounds. As his messianic conviction that he alone held the truth grew, so his refusal to admit that, at least on occasion, he might be wrong became more obdurate.

Perhaps the most extraordinary instance of this occurred in connection with the incidents described in Doyle's book *The Coming of the Fairies*. In May 1920, Doyle heard from a friend, Miss Felicia Scatcherd, a well-known 'sensitive', that 'two photographs of fairies had been taken in the North of England under circumstances which seemed to put fraud out of the question'.[49]

The appearance of spirits on photographs was by this time nothing new. The first such photographs had been produced by a photographer named Mumler in Boston, Mass., in 1860; he was later successfully prosecuted for fraud. However, the fashion had caught on, and there was no stopping it. Everywhere, spirit 'extras' began to appear on photographs. Shadowy figures, readily identifiable as dead relatives, hovered behind live sitters. Sometimes the face was not blurred, but perfectly recognizable. In these cases, it almost certainly strongly resembled the face in an existing photograph.

The ease with which such photographs could be faked – by double exposure, or prepared plates – was admitted by all. Determined sitters went to the photographer armed with their own, marked, plates; even so, the spirit 'extras' often appeared. The usual people – Houdini, Maskelyne – showed, time and again, exactly how simple the production of such photographs was. All the best-known photographers specializing in these productions, notably Mumler and Hudson in the United States, Boursnell and Hope in England, were shown up as frauds more than once, but, as usual, this did not deter enthusiasts.

One such was W.T.Stead. One of Stead's proudest possessions was a photograph taken by Boursnell showing the seated Stead in front of a shadowy figure later determined to be the Boer commander Piet Botha. The photograph was taken in 1902; Botha died in 1899. Stead, always much interested in South African affairs and a supporter of the Boer cause, knew several Bothas but no Piet. The photographer, however, insisted that this Botha was the deceased general. 'That's what he says,' he repeated doggedly. Subsequently, Stead sent a copy of the picture to Botha's relatives, who confirmed that it was indeed he. Stead asserted that no one in England could have had access to a portrait of Botha, and that indeed nobody had even known he existed.

This claim was taken up by J.N.Maskelyne, who found that after Botha died at the siege of Kimberley on 24 October 1899, news of the event was reported in the *Daily Graphic*, together with a portrait of the deceased. This finding was ignored by Stead and his fellow enthusiasts. 'Maskelyne . . . had the usual qualifications of "experts." [He] possessed no knowledge whatever of the subject but made up for that with abundant animus,' said one.[50] Stead himself commented:

I am quite willing to admit . . . that it is absolutely impossible to prevent a clever photographer, who is also a skilful conjurer, producing faked photographs which have the appearance of spirit pictures. I am also willing to admit, although it is quite contrary to reasonable commonsense, that even if you take your own plates, place them yourself in the camera, and afterwards develop them yourself, without allowing a photographer to have access to them, it is still possible that the spirit picture which appears on the negative may be the result of fraud. But when all that is said and done, my faith in the reality of some spirit photographs is invincible, and for this reason. Fraud can do many things, conjurers can deceive the eye of the most vigilant observer, but there are limits to fraud and conjuring. . . . The story of the Piet Botha photograph is well known. When I went to sit with Mr Boursnell I did not know that Piet Botha was dead. He appeared, much to Mr Boursnell's surprise, in the studio, was photographed standing behind me, and when asked by Mr Boursnell, at my suggestion, what was his name, he said it was Piet Botha. Subsequent research proved that a Botha, whose name was not given as Piet, had been killed at an early period of the Boer War. A portrait of this Botha had been published in a London illustrated paper. It bore not the least resemblance to the Piet Botha on the Boursnell picture.[51]

Such were typical claims and counter-claims in the spirit photographs controversy: and it will come as no surprise to learn that Conan Doyle was wholeheartedly on the supporters' side against that of the sceptics. He was much excited by Miss Scatcherd's report. He himself was very busy at the time – he was just off on one of his tours, this time to Australia – so he sent off a trusted friend, a Mr Edward Gardner, a member of the Executive Committee of the Theosophical Society, to investigate.

The fairies had been encountered by Frances Griffiths, aged ten, and her cousin Elsie Wright, then sixteen, in the countryside around the Griffiths family home at Cottingley in Yorkshire. When Gardner first visited the girls in 1920, it was three years since the pictures had been taken. His report was all enthusiasm. He found out the names and address of the girls, and wrote to them asking to see copies of the photographs.

> The correspondence that followed seemed so innocent and promising that I begged the loan of the actual negatives – and two quarter-plates came by post a few days after. . . . The negatives proved to be truly astonishing photographs indeed, for there was no sign of double exposure nor anything other than ordinary straightforward work. I cycled over to Harrow to consult an expert photographer of thirty years' practical experience whom I knew I could trust for a sound opinion. Without any explanation I passed the plates over and asked what he thought of them. After examining the 'fairies' negative carefully, exclamations began: 'This is the most extraordinary thing I've ever seen!' 'Single exposure!' 'Figures have moved!' 'Why, it's a genuine photograph! Wherever did it come from?'[52]

It may be stated at once that the photographs were, as might be imagined, fakes. The 'fairies' were cardboard cut-outs, the originals being taken from a drawing illustrating a poem by Alfred Noyes entitled 'A Spell for a Fairy' in *Princess Mary's Gift Book*, published 1915.

(For a detailed examination of the whole Cottingley business, the techniques used and how the fakery was proved, readers are referred to the relevant chapter in James Randi's *Flim-Flam.*) It is anyway clear that, if cut-outs were being used, there would be no need for double exposure. However, Gardner, being assured that on the contrary everything was genuine, was naturally much excited. He travelled up to Yorkshire and asked Frances and Elsie if they could repeat their earlier photographic feat. Unexpectedly, they said they could, so long as they were left to themselves and not disturbed by extraneous observers. The reasons for this are of course now obvious, but Gardner suspected nothing, and was delighted when three more photographs were forthcoming.

Doyle was so enchanted with all this that, on his return, he immediately published an article about the fairies. This appeared in the Christmas 1920 number of *The Strand Magazine*, illustrated with the first two photographs of the fairies. The article was not received uncritically. Some papers just laughed. *Truth* begged Elsie, now that she had made her effect, to come clean and tell the eager public how it was all done. The *Westminster Gazette* conducted its own investigation, which ended non-committally: 'There is an old saying in Yorkshire: "Ah'll believe what Ah see," which is still maintained as a valuable maxim.'[53] Conan Doyle was deluged with fake photographs of fairies, some of which, he said, were excellent in their way, but none of which passed the eagle-eyed scrutiny of Gardner and himself. There was 'a weird but effective arrangement' done by Judge Docker, of Australia; the elves of Miss Ida Inman, of Bradford, were so good that the two fairy-seekers were, for some weeks, in two minds as to their authenticity, but, finally, 'clever as they were, there was nothing of the natural grace and freedom of movement which characterize the wonderful Cottingley fairy group'.[54] But what finally stilled Doyle's doubts was the conviction that two little girls, inexpert photographers at that, could never have hatched and carried through so complex and professional a trickery.

It was the old, old story – the story, indeed, with which this book began; and, like the Fox sisters, Frances and Elsie saw their childish prank grow and ramify until it took on a life of its own, making it increasingly impossible for them to back out. For, not content with his article, Doyle now prepared to publish a book on the subject. *The Coming of the Fairies* was published in 1922. It contained a full account of the affair, and had in addition chapters entitled 'Independent Evidence for Fairies', 'Some Subsequent Cases' and 'The Theosophic

View of Fairies'. For added corroboration, a clairvoyant had been taken to the scenes of the original fairy appearances and had, inevitably, seen the creatures for himself.

How could he do it? How could this intelligent, gifted man allow himself to be carried away by such childish fantasies, how to such a degree abandon ordinary sense and expose himself to ridicule? For this was surely of an order different from anything Stead or Lodge had done or written. The answer is perhaps to be found in Doyle's self-view, and sense of his message, compared to theirs. Both Stead and Lodge had essentially been conveying a personal message. Being successful, confident members of the most successful, confident nation on earth, they were not particularly concerned with what people thought of them. They had received this revelation, and they published it because it might help others, as indeed it did. The difference between them was that, by the time Lodge came upon his truth, the whole desperate world was agog for something of the sort.

But Doyle had passed beyond this realm to something altogether larger and more grandiose. He saw himself, increasingly, as a prophet of the future of the whole world. The cataclysm of the First World War had revived occult interest in the fate of Atlantis, and the lessons to be drawn from this earlier catastrophe. The Doyles were now put in personal contact with a guide to this uncertain future, an Arabian spirit called Pheneas who communicated through Jean Doyle's automatic writing. In 1923 Pheneas told the Doyles that the world was 'sinking into a slough of evil and materialism' because of the presence on earth of thousands of evil spirits who had never gone beyond the first of the spiritual planes. 'God's own light must descend and burn up the evil fumes,' he said, and to this end a band of spiritual scientists was already at work 'connecting vibratory lines of seismic power' to produce the tidal waves and earthquakes which would herald the end. Doyle had his particular place in this programme. He must 'prepare men's minds so that when the awakening comes they shall be ready to receive it'. He would act as 'a battery to others' and 'the whole world . . . in its great extremity' would 'cling' to his record of the revelations.

By 1925, Pheneas was giving specific details of the coming calamities. Central Europe was to be engulfed, from west to east, by storms and earthquakes, followed by 'a great light from on high'. America would be riven once more by civil war. Russia would be destroyed, Africa flooded, Brazil would suffer 'an eruption of an extraordinary kind', and the Vatican, 'that sink of iniquity', would be wiped off the earth. In this dark world, England would be the 'beacon light'. The beacon would flash especially strongly from the 'power-station' which was being erected round the Doyle home in Sussex. This had already been approached by Christ, and he would soon make his presence known there, before retiring to make his preparations for the second coming. Doyle kept a small notebook entitled *Prophesied Course of Events*, in which he recorded that 'the whole process will take some years, but I shall survive till the end, then pass over with my whole family'. But 1925 passed without any untoward happenings. Pheneas explained that preparations were taking longer than expected, as the enemy's strength had been underrated. English spiritualists mean-while prepared for the catastrophe: they seriously considered how they would distribute their literature when it happened, in the event of 'interruption of railway communication'.[55]

Shortly before his death in 1930, Doyle wrote to a friend that he had begun to wonder if he and Jean had been 'victims of some extra-ordinary prank played upon the human race from the other side', since none of the Pheneas predictions had yet been fulfilled. But he had little time left to worry about this. On 7 July 1930 he died, surrounded by his family. Four days later, they gave a garden party to celebrate his translation to the other side.

8

The Rejection of Disbelief

First objection: 'These manifestations are produced by machinery, trickery or deception.' – This has long since been discarded. No one who has examined the manifestations, will for a moment doubt that they are produced independent of all human agency. – JOHN S. ADAMS, *Answers to Seventeen Objections Against Spiritual Intercourse and Inquiries*, 1853

Don't you see, my friends, that if the evidence of Spiritualism was so abundant as they declare, there could be no sceptics? – PROF. J.STANLEY GRIMES, Boston, 1864

On 21 October 1888 a momentous event in the history of spiritualism took place. On that day, in the New York Academy of Music, in front of a packed house including representatives of all the American press, Maggie Fox publicly confessed that spiritualism, as far as she was concerned, had been nothing but an imposture from the beginning.

The confession could not have been more detailed and circumstantial. Barefooted, Maggie demonstrated time and again that the mysterious 'Rochester raps' had been produced by nothing more than a cultivated abnormality of her big toe. A committee of five doctors was invited on to the platform to hold her foot and confirm – as those other committees forty years previously had so signally failed to confirm – the truth of this statement. Maggie's sister, Kate Fox, sitting in a box overlooking the stage, confirmed the truth of everything Maggie was saying. The raps so produced sounded, according to Moncure Conway, who was present, like 'a muffled hammer, but I heard every stroke from the farthest part of the balcony'.[1] The effect of the show, he reported, was in a way comic, and some of the younger members of the audience laughed; but it was not without its tragic side, as spiritualists throughout the house cried out at having to face again the loss of loved ones they had thought restored to them for ever through the ministrations of those who had followed the Fox sisters.

Why had Maggie suddenly felt impelled, after so long, to take this astonishing action, which – quite apart from anything else – instantly destroyed her livelihood? The answer was that this was no sudden decision. For many years now, both she and Kate, to whom she remained much attached, had been leading hellish lives. While Leah moved from strength to strength, they declined into squalor. Both, now, were miserable drunkards; both, now widows – if, indeed, Maggie had ever been married. Dr Kane was a hazy memory, a constantly frustrating consciousness of promises unredeemed. Mr Jencken, Kate's husband, had died in 1881, and with him any hope of stability for her or her two children. Early in 1888 the New York Society for the Prevention of Cruelty to Children had taken charge of these boys, Ferdy and Henry, when their mother was arrested for drunkenness and idleness. Maggie, by a ruse, had got them out of this custody and over to England, where she then was, and where their uncle Edward, their legal guardian, resided. She had then taken ship for America, and had experienced the greatest difficulty in resisting the urge to commit suicide by jumping overboard during the voyage. The only thing which had sustained her was the knowledge that, at long last, she was going to get her own back on Leah. She gave a reporter who interviewed her a short while before the lecture a demonstration of her powers. Rappings sounded under her feet, then under the chair on which the reporter sat, then under a table on which he was leaning. When he sat at the piano, the instrument reverberated. He, like so many before him, was dumbfounded. 'How do you do it? Is it all really a trick?' he asked. 'Absolutely. Spirits? Is he not easily fooled?' she replied bitterly.[2]

Did this bombshell, which received great publicity, then mark the end of spiritualism? Readers will know that it did not. Too much had been invested by too many people for the ravings of a poor alcoholic to be credited if they could be dismissed – and what could be easier to dismiss than the ravings of a poor alcoholic? Leah continued opulently on her way, turning in disgust from the degradation of her sisters. The Society for Psychical Research, which had recently been founded, was at its most active. The great days of Paladino were about to begin. Maggie and Kate Fox, however, were finished. Kate and her sons had been receiving some financial help from her old friend the banker Horace Livermore, whose wife she had 'materialized' at the beginning of the 1870s, but this now ceased. Maggie had had no such friend, and had relied on giving shows for a living, occasionally helped out by Kate. She was soon destitute. She appealed to Henry Newton, a kind and wealthy man and a leading spiritualist, to help restore her standing with the movement. She offered to recant her lecture in a written confession which he could publish. He accepted the offer, but the confession was so incoherent that it was never published – only a statement that she had retracted. For a while Newton allowed her to live in an apartment he owned on 51st Street, but her drunken ways soon became an embarrassment, and she went to live with an old friend, Emma Ruggles, in Brooklyn. There she died in 1895, and was buried in a pauper's grave, where she was very soon joined by her sister Kate.

The Fox sisters' hopeless end was all of a piece with the rest of their lives. Who knows what they must have felt in those days when it became apparent that, far from destroying spiritualism, they had barely made a dent in the edifice? Fury? Relief? Shame? A sort of pride in the indestructibility of their creation? Was it possible that people perhaps knew something which had never been made manifest to them? Judging from their personal experience that must have seemed doubtful. But what more could they do? They had begun it all; they should know the truth of the matter. They could not force people to believe them.

In their state of degradation at the time this confession was made it was not, of course, hard to discredit it and them. But what is perhaps surprising is the absolute refusal of modern commentators to accept that Maggie and Kate were ever to be believed on the different occasions when they were moved to confess to fraud. It will be remembered that, very early on, Kate had explained to her aunt, Mrs Culver, exactly how the raps were produced. Brian Inglis, writing in 1977, dismissed this as 'sheer invention on Mrs Culver's part', preferring to believe a friend of Leah's and contemporary promoter of spiritualism, E.W.Capron.[3] The 1888 confession is dismissed equally peremptorily: 'Anybody with even a slight acquaintance with [Margaret Fox's] history could have seen that it was spurious.'[4] Another learned and exhaustive historian of the movement, Alan Gauld, is also dismissive of both confessions, and goes on to explain why:

> The trouble with all toe, ankle and knee theories [of rappings] is the absolute failure of their proponents (including Margaret Fox) to tell precisely how the joints or members could be manipulated so as to reproduce the famous rappings in a convincing way. Quite a few people who could crack their toes or their knees came forward to give public demonstrations

of their powers; but no toe-cracker of whom I have heard could tap out a rhythm in the least comparable to that which any one of the Fox sisters could produce on a good day. The sisters could obtain not just regular rappings, but arpeggios and cadenzas of raps at a rate not unlike that of a musician playing a fast passage.[5]

It is difficult, concludes Dr Gauld, to imagine that such performances could ever have been coaxed from mere human toes. So it is; but one may perhaps wonder on exactly what evidence Dr Gauld bases his certainty that the Fox sisters produced such performances? One thing is certain – he never, unless in a previous incarnation, heard them himself. As for the accounts of excited witnesses, the history of both psychical research and psychology has shown time and again wild discrepancies between the extraordinary feats described by observers after an event and the relatively disappointing reality of what took place as noted and recorded at the time.

In both these respects – the anticlimatic nature of their later career, and the fact that they confessed only to retract when it became apparent that nobody was going to believe them anyway – the Fox sisters were typical of many other mediums; although in both respects their experience was more extreme than that of the others.

In fact the only medium of any note never either to confess or be exposed was D.D.Home, but having scaled the heights of his career and mystified all comers in the early 1870s, he went, literally, into a decline. The tuberculosis which had been his first reason for leaving America and coming to Europe finally caught up with him, having already killed his first wife. The second Madame Home, also a Russian lady, survived him, and spent the best part of her time thereafter writing up the story of her late husband's miraculous life and career. He remains the one case invariably cited by those who wish to adduce the supernatural nature of the 'physical manifestations' so popular in the nineteenth century. But others, even when apparently discredited, retain their adherents.

It might, for example, seem impossible that anyone could still have faith in Florence Cook and 'Katie King' in the face not only of numerous exposures but also of the circumstantial confession discussed in an earlier chapter. But in a long examination of the affair published in the *Proceedings* of the SPR in 1964, two respected psychical researchers, Dr Medhurst and Mrs Goldney, are obviously much inclined to dismiss all the contrary evidence and give Miss Cook the benefit of the doubt. In the course of their discussion they touch upon the work of the Seybert Commission in Philadelphia and the damning, though utterly good-natured, indictment of 'materializing mediums' by its diligent secretary, Dr Furness:

> Before me, as far as I can detect, stands the very Medium herself, in shape, size, form, and feature true to a line; and yet, one after another, honest men and women at my side, within ten minutes of each other, assert that she is the absolute counterpart of their nearest and dearest friends, nay that she *is* that friend. It is as incomprehensible to me as the assertion that the heavens are green and the leaves of the trees deep blue.

To which Dr Medhurst and Mrs Goldney add the rider, 'It should be added that we have no information regarding Dr Furness's abilities as an observer. He says of himself that he found it difficult to attend seances without being recognized because "my ear-trumpet soon makes me a marked man", though of course his *vision* may have been acute.' What could be more childish than such a comment?

Other defensive reactions go beyond childishness into the realms of the most extraordinary casuistry. At the trial of a certain notorious Dr Monck, whose luggage, on examination, revealed two large boxes and a travelling bath filled with trick apparatus, including spirit hands, spirit masks, a large quantity of gauzy material (for producing the emanations from which the materialized spirit emerged), a spirit bird, apparatus for floating tambourines, bells and spirit lamps, it was alleged that while he was staying at Huddersfield he had refused to be searched by his host, a Mr Lodge. When the other sitters begged him to submit to the search, he rushed at Mr Lodge, tried to punch him on the nose, then bolted upstairs, locked himself into his room, and let himself out of the window by a rope made of the bed-sheets. When the door was eventually opened the whole bag of tricks lay revealed. Testifying for Monck at the trial, Alfred Russel Wallace was asked, 'Have you ever heard of a medium who was not exposed in the end?' He replied, 'On the contrary, I have heard of very few who were exposed. Monck was not caught in the act of trickery. Monck was a guest on that occasion, and a demand was made that he should be searched, and he departed through the window.'[6]

Many more such examples could be cited, but perhaps the most interesting of all the discounted confessions is that which was made by Mrs Piper. For a great many people who found themselves quite unconvinced by the Fox sisters, Paladino, even Home, nevertheless retained their faith in the possibility of supernormal manifestations on account of Mrs Piper.

On 20 October 1901, the *New York Herald* devoted two and a half

pages to a statement by Mrs Piper. The piece had the headline: I AM
NO TELEPHONE TO THE SPIRIT WORLD. In it Mrs Piper did not,
indeed, say that she had ever cheated. What she did say was that she
was not a spiritualist, had never had any convincing proof of the
possibility of spirit return, and 'am inclined to accept the telepathic
explanation of the so-called psychic phenomena, but beyond this I
remain a student with the rest of the world'. What is to be made of this
effusion? Commenting on the subject, the psychologists Hans Eysenck
and Carl Sargent tell us that this 'sensationalised "Confession"
should not be taken too seriously.'[7] But there seems no reason to
dismiss it out of hand. The packaging is sensational, certainly, but the
text is perfectly sober.

Richard Hodgson and William James were the investigators who
were principally concerned with Mrs Piper at this time. James, questioned by the *Herald* about the spiritualistic hypothesis, said that he
was still 'sitting on the fence', and referred them to an article he had
written three years previously for the *Psychological Review* about Mrs
Piper. In this, James had discussed the various possible hypotheses
which might account for the Piper phenomena. Of these hypotheses,
he said,

> each seems more unnatural than the rest. Any definitely known form of
> fraud seems out of the question; yet undoubtedly, could it be made prob-
> able, fraud would be by far the most satisfying explanation, since it would
> leave no further problems outstanding.
>
> The spirit hypothesis exhibits a vacancy, triviality and incoherence of
> mind painful to think of as the state of the departed; and coupled there-
> withal a pretension to impress one, a disposition to 'fish' and face round
> and disguise the essential hollowness which are, if anything, more painful
> still. Mr Hodgson has to resort to the theory that, although the communi-
> cants probably are spirits, they are in a semi-comatose or sleeping state
> while communicating, and are only half aware of what is going on, while
> the habits of Mrs Piper's neural organism largely supply the definite form
> of words, &c., in which the phenomenon is clothed.

Other possibilities were that the whole thing was a result of the cavort-
ings of Mrs Piper's unconscious mind, 'using its preternatural powers
of cognition and memory for the basest of deceits', which James
thought fairly probable but, if true, distressing: 'The humbugging and
masquerading extra-marginal self is as great a paradox for psychology
as the comatose spirits are for pneumatology.' And finally there was
the possibility of 'a sort of floating mind-stuff in the world, intra-human,
yet possessed of fragmentary gleams of super-human cognition,

unable to gather itself together except by taking advantage of the trance-states of some existing human organism and there enjoying a parasitic existence, which it prolongs by making itself acceptable and plausible under the improvised name of a spirit control'.[8]

For James, then, Mrs Piper, in saying that she did not communicate with spirits, was simply ruling out one of several possibilities. As to other opinions, Houdini thought she was certainly fraudulent; but Houdini thought that about all mediums, presumably extrapolating from what his own actions would have been in similar circumstances, and he never seems actually to have met Mrs Piper. And, as we have seen, her seances while staying with Oliver Lodge seem to have indicated adroit fishing and deduction, rather than downright fraud. But as far as the general public was concerned – and Mrs Piper was among the most famous mediums of her day, and by now made a very substantial living in this way – the confession was a bombshell: for her quite unequivocal claim in the period immediately before this was that she had been in communication with departed spirits, notably that of one George Pellew, known as G.P.

Many people saw Mrs Piper's G.P. control as perhaps the strongest proof yet adduced of the possibility of communing with departed spirits. Pellew, in life, had been a young New York lawyer and lit-térateur of great promise. He had died in an accident, and among Mrs Piper's clients were many who had known him in life. Some of these affirmed that spirit return could be the only explanation of Mrs Piper's feats of recall concerning Pellew's ways and life; the instance most generally put forward being an occasion on which she had correctly said that some papers, which had been lost, were to be found in a certain tin box whose whereabouts she gave. But Pellew's family could never accept that Mrs Piper's G.P. had anything to do with their son and brother, and even discounted the tin box story: the box, it seemed, had indeed been where Mrs Piper said it was, but it was empty – Pellew had given those papers to a friend shortly before his death. Pellew's brother commented, 'This was almost the only time Mrs Piper ever came near, so far as I know, to saying anything that might conceivably have come from my brother.'

Richard Hodgson was quite convinced of the Pellew identity, 'as was every other intelligent and unprejudiced reader', as he wrote to Pellew's parents. Pellew's mother, however, could not agree with Hodgson. Her son had been exceptionally brilliant in life, hampered only by a weak body. Once freed from that, she was sure that his soaring intellect would have known no bounds, and could certainly not, as his brother put it, 'under any conceivable circumstances, have given vent to such utter drivel and inanity as purported, in those communications, to have been uttered by him'.[9]

Be that as it may, it is clear that Hodgson was by no means able to share James's detachment as to the source of Mrs Piper's strange powers. He was sure that she was in touch with the spirit world, and that his experiments with her proved its existence; and this knowledge was of the greatest personal importance to him. James, his friend and mentor, noted the calm and serenity, the improvement in looks and character, which his studies in the field of psychical research had given him – an effect similar to that which they had had upon F.W.H.Myers. This alone was enough to convince James, who held these two in the highest regard, that there was something in it all, and something supremely worth knowing.

For Hodgson, then, Mrs Piper's statement that she was not a spiritualist must have come as an absolute bombshell. He immediately set about rectifying the damage. Five days after the *Herald* piece had appeared, on 25 October 1901, the *Boston Advertiser* printed a statement: 'I did not make any such statement as they published in the *New York Herald* to the effect that spirits of the departed do not control me. . . . Spirits of the departed may have controlled me and they may not. I confess that I do not know.' And next day, on 26 October, Hodgson announced in the *Westminster Gazette* that 'Mrs Piper had not discontinued her sittings for the society and that the statement made by her represented simply a transient mood'. It is perhaps not surprising that when Hodgson himself died in 1906 his spirit, together with that of Myers, should have become one of Mrs Piper's most constant visitants. She never again expressed any doubts about the authenticity of her spirit visitors, but went on receiving them, and passing on messages from the other world through their good offices, until her career ended peacefully with her death in 1919. (It may be remembered that it was she, through the agency of Myers, who first passed on messages about Raymond to Sir Oliver Lodge in 1915.) As for her personal opinions, she kept these to herself henceforth.

There are various features which link this string of confessions and discredited mediums – whether they were discredited out of their own or other people's mouths. The most obvious is that, although each of them may have disillusioned a certain number of people with spiritualism in general or, more specifically, with the particular medium in question, they did not stop the forward march of the spiritualist movement or of psychical research in general. Margaret Fox's confession was later expanded into a book, hopefully entitled by its author, Reuben Davenport, *A Death-Blow to Spiritualism*; but it was, of course, nothing of the sort – merely a death-blow to the unfortunate Fox sisters. The new-found faith of the hitherto hyper-critical Richard Hodgson was unshaken by Mrs Piper's aberration, which he soon took steps to correct. Paradoxically, the fact that these people were the original source of faith had, as it turned out, nothing to do with the faith itself, which soon became larger than they were and took over as an entity in its own right.

This was fortunate; for the outstanding characteristic of the leading spiritualist mediums was their singular lack of prophetic stature. Who could build a faith on the Fox sisters? What had D.D.Home to offer other than an exceptional range of conjuring tricks? Were Paladino or Eva C. credible fountainheads of a new revelation? Each had a particular and limited repertoire which soon, and inevitably, began to pall as fresh novelties were produced. By that time it was relatively unimportant if they faded away, like Eva (who got married and disappeared from view in 1920), or, like the Fox sisters and Paladino, sank further and further out of the public's view and into a slough of general discredit and lack of interest. There could be no greater contrast than that between the stature and earnestness of most of the leading psychical researchers and the often grotesque triviality of their subject.

The one shining exception to this rule was, as usual, Madame Blavatsky. This is not, of course, to say that she was never exposed as a fraud, or never confessed. On the contrary, she was shown up perhaps more comprehensively than any other single medium, by Hodgson in his report to the SPR in 1885; while as for confessions, she was always making them with a brazenness that amounted almost to pleasure. But her personal stature, intelligence and charisma were such that none of this seemed to matter in the least. Thus Henry Sidgwick wrote in 1885, while Hodgson was in Madras conducting his investigations:

> We talked over Theosophy, of which Hodgson keeps us amply informed by weekly accounts of his investigation. His opinion of the evidence seems to be growing steadily more unfavourable; but there are still some things difficult to explain on the theory of fraud. I have no doubt, however, that Blavatsky has done most of it. She is a great woman.

And a month later he reported:

> Hodgson came back from Madras. He has no doubt that all Theosophic

marvels are and were a fraud from beginning to end. He thinks Madame Blavatsky a remarkable woman, possibly working for motives of Russian patriotism and Russian pay to foment native discontent. . . .[10]

This is not to say that Madame Blavatsky acquiesced, then or ever, with Hodgson's accusations. On the contrary, she angrily rejected them – being especially indignant at the notion that she might be thought a Russian agent. Generally, though, and not surprisingly in view of their sober, painstaking and circumstantial nature, they were believed. But – and this is where Madame Blavatsky was unique – her personal standing was in no way affected by them. The most usual reaction was that evinced by Sidgwick and Hodgson. Thus W.B.Yeats, meeting her some years later, compared her to William Morris, who was then his great hero. He admired them both, he said, for the same reason:

> They had more human nature than anybody else; they at least were unforeseen, illogical, incomprehensible. Perhaps I escaped when I was near them from the restlessness of my own mind. She sat there all evening, talking to whoever came – vast and shapeless of body, and perpetually rolling cigarettes – humorous and unfanatic, and displaying always, it seemed, a mind that seemed to pass all others in her honesty. Unlike those about her, I had read with care the Psychical Research Society's charge of fraudulent miracle-working. 'She is a person of genius,' Henley had said to me, 'but a person of genius must do something – Sarah Bernhardt sleeps in her coffin.' I could not accept this explanation, but finding those charges, so weightily supported, incompatible with what I saw and heard, awaited with impatience the explanation that never came. To her devout followers she was more than a human being. . . .[11]

Yeats himself witnessed some miracles, or apparent miracles, while in her presence – a picture in the next room was there one moment, gone the next. Madame Blavatsky herself accepted this occurrence in the most matter-of-fact way. It is highly possible that it was the effect of hypnotic suggestion working on a willing mind. On another occasion J.N.Maskelyne saw her, in conversation with a nervous gentleman whom she wished to convert to theosophy, roll up her handkerchief and throw it on the floor saying it was a poisonous snake. The man ran away in terror and it was long before he would believe he had not seen a snake.

Hodgson alleged, among other things, that mysterious letters purporting to come from the Tibetan Mahatmas who were at the core of theosophical teaching were one and all written by Madame Blavatsky herself, and that mysterious phenomena taking place at the theosophists' central shrine at their headquarters in India were also produced by H.P.B, whose bedroom conveniently backed on to the shrine. The

shrine itself was a cedarwood cupboard, about four feet square and
fifteen inches deep, lacquered in black. It was placed against the wall
which divided Madame Blavatsky's bedroom from the occult room,
and was suspended by thick wires from hooks in the ceiling. Around it
were curtains seven feet high which were drawn aside when anyone
wished to consult it. When Hodgson voiced his suspicions a devout
theosophist called T. Vijiarghava Charlu struck the back of the shrine
with his hand, saying, 'You see, it's quite solid.' At this, the middle
panel of the back flew up. The shrine was removed forthwith, and
broken to pieces and burned next night. The walls of the occult room
were then replastered, but traces of the aperture which had originally
existed between the two rooms still remained.[12]

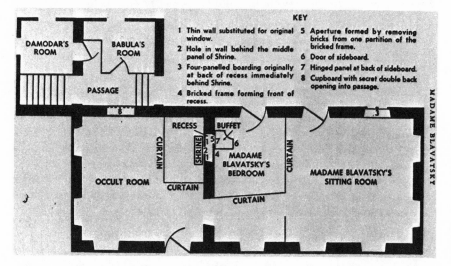

Plan showing the layout of the 'shrine' at the Theosophical Society
headquarters in India

All these things (and there were a great many more) should have
been utterly damning. Yet somehow they seemed almost irrelevant. As
a Blavatsky follower wrote many years later, in a book which set out to
answer Hodgson's charges, 'The S.P.R. Report cannot today – nor,
indeed, did it at the time – make any difference to those for whom
Theosophy, the *Ancient Wisdom Religion*, has been the great TRUTH.'[13]
And indeed H.P.B herself was entirely unabashed by it. When Annie
Besant, later to take over as the society's leader, first proposed to join
the theosophists, Madame Blavatsky asked her: 'Have you ever read

the report about me by the S.P.R?' 'No,' said Mrs Besant, 'I never heard of it.' 'Then go and read it, and if after reading it you come back – well.' Mrs Besant took a copy home and read it. She says, 'I laughed aloud at the absurdity, and flung the report aside with the righteous scorn of an honest nature that knew its own kin when it met them, and shrank from the foulness of a lie.' She went back to Madame Blavatsky and literally flung herself into her arms. After the embrace Madame, looking into Mrs Besant's eyes, said: 'You are a noble woman. May Master bless you!'[14]

At the time the Hodgson report appeared, Madame Blavatsky had yet to write *The Secret Doctrine* (the work which converted Mrs Besant to theosophy), *The Key to Theosophy*, and *The Voice of the Silence*. Her description of her technique in writing these and other theosophical works, notably *Isis Unveiled*, very much recalls W.T.Stead in its severely practical view of the uses to which occult gifts may be put:

> I make what I can only describe as a sort of vacuum in the air before me and fix my sight and my will upon it, and soon scene after scene passes before me like the successive pictures of a diorama, or, if I need a reference or information from some book, I fix my mind intently, and the astral counterpart of the book appears, and from it I take what I need.

If her mind was distracted, however, she complained that the quotations tended to be wrong.[15]

The paradoxical thing about Madame Blavatsky was that although her signal qualities were recognized by everyone, including (as we have seen) the most high-minded thinkers, she never interested them, even when they believed in her, as much as did such relatively trivial performers as Home, Paladino and Eva C. Possibly this was because she supplied her own weird philosophy, while the mere wonder-workers, in their various ways, provided a clean sheet upon which interested persons could inscribe their own personal systems and arabesques. When Madame Blavatsky died in London in 1891, she had the satisfaction of knowing that a woman of the calibre of Annie Besant was waiting to pick up the torch. But theosophy remained the preserve of a few dedicated occultists, while spiritualism, in its various forms, continued to attract the attention and avid interest of some of the most brilliant minds of the age.

'Religion', wrote William James, 'is the great interest of my life'; and, as we have seen, he thought that spiritualism if it were true, presented the great way forward for religion, unlikely as that might seem. He recognized its absurdities – he had, he wrote in the preface to his collection of essays *The Will to Believe*, first been attracted to psychical research by 'my love of sportsmanlike fair play in science' – but they did not particularly worry him. In the eponymous first essay of that collection he wrote: 'Our errors are surely not such awfully solemn things. In a world where we are so certain to incur them in spite of all our caution, a certain lightness of heart seems healthier than this excessive nervousness on their behalf.'

James, then, began with a certain philosophical disposition towards spiritualism which was to be at least partially confirmed by his experiences with Mrs Piper, his 'one white crow'. And there were some other psychical researchers, notably F.W.H.Myers, who trod a very similar path – from inclination to confirmation. Myers wrote:

> I look upon Christ as a Revealer of immortality absolutely unique, as the incomparable Pioneer of all wisdom that shall be learnt concerning unseen things. But, like the Norseman's discover of America, his work grows more and more remote, and there are no other sea-marks for others to follow along the legendary way. A new discovery is needed . . . by the devotion of a world-wide labour to the deciphering of that open secret which has baffled the too hasty, or too self-centred wonder and wish of men . . . I believe, then, that Science is now succeeding in penetrating certain cosmical facts. . . . The first, of course, is the fact of man's survival of death. The second is the registration in the universe of every past scene and thought. This I hold to be indicated by the observed facts of clairvoyance and retrocognition; and to be itself probable as a mere extension of telepathy, which, when acting unrestrictedly, may render it impossible for us to appear as other than we are.[16]

(This, of course, is the consideration which makes many of us so thankful that telepathy, if it does exist, works so inefficiently!) For Myers, too, the Piper experiments were of the utmost importance – especially after the Paladino myth seemed to have been exploded; and it was surely this fundamental sympathy of approach which was the basis of James's great admiration for his work.

But this highly intellectual path was not the only way, or at all the most usual, in which people came to believe in spiritualism or its related phenomena – or, as it is more generally known today, psi. Then as now, the most usual way was that something strange and otherwise seemingly inexplicable had happened to them. The physicist Ernst Mach, yet another of the scientists who, at the turn of the century, interested themselves in such things, observed that 'the mere happening of an extraordinary event is in itself not marvellous; the marvel is to be sought, not in the event, but in the person observing the event.' When, asked Mach, does a phenomenon seem to be marvellous? It is 'when one's entire mode of thought is disturbed by it and forced out of its customary and familiar channels'. The astonished victim of such a happening is quite unable to accept that there is no connexion between the new happening and other phenomena, but since he can discern no such connexion, 'he is led, in the nature of the case, to adopt extra-ordinary conjectures'.

Mach, in the same article, goes on to tell the story of the 'girl struck by lightning' who ever afterwards, as a consequence, gave off electrical sparks. This girl was exhibited with other marvels at a fair, where she was seen by an old gentleman of Mach's acquaintance. He, much impressed, persuaded Mach to go along with him and view the girl. Mach 'recognised the sparks as those of a small Ruhmkorff coil, but was unable to discover the connexions, despite the fact that I had brought along with me a cane covered with a strip of tinfoil'. Where the physi-cist was stumped, however, his resourceful machinist was not. A good amateur conjurer, he soon worked out how the device functioned, fixed up his son in a similar manner, and was soon able to exhibit to the old gentleman the phenomenon of the 'boy struck by lightning'. The old gentleman was delighted, but when he was shown the simple device by which the effect was obtained, he refused to believe it, and went off declaring, 'No, that was not the way it was done!'[17]

In this resistance to explanation, the old gentleman was absolutely typical. Once they have decided that something is caused by a miracle, or by the supernatural, people are generally reluctant to relinquish this explanation in favour of something more humdrum. This reluc-tance has been exhibited time and again in the course of this book. But it is more than mere reluctance; it is a positive desire to believe that the magical thing has happened. An extreme example of this way of thinking is discussed by the novelist Henry James, brother of William, in one of his more superbly convoluted passages:

If once we lend ourselves to the hypothesis of posthumous renovation at all, the fact that our ex-fellow-mortals would appear to have taken up some very much better interest than the poor world they left might pass for a positively favourable argument. On the basis of their enjoying another state of being, we have certainly to assume that this is the case, for to the probability of a quite different case the inveteracy of their neglect of the previous one, through all the ages and the spaces, the grimness of their utter refusal, so far as we know it, of a retrospective personal sign, would seem directly to point.

Or, in other words, the fact that the dead do not communicate with the living does not necessarily mean there is no life after death. James, presumably with his brother in mind, went on to add, 'I can only treat here as absolutely not established the value of those personal signs that come to us through the trance medium. These often make, I grant, for attention and wonder and interest – but for interest above all in the medium and the trance.'[18]

The most likely path to firm belief, then, is personal experience of the apparently miraculous; and the fact is that some such experience is likely to happen to almost all of us. Andrew Lang, the writer and anthropologist, and an early and prominent member of the SPR, said, 'No-one is talking about "the supernatural". We are merely discussing the rather unusual.' But the kind of phenomena we are discussing are not particularly unusual. This was fully recognized by William James, who said, 'The first difference between the psychical researcher and the inexpert person is that the former realizes the commonness and typicality of the phenomenon here, while the latter, less informed, thinks it so rare as to be unworthy of attention. *I wish to go on record for the commonness.*'[19]

The phenomenon James was talking about was the tendency of the subconscious to be dominated by some external force 'impelling us to personation'; in other words, to be taken over by a 'control'. But a much more usual experience, and the one cited by most people as the reason why they believe that there are some things which simply cannot be explained, except by psi, or ESP, or whatever, is some extraordinary and quite inexplicable coincidence. Some such event seems to be the thing that sets most psychical researchers off on their chosen field.

An example of the extreme difficulty of seeing such experiences in any sort of detached light is given by a doctor who was a medical officer in the First World War. Just before an attack, it was not unusual for officers to bring him letters addressed to people at home, with the request that he should post them if the senders did not survive. 'Most of them stated quite clearly as a reason for this procedure a conviction which they were quite unable to explain, but which was of so overwhelming a character that, as they expressed it, they knew they were "for it" that night.' Sometimes this was of course true, but, even in the Great War, in the large majority of cases it was not. When survivors returned they took back the letters which were, happily, no longer applicable. 'Yet had I argued from any of the isolated cases where the letter was indeed posted by me, a clear case could undoubtedly have been made for a premonition having occurred,' wrote the MO.[20]

We may be thankful that such a generalized and multifarious overview of this kind of event is given to few people, but without it, the notion that one has undergone a unique and extraordinary experience is almost impossible to avoid. A compendium of such occurrences was one of the earliest substantial publications of the SPR. Entitled *Phantasms of the Living*, it was compiled by Myers, Frank Podmore and Edmund Gurney, and recorded cases where people had experienced hallucinations – auditory, visual, or of any other sort – of other people who were not in fact present but who were undergoing some traumatic event, such as death, accident or illness, at the time.

What the book shows is the deep and lasting impression made by this kind of experience, which often – indeed usually – sticks in the mind for a lifetime. What it does not offer is any proof of the prophetic or simultaneous nature of these events, except as existing in the mind of the recorder. Naturally Gurney, Myers and Podmore were eager to find this kind of confirmatory proof – for instance, dated letters describing an incident from both sides. And indeed in a few cases they stated that such proof existed, but it was found that none of the letters mentioned could actually be produced. In 1887, the year after the book was published, an article entitled 'Where Are the Letters?' appeared in *The Nineteenth Century*. The author, a Scottish lawyer named Taylor Innes, happened to know the family in which one of the incidents mentioned in the book, and described as having been confirmed by crossing letters, had taken place. An elder brother, according to the story, had dreamed that his younger brother had fallen and been spiked on some railings; an incident which had actually occurred, and which was confirmed in a letter from the mother to the elder brother describing the dream. Taylor Innes describes how he asked his acquaintance:

'Dr M—, where are the two letters which crossed?'
    There was no answer, but a long pause, for all the mind was for the first time troubled with a doubt. I ventured to press my question.
    'I remember your mother. There was no more intelligent lady in the north of Scotland. Had she received such a letter as you now believe you wrote, she would sooner have thrown a hundred-pound note into the fire than have destroyed it.'
    'You mean', he said slowly, 'that I also, at the other end of the circuit, in Aberdeen, would have done anything rather than part with the letter from my mother which I described, had I really received it.'

> I replied cautiously that what I meant rather was, that if the two letters with their postmarks could now be got, they would absolutely prove the case. . . . From that date I have never doubted that there are cases in which the absence of documentary evidence is nearly as conclusive against a story as the presence of such evidence would be in its favour.

And Innes then goes on to describe how none of the letters or documents mentioned in the book – not even where the authors say they have 'seen or ascertained' their existence – can actually be produced.

Undoubtedly, however, the incidents themselves do occur. People have seemingly prophetic dreams, unnerving experiences of hauntings or visitations; and they do remember these things – whether or not perfectly accurately as to points of timing, etc., is another question. How, if not by some sort of ESP, are they to be explained?

In the course of their fascinating book *The Psychology of the Psychic* two psychologists, David Marks and Richard Kammann, go into this very question. It so happens that Kammann experienced a dream of this sort. He had a nightmare in which he was continually running into the bathroom where his seven-year-old daughter was playing in the tub, and every time he was only just in time to prevent her from drowning because she was constantly slipping under the water. He mentioned this dream to his wife next day, and then forgot about it. A couple of weeks later the Kammanns were invited to a pool party at the home of some friends, in the course of which he suddenly noticed his daughter struggling in the deep end of the pool – she was unable to swim. He leapt in and pulled her out, and it was only later that he remembered his dream. 'The idea that the dream caused the pool incident seems absurd – if anything the dream should have made me more careful to prevent any accident. Nor could my memory of the dream have been revised to fit the facts, since I had already told it to my wife. After much discussion, I could only guess that it was precognition, but whatever it was, I never forgot it.'[21]

The explanation Kammann and Marks propose is the theory of what they call *oddmatches*. Here are two events, the dream and the pool incident, each containing very similar ingredients. They are thus a *match*. They are also an unexpected match, unlike the kinds of match which occur all the time in life, as when a key fits a door. In fact this type of match is distinctly odd, because it is not readily susceptible of explanation; and because of this quality it catches the imagination and is remembered. The greater the oddity, the longer it is remembered.

The question is whether this kind of event is likely to arise in the

course of life purely by chance, or whether (as parapsychologists believe) it is part of a whole system, or alternative universe, of such
events that time and systematic application must uncover. Kammann
and Marks do not believe this. They point out that 'it is a simple
deduction from probability theory that an event that is very improbable in the *short run* of observations becomes, nevertheless, highly probable somewhere in a *long run* of observations'. And what is a longer run
of observations than the whole of life? Small events are taking place in
our lives all the time. Mostly we have no cause to remember them;
but if two occur near enough together and like enough to make an
oddmatch, then we will remember them. Kammann and Marks point
out that 'even if we allowed only 10 events a day, and only 5 years, and
only 100 people, we still get a long run of over 8 million pairs of events'
which are statistically likely to give rise to a certain number of odd-
matches. And any oddmatch is liable to make a good psychic
mystery.[22]

It all seems so simple seen like this; and it can all seem so mysterious and extraordinary when seen as, for example, Arthur Koestler
sees it in such books as *The Roots of Coincidence*. And there can be no
doubt how most people want, and always have wanted, to see such
things. To make the point using the examples under discussion, *The
Roots of Coincidence* is a best seller that has gone through numerous
editions; *The Psychology of the Psychic*, an extraordinarily interesting
book, was turned down by sixteen publishers before it eventually saw
print.

What is it? What is this compulsion? Why are people so desperate
to believe in the supernatural that, even in the most extreme circumstances, the benefit of the doubt is *always* given? In his *Last Report*, in
which he summed up his feelings after his many years of research into
psychic phenomena, William James admitted that the absolute stasis,
the complete lack of progress, on the entire subject was an enormous
stumbling block. Henry Sidgwick had felt the same way: 'I heard him
say, the year before his death, that if anyone had told him at the outset
that after twenty years he would be in the same identical state of doubt
and balance that he started with, he would have deemed the prophecy
incredible. It appeared impossible that that amount of handling evidence should bring so little finality of decision.' Of himself James
said:

My own experience has been similar to Sidgwick's. For twenty-five years I
have been in touch with the literature of psychical research, and have had

acquaintance with numerous 'researchers'. I have also spent a good many hours (though far fewer than I ought to have spent) in witnessing (or trying to witness) phenomena. Yet I am theoretically no 'further' than I was at the beginning; and I confess that at times I have been tempted to believe that the Creator has eternally intended this department of nature to remain *baffling*, to prompt our hopes and curiosities and suspicions all in equal measure, so that, although ghosts and clairvoyances, and raps and messages from spirits, are always seeming to exist and can never fully be explained away, they also can never be susceptible of full corroboration.

James's reaction, however, was not downhearted. He wrote,

It is hard to believe, however, that the Creator has really put any big array of phenomena into the world merely to defy and mock our scientific tendencies; so my deeper belief is that we psychical researchers have been too precipitate with our hopes, and that we must expect to mark progress not by quarter-centuries, but by half-centuries or whole centuries.[23]

In this extraordinary passage James, perhaps the greatest mind ever to concern himself seriously and in detail with spiritualism and psychical research, shows how far he is prepared to go in order to preserve his belief that something is there at the bottom of it all. It is not so much that he knows there is something as that he is absolutely determined that there cannot be nothing.

In this as in all his other writings James is disarmingly, transparently and beautifully honest. In this passage it is quite clear that he is referring to that essentially religious impulse which he himself called 'the will to believe', at once the most exalted of motives for pursuing these researches and (as we have seen) for various reasons the one most often dissembled. Yet immediately, in the very next paragraph, he is pushed up against the baseness of so much of his research material. Just recently, he says, it has begun to seem as though much of the waiting may have been justified after all.

[A] faint but distinct step forward is being taken by competent opinion in these matters. 'Physical phenomena' . . . have been one of the most baffling regions of the general field (or perhaps one of the most baffling *prima facie*, so certain and great has been the part played by fraud in their production); yet even here the balance of testimony seems slowly to be inclining towards admitting the supernaturalist view.

And what, or who, was the basis for this renewed hope? None other than – Eusapia Paladino!

James was writing this in 1909, when, after a long period of decline and almost eclipse, Eusapia was once again in the front line of interest. Her most recent converts included three people hitherto extremely sceptical about her: two eminent Italian professors, Morselli, a psychiatrist, and Botazzi, a physiologist; and Hereward Carrington, a psychical researcher who had published a generally scathing book on *The Physical Phenomena of Spiritualism*. Did this mean, wondered James, that her dismissal by Hodgson and the Sidgwicks could now be overlooked?

> If Mr Podmore, hitherto the prosecuting attorney of the S.P.R. so far as physical phenomena are concerned, becomes converted also, we may indeed sit up and look around us. Getting a good health bill from 'Science,' Eusapia will throw retrospective credit on Home and Stainton Moses, Florence Cook ... and all similar wonder-workers. The balance of presumptions will be changed in favor of genuineness being possible at least, in all reports of this particularly crass and low type of supernatural phenomenon.[24]

The *Last Report* really does represent James's ultimate thoughts on spiritualism, for later in 1909 he died, his place at Harvard being taken by Hugo Muensterberg, who although he was a friend and protégé of James's did not share his views on psychical research. He was interested in it and its various manifestations as psychological phenomena, but was inclined to scepticism. When, in November 1909, Carrington brought Eusapia over to the United States to make a triumphant and confirmatory tour, Muensterberg welcomed the chance of testing her. So did another interested psychologist, Joseph Jastrow.

Muensterberg and Jastrow both adopted similar tactics. Muensterberg hid a confederate inside the cabinet, to see what transpired, while Jastrow hid his accomplice, dressed in black, under the seance table. In the middle of the seance Muensterberg's man caught hold of a foot which was picking up objects out of the alcove, and which turned out to be attached to Eusapia (both of whose feet were of course supposed to be 'controlled' at the time). Jastrow's man also observed her using her foot to pull objects out of the cabinet. This foot was also used to give a quick kick to the cabinet curtains, so that they bulged out towards the sitters (a well-known phenomenon of Eusapia's, and one which had mystified numerous sitters). Although the lights had by now been turned down the observer, Joseph Rinn, remarked that 'This was done several times so daringly that under the chairs where I lay it seemed impossible that the people above the table could not have observed it.'[25] Before this, she had used her free foot to jiggle the table in the time-honoured manner.

Of course none of this is, or was, new. Not surprisingly, this tour, far from confirming Eusapia's triumphant return, finally destroyed her reputation in the eyes of the general public. She retained the support of Carrington, and went on touring and giving her seances until not long before her death in in 1920, there being no other way she knew of making a living. But this poor creature bore little relation to the dominant and strangely alluring figure of the 1880s and 1890s.

In view of the Jastrow and Muensterberg findings, so clear-cut and which so strongly confirm each other, Eusapia's final discrediting cannot seem surprising. There is little of interest there. What is interesting is that the legend of her supernatural abilities was not destroyed by them but still survives; and the terms on which it survives throw a curious light on the phenomenon of bending over backwards in order to sustain belief.

Once again the most reasoned, and one of the most recent, discussions of these matters from the believer's point of view is to be found in Brian Inglis's book *Natural and Supernatural*. Of the débâcles of 1909 and 1910 he has this to say:

> Eusapia made no attempt to deny that if she was given the opportunity to cheat, in her trances, she might take it – particularly if that was what witnesses wanted; 'they think of tricks, nothing but tricks; they put their mind on the tricks and I automatically respond.' Yet in the light of what had been discovered in the course of the European investigations, it was far from certain that what had been described as 'feet' were Eusapia's feet. Neither Muensterberg nor Jastrow would have taken the 'pseudopod' hypothesis seriously; and their assistants were unlikely even to have heard about it. But given the possibility that she could produce psychic elongations, the experiments were simply not designed to distinguish between them and her arms and feet.[26]

Far more unlikely than the production of pseudopods, in Inglis's opinion, is the possibility that Eusapia, by now a 'fat, elderly lady', could have managed the contortions necessary to perform the actions observed by Jastrow and Muensterberg with her own limbs.

As between these two views of what was or was not most likely to be going on, it is hard to see that there can be any reasoned argument – given that argument can only take place if there is a certain common ground conceded. Is it really only a hardened and blind sceptic who finds it easier to believe that an elderly lady who has been doing the same tricks all her adult life may have retained a certain strength and suppleness, at least in regard to those particular contortions, than that she is capable of producing supernatural limbs about her person? (For a detailed description of Eusapia's techniques, and of her outstanding strength and suppleness when in her prime, see Maskelyne's account of her Cambridge seances in the appendix.)

The spiritual world got its own back on Muensterberg, at least. In the *Pall Mall Gazette* for 18 January 1917, it was recounted that Miss Caroline Pillsbury of Brookline, Mass., editor of *Boston Ideas*, claimed to have received a spirit message from the now defunct psychologist in which he said: 'Although I have been in the spirit world but a brief time, I have received absolute proof that excarnate beings can and do communicate with their earth friends. However valuable the messages I may bring in future time, this one today is important. Spirit return is truth. I am Hugo Muensterberg.'

The slightly crazy feeling arising from arguments of this sort – which may be taken to include nearly all the controversies we have looked at in the course of this book – arises from the application of a kind of mad logic to situations which are fundamentally not logical. The logical world is simply not what they are about. These controversies are therefore, and almost invariably, deeply unsatisfactory. They get bogged down in trivia of the basest and crassest sort, to borrow two eminently suitable adjectives from William James. Was the ectoplasm really regurgitated muslin? Was that a phantom, or the medium, or the medium's accomplice? And if a phantom, why should phantoms wear stays, or indeed clothes of any sort? How are the phantoms of savages dressed, if at all? How, if not supernaturally, could the medium have come by this information? Can this respected scientist really not be trusted to detect a simple conjuring trick?

Red herrings abound. Pseudo-science presents its offerings. *The Body of the Future Life – Is It Electrical?* – asks a gentleman in 1903. ('The thought that the body of the future life may be electrical was suggested to the writer by the wireless message and the flight of the angel Gabriel as mentioned in Daniel ix. 21. It is only a surmise. It does not amount to a conviction. . . . At the same time it cannot be denied that Scripture seems to support the postulate here presented in a startling manner.'[27])

On the one hand the enthusiasts seek to prove their particular points; on the other, enraged rationalists seek to disprove them and show the whole farrago up for – a farrago. Thus, Sir William Barrett, a leading light of the SPR, put the impatience of orthodox science with spiritualism and psychical research down to 'the difficulty of finding any explanation of the phenomena which is related to existing scientific knowledge'.[28] And in the opposing camp Joseph Jastrow drew the moral of witch-points, those insensitive areas, tested by special pins, the existence of which on the body proved that the person under examination was a witch. It was now known, he pointed out, that these anaesthetic areas occur in cases of hysteria. 'The fact was a real fact.'[29] So might other apparent mysteries be cleared up as science uncovered more such facts.

Perhaps the most marked characteristic of all this striving is the sense of disproportion it engenders. Two little girls play a game: in less than five years, millions of people are caught up in quasi-religious enthusiasm. Some of the best intellects of the day apply themselves in the most strenuous manner to testing the veracity of con-men and conjurers. Above all, the passions aroused, on both sides, seem much too large for the phenomena under investigation. How can such dreadful trivia arouse such deep emotions?

The disproportion picked out in this last question was from the first a recognized bone of contention. It was undeniable, and hard to counter satisfactorily. Perhaps the most astringent expression of this doubt was the famous piece of scorn from T.H.Huxley, on the occasion of his declining to take part in the Dialectical Society's investigation of spiritualism. He wrote:

> I regret that I am unable to accept the invitation of the Committee of the Dialectical Society. . . . I take no interest in the subject. The only case of 'Spiritualism' I have ever had the opportunity of examining into for myself was as gross an imposture as ever came under my notice. But supposing the phenomena to be genuine – they do not interest me. If anybody would endow me with the faculty of listening to the chatter of old women and curates in the nearest provincial town, I should decline the privilege, having better things to do. And if the folk in the spiritual world do not talk more wisely and sensibly than their friends report them to do, I put them in the same category. The only good that I can see in the demonstration of the 'Truth of Spiritualism' is to furnish an additional argument against suicide. Better live a crossing-sweeper, than die and be made to talk twaddle by a 'medium' hired at a guinea a Seance.[30]

To this, William James made a valiant attempt at a reasoned reply. He said,

> The odd point is that so few of those who talk in this way realize that they and the spiritists are using the same major premise and differing only in the minor. The major premise is: 'Any spirit-revelation must be romantic.' The minor of the spiritist is: 'This is romantic'; that of the Huxleyan is: 'This is dingy twaddle' – whence their opposite conclusions![31]

He was right – up to a point. But it still does not go to the heart of the matter. *Why* does the spiritist find the dingy twaddle romantic? How can he possibly do so? The answer must lie in its associations; and of these the chief is immortality. Immortality and miracles – always we come back to religion. But why should religion need such desperate and painstaking proof? Is this not the realm of the act of faith? What has religion to do with the laboratory bench at Duke University or the metal-bending tests at Birkbeck College or the Stanford Research Institute, with Schrenck-Notzing probing through the knitted leotard, with D.D.Home solemnly juggling William Crookes's balance?

As we have seen, the answer of the experimenters on these occasions would have been 'Nothing at all'; but – as we have also seen – this answer is by no means always to be trusted. And if what they are dealing with is not some kind of mystical or quasi-religious manifestation, what is it?

The answer often presented is that this is science, a science offering unique possibilities for the extension of our consciousness and understanding of this world and, possibly, the next. Researchers in the field of the paranormal have always liked to think that they are unreasonably ostracized by orthodox science. They still think this. Thus Hans Eysenck and Carl Sargent, writing in 1982, remark with a certain disingenuousness:

> Over 75 per cent of the general population believe in ESP ... and a majority believe in 'dreams that come true'.... Yet if we look at the scientific community we find that only some 10 per cent of them believe that ESP is an established fact. Is this because the scientific studies simply have not been done which would persuade them that ESP is at the least highly probable? Or are they just ignorant of the facts?[32]

Anyone who has read this book will, I hope, realize that neither of these propositions is true. Scientific studies without number have been done, and many scientists are only too aware of the facts. The people who are not so aware – or, rather, refuse the awareness – are more often the psychical researchers. Anyone who reads widely in this field must be shocked when he arrives at some of the weightiest tomes by some of the most highly respected of the researchers. Quite simply, all the facts are never mentioned – or, if they are, only in the most slanted way, so that those undermining the desired evidence will be dismissed. This may be excellent propaganda, but it is not science.

So – once again – why? Why do they do it? Why go to all this bother to dress something up as science when it is clearly not science but, in one sense or another of that word, magic? Is it that the Victorians and, even more so, our own age were and are unable to accept their magic undiluted but must feel they have a basis of rational justification, a factual underpinning? Clearly, as that other magic which goes under the name of 'orthodox science' progresses into ever more arcane and unimaginable spheres, there is a deep wish for the irrational to triumph.

The paradoxical fact of the matter is that ever since Darwin seemingly staked out their territories in such clear and discrete opposition, the roles of science and religion have been getting more and more muddled and intermingled. Darwinism seemed to undermine the foundations of Christian religious belief – and what was religion's response? It might have retreated further into those spheres of mysticism and mystery which are unaffected by science; but it did not do so. Instead it sought to beat science at its own game. This trend soon became clear. In 1896 Paul Carus, a clergyman and editor of a magazine, *Open Court*, published in Chicago, which particularly interested itself in these questions and which consistently carried distinguished and interesting articles, wrote:

> The truth is that the confidence in science has already become a religious conviction with most of us. The faith in the scientifically provable has . . . taken root in the hearts of men. Today it is the most powerful factor of our civilization, in spite of various church dogmas which are declared to be above scientific critique and argument; for these dogmas are becoming a dead letter. There are several conservative and prominent churchmen who publicly confess that the dogmas of the Church must be regarded as historical documents and not as eternal verities.

This trend still continues. The desire for clarity and demystification has led to the grotesque austerities of the New English Bible, which turns its back on one of the great poetic monuments of the English language.

But if poetry, mystery and the irrational are abolished from today's religion, that is not to say that most people prefer to do without them. The corollary of that rationalism which seemed the natural heir to the post-Darwinian world is that, since no divine authority is on hand to bail us out of trouble, we alone must accept responsibility for ourselves and what we do. Some would ask nothing better; but for many this is a hard position to accept. To take complete responsibility for yourself and your actions is not easy.

But neither is it particularly easy or logical to turn for authority to some other merely human source. And clearly many of the manifest-ations of the super-normal do fulfil this craving for some sort of appar-ently super-human authority. As C.G.Jung wrote, 'There is a deep need in the world just now for guidance – almost any sort of spiritual guidance. Look at the popularity of astrology just now. People read about astrology because it offers them one form of astral inspiration, perhaps a form with limitations, but at least it's better than nothing at all.'[33] That was in 1960, since when the popularity of astrology and related topics has done nothing but increase. A new edition of the prophecies of Nostradamus, 'recoded by computer' to give the requi-site scientific gloss, recently sold 100,000 copies in France alone.

Jung himself was by no means immune to the attractions of the supernormal. His doctrine of the 'collective unconscious' had of course much in common with that vitalism which was and is such an essential element in the intellectual attraction of spiritualism; and indeed he was led to formulate it in the classic way, by a succession of 'odd-matches' or prophetic dreams in which, during 1913 and 1914, he saw what he later realized to have been the coming of the Great War. But also, on a more elementary level, he was quite ready to believe in such supernatural manifestations as flying saucers. Lindbergh, the aviator, talking to Jung, was convinced that he believed in them as facts, not just as psychological phenomena – at any rate, Jung got very cross when Lindbergh suggested they couldn't really exist.[34]

There are many who would share Lindbergh's amazement at this. Vitalism is one thing, but flying saucers . . . ! The notion is absurd. And therein, maybe, lies its attraction – and the attraction of psi phenomena in general, especially for those many scientists and intellectuals whose beliefs remain unshaken despite repeated expla-nations and disproofs. If science, in its various aspects, has now usurped the position and authority once held by religion and magic, and if religion itself, in response, is assuming an increasingly prosaic and quasi-scientific posture, what room is left for the act of faith, for Camus's 'leap into the absurd'? Seemingly very little; and yet there is no reason to suppose that this is not as attractive, even essential, to a great many people as it ever was.

In this situation, psi, parapsychology, psychical research, present a way out of the dilemma. The act of faith is transferred to the realm of science itself. And how much more emotionally satisfying it is than the arid wastes of rationalism! Take, for instance, the story of Ruth Pierce, recounted by a militant sceptic distressed at the lack of impact made by repeated unmaskings and debunkings. Ruth Pierce is

commemorated by a plaque in the market place of the Wiltshire town
of Devizes. On that spot she called on God to strike her dead if she was
not speaking the truth – whereupon she instantly fell dead and was
subsequently shown to have been lying. This was not so extraordinary
as it might seem, pointed out the sceptic: there are 'numerous instances where fear of the terrible consequences of some act had led to
syncope – sudden stoppage of the heart – and death'.[35] So there are;
but it seems naive not to see why a great many people would not wish
to be made aware of this explanation but would prefer to see the fate of
Ruth Pierce as a latter-day miracle and act of God, or some such higher
authority.

The reaction of many scientists to the fact of this attraction – their
difficulty in admitting the real basis of their interest in 'phenomena',
even to themselves, and the elaborately scientific, or scientistic,
apparatus built up around their investigations – has been discussed
in detail in earlier chapters. Clearly, once they had 'come out' in favour
of the spiritualistic hypothesis, or one of its offshoots, they had a
double interest in resisting its destruction: both intellectual commit-
ment and reputation and deep personal feelings were involved.

The cases discussed in the course of this book almost all took place
many years ago, and most of the protagonists are now dead. But,
despite everything, the controversies they aroused have not died
away; nor have the terms in which they are discussed substantially
changed. Today, of course, produces its own crop of supernormalities
over which debate rages as fiercely as ever, together with its new
generation of debunkers. Charlatans are unmasked as regularly and
unavailingly as ever they were. As with those other 'miracles', the
show goes on regardless. Passions run as high as ever they did. The
spirits are willing, and the flesh is weak.

Appendix
The Machine in the Ghost

All wonder is the effect of novelty on ignorance. – DR JOHNSON

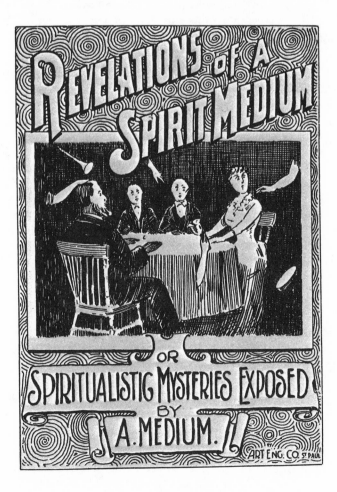

EUSAPIA PALADINO

The most thorough account I have found of Eusapia's methods is that
given by J.N.Maskelyne in the *Daily Chronicle*, 29 October 1895,
shortly after the Cambridge seances which discredited Eusapia in the
eyes of many leading members of the SPR Andrew Lang had demanded that Maskelyne reproduce certain of Eusapia's phenomena.
Maskelyne replied that, although he could doubtless reproduce all
that Eusapia really did, the reproduction of what she was supposed to
have done was quite another matter. Lang said this 'amounted either
to a charge of malobservation or collective hallucination on the part of
a large number of eminent men. How was it possible that such men as
Lodge, Schiaparelli, Richet, Ochorowicz, Lombroso, etc., could all be
deceived?' Maskelyne 'knew from experience that no class of men can
be so readily deceived by simple trickery as scientists. Try as they may,
they cannot bring their minds down to the level of their subject, and
are as much at fault as though it were immeasurably above them.'
Subsequently, Lang and Lodge visited Maskelyne, and told him more
about Eusapia. From what Lodge said, Maskelyne was almost convinced that she really had supernormal – though not necessarily spiritual – powers. Accordingly Maskelyne and his son went to Cambridge
to attend the seances there and see for themselves.

> There is not the least doubt that at the date of our visit to Cambridge the
> whole of the investigators were thoroughly impressed with the genuineness
> of the phenomena. And we were particularly desired to enter into the spirit
> of the thing as far as possible and to do all we could to encourage the
> medium and her 'control' ... also ... to express approval of the
> phenomena as they occurred in terms such as 'Bene!' or 'Molto bene!' ...
> We were warned that, before going into the trance state, the medium was
> given to performing little tricks which were quite palpably spurious. This
> was condoned. ... But the really important manifestations came in the
> trance.

Eusapia was dressed as usual in a black, light dress and felt slippers.
Her control, the ubiquitous John King, objected to silk because it
spoilt the spirit influence – but Maskelyne thought the greater objection was that it might rustle at the wrong moment. There was too
much light in the room, though only one small window was left uncur-
tained. This was then curtained, but it was still possible to see.

As 'trance' approached, Eusapia sighed heavily and was very restless. Then she deliberately rapped three times with her right hand on
the centre of the table. She then placed this hand palm down on the

table, and Lodge, who was on her right, put his hand on the back of it. There were three faint answering raps. This was done several times. Maskelyne commented:

J.N.Maskelyne

Well! I have rarely seen anything more barefaced than this, even among spirit mediums. . . . I distinctly saw her produce the 'answering' raps by the well-known dodge of 'skidding' her finger along the table. While engaged in this manoeuvre she happened to catch my eye; and although I was trying my utmost to discharge all expression from my features . . . she became very angry with me at times afterwards.

After this there was table-lifting. 'While this was going on, I learnt that Eusapia understands her business well [and knows] how to adapt her proceedings to any circumstances that may arise. I will undertake to say that she has more methods of lifting a table than any furniture remover has ever dreamt of. Fingers, wrists, toes, knees, calves, abdomen: she knows how to use them all.' The table was a small rectangular one made of deal, with four legs. Maskelyne was on Eusapia's left, Lodge on her right. 'While the table was tilting in my direction I could not for the life of me refrain from projecting my leg slightly to keep her calf away from the table leg nearest me. And, when the tilting was in the other direction, I could not help just slightly opposing the motion by a few ounces of pressure. And a very few ounces prevented the movement entirely.' Eusapia then swore at Maskelyne in Italian, and he behaved himself thereafter.

> Finally, the table reared up at the medium's end, and, by a supreme effort on her part, the two legs at the other end were also lifted off the floor, the table thus appearing to be supported on nothing . . . Dozens of scientific men have declared that they have seen her lift a table with only the tips of her fingers touching it. All I can say is, that when *I* saw her lift a table, there was a vast deal more than her fingers in contact with it. . . . Pushing the table-top forward with her wrists, the table was caused to rear upon the two further legs to such a degree that it was almost balanced upon them. This brought the two near legs to such a position that they crossed the sides of her thighs. In this position the table remained for a second or so. Then, suddenly spreading her thighs somewhat, she pressed them firmly against the inner sides of the table-legs. Simultaneously she threw her body back, and drew the table-top towards her. Thus, using her thighs as a fulcrum, she levered the farther pair of legs off the ground. Naturally, she had not enough strength to maintain the strain involved, and the table-legs slipped rapidly past her thighs. Extending her legs, she caught the descending table upon her left toe, and, holding her hip-joints rigid, allowed the weight to bring her body into an erect position, by which time the table-legs were again on the floor. . . . As the table went up, Eusapia favoured us with the first of a series of little sardonic laughs, to which she generally gave vent when anything was about to happen. Really, it sounded just as though she were laughing in her sleeve at our simplicity.

'John King' now arrived on the scene. The room was darkened progressively as he took over; when it was only lit by the note-taker's reading-light the fun began. A little table with a zither on it approached Eusapia's chair, Lodge was 'touched', the little wicker table on Eusapia's right was lifted bodily by an unseen agency and put upside-down on the seance-table. The zither was placed on the seance table. Hands pinched and poked Maskelyne and Lodge. Then Maskelyne's son took Lodge's place and was felt and touched very often, though Maskelyne himself was hardly touched at all.

Maskelyne's son was told he could see the 'prominences' if he would promise not to touch. Of course, he promised. Myers took Eusapia's right hand, Maskelyne's son stood behind her and could just see –

> by stooping he could bring the right shoulder of Eusapia between the little

patch of illuminated ceiling and his eyes. . . . Then she commenced to make a little blowing noise, and my son saw projecting gradually from her right shoulder what appeared to be a hand which, having become completely visible as a silhouette, was immediately withdrawn. This was repeated several times, and my son has not the slightest doubt that what he saw was a solid hand and not merely a dummy.

Maskelyne concluded that everything rested on the question whether Eusapia could get a hand or foot free occasionally. She wriggled so much that it was impossible to control her properly throughout. If she could get one hand, and sometimes a foot, free, everything could be explained. And 'really one might as well try to make sure of holding an eel in the dark'.

Eusapia was held when the little wicker table was lifted; she did it by leaning far back and lifting it with her teeth.

She freed her left hand by making sure that her right hand was always held so that the fingers were free. She then placed her left hand-holder's hand on the table (taking care that it was in the correct position) and ran her fingers over the back of it, finally pressing down firmly – but with the fingers of the right hand.

D.D. HOME

D.D. Home was never exposed in fraud, and the essence of his reputation lies in the intellectual quality of those who tried so to expose him – or anyway set out to examine his phenomena in detail – and failed to detect any trickery. Of these the most persistent and eminent was Sir William Crookes, later to become President of the Royal Society. The two particular feats studied by Crookes were the movement of a balance by 'psychic force' and Home's resistance to heat, as for instance his ability to handle hot coals with no deleterious effects. His other famous effect was, of course, levitation (see Chapter 2).

The scientists were in no doubt whatever about the correctness of their diagnosis that the resistance to heat was a supernatural power. Sir William Barrett wrote: 'It is impossible to explain this [Home's grasping a red-hot coal] by some fire-resisting substance, surreptitiously put over the skin by Home, for Sir William Crookes, than whom no higher authority on Chemistry can be cited, tells us he knows of no chemical preparation that will accomplish this.'[1] Crookes himself commented (in 1893, referring to a 'fire test' given by Home to F.W.H. Myers twenty years earlier in 1873):

I do not believe in the possibility of the ordinary skin of the hand being so prepared as to enable hot coals to be handled with impunity. Schoolboys' books and mediaeval tales describe how this can be done with alum or certain other ingredients. It is possible that the skin can be so hardened and thickened by such preparations that superficial charring might take place without the pain becoming great, but the surface of the skin would certainly suffer severely. After Home had recovered from the trance I examined his hand with care to see if there were any signs of burning or of previous preparation. I could detect no trace of injury to the skin, which was soft and delicate like a woman's. Neither were there signs of any preparation having been previously applied.

I have often seen conjurers and others handle red-hot coals and iron, but there were always palpable signs of burning. A negro was once brought to my lab., who professed to be able to handle red-hot coals with impunity. I was asked to test his pretensions and I did so carefully. There was no doubt that he could touch and hold for a brief time the red-hot iron without feeling much pain, and supposing his feet were as resisting as his hands, he could have triumphally passed the 'red-hot ploughshare' ordeal. But the house was pervaded for hours with the odour of roast negro.[2]

In fact, Crookes's confidence was not necessarily justified. Conjurers have used various methods over the past centuries to fireproof themselves. Houdini gives a number of these in his book *Miracle-Mongers and their Methods*. Here is one:

From *Hocus-Pocus*, 1763: HOW TO WALK ON A HOT IRON BAR WITHOUT ANY DANGER OF SCALDING OR BURNING.
Take half an ounce of samphire, dissolve it in two ounces of acquavitae, add to it one ounce of quicksilver, one ounce of liquid storax, which is the droppings of Myrrh and hinders the samphire from firing; take also two ounces of hematitus, a red stone to be had at the druggist's, and when you buy it let them beat it to powder in their great mortar, for it is so very hard that it cannot be done in a small one; put this to the aforementioned composition, and when you intend to walk on the bar you must anoint your feet well therewith, and you may walk over without danger; by this you may wash your hands in boiling lead.

Another method given is from 1827, as used by a famous magician of the day:

It consisted only in rubbing the hands and thoroughly washing the mouth, lips, tongue, teeth and other parts which were to touch the fire, with pure spirits of sulphur. This burns and cauterizes the epidermis or upper skin, till it becomes as hard and thick as leather, and each time the experiment is tried it becomes still easier. But if, after it has been very often repeated the upper skin should grow so callous and hard as to become troublesome, washing the parts affected with very warm water, or hot wine, will bring away all the shrivelled or parched epidermis. The flesh, however, will continue tender and soft for such business till it has been frequently rubbed over with the same spirit.

This preparation may be rendered much stronger and more efficacious by mixing equal quantities of spirit of sulphur, sal ammoniac, essence of rosemary and juice of onions. The bad effects which frequently follow swallowing red-hot coals, melted sealing-wax, rosin, brimstone and other calcined and inflammable matter, . . . were prevented by drinking plentifully of warm water and oil, as soon as he left the company, till he had vomited it all up again.

Houdini also quotes the experiments of a Professor Sementini in Naples, who practised various methods on himself until he found those which worked best.

He found that by friction with sulphuric acid diluted with water, the skin might be made insensible to the action of the heat of red-hot iron; a solution of alum, evaporated till it became spongy, appeared to be more effectual in these frictions. After having rubbed the parts which were thus rendered in some degree insensible, with hard soap, he discovered, on the application of hot iron, that their insensibility was increased. He then determined on again rubbing the parts with soap, and after that found that the hot iron not only occasioned no pain but that it actually did not burn the hair.

Being thus far satisfied, the Professor applied hard soap to his tongue until it became insensible to the heat of the iron; and having placed an ointment composed of soap mixed with a solution of alum upon it, burning oil did not burn it; while the oil remained on the tongue a slight hissing was heard, similar to that of hot iron when thrust into water; the oil soon cooled and might then be swallowed without danger . . .

Liquid storax is now used to anoint the tongue when red-hot irons are to be placed in the mouth. It is claimed that with this alone a red-hot poker can be licked until it is cold.

Another formula is given by Griffin, as follows: 1 bar ivory soap, cut fine, 1 pound of brown sugar, 2 ounces liquid storax (not the gum). Dissolve in hot water and add a wine-glassful of carbolic acid. This is rubbed on all parts liable to come in contact with the hot articles. After anointing the mouth with this solution rinse with strong vinegar.

Houdini adds, 'No performer should attempt to bite off red-hot iron unless he has a good set of teeth.'[3]

An investigation conducted by the veteran psychical researcher and magician Harry Price into fire-walking showed that this feat could be performed without resorting to trickery or chemical preparation or wetting of the feet. All that was needed was a cool approach and the balance of mind essential to ensure that the walking was absolutely controlled. A man was burned crossing a trench of coals in six steps, but another who crossed the same trench in four steps was unharmed. This was at a trench temperature of 740 °C.[4]

The Home phenomenon which most impressed Crookes scientifically speaking was, it will be remembered, his demonstration of 'psychic force' when he depressed a spring balance without apparently touching it at all. Various explanations have been offered for this. Frank Podmore and others thought the trick was worked by using hairs or thin silk thread to move the balance, the attention of Crookes and any other observers having first been distracted (for comments on techniques of misdirection see Section 5 of this Appendix). It was remarked that Crookes was very short-sighted. The hairs and threads could also have been used to stop objects sliding off a tilted table, another favourite effect of Home's.

Another explanation offered was that of static electricity. A Dr William A. Hammond, a neurologist, described this experiment in 1876:

> Place an egg in an egg-cup and balance a long lath upon the egg. Though the lath be almost a plank it will obediently follow a rod of glass, gutta percha or sealing-wax, which has been previously well dried and rubbed, the former with a piece of silk, and the two latter with woolen cloth. Now, in dry weather, many persons within my knowledge, have only to walk with a shuffling gait over the carpet, and then approaching the lath hold out the finger instead of the glass, sealing wax or gutta percha, and instantly one end of the lath rises to meet it, and the other end is depressed. Applying these principles, I arranged an apparatus exactly like that of Prof. Crookes, except that the spring balance was such as is used for weighing letters and was therefore very delicate, indicating quarter ounces with exactness, and that the board was thin and narrow.
>
> Applying the glass rod or stick of sealing wax to the end resting by its foot on the table, the index of the balance at once descended, showing an increased weight of a little over three quarters of an ounce, and this without the board being raised from the table.
>
> I then walked over a thick Turkey rug for a few moments, and holding my finger under the board near the end attached to the balance, caused a fall of the index of almost half an ounce. I then rested my finger lightly on the end of the board immediately over the foot, and again the index descended and oscillated several times, just as in Mr Home's experiments. The lowest point reached was six and a quarter ounces, and as the board weighed, as attached to the balance, five ounces, there was an increased weight of one

and a quarter ounces. At no time was the end of the board raised from the table.

I then arranged the apparatus so as to place a thin glass tumbler nearly full of water immediately over the fulcrum, as in Mr Crookes' experiment, and again the index fell and oscillated on my fingers being put into the water.

Now if one person can thus, with a delicate apparatus like mine, cause the index, through electricity, to descend and ascend, it is not improbable that others, like Mr Home, could show greater, or even different electrical power, as in Prof. Crookes' experiments.[5]

As to the famous levitation incident recounted in Chapter 2, the conflicting reports of the observers have been generally remarked upon. For instance, Lord Lindsay said that he saw Home float out of the window horizontally; but he also said that what he saw was not the man himself but his shadow, cast by the new moon (it was then two days old), which would imply that he had his back to the window at the time. Lord Adare, on the other hand, saw Home 'standing upright outside our window'.

One commentator remarked:

It is a familiar fact of physiological optics that, in a faint light, if the eyes are fixed upon an object, the latter gradually becomes clouded and finally disappears entirely. Then it requires only a little heightening of a not unusual imagination to believe that, if the object that disappeared was a man, he wafted himself through the air and went out of the window.[6]

SMITH AND BLACKBURN

Douglas Blackburn and G.A.Smith were two young men in Brighton who were discovered by Edmund Gurney and F.W.H.Myers doing a professional thought-reading act and who were enthusiastically taken up by members of the SPR Smith subsequently became Gurney's secretary. Trevor Hall, in his book *The Strange Case of Edmund Gurney*, suggests that Gurney's death, which was almost certainly suicide, may have been precipitated by the realization that they had all been gulled and that Smith and Blackburn had been systematically tricking them. But if he did think this, his opinion was never shared, at least so far as we know, with his fellow investigators, for many of whom, including Mrs Sidgwick, Miss Alice Johnson and Frank Podmore, Smith and Blackburn remained one of the few examples of good evidence for psychical powers which stood up through thick and thin.

Smith continued to be employed in a secretarial capacity by the

SPR for some time after the dissolution of his partnership with Blackburn, who went to South Africa where he became a successful writer. In 1911, many years after the events in question (Blackburn's last tests for the SPR took place in 1883), Blackburn published a confession of how it had all been done. This appeared in the *Daily News* for 1 September 1911:

> I am the sole survivor of that group of experimentalists, and as no harm can be done to anyone, but possible good to the cause of truth, I . . . now declare that the whole of those alleged experiments were bogus, and originated in the honest desire of two youths to show how easily men of scientific mind and training could be deceived when seeking for evidence in support of a theory they were wishful to establish [he wrote]. And here let me say I make this avowal in no boastful spirit. Within three months of our acquaintance with the leading members of the Society for Psychical Research Mr Smith and myself heartily regretted that these personally charming and scientifically distinguished men should have been victimized; but it was too late to recant. We did the next best thing. We stood aside and watched with amazement the astounding spread of the fire we had in a spirit of mischief lighted.

Blackburn went on to give the history of the partnership.

> Brighton, where I was editing a weekly journal, became a happy hunting ground for mediums of every kind. I had started an exposure campaign, and been rather successful. . . . In 1882, I encountered Mr G.A.Smith, a youth of 19, whom I found giving a mesmeric entertainment. Scenting a fraud, I proceeded to investigate, made his acquaintance, and very soon realised that I had discovered a genius in his line. . . . He had the versatility of an Edison in devising new tricks and improving on old ones. We entered into a compact to 'show up' some of the then flourishing professors of occultism, and began by practising thought-reading. . . . One of our exhibitions was described very fully and enthusiastically in *Light* and on the strength of that Messrs. Gurney, Myers and Podmore called on us. . . .

They had never, said Blackburn, been paid by the Society, and did not at first realize the seriousness of its intentions.

> We saw in them only a superior type of spiritualistic crank. . . .
>
> Our first private seance was accepted so unhesitatingly, and the lack of reasonable precautions on the part of the investigators was so marked, that Smith and I were genuinely amused, and felt it our duty to show how utterly incompetent were these 'scientific investigators'. Our plan was to bamboozle them thoroughly, then let the world know the value of scientific research. . . .

Starting with a crude set of signals produced by the jingling of pince-nez, sleeve-links, long and short breathings, and even blowing, they developed their technique to a degree little short of marvellous. 'To this day no conjurer has succeeded in approaching our great feat, by which Smith, scientifically blindfolded, deafened, and muffled in two blankets, reproduced in detail an irregular figure drawn by Mr Myers and seen only by me.'

Blackburn had stirred up more of a hornet's nest than he realized with this article, for although Gurney, Myers and Podmore were long since dead, and although repeated attempts to contact Smith had failed and he had been told that his old friend, too, had died, this was not the case. Smith was found by the *Daily News*, and, in an interview printed on 4 September 1911, absolutely denied that he and Blackburn had ever cheated. Blackburn was left with no choice but to contradict his old friend and prove that he, Blackburn, was telling the truth and Smith was perpetuating a lie. This he did with great regret, but incontrovertibly, by describing in detail the workings of their high point of trickery to which he had referred previously. This description appeared, also in the *Daily News*, on 5 September 1911:

> The committee had realised the possibility of conveying by signals a description of a regular figure or any object capable of being described in words . . . but the more irregular and indescribable. . . . the greater and wider were the discrepancies between the original and the copy. . . . I had a signal, which I gave Smith when the drawing was impossible. We made a pretence of trying hard, but after a time would give up. . . . As a matter of fact the committee were beginning to have grave doubts when the 'great triumph' I shall now describe saved our reputations. . . .
>
> The conditions of the trick were these: Smith sat at a table. His eyes were padded with wool and, I think, a pair of folded kid gloves, and bandaged with a thick, dark cloth. His ears were filled with a layer of cotton-wool, then pellets of putty. His entire body and the chair on which he sat were enveloped in two very heavy blankets. I remember, when he emerged triumphant, he was wet with perspiration, and the paper on which he had successfully drawn the figure was so moist that it broke during the examination by the delighted observers. Beneath his feet and surrounding his chair were thick, soft rugs, rightly intended to deaden and prevent signals by feet shuffles – a nice precaution. . . . At the farther side of . . . a very large dining-room, Mr Myers showed me, with every precaution, the drawing that I was to transmit to the brain beneath the blankets. It was a tangle of heavy black lines, interlaced, some curved, some straight, the sort of thing an infant playing with a pen or pencil might produce. . . . I took it, fixed my gaze on it, pacing the room meanwhile . . . but always keeping out of

touching distance of Smith. These preliminaries occupied perhaps ten minutes, for we made a point of never hurrying. I drew and redrew the figure many times, openly in the presence of the observers, in order, as I explained and they allowed, to fix it in my brain. I also drew it secretly on a cigarette paper. By this time I was fairly expert at palming, and had no difficulty while pacing the room collecting 'rapports' in transferring the cigarette paper to the tube of the brass protector on the pencil I was using. I conveyed to Smith the agreed signal that I was ready by stumbling against the edge of the thick rug near his chair.

Next instant he exclaimed 'I have it.' His right hand came from beneath the blanket, saying, according to the arrangement, 'Where's my pencil?' Immediately I placed mine on the table. He took it and a long and anxious pause ensued. . . .

Smith had concealed up his waistcoat one of those luminous painted slates which in the dense darkness gave sufficient light to show the figure when the almost transparent cigarette paper was laid flat on the slate. He pushed up the bandage from one eye and copied the figure with extraordinary accuracy. It occupied over five minutes. During that time I was sitting exhausted with the mental effort quite ten feet away.

Presently Smith threw back the blanket, and excitedly pushing back the eye bandage produced the drawing, which was done on a piece of notepaper and very nearly on the same scale as the original. It was a splendid copy.

Of this exploit Smith said, 'It was a bona fide experiment and the successful result was either due to chance or telepathy. I think it most unlikely that it was due to chance.'

THE ADVANTAGES OF EDUCATION IN PSYCHIC INVESTIGATION

It was often argued that Smith and Blackburn, in particular, could not have been cheating because the people who investigated them would have been exceptionally difficult to deceive. They were, after all, leading intellectuals of the highest order. Among them were Mrs Sidgwick, soon to become Principal of Newnham College, Cambridge, and her colleague Miss Alice Johnson, a gifted scientist. Of these two ladies Professor C. D. Broad wrote in 1962:

I have no hesitation in expressing the opinion, for what it is worth, that there was no abler *woman*, and few if any abler *persons*, in the England of her time, than Mrs Sidgwick. . . . [Miss Johnson] had been trained for her work by Mrs Sidgwick, was brought up in the extremely high standards of intellectual and moral integrity so characteristic of the Sidgwicks, and was herself distinguished for the meticulous care and the critical acumen with which she appraised evidence. . . . A reference to the qualifications of the writers is in place as a warning against lighthearted general criticism without careful attention to specific details. It really is not very likely that the kind of objection which would arise in the mind of any assistant in a psychological laboratory while shaving would have escaped the notice of Sidgwick, of Mrs Sidgwick and of Miss Alice Johnson. Those who indulge in that kind of criticism . . . will amost certainly find themselves in the embarrassing company of those who undertake to teach their grandmothers to suck eggs.[7]

This may be taken as the received position of educated psychical researchers, and indeed it does not seem at all unreasonable. But it does not correspond with the opinion held by professional mediums. David Abbott, who had been a medium and was a professional conjurer, and who was much concerned with these questions, said:

A medium once told me that . . . really mediums do not care for performing for spiritualists so much, as they expect so much for their money; and if given a fine piece of work, they accept it as a matter of course. Mystery, he said, has become commonplace to such people. It is the more intelligent class, who call themselves 'investigators', that are willing and able to pay 'good money' for a medium's services.[8]

And Max Dessoir, in *The Psychology of Legerdemain*, said:

The uneducated person is far more difficult to deceive than the cultivated; for the former sees at every turn an avowed mistrust of his intelligence, an attempt to dupe him, against which he contends with all his strength, while the latter surrenders himself without resistance to the illusion, for he has come with the sole purpose of being deceived. One can hardly believe what artlessness is occasionally displayed by these cultured people. I have heard a professor, in the well-known ring game, declare that he had tested all eight rings, when in reality he had received only two in his hand [this was the game which convinced Professor Zollner of the existence of a fourth dimension]; and I myself have often ventured to count a number of cards in the reverse order from that agreed upon, without anyone making any objection.

A parallel might perhaps be drawn with the more recent testing of young metal-benders, post-Geller, by Professor John Taylor of Birkbeck College, London, and his noting of the amazing *shyness effect* which meant that the metal never would bend while anyone was looking, but did so when the attention of observers was distracted.

THE TECHNIQUES OF DISTRACTION

These are of course some of the fundamental techniques of the conjurer. Robert-Houdin, the first of the great prestidigitators, (after whom

Houdini, *né* Ehrich Weiss, named himself) gave it as one of his rules never to announce beforehand the nature of the effect which he intended to produce, so that the spectator would not know where to fix his attention. To give a basic example of this technique of misdirection, when the conjurer calls 'One, two, three' and on 'three' something vanishes, the real vanishing must be done before 'three' is called; the attention of the audience will be fixed on the 'three'.

The medium is not quite in the same position as the conjurer vis-à-vis his audience and, as readers will have noted, does not use quite this technique. Rather, expert practitioners such as Home used to make announcements such as 'Now I am rising' or 'Now I shall elongate' in order to implant a suggestion in the audience's mind of what was going on. Jastrow has pointed out that in this respect the medium's performance is much more akin to that of the necromancer who induces awe and a sense of magic in his spectators, who are not quite sure what interpretation they should place upon what they see, or who are more or less determined to see in everything the evidence of the supernatural.[9]

This is not, however, to say that mediums did not use their own techniques of misdirection. A classic one is described by the author of *Revelations of a Spirit Medium*, a publication which appeared in 1891 and was immediately bought up *en masse* by alarmed mediums in order to prevent their trade secrets being made available to the public. The book was reissued in 1922, edited by Harry Price and E.J.Dingwall. In talking about the most effective ways to search a medium's cabinet for hidden trapdoors and hiding-places for accessories, the anonymous author urges:

> Do not forget the 'manager' in your search. He or she is never searched, or never has been, up to date, which has been the cause of many a failure to find the 'properties' of the 'medium' when the 'seance' was given in a room and 'cabinet' furnished by a stranger and skeptic. Do not be deceived into a belief that each one of the 'sitters' are strangers to the 'medium'. There may be from one to five persons present who pay their money the same as yourself, and who may appear to be the most skeptical of any one in the room. They will generally be the recipients of some very elegant 'tests'. . . . They are the most careful of investigators and when the 'medium's' trap is located in the door-jamb, will pound the walls, and insist on the carpet being taken up, when they will get upon hands and knees and make a most searching examination of the floor. They are the closest and most critical of investigators, but they are very careful to examine everywhere except where the defect is located.[10]

A lot of the medium's technique, particularly in the case of someone like Home, lay and lies in skilful suggestion. This may be carried to a fine art, as with Home, but it is also the basis for some of the most simple tricks whose effect lies in induced hallucination in the spectator. Such hallucinations may be positive: if three oranges are thrown in the air by a juggler who continues juggling, we may see a fourth where none exists. Conversely, we may look in vain for an object which is lying before our eyes, see the conjurer changing cards, etc. – and simply not register what we are seeing. The aspiring magician, or medium, is advised to practise in front of a mirror, and to watch closely the positions and movements of his hands, so that all distinctions between reality and illusion are rendered invisible. Above all, he must get used to following with his eyes the hand that seems to contain the objects in question – this is the surest way of directing the eyes of the audience in the same direction.

Illusions and misdirections do not always involve anything happening. One of the aspects of D.D.Home which people found most convincing was that by no means all his seances produced phenomena. Thus Dr James Edmunds reported to the Dialectical Society of London:

> Mr Home was most frank in everything. He insisted upon my examining him personally, and went into my study for that purpose . . . Mr Home afterwards wore a suit of clothes with which, at his instance, I provided him. The seance commenced at 8.30 p.m., and lasted several hours, the room being fully lighted by Mr Home's direction. Nothing whatever occurred, except that Mrs Edmunds became a little faint and nervous at one part of the evening. Three other seances, I think, occurred without noteworthy result. They were then discontinued in consequence of Mr Home having other engagements, and Mr Home did not appoint any time for resuming them. Mr Home possesses a very lithe, elastic and muscular frame, and he is a gentleman of exceptional mental gifts and personal accomplishments.[11]

Others commented that, even after a blank sitting, Home was always exhausted. This spasmodic lack of results in no way detracted from his reputation, while it allowed him (as has been shown) carefully to pick the audiences before whom he did perform. With regard to this technique, S.J.Davey, an investigator and colleague of Richard Hodgson, who became so skilled at producing phenomena that a great many people refused to believe that he was not psychic even though he continually assured them that all his results were achieved by trickery, wrote: 'I have found . . . that a blank sitting occasionally with an investigator who at other times gets good results, makes the phenomena look more mysterious than ever, and forms an additional reason in his mind for not attributing the phenomena to conjuring.'[12]

'CHEATING'

One very curious aspect of the relationship between conjurers and spiritually inclined spectators is the notion (held by the audience) that the conjurer was in some way cheating if he suggested that his feats were performed by trickery rather than by supernormal powers. The outstanding example of this was Conan Doyle, particularly vis-à-vis Houdini – the more extraordinary when one considers that Conan Doyle made his literary reputation by using logic to explain mysteries. And indeed, such were Houdini's powers, and such his fabled reputation, that people are still palpably disappointed when the mechanical secrets behind his feats are laid bare. Not being suicidally inclined, Houdini of course always made quite sure that all his 'impossible' feats were quite possible before he performed them in public – though this did not mean that some of them were not extremely difficult.

Many of his tricks required some help or collusion, and this was provided by his manager and various aides, many of whom were bound to strict secrecy under a notarial oath; this trust was betrayed only in one trifling instance. Many others seem, when explained, childishly simple. For instance, there was the one which particularly amazed Conan Doyle, where the conjurer walked through a brick wall on stage. First, a sheet of glass covered the stage, to make sure that no trapdoor could be used. Then a team of bricklayers came on and built a brick wall. On one side of this a small screen was erected. Houdini walked on in evening dress, bowed, went behind the screen, where his arms could be seen waving while he shouted, 'Here I am!' Then a team of workmen came on, removed the screen and carried it round to the other side of the wall. No Houdini. But almost at once the magician's arms were seen waving again from behind the moved screen, and he walked out and presented himself once more to the audience. The secret lay in the fact that on the back of the screen were a hook with some workmen's overalls and a pair of false arms worked by strings. Houdini put on the overalls, worked the arms, and crossed the wall as one of the workmen carrying the screen (a similar trick was used by the late Howard Hughes when he pretended to be one of his own stretcher-bearers). There were also various other methods of carrying out this trick: no one was more adept than Houdini at varying his techniques.

Another revealing instance of his approach is the way in which he would escape from a locked bank-vault. When he was due to perform this feat, Houdini would insist on being shown the vault beforehand – a perfectly reasonable request. He or his aide would take the opportunity of secreting a screwdriver somewhere within it. After he was locked in, Houdini (an expert locksmith) would unscrew the lock from the inside, adjust the combination until it opened, screw the plates back on, open the door, and walk out triumphantly. He was a master of showmanship. When he performed a similar trick on stage (he would challenge any firm of safemakers wherever he went to produce a safe from which he could not escape), he would enter the safe, assuring his audience that he must escape within an hour or he would suffocate, as the air inside it would run out. A screen would be drawn in front of the safe. Time would pass. Tension in the audience would rise. After forty-five minutes or so, this tension would become unbearable. Would the magician have to call for help, as he had said he would if he failed in his task? Was he, perhaps, already too weak . . . ? – Just before the hour was up, Houdini would appear, smiling and bowing. The house would go wild. In fact he had usually escaped within the first ten minutes and had been sitting comfortably behind the screen playing cards and waiting for the time to elapse.

That he was only too human was proved by the way in which he died. He was, as might be expected, superbly fit, and was particularly proud of his muscular control, which was of course an essential part of his technical equipment. In 1926 he was lecturing to some students on this subject, and boasted, among other things, that he could withstand any blow to the stomach so long as he was prepared to receive it. After the show some of the students went round to see him in his dressing-room, and one of them, without any warning, suddenly hit him in the stomach. Houdini was in considerable pain, but he had to do a show in Detroit that night and insisted that it must go ahead. Afterwards, when the pain became unbearable, he was rushed to hospital where he was found to have peritonitis. He died next day. His wife, Bessie, was distracted with grief. They had arranged an agreed message which whoever of them died first was to send the other, should spirit survival prove really to be true. Bessie spent the rest of her life going from medium to medium in an effort to receive this message from her husband. It never came.

LEVITATION

We have seen how practitioners such as D.D. Home were able to con-vince people most effectively by force of suggestion that they were

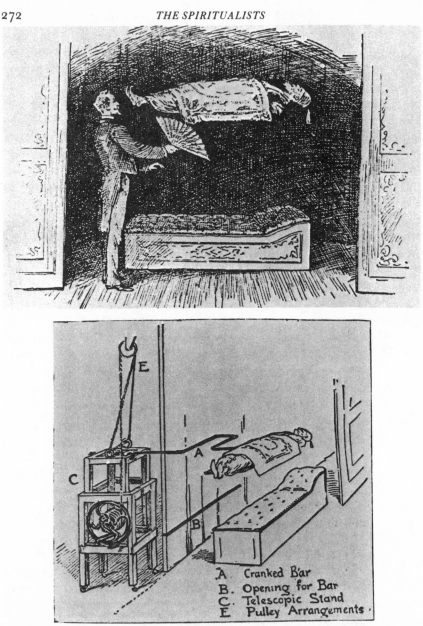

A   Cranked B'ar
B. Opening for Bar
C. Telescopic Stand
E   Pulley Arrangements

"LEVITATION"—HYPNOTISM OR MECHANISM?—WHICH?

levitating. (William Crookes published a list of successful levitators in the *Quarterly Journal of Science*, beginning with the prophet Elijah and including Home.) But illusionists such as Robert-Houdin and Harry Kellar went much further than this. They actually showed levitation on stage. A lady entered, lay down on an ottoman, and rose gently into the air, where a hoop would be passed right round her body; she then returned to earth. Indian fakirs perform a very similar trick, though less complicated; they disappear behind a screen which is removed to reveal the fakir lying in mid-air.

Kellar's apparatus for this trick was highly ingenious. The top of the ottoman was attached to an iron bar worked by a pulley from backstage. Draperies concealed the rigid platform on which the performer lay, and the bar was painted the same colour as the backdrop. In order that a hoop might go – or appear to go – right round the body in mid-air, a U-bend was constructed in the bar connecting the pulley to the ottoman. The hoop could be drawn into the bend, flipped round, appear to have turned right round the body, and then be drawn back again.

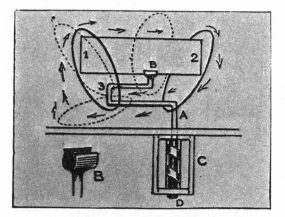

"LEVITATION"—HOW THE HOOP IS PASSED OVER THE BODY.

The Indian fakir's hand rests lightly on a bamboo strut. The secret of the trick is that inside the bamboo runs an iron bar bent at right angles at the top. Attached to this is a metal bracket to support the body. The metal support and the iron stay are covered by the clothes and sleeves of the magician. In this trick the actual preparations must always be carefully screened since often, when no other method is readily available, a deep hole must be dug to hold the base of the bamboo-covered iron rod.

MEDIUMISTIC TECHNIQUES

Some of the methods used by mediums to produce an effect at a seance

were of the crudest, as is shown by the following verbatim account of
the testimony of an accomplice, the mediums in this case having been
caught and brought to trial:

COUNSEL: How many people came to the seance?

MADDOCKS [the accomplice]: Five or six besides Mr and Mrs Fletcher
[the mediums].

COUNSEL: What was done?

MADDOCKS: I sat near the end of the table with Mr Fletcher on my right
and Mrs Fletcher on my left, and the rest of the company sat round the
table, joining hands. Mr Fletcher then put the lights out. They were
candles. He then released my hand, and I got up and went to the musical
box. It was a very large one and the winding up made a noise.

COUNSEL: Did the people say anything?

MADDOCKS: Yes; they said 'How marvellous! What power the spirit
has!' (loud laughter)

COUNSEL: What happened then?

MADDOCKS: The tube was used to tap the guests with. On touching
some of them with it they said 'Thank you, dear spirit' and others said 'Oh,
I am so nervous, don't touch me'. (laughter)

COUNSEL: Who used the tube?

MADDOCKS: I did sometimes, and when I was standing up using the
tube, I accidentally trod on some matches. They ignited and showed my
face. I thought the people would discover who I was, and I sat down, but to
my surprise a lady said she recognised me as the spirit of her uncle or
cousin, I forget which, and was highly delighted. (loud laughter)

COUNSEL: And then you did something with the coal scuttle?

MADDOCKS: Yes. Mrs Fletcher asked the spirits to do something, and I
placed the coal scuttle on the table, and then I took one of the candles from
the candlestick and touched them all round with that.

COUNSEL: Did the table move at all?

MADDOCKS: Oh, yes, we pushed the table backwards and forwards.

COUNSEL: Did you use the phosphorus?

MADDOCKS: Yes, I walked about the room with a bottle of phosphorescent oil to show the spirit lights, and Mrs Fletcher made some small
lights. I showed a phosphorescent light about the size of a half-crown.[13]

This was all pretty knockabout stuff. But some of the methods used
involved great skill both in sleight of hand and psychology.

A contrast between the sitter's view and that of the sceptic is provided by Mr J.Arthur Hill, the friend and confidant of Sir Oliver
Lodge, and Edward Clodd. In the *Nineteenth Century* for June 1917, Hill
wrote: 'A sitting often contains a number of apparently unconnected
statements, the connection or the rationale of which becomes apparent
only by having a series of sittings and carefully collecting the reports,

hence the importance of contemporaneous verbatim notes which I make in shorthand.' Clodd comments: 'In plain English, the medium must have a chance of filling up the gaps in his knowledge about the inquirer between his succeeding visits.'[14] Looked at in this way, the workings of Mrs Piper and many others may be seen in a new light.

David Abbott gives a revealing example of the use of psychology. The medium will give the name of a real dead person from among five or six others all written down at the same time.

A page of writing-paper is divided into six spaces, one beneath the other, one name to be written in each by the sitter. The process has seven steps:

1) The medium gets the sitter to select unconsciously the name of the dead person in advance. This is easily done by adroit suggestion.

2) As they write the names, they will pause before each one except the one selected, especially if hurried along.

3) If left to themselves, they will in about half the cases write the name in the third space from the top. This is especially true if the instructions are to 'mix the dead person's name in among the others, where you cannot know where it is'. The rest of the cases will probably write the name first or last.

4) Talk continuously and distract their attention until the proper moment, when they have reached the space you want – the third space is best, as this is the one they would choose. Just as they start on the first name, say 'Now be sure and select names of living persons I couldn't possibly know.' This will probably ensure that the name of a living person comes first. When the second name is done, say, 'Now write as rapidly as possible.' Then if they pause on the fourth you will know it's the third. If there is no pause before the fourth name, you may still be uncertain – but this should not happen if an expert manner is used.

5) If, despite all this, you are reduced to guesswork, you stand a 1 in 6 chance of success; at the second go, this is reduced to 1 in 3.

6) Cut up the sheet and fold the billets, folding the third, or whichever contains the right name, slightly differently from the rest, so that it can be picked out when the billets are thrown on the table. If you are doubtful, fold the second choice slightly differently again. Memorize these names.

7) Give the dead man's name.

Do not appear to watch while the person is writing. Get the person to cut the paper into slips himself. Help fold the slips, then put on the table, in a hat, etc.

Mediums, however, did not have to rely on bullying, conjuring, or psychological skills to make their effect; nor did they have to cheat so crudely as the Fletchers. One of the biggest bombshells dropped by the author of the *Revelations of a Spirit Medium* was his confirmation of the existence of what was known as the *Blue Book*.

> It was during the third year of the writer's travels that he became a member of an organization of 'mediums' that discovered to him the manner in which the first 'medium' visited by him came by the information he possessed regarding the writer and the writer's family. . . . The writer was asked how he was fixed for 'tests', and had to admit he had none that he had kept track of. Well, the organization was for the purpose of keeping each other posted on 'tests' in the territory in which we traveled. . . . He was supplied with all the 'tests' known by from one to twenty 'mediums' who had done the territory he intended covering, and was expected to make notes of any new 'tests' he should discover.

The writer then went on to give a selection of 'tests' for the city of Cincinnati, Ohio:

> G.A.WILSON (Merchant)
> Spt. Dau. Elsie – Died '76, age 14 mos. diphtheria, blonde, blue eyes.
> Spt. Moth. Elenor Wilson – Died '67, consumption, age 56, dark.
> Spt. Fath. Nathan E. Wilson – Died '71, pneumonia, age 64, light.
> Spt. Friend. Andy Nugent, schoolmates at Oberlin, O. . . .
> R.B.YOUNG, rich
> Spt. Dau. Alice E., aged 19, pneumonia, '79, upper front teeth gold filled. Extraordinarily long hair. Quite an artist, and one of her landscapes hangs in parlor in gilt and gold frame. Spirit painting of her in the sitting room, that is kept curtained. She is an artist in spirit world. Supposed to have a son in spirit that had no earth life named Egbert O.
> Spt. Son – Egbert O., never had earth existence, an inventor in spirit life and supposed to work through Thos. Edison. Is especially interested in electrical work . . .
> Remarks – A good mark for private seances at his home, and will pay well. Dead gone on physical manifestations and materializations. Will get up lots of seances. Agree with everything he says and you are all right.[15]

With such a source of information, what medium could fail?

GADGETS

Some of the gadgets in use by mediums and illusionists were, and still are, relatively complex to set up. For instance, the special chairs used by 'mind-readers' involved at least one accomplice and a special wiring system connected to the chair, terminating in a 'buzzer' which could be felt or heard by the mind-reader, and on which numbers, or letters in the morse code or any other code worked out beforehand, could be transferred. But not all equipment was as complicated as this. The indefatigable David Abbott gave a run-down of mediumistic gadgetry varying from the simplest to the most ingenious.

He began with the simple reaching-rod, telescopic, made of aluminium, little larger than a lead pencil when closed, and extending to six feet or more. This was used for making raps; it could also have a hook on the end for hooking into the handle of a trumpet or any other object which was to be 'floated'. This rod was sometimes made as a tube into which the medium could whisper, the voice 'materializing' at the other end, wherever that might be – for example, through the mouth of the trumpet.

In some 'trumpet' seances the lights are not put out but merely lowered until the room is quite dim. The trumpet is laid on the floor in front of the cabinet, and voices come out of it. This is done by a concealed rubber tube lying under a loose rug; when the trumpet is laid on the floor, the tube is secretly slipped into the small end. If the medium hears a sudden movement among the spectators, she quickly draws the tube into the cabinet and hides it in her clothing.

In some cases the trumpet is laid on a chair in front of the cabinet, and voices come out of it. In this case the medium in the cabinet has a second telescopic trumpet hidden in her clothes. When the curtain is closed, she secures this and extends it, holding it near the curtain directly behind the other one. It is a perfect illusion: the sounds have the trumpet tone, are in line behind the visible trumpet, and the attention is directed to the trumpet in the chair, just as with a ventriloquist's trick and the 'figure'.

Mediums working in their own home may have speaking tubes hidden in the moulding, etc., leading to a confederate who by a switch system sends sound into the room by any or all the tubes. This sound is very hard to locate. This technique may even be used outside: a small iron pipe could be laid underground from a hose and terminate, for instance, near a well – so that the medium could converse with the 'independent voice' even outside. This pipe may be corked to keep moisture out when it is not in use. Of course, it should be used in the evening, in a dim light, and then used but sparingly. After use, it should be recorked and covered with earth, and grass should be rearranged over it.

At one time I filled up my home with a number of mechanical rappers under the floor in different positions. The threads that operated them all entered the room through some tiny holes in the floor back of a couch. My wife lay on this couch, apparently resting and secretly manipulating the threads. I had most marvelous raps, which would seem to move to any position asked for by the spectators, and would answer questions

intelligently. . . . I had one set of strings which caused a piano to voluntarily
strike chords when I should desire. . . .[16]

(The self-playing piano was one of D.D.Home's most apparently
miraculous effects.)

Very similar gadgets are still in use today. For instance, trumpets,
planchettes, crystal balls, ouija boards, pendulums and radiaesthesia
appliances were advertised for sale from an address in Bournemouth in
Psychic News for 5 December 1981.

Even more basic were the discoveries made by E.J.Dingwall with
regard to the famous Zener cards used by J.B.Rhine in his parapsy-
chological card-guessing experiments. In 1970 he wrote:

In 1934 ESP in its modern fashionable attire was born, and tens of
thousands of people started guessing cards and getting extraordinary
results. . . . I was, I admit, wholly unmoved by the flood of propaganda put
out by the parapsychologists in support of these claims. I did not believe in
their stories since the conditions seemed to me to be far from adequate and
allowed plenty of scope for normal methods to operate. However, I was
hardly prepared for what I found one day lying on a table in New York. It
was, it appeared, one of the famous cards used in certain card-guessing
experiments which were supposed to suggest ESP. This card was so crudely
made that a mere glance at the back was sufficient to determine what was
on the front. Although I knew that the cards used in the early experiments
at Duke were so badly made that they were not in some cases even of the
same shape, it was an additional shock to discover that some of the cards
were almost transparent. Evidently some, at least, of the astonishing
beyond chance successes could easily be explained.

 . . . It might have been thought that after an exposure of this sort the
ESP propagandists would have quietly repaired the damage, and seen
to it that no such scandal again arose. The officials of the S.P.R. in
London were, it is true, somewhat disconcerted by these discoveries
and succeeded in having cards made which could not be read from the
back, which at least removed one source of error. Later, however, the
Society, having apparently sold their stock of the opaque cards, began
selling again the packs patented by Dr Rhine in 1937. During tests in
1960 by a S.P.R. working group remarkable hits in clairvoyance runs
were obtained, but it soon emerged that the transparent nature of the
cards offered an easy solution. The handbook supplied with the cards
in 1937, which was arranged and edited by members of the Duke
University Parapsychology Laboratory, is quite clear as to how the
cards were to be used and in the single card calling test the amateur is
instructed to test his ESP by having the pack in front of him and calling
the cards one after another.

After the lapse of thirty years the transparent cards are still being sold.[17]

The spiritoscope, from Professor Robert Hare's *Experimental Investigation of the Spirit Manifestations* (New York, 1855). This was an apparatus which, being contrived to determine whether spirit manifestations were genuine, led to the author's conversion.

In an edition of *The Unexplained* magazine in spring 1982, a set of these cards was printed to be cut out and used for testing ESP. These, too, proved to be quite transparent. The author and all her friends and acquaintances scored 100 per cent hits in tests using them.

MATERIALIZING PHANTOMS

The author of *Revelations of a Spirit Medium* goes into some detail about this, an important part of the stock-in-trade of every successful Victorian medium. Some of the techniques involved have already been discussed (see Chapter 4). *Revelations* describes a specially made guitar, with panels that could be displaced, giving storage space for, among other things, all that a well-dressed phantom could need. This guitar had, apart from this useful feature, the machinery from a small one-tune spring musical box fixed to the wood forming the top, just under the strings.

> Wind this up, set it in motion, take your reaching-rod and insert it in the hole in the neck of the instrument, raise it into view, slowly turning it round and round and waving it back and forth and you present the strange phenomena [*sic*] of a guitar floating in the air and playing a tune upon itself. It does not sound exactly as though the music was produced on the strings; but near enough so that the true explanation, or any explanation the 'medium' is supposed to offer has ever been advanced for it.[18]

(Cf. D.D.Home's accordion, which always played either *Home Sweet Home* or *The Last Rose of Summer*.)

The spirit clothes were made of fine white netting, so fine that

> enough of it could be compressed into a space no larger than an ordinary tin blacking-box to furnish a full evening suit for the largest spirit. Enough more can be carried in a hollow boot-heel to dress up a couple more with an abundance of clothing. In the other boot-heel can be carried an assortment of netting-masks with which to transform your own face half-a-dozen times. In the envelopes supposed to contain letters you have the water-color faces for completing the forms, when their relatives are in attendance.[19]

The art of producing phantoms had, however, been raised to an even higher level than this. Whole processions of them appeared at the better seances, left the cabinet, walked round and talked with the sitters, and the 'medium' could be seen sitting in his chair the while. How was this done? The author of the *Revelations* describes a seance in which eight persons were concerned, seven upstairs in the house and the medium down below in his cabinet, which was constructed in the corner of a room out of lath and plaster with a false ceiling containing a trapdoor.

> Of course it was not necessary that the 'medium' get out of his fastenings, and the facts are that he did not. The table was placed across the cabinet door, not to lay the instruments on, but to be very much in the way should any one make a rush and 'grab' for the 'materialized forms'. In case this occurred, the 'spooks' above would close the light, making the room per-fectly dark, and the manager would do his utmost to turn the table on end, or side, with the legs out in the room. Before the 'grabber' could get the lay of things and get past it, the 'spooks' would have gone through the trap, pulled up the ladder and have closed it.[20]

Clearly, things had moved on considerably since the days of Florence Cook and 'Katie King'.

Not all the phantoms were dressed in white netting. A considerable effect was made by having one of them dressed in black tights from head to toe, with only one arm visible which had been powdered with pulverized luminous paint. This spirit arm was of course capable of anything which an ordinary arm could do, and if anyone seemed to be getting too curious, it could be covered with a long black glove. The arm could even be made to float near the ceiling, if the bearer climbed on to the table. Other spooks could appear and perform at will, variously and appropriately arrayed.

The trapdoor for admitting the ghosts was not always in the ceiling – indeed, this was never possible except where a false ceiling had been constructed. It might be in the floor, but this was risky, as it might easily be discovered. A wide skirting-board was a likely spot; if that was where it was, 'you will find upon examination that there is a joint in it near the corner of the "cabinet", but you will find it solidly nailed with about four nails each side of the joint. . . . The nails are not what they appear, but are only pieces about one-half inch in length and do not even go through the board.'[21] This aperture connected with a corresponding one in the skirting of the next room. It was not really ideal, as the opening could never be very big, and spooks could not escape in a hurry and might tear their robes. Panelling, of course, provided an ideal site for hidden traps in the wall.

FURNITURE-MOVING

One of the most constant features of poltergeist phenomena and other such manifestations is furniture moving apparently of its own accord, and following the medium or (in the case of poltergeists) the focus of the phenomena round the room. Stuart Cumberland reveals at least one way in which this was achieved. In this case a table followed the medium round the room, and it turned out that she was connected to it by a piece of invisible Chinese silk thread – not only invisible, but very strong. At each end of the thread was a bent pin. One pin was attached to her shoe, the other fixed to the table when she passed her hands over it in invoking the spirits. When she sat down and pulled the thread (her long skirt covering her manoeuvres) the spirits worked and the table moved on castors. Castors were essential for the successful execution of this trick, for without them the table would wobble, not glide.[22]

RAPPING

Various methods of producing raps have been noted in the course of the book. The author of *Revelations of a Spirit Medium* gives a few more.

He discounts the theories produced to account for the Fox sisters' phenomena, that they snapped their toe joints, threw small shot against walls and ceiling, and had leaden weights attached to their skirts. There are, he says, much simpler methods of achieving the desired end. The medium

> merely seats himself at the table, spreads his hands on the top, and the 'raps' come without the least particle of trouble. . . . In spreading the hands on the table . . . be careful to bring the thumbnails in contact, one with the other. Press them together tightly and slip them a little at a time. You will find that every time you slip them, one against the other, quite a loud 'rap' will be heard.
>
> Another way is to place your shoe against the leg of the table, and by slipping it backward or forward 'raps' will be produced that will appear to proceed from the table top. Your knee will also furnish 'raps' if pressed against the table leg and moved slightly one way or the other. You can produce 'raps' on a slate or book by holding it in such a way that the nails of the forefingers are in contact, one with the other, and slipping them as in 'rapping' on a table.
>
> In you own room it is an easy matter to so fix a chair or table that by wrenching it one way or another you can get an elegant variety of raps.[23]

FREEING A HAND OR FOOT

This was one of the most necessary and fundamental techniques for a successful medium to acquire. If a hand or foot could be freed while seemingly still remaining under 'control' then any number of otherwise inexplicable tricks could be performed. The simplest way to achieve this was of course to have an accomplice seated on one side. But if this could not be done, there was no need to despair.

The first essential was not to stay still. Eusapia, one of the great practitioners of this art, wriggled and shuffled about incessantly throughout her seances so that those who were trying to keep hold of her anyway had their work cut out. The essence of the trick, however, lies in the fact that a hand consists of both a wrist and fingers; a foot, of both toes and ankle. Moreover, in the case of hands, control may consist of holding or being held – both equally valid.

To free one hand, therefore, the medium holds the wrist of the sitter on one side and is held in the same way by the sitter on the other side. The hands are then manoeuvred closer and closer together until it is possible to combine both sets of control using one hand only. To free both hands, the sitters should be manoeuvred until they are controlling each other, with the medium in the middle.

But how can such a manoeuvre be accomplished when everyone is concentrating on tight control and not letting go? It is surprising how even under these conditions the move may be accomplished quite naturally. The medium, for instance, may need to blow his nose; when he has done this he returns his hand at once – but to a position much closer to the other one. Or he may have to indicate where something should be placed. . . .

Various gadgets were in use to simulate grips of different sorts. Henry Ridgely Evans, in *Hours with the Ghosts*, describes a spring clasp with simulated fingers and thumb, which could be worked by means of wire rings in which the medium's first finger and thumb were inserted and, when the clasp was in position, withdrawn; it was removed in the same way and concealed in the vest pocket. A similar device, a fake clasping hand made of lead, is described in the *Revelations of a Spirit Medium*, but no indication is given of how this was removed once in position. Seeing how easily the feat could be accomplished without resource to gadgets, these seem rather to have been a case of gilding the lily.

TYING WITH ROPES

One commonplace way of making sure the medium was secured was to have him or her (or, in the case of the most famous practitioners of this art, the Davenport Brothers, them) securely tied to the seat by members of the audience. At the end of the show, after all the wonderful phenomena had taken place, the lights would go up and there they would be, still securely tied up.

The art of evading secure tying up is an ancient and complex one. Its essence lies in the inequality of the contest between the unskilled amateur doing the tying and the skilled professional being tied. Robert-Houdin, in a pamphlet on the Davenports, put it like this:

> The ropes used by the Davenport Brothers are of a cotton fibre; and they present therefore smooth surfaces, adapted to slip easily one upon another. Gentlemen are summoned from the audience to tie the mediums. Now, tell me, is it an easy task for an amateur to tie a man up off-hand with a rope three yards long, in a very secure way? The amateur is flurried, self-conscious, anxious to acquit himself well of the business, but he is a gentleman, not a brute, and if one of the Brothers sees the ropes getting into a dangerous tangle, he gives a slight groan, as if he were being injured, and the instantaneous impulse of the other man is to loosen the cord a trifle. A fraction of an inch is an invaluable gain in the after-business of loosening the ropes. Sometimes the stiffening of a muscle, the raising of a shoulder, the crooking of a knee, gives all the play required by the Brothers in ridding themselves of their bonds. Their muscles and joints are wonderfully supple, too; the thumbs can be laid flat in the palm of the hand, the hand itself rounded until it is no broader than the wrist, and then it is easy to pull through. Violent wrenches send the ropes up toward the shoulder, vigorous shakings get the legs free; the first hand untied is thrust through the hole in the door of the cabinet, and then returns to give aid to more serious knots on his own or his brother's person. In tying themselves up the Davenports used the slip-knot, a sort of bow, the ends of which have only to be pulled to be tightened or loosened.[24]

The most thorough exposure of the Davenports took place in 1868, in Liverpool, when some knotsters as expert as they set about the tying and were resisted by the brothers. But this was an altogether untypical occasion.

Other techniques were also used. Some mediums cut their bonds once they were in the cabinet, having ready-prepared ties with slip-knots to don at the end of the seance before the lights went up again. In some tricks (such as a performance of sawing the lady in half recently seen on British television) the sensational presentation of the trick was so skilfully done that nobody even thought of checking what had happened to the bonds at the end.

Houdini always advised anyone trying to make sure that a medium could not escape once tied up to insist on using, not rope, which can almost always be manoeuvred, but cotton thread. After all, what is needed is not brute force – merely an assurance that the performer is genuinely unable to move. Certainly when this method was suggested to Eusapia, she indignantly rejected it.

SPIRIT PICTURES

One of the most effective tricks in the medium's repertoire was the materialization, before the astonished eyes of the audience, of spirit pictures on a blank canvas.

One crude method of achieving this effect was to have two canvases, one of which had on it a still-wet oil painting. A blank face was presented to the public; when the 'picture' was covered and the cover removed, the top canvas was also removed, and the picture had been transferred to the bottom one. Another method was to paint over a picture a thin layer of easily dissolved white, which could be sprayed off with a solvent.

THE DAVENPORT BROTHERS IN THEIR CABINET.

David Abbott, however, gave a rather more effective recipe for achieving this effect.

If a canvas of unbleached muslin have a portrait painted on it with the solutions given below, it will appear to be unprepared, as the chemicals will be invisible when dry. If sprayed with a weak solution of tincture of iron, the picture gradually appears:

Sulphocyanide of potassium – red
Ferrocyanide of potassium – blue
Tannin – black
or
Sulphate of iron – blue
Nitrate of bismuth – yellow
Copper sulphate – brown
– these should be sprayed with a solution of prussiate of potash.

Music can be played to cover the noise of the atomizer. Or passes can be made to speed up the results, while using an atomizer concealed in the sleeve.[25]

Notes

1 KNOCK, KNOCK, WHO'S THERE?

1. Davenport, pp. 91–2.
2. Ibid.
3. Capron and Barron, pp. 15–16.
4. The account of events in Rochester is from Cadwallader, *Hydesville in History*, as recounted by Leah, then Mrs Underhill, to the author, a friend of hers.
5. Ibid.
6. Davenport, pp. 103–4.
7. Capron, *Modern Spiritualism*, p. 421.
8. Ibid., p. 422.
9. Ibid., pp. 220–4.
10. E.A. Poe, 'The Facts in the Case of M. Valdemar', from *Tales of Mystery and Imagination*, pp. 280–9.
11. For a full and clear discussion of mesmerism and its associated movements, see Podmore, I, pp. 51–176.
12. Conway, I, p. 260.
13. Quoted Podmore, I, p. 163.
14. Davenport, p. 127.
15. Symonds, p. 220.
16. Davenport, p. 127.
17. Ibid., p. 106.
18. Capron, *Modern Spiritualism*, p. 72.
19. Ibid., pp. 88–9.
20. Ibid., p. 89.
21. This account taken from Capron, pp. 91–7.
22. *Spiritual Telegraph*, Boston, Vol. I, No. 1, July 1850.
23. Davenport, pp. 144–5.
24. *Holden's Dollar Magazine*, September 1850.
25. Letter from John Hurn, *New York Tribune*, 12 March 1850.
26. Flint et al., p. 5.
27. Page, p. 5.
28. Britten, *Modern American Spiritualism*, p. 155.
29. Ibid., p. 152.
30. Fox, *Memoir and Love Life of Dr Kane*, p. 22.
31. Ibid., All quotations from letters between Maggie Fox and Dr Kane are taken from this collection.
32. *New York Tribune*, 6 November 1855.
33. *Blackwood's Edinburgh Magazine*, May 1853.
34. Hatch, p. 12.
35. Ibid.
36. Elder, *Life of Elisha Kent Kane*.
37. Fornell, p. 109.
38. Britten, *Modern American Spiritualism*, p. 132.
39. Ibid., p. 546.
40. Truesdell, p. 315.
41. *New York Times*, 6 December 1858.
42. Edmonds and Dexter, p. 56.
43. *New York Times*, 29 November 1858.
44. *New York Times*, 6 December 1858.
45. Britten, *Autobiography*, p. 106.
46. Ibid., p. 40.

2 MR SLUDGE AND OTHER MEDIUMS

1. Figures given by a correspondent of *The Spiritual World*, quoted Podmore, I, p. 183.
2. C.F.Browne: 'Among the Spirits', *Complete Works of Artemus Ward*.
3. Strong, *Diaries*, II.
4. de Morgan, preface, p. x.
5. Sidgwick, *H.S.*, p. 385.
6. *Spiritual Magazine*, November 1860.
7. Guppy, *Mary Jane*.
8. Truesdell, p. 316.
9. Dialectical Society, *Report*, p. 204.
10. Conway, II, p. 312.
11. Britten, *Autobiography*, pp. 2–3.
12. Adams, pp. 11–12.
13. Taylor, 'Confessions of a Medium'.
14. Dunne, '*Intrusions*', pp. 95–6.
15. E.B.Browning, *Letters to her Sister*.
16. Dialectical Society, *Report*.
17. Home, *Incidents in My Life*, pp. 18–19.
18. Wallace, *My Life*, II, p. 281.
19. *Spiritual Magazine*, May 1860.
20. Archives of the Swedenborg Society, cited Gauld, p. 67.
21. Letter to Mrs Trollope, 19 June 1855, cited Henry Dickens, p. 63.
22. Charles Dickens, cited Porter, p. 17.
23. Henry Dickens, p. 63.
24. Burton, p. 143.
25. Mrs Home, *D.D.Home, His Life and Mission*, p. 25.
26. Letter from Robert Browning to Mrs Elizabeth Kinney, now in Yale library.
27. Elizabeth Barrett Browning, letter to her sister Henrietta, 17 August 1855.
28. Letter to Mrs Kinney.
29. Letter to Henrietta.
30. Letter to Mrs Kinney.
31. E.B.B. to Henrietta, 18 November 1856.
32. Letter to Mrs Kinney.
33. Ibid.
34. This story is recounted in Dingwall, *Some Human Oddities*, which contains an excellent account of Home's sojourn at the French court.
35. *Harper's Weekly*, 25 April 1857.
36. In most detail, by Dingwall.
37. Ibid., p. 121.
38. E.B.B. to Henrietta, 1858.
39. Dialectical Society, *Report*, p. 207.
40. Ibid., pp. 207–8.
41. Dunraven, *Experiences in Spiritualism with D.D.Home*.
42. Ibid., pp. 148–9.
43. Ibid., pp. 152–3.
44. Ibid., p. 155.
45. Ibid.
46. Dialectical Society, *Report*, p. 214.
47. Houdini, *Magician Among the Spirits*, p. 48.
48. Dunraven, pp. 155–6.
49. Podmore, II, p. 245.
50. Dickens, p. 64.
51. Evans, *Hours with the Ghosts*, p. 109.
52. Rinn, *Searchlight on Psychical Research*.
53. Carpenter, *On Fallacies Respecting the Supernatural*.
54. Hall, *New Light on Old Ghosts*, p. 110.
55. Dunraven, p. 157.
56. Ibid.

3 SCIENTISTS AND SPIRITS

1. *Quarterly Journal of Science*, July 1870.
2. Fournier d'Albe, *Life of Crookes*, pp. 197–8.
3. Ibid., p. 203.
4. *Quarterly Journal of Science*, July 1871.
5. Fournier d'Albe, op. cit., p. 207.
6. Ibid.
7. *Quarterly Journal of Science*, January 1874.
8. Fournier d'Albe, *Life of Crookes*, p. 200.
9. Ibid., p. 215.
10. Sidgwick, *H.S.*, pp. 290–1.
11. Fournier d'Albe, *Life of Crookes*, p. 193.
12. Dr A.Lehman, SPR, *Journal*, November 1900, p. 323.
13. M.Petrovo Solovovo, ibid., p. 324.
14. *Light*, 26 September 1885.
15. Sidgwick, *H.S.*, p. 53.
16. Ibid., p. 160.

17. Ibid., p. 347.
18. Ibid., p. 387.
19. Anon, *Extra Physics*, pp. 15–16.
20. Wallace, *My Life*, II, p. 296.
21. Popper, *The Logic of Scientific Discovery*, p. 280.
22. Ibid., p. 279.
23. Driesch, *Psychical Research*, pp. xii–xiii.
24. Dunne, *An Experiment with Time*, p. 87.
25. Dunne, '*Intrusions*', p. 86.
26. Ibid., p. 108.
27. Rhine, pp. 143–4.
28. Ibid., pp. 196–202.
29. Inglis, p. 445.
30. Ibid., p. 360.
31. Ibid., p. 451.

4 THE GHOST-GRABBERS

1. W.H. Evans, *How to be a Medium*, p. 81.
2. Report in *The Nation*, cited Fornell, pp. 145–6.
3. Seybert Commission, *Report*, pp. 150–1.
4. David Abbott, *Open Court*, March 1907.
5. Seybert, *Report*, pp. 153–4.
6. *The Spiritualist*, 13 November 1874.
7. *New York Sun*, 1892.
8. Wallace, II, pp. 278–9.
9. SPR, *Proceedings*, 3 May 1886.
10. Samuel Guppy, *Imitations of Spiritual Phenomena*, p. 8.
11. Davies, p. 310.
12. Ibid., p. 312.
13. Cited Hall, *The Spiritualists*, p. 29.
14. Cited Medhurst and Goldney, 'William Crookes and the Physical Phenomena of Mediumship', p. 58.
15. Ibid., p. 59.
16. *The Spiritualist*, 6 February 1874.
17. *The Spiritualist*, 16 January 1874.
18. *The Spiritualist*, 6 February 1874.
19. Fournier d'Albe, *William Crookes*, p. 223.
20. Medhurst and Goldney, 'William Crookes', pp. 41–2.
21. SPR, *Proceedings*, 3 May 1886.
22. Fournier d'Albe, *Life of Crookes*, p. 225.
23. *The Spiritualist*, 3 April 1874.
24. *The Spiritualist*, 5 June 1874.
25. Davies, p. 318.
26. *The Spiritualist*, 2 January 1874.
27. Davies, p. 316.
28. *Light*, 16 September 1882.
29. Davies, p. 319.
30. *The Spiritualist*, 5 June 1874.
31. Fornell, p. 145.
32. e.g., *New York Times*, 14 September 1979.
33. Cited Hall, *The Spiritualists*, p. 102.
34. Cited Medhurst and Goldney, 'William Crookes', p. 113–14.
35. Ibid., p. 117.
36. Conway, II, p. 332.

5 WHY ECTOPLASM?

1. For a remarkably interesting discussion of this aspect of Victorian life, see Steven Marcus, *The Other Victorians*, London, 1967.
2. *The Spiritualist*, 2 and 15 August 1873.
3. Lodge, *Past Years*, p. 296.
4. Ibid., p. 298.
5. Ibid., p. 302.
6. See also the discussion of this topic in Moore, *In Search of White Crows*; also Rawcliffe, and Alcock, *passim*.
7. Foreword to Mackenzie, *Hauntings and Apparitions*, and three other volumes, all printed for the SPR, London, 1982.
8. Richet, *Thirty Years of Psychical Research*, pp. 543–4.
9. Ibid., p. 467.
10. *Daily Chronicle*, 29 October 1895.
11. For example, in the number-guessing experiments conducted with Basil Shackleton by the mathematician S.G. Soal. The fact that Soal cheated in these experiments has only recently been proved – being an expert mathematician, he did so very cleverly. And how much confidence can be placed in any findings by Sir Cyril Burt, considering that he even

cheated in his own field of
psychology?
12. See the discussion of Bien Boa's
   'psychogenesis' in Flournoy,
   pp. 488–9.
13. *Annals of Psychical Science*, Vol. II,
   No. 5, 1905, p. 283.
14. Ibid., p. 272.
15. Tuckett, p. 92.
16. *Annals of Psychical Science*, Vol. II,
   No. 5, pp. 273, 274.
17. Ibid., pp. 283–4.
18. Ibid., p. 286.
19. Ibid., p. 288.
20. *Annals of Psychical Science*, Vol. III,
   No. 4, 1906, p. 206.
21. *Le Matin*, 3 January 1914.
22. *Annals of Psychical Science*, Vol. III,
   No. 4, pp. 207–8.
23. Schrenck-Notzing, p. 38.
24. Ibid., p. 39.
25. Ibid., p. 30.
26. Ibid., p. 31.
27. e.g. p. 82; but *passim*.
28. Ibid.
29. Crawford, pp. 133–4.
30. Ibid., p. 149.
31. Schrenck-Notzing, p. 15.
32. Ibid., p. 116.
33. Ibid., pp. 143–4.
34. Ibid., pp. 188–9.
35. Ibid., p. 221.
36. Ibid., p. 293.
37. Ibid., pp. 304–5.
38. Ibid., pp. 337, 340.
39. Houdini, *Magician Among the Spirits*,
   p. 174.
40. Ibid., p. 175.
41. Crawford, p. v.
42. Jastrow, *Wish and Wisdom*, p. 380.
43. All cited by Alcock, p. 119.

6 MAGICIANS AMONG THE SPIRITS

1. Rinn, p. 113.
2. Houdini, *Magician Among the Spirits*,
   pp. 141–2.
3. Doyle, *Our American Adventure*, p. 190.
4. Ernst and Carrington, p. 159.

5. Houdini, *Magician Among the Spirits*,
   p. 150.
6. Ibid., p. 151.
7. Ernst and Carrington, pp. 165–8.
8. Ibid., pp. 162–3.
9. Ibid., p. 171.
10. Ibid., p. 174.
11. Ibid., p. 174.
12. Cited Ernst and Carrington,
   pp. 180–1.
13. Doyle, *On the Edge of the Unknown*, cited
   Ernst and Carrington, p. 167.
14. Ibid., p. 147.
15. Houdini, *Magician Among the Spirits*,
   pp. 159–60.
16. Christopher, pp. 187ff.
17. Correspondence quoted Meikle,
   p. 33.
18. Houdini, *Margery* pamphlet, p. 7.
19. Ibid., pp. 7–8.
20. Ibid., pp. 13–18.
21. *Boston Herald*, 22 December 1924.
22. *Boston Herald*, 26 January 1925.
23. Ibid.
24. *Progressive Thinker*, 18 April 1925.
25. Unpublished letter in Harry Price
   Library.
26. *Boston Evening Transcript*, 18 February
   1925.
27. *Boston Herald*, 9 February 1925.
28. Ibid.
29. Doyle, *Edge of the Unknown*, p. 13.

7 WHISKY AND CIGARS ON THE OTHER SIDE

1. Meikle, p. 24.
2. Harper, pp. 23–4.
3. Letter in possession of University of
   Iowa Library.
4. E. Stead, *My Father*, pp. 103–6.
5. Ibid., pp. 132–6.
6. Ibid., p. 173.
7. Robertson-Scott, p. 245.
8. W. T. Stead, *Real Ghost Stories*, pp. 4–6.
9. Harper, p. 43.
10. Cited Harper, p. 36.
11. W. T. Stead, *Real Ghost Stories*,
   introduction.

12. Ibid., pp. 26–7.
13. Harper, pp. 39–41.
14. Robertson-Scott, pp. 192–3.
15. *Daily Chronicle*, 1 November 1909.
16. E.Stead, pp. 198–9.
17. Harper, pp. 50–1.
18. Ibid., p. 24.
19. Ibid., pp. 129–32.
20. E. Stead, p. 333.
21. Ibid., p. 341.
22. Ibid., p. 343.
23. Hill (ed), *Letters from Sir Oliver Lodge*.
24. Ibid.
25. James, 'What Psychical Research has Accomplished', in *The Will to Believe*, pp. 222–38.
26. Ibid., p. 235.
27. Ibid., p. 236.
28. James, *The Will to Believe*, Introduction, p. xxxvii.
29. *Open Court*, March 1907.
30. SPR, *Proceedings*, Vol. VI, p. 465; cited Tuckett, p. 337.
31. *Open Court*, March 1907.
32. SPR, *Proceedings*, Vol. VI, pp. 534, 5; cited Tuckett, p. 330.
33. Tuckett, p. 331.
34. Murphy and Ballou, p. 205.
35. Lodge, *Raymond Revised*, pp. 8–9.
36. Ibid., pp. 56–7.
37. Hill, p. 143.
38. Lodge, *Raymond Revised*, pp. 61–2.
39. Ibid., pp. 112–13.
40. Hill, pp. 114–15.
41. Cited Clodd, p. 182.
42. Lodge, *Raymond Revised*, p. 189.
43. Ibid., p. 214.
44. Cited Alcock, pp. 109–10.
45. Meikle, p. 28.
46. Cited Alcock, p. 14.
47. Doyle, *Our American Adventure*, p. 19.
48. Ibid., p. 43.
49. Doyle, *Coming of the Fairies*, p. 29.
50. Coates, *Photographing the Invisible*, p. 92.
51. Ibid., pp. 95–6.
52. Doyle, *Coming of the Fairies*, pp. 32–3.
53. Ibid., p. 50.
54. Ibid., p. 52.
55. Meikle, pp. 35–7.

8 THE REJECTION OF DISBELIEF

1. *Open Court*, 8 November 1888.
2. *New York Herald*, 24 September 1888.
3. Inglis, p. 209.
4. Ibid., p. 370.
5. Gauld, pp. 25–6.
6. *The Times*, 27 April 1907.
7. Sargent and Eysenck, p. 168.
8. *New York Herald*, 20 October 1901, Section 5, p. 2.
9. Correspondence between the Pellew family and Edward Clodd, cited Rinn, pp. 125–6.
10. Sidgwick, *H.S.*, pp. 405, 410.
11. Yeats, p. 24–5.
12. Symonds, pp. 210–11.
13. Kingsland, p. 5.
14. Maskelyne, *Modern 'Theosophy'*, p. 59.
15. Symonds, p. 238.
16. Myers, *Fragments*, p. 46.
17. *Open Court*, September 1900, pp. 539 ff.
18. Henry James, 'Is There a Life after Death?'
19. William James, *Last Report*, Murphy and Ballou.
20. Undated cutting, Harry Price Library.
21. Marks and Kammann, p. 157.
22. Ibid., pp. 164–7. G. Spencer Brown, also discussing the question of probability theory as it relates to psychical research, points out the importance of the point at which it is decided to stop a run (e.g., in Rhine's card-guessing experiments) in order to work out the results relative to the expected average.
23. James, *Last Report*, Murphy and Ballou, p. 310.
24. Ibid., p. 311.
25. *Collier's Weekly*, 14 May 1910.
26. Inglis, p. 430.
27. Charles Hallock, MBS, *Open Court*, November 1903.
28. Barrett, p. 10.
29. Murchison, pp. 286 ff.: 'The Animus of Psychical Research'.

30. Huxley, *Life and Letters of Huxley I*,
    p. 240.
31. W. James, *Last Report*, Murphy and
    Ballou, p. 315.
32. Sargent and Eysenck, p. 6.
33. McGuire and Hull, p. 398.
34. Ibid., pp. 364ff.
35. Tuckett, p. 21.

APPENDIX: THE MACHINE IN THE GHOST

1. Barrett, p. 77.
2. Medhurst, Goldney and Barrington,
   p. 217.
3. Houdini, *Miracle-Mongers and their
   Methods*, pp. 101–110.
4. Harry Price, University of London
   Council for Psychical Investigation,
   Bulletin, II, 1936: 'Two Experimental
   Firewalks'; *Bulletin*, IV, 1938: 'Three
   Experimental Firewalks'.
5. H. R. Evans, *Hours with the Ghosts*,
   pp. 132–5.
6. Newcombe, 'Modern Occultism',
   Nineteenth Century, 383, p. 137.
7. Broad, pp. 101–2.

8. *Open Court*, March 1907.
9. Jastrow, *Fact and Fable in Psychology*,
   p. 130.
10. Dingwall and Price, *Revelations of a
    Spirit Medium*, pp. 302–3.
11. Dialectical Society, *Report*, p. 74.
12. SPR, *Proceedings*, 1887, pp. 46–7.
13. This account is taken from Trevor
    Hall, *The Spiritualists*, pp. 128–9. It
    was first printed in the *Dailly News*,
    29 January 1881.
14. Clodd, p. 185.
15. Dingwall and Price, op. cit.,
    pp. 107–9.
16. *Open Court*, January 1907.
17. *Parapsychology Review*, November–
    December, 1970, pp. 16–17.
18. Dingwall and Price, op. cit., p. 116.
19. Ibid., p. 117.
20. Ibid., pp. 290–3.
21. Ibid., p. 300.
22. Cumberland, pp. 72–3.
23. Dingwall and Price, op. cit.,
    pp. 171–2.
24. Quoted H. R. Evans, *Hours with the
    Ghosts*, pp. 141–2.
25. *Open Court*, April 1907.

Bibliography

Abbott, David P.: *Behind the Scenes with the Mediums*, Chicago, 1907.

Abbott, David P.: 'Independent Voices, Movement of Objects without Contact, and Spirit Portraits', *Journal* of the ASPR, April 1911.

Abbott, David P.: 'The History of a Strange Case', reproduced from *Open Court* for May and June, 1908.

Adams, John S.: *Answers to seventeen objections against Spiritual Intercourse and Inquiries relating to the Manifestations of the Present Time*, New York, 1853.

Alcock, James E.: *Parapsychology: Science or Magic? A psychological perspective*, Oxford, 1981.

Appleton, Thomas Gold, *A Sheaf of Papers*, Boston, 1875.

Baggally, W.W.: *Telepathy, Genuine and Fraudulent*, London, 1917.

Balfour, Countess of: 'The Palm Sunday Case: New Light on an Old Love Story', *Proceedings* of the SPR, Vol. 52, Part 189, February 1960.

Barnum, P.T.: *The Humbugs of the World*, London, 1866.

Barrett, Sir William F., FRS: *On the Threshold of the Unseen*, London, 1920 (3rd edition).

Barber, Theodore X.: *Pitfalls in Human Research*, Oxford and New York, 1976.

Beatty, James McGregor: *Illustrious Madmen of the Ages*, Los Angeles, 1919.

Bisson, J.A.: *Les phénomènes dits de matérialisation*, Paris, 1914.

Blackburn, Douglas: *Daily News*, 1 and 5 September 1911, confessions *re* Smith and Blackburn frauds.

Blackburn, Douglas: 'Sir Oliver Lodge's Innocence', letter, *Sunday Times*, 16 September 1917.

Blavatsky, H.P.: *Letters to A.P.Sinnett*.

Britten, E. Hardinge: *Autobiography*, Manchester, 1900.

Britten, E. Hardinge: *Modern American Spiritualism: A Twenty Years' Record of the Communion between Earth and the World of Spirits*, New York, 1870.

Broad, C.D.: *Lectures on Psychical Research*, London, 1962.

Brown, G. Spencer: *Probability and Scientific Inference*, London, 1957.

Browne, Charles Farrar ('Artemus Ward'): 'Among the Spirits', *Complete Works of Artemus Ward*, London, 1884.

Browning, Elizabeth Barrett: *Letters to her Sister, 1846–59*.

Browning, Robert: 'Mr Sludge "The Medium"'.
Burr, George Lincoln (ed.): *Narratives of the witchcraft cases 1648–1706*, New York, 1914.
Burr brothers: *Knocks for the Knockings*, Rochester, 1851.
Burton, Jean: *Heyday of a Wizard*, London, 1948.
Cadwallader, Mary: *Hydesville in History*, Lily Dale, N.Y., 1911.
Campbell, Elder C.: *The Spiritual Telegraphic Opposition Line; or, Science and Divine Revelation against Spiritual Manifestations*, Springfield, Illinois, 1853.
Campbell, John L., and Trevor H. Hall: *Strange Things: the Story of Fr. Allen McDonald, Ada Goodrich Freer, and the Society for Psychical Research's Enquiry into Highland Second Sight*, London, 1954.
Cannell, J.C.: *The Secrets of Houdini*, London, 1932.
Capron, E.W.: *Modern Spiritualism, Its Facts and Fanticisms, its Consistencies and Contradictions*, Boston, 1855.
Capron, E.W., and H.D. Barron: *Explanation of the mysterious Communion with Spirits*, Auburn, N.Y., 1850.
Carpenter, W.B.: 'On Fallacies of Testimony in Relation to the Supernatural', *Contemporary Review*, January 1876.
Chevreul, M.-E.: *De la Baguette divinatoire, du pendule dit explorateur, et des tables tournantes au point de vue de l'histoire, de la critique et de la méthode expérimentale*, Paris, 1854.
Christopher, Milbourne: *Houdini: The Untold Story*, New York, 1969.
Clark, Franklin W.: 'The Rochester Rappers' (Master's thesis, unpublished), Rochester, 1933.
Clemens, Samuel (Mark Twain): *Life on the Mississippi*, New York, 1883.
Clodd, Edward: *The Question: If a man die, shall he live again?* London, 1917.
Coates, James (ed.): *Has W.T. Stead Returned? A Symposium*, London, 1913.
Coates, James: *Photographing the Invisible*, New York, 1912.
Conway, Moncure: *Autobiography* (2 vols), London, 1904.
Cooke, Parsons: *Necromancy, or, a Rap for the Rappers*, Boston, 1857.
Crawford, W.J.: *The Psychic Structures of the Goligher Circle*, London, 1919.
Crowe, Catherine: *The Night Side of Nature or, Ghosts and Ghost Seers*, London, 1854.
Cumberland, Stuart: *That Other World: Personal Experiences of Mystics and their Mysticism*, London, 1918.
Davenport, R.B.: *The Death-Blow to Spiritualism*, New York, 1888.
Davies, C.M.: *Mystic London*, London, 1875.
de Morgan, Mrs C. (preface by August de Morgan): *From Matter to Spirit*, London, 1863.
Dessoir, Max: *The Psychology of Legerdemain*, Chicago, 1893.
Dickens, Sir Henry: *Recollections*, London, 1934.
Dingwall, E.J.: *The Critics' Dilemma*, Crowhurst, Sussex, 1966.
Dingwall, E.J.: 'Responsibility in Parapsychology', *Parapsychology Review*, Nov.–Dec., 1970.
Dingwall, E.J.: *Some Human Oddities*, London, 1947.
Dingwall, E.J., K.M. Goldney and T.H. Hall: *The Haunting of Borley Rectory*, London, 1956.
Dingwall, E.J., and Harry Price (eds): *Revelations of a Spirit Medium*, St Paul, Minnesota, 1891; facsimile edition, London, 1922.
Doyle, A. Conan: *Memories and Adventures*, Boston, 1924.

Doyle, A.Conan: *On the Edge of the Unknown*, London, 1930.

Doyle, A.Conan: *Our American Adventure*, New York, 1923.

Doyle, A.Conan: *Our Second American Adventure*, London, 1923.

Doyle, A.Conan: *The Coming of the Fairies*, London, 1922.

Driesch, Hans: Presidential Address to the Society for Psychical Research, 1926 (SPR, *Proceedings*, XXXVI, pp. 171 ff.).

Driesch, Hans: *Psychical Research, the science of the super-normal* (tr. Theodore Besterman), London, 1933.

Ducasse, C.J..: *Is life after death possible?* Los Angeles, 1948.

Ducasse, C.J.: *The belief in a life after death*, Chicago, 1961.

Dunne, J.W.: *An Experiment with Time*, Papermac edition, London, 1981.

Dunne, J.W.: '*Intrusions*', London, 1955.

Dunraven, Earl of: *Experiences in Spiritualism with Mr D.D.Home*, London, 1869 or 1870; reprinted 1924 as part of Vol. XXXV of the *Proceedings* of the SPR and for the SPR as a book in Glasgow, with introduction by Sir Oliver Lodge.

Edmonds, John Worth, and Geo. T.Dexter: *Spiritualism*, New York, 1853.

Edmunds, Simeon: *Spiritualism: A Critical Survey*, London, 1966.

Elder, William: *Life of Elisha Kent Kane*, Philadelphia, 1857.

Ernst, Bernard M.L., and Hereward Carrington: *Houdini and Conan Doyle*, London, 1933.

Evans, Henry Ridgely: *Hours with the Ghosts*, Chicago, 1897.

Evans, Henry Ridgely: *The Old and the New Magic*, Chicago, 1909.

Evans, Henry Ridgely: *The Spirit World Unmasked*, Chicago, 1902.

Evans, Hilary: *Intrusions – Society and the Paranormal*, London, 1982.

Evans, W.H.: *How to be a Medium*, Philadelphia, n.d.

Ewer, F.C.: *The Eventful Nights of August 20th and 21st, 1854; and how Judge Edmonds was Hocussed; or, Fallibility of 'Spiritualism' Exposed*, New York, 1854.

Flint, A., C.A.Lee and C.B.Coventry: *Discovery of the Source of the Rochester Knockings*, Buffalo, 1851.

Flournoy, Théodore: 'Esprits et médiums', in *Mélanges de métapsychique et de psychologie*, Geneva and Paris, 1911.

Fornell, E.W.: *The Unhappy Medium: Spiritualism and the Life of Margaret Fox*, Austin, Texas, 1964.

Fournier d'Albe, E.E.: *Life of Sir William Crookes*, London, 1923.

Fournier d'Albe, E.E.: *New Light on Immortality*, London, 1908.

Fox, Margaret: *Memoir and the Love-life of Doctor Kane: Containing the Correspondence, and a History of the Acquaintance, Engagement and Secret Marriage between Elisha K.Kane and Margaret Fox*, New York, 1866.

Freer, Ada Goodrich: *Essays in Psychical Research*, London, 1899.

Gauld, Alan: *The Founders of Psychical Research*, London, 1968.

Geley, Dr Gustave: *Clairvoyance and Materialisation*, London, 1927.

Gettings, Fred: *Ghosts in Photographs*, London and New York, 1978.

Goldston, Will: *Exclusive Magical Secrets*, London, 1912.

Gould, Stephen Jay: *The Panda's Thumb*, New York and London, 1980.

Gridley, J.A.: *Astounding Facts from the Spirit World*, Southampton, Mass., 1854.

Grimes, Prof. J.Stanley, and Leo Miller, Esq: *Great Discussion of Modern Spiritualism at the Melodeon, Boston, reported, verbatim, for the Banner of Light*, Boston, 1860.

Guppy, Samuel: *Imitations of Spiritual Phenomena, with comments thereon*, London, 1873.

Guppy, Samuel: *Mary Jane; or, Spiritualism Chemically Explained, with Spirit Drawings*, London, 1863.

Hall, Trevor H.: *New Light on Old Ghosts*, London, 1965.

Hall, Trevor H.: *The Spiritualists*, London, 1962.

Hall, Trevor H.: *The Strange Case of Edmund Gurney*, London, 1964.

Hansel, C.E.M.: *E.S.P. – A scientific evaluation*, London, 1966.

Harper, Edith K.: *Stead the Man*, London, 1914.

Hatch, Benjamin F.: *Spiritualists' Iniquities Unmasked and the Hatch Divorce Case*, New York, 1859.

Hawthorne, Nathaniel: *American Notebooks*, Boston, 1868.

Hill, J. Arthur (ed.): *Letters from Sir Oliver Lodge*, London, 1932.

Hodgson, Richard: 'The possibilities of mal-observation and lapse of memory, from a practical point of view', *Proceedings* of the SPR, 1886–7, Vol. 4, pp. 38ff.

Home, D.D.: *Incidents in my Life*, London, 1864.

Home, D.D.: *Lights and Shadows of Spiritualism*, London, 1877.

Home, Mrs D.D.: *D.D. Home. His life and Mission*, London, 1888.

Home, Mrs D.D.: *The Gift of D.D. Home*, London, 1890.

Houdini, Harry: *Houdini Exposes the Tricks Used by the Boston Medium "Margery"*, New York, 1924.

Houdini, Harry: *A Magician Among the Spirits*, New York, 1924.

Houdini, Harry: *Miracle-Mongers and their Methods*, New York, 1920.

Howells, William Dean: *Impressions and Experiences*, New York, 1896.

Howells, William Dean: *The Undiscovered Country*, New York, 1880.

Howells, William Dean: *Thoughts on the Future Life*, New York, 1910.

Human Nature, monthly, ed. John Burns, London, April 1867.

Huxley, L.: *Life and Letters of Huxley, Vol 1*, London, 1900.

Huxley, T.H.: *Collected Essays*, London, 1893–4.

Inglis, Brian: *Natural and Supernatural*, London, 1977.

Innes, Taylor: 'Where Are the Letters?', *Nineteenth Century*, London, Vol. XXII, pp. 174–94.

James, Henry: 'Is There a Life after Death?,' essay in W.D. Howells (ed), *In After Days, Thoughts on the Future Life*, New York, 1910.

James, William: *Letters*, ed. Henry James, London, 1926.

James, William: *The Will to Believe*, Harvard UP edition, 1979.

Jastrow, Joseph: *Fact and Fable in Psychology*, New York, 1900.

Jastrow, Joseph: *The Psychology of Conviction*, New York, 1918.

Jastrow, Joseph: *Wish and Wisdom – Episodes in the Vagaries of Belief*, New York and London, 1935.

Jung, C.G.: *Flying Saucers: a Modern Myth of Things Seen in the Skies* (tr. R.F.C. Hull), London, 1959.

Kerr, Howard: *Mediums and Spirit-rappers and Roaring Radicals – Spiritualism in American Literature 1850–1890*, Chicago, 1972.

Kingsland, William: *Was She a Charlatan?* London, 1923.

Koestler, Arthur: *The Ghost in the Machine*, London, 1967.

Koestler, Arthur: *The Roots of Coincidence*, London, 1972.

Lang, Andrew: *Cock Lane and Common-sense*, London, 1894.

Lathrop, Rose Hawthorne: *Memories of Hawthorne*, New York, 1897.

Lodge, Sir Oliver: *Past Years*, London, 1931.

Lodge, Sir Oliver: *Phantom Walls*, London, 1929.

Lodge, Sir Oliver: *Raymond, or Life after Death*, London, 1916.

Lodge, Sir Oliver: *Raymond Revised*, London, 1922.

London Dialectical Society: *Report of an investigation into spiritualism*, 1871.

Mach, Ernst: 'The Propensity towards the Marvellous', *Open Court*, Chicago, September 1900, pp. 539–50.

Marks, David, and Richard Kammann: *The Psychology of the Psychic*, Buffalo, N.Y., 1980.

Maskelyne, J.N.: *Modern Spiritualism*, London, 1876.

Maskelyne, J.N.: *The fraud of modern 'Theosophy' exposed*, London, 1913.

Mattison, Rev. H.: *Spirit Rapping Unveiled*, New York, 1853.

McDougall, William: *Body and Mind*, New York, 1908.

McGuire, William, and R.F.C. Hull (eds): *C. G. Jung Speaking – Interviews and Encounters*, London, 1978.

Medhurst, R.G. (ed. with K.M. Goldney and M.R. Barrington): *Crookes and the Spirit World*, London, 1972.

Medhurst, R.G., and K.M. Goldney: 'William Crookes and the Physical Phenomena of Mediumship, – SPR *Proceedings*, Vol. LV, Part 195, March 1964.

Meikle, Jeffrey: '"Over There": Arthur Conan Doyle and Spiritualism', University of Texas at Austin Library *Journal*, 1974.

Moore, L.: *In Search of White Crows*, Oxford, 1977.

Muensterberg, Hugo: *Psychology and Life*, New York, 1899.

Muensterberg, Hugo, *et al.*: *Subconscious Phenomena*, Boston, 1910.

Murchison, Carl (ed.): *The Case for and against Psychical Belief*, Worcester, Mass., 1927.

Murphy, G., and R.O. Ballou: *William James on Psychical Research*, London, 1960.

Myers, F.W.H.: *Human Personality and its Survival of Bodily Death*, London, 1907.

Myers, F.W.H.: *Fragments of Prose and Poetry*, London, 1907.

O'Brien, Fitz-James: *The Diamond Lens*, New York, 1918.

Open Court Magazine, Chicago, Open Court Publishing Co., 1886–1936.

Owen, Robert Dale: four autobiographical articles, *Atlantic Monthly*, July 1874, November 1874, December 1874, January 1875.

Page, Charles G.: *Psychomancy – Spirit rappings and Table-tippings exposed*, New York, 1853.

Pedler, Kit: *Mind over Matter*, London, 1981.

Phelps, William Lyon: 'Robert Browning on Spiritualism', *Yale Review*, New Series, XXIII, pp. 125–38.

Pinkerton, A.: *The Spiritualists and Detectives*, New York, 1877.

Podmore, Frank: *Modern Spiritualism*, (2 vols) London, 1902.

Poe, E.A.: *Tales of Mystery and Imagination*, Everyman edition, London, 1966.

Popper, K. R.: *The Logic of Scientific Discovery*, London, 1972.

Powell, Nicolas: *Fuseli: The Nightmare*, London, 1973.

Porter, Katherine H.: *Through a Glass Darkly: Spiritualism in the Browning Circle*, Lawrence, Kansas, 1958.

Quinn, David ('A Citizen of Ohio'): *The Interior Causes of the War: The Nation Demonized and its President a Spirit-Rapper*, New York, 1863.

Randi, James: *Flim-Flam ! – The Truth about Unicorns, Parapsychology and Other Delusions*, New York, 1980.

Rasputin, Mariya Grigoriyevna: *My Father*, London, 1934.

Rawcliffe, D.H.: *The Psychology of the Occult*, London, 1952.

Rhine, J.B.: *The New World of the Mind*, London, 1954.

Richet, Prof. Charles: *Metapsychics*, London, 1905.

Richet, Prof. Charles (tr. Fred Rothwell): *Our Sixth Sense*, London, 1929.

Richet, Prof. Charles: *Thirty Years of Psychical Research*, London, 1923.

Rinn, Joseph Francis: *Searchlight on Psychical Research: a record of sixty years' work*, London, 1954.

Robertson-Scott, J.W.: *The Life and Death of a Newspaper*, London, 1952.

Sage, M.: *Mrs Piper and the Society for Psychical Research*, London, 1903.

Sargent, Carl, and Hans Eysenck: *Explaining the Unexplained*, London, 1982.

Sargent, E.: *Proof Palpable of Immortality*, Boston, 1876.

Schrenck-Notzing, Baron von: *Phenomena of Materialisation*, London, 1920.

Seybert Commission: *Preliminary Report of the Commission Appointed by the University of Pennsylvania to investigate Modern Spiritualism in accordance with the request of the late Henry Seybert*, Philadelphia, 1887; reprinted with preface by H.H. Furness, Jr., 1920.

Shufeldt, Geo. A., Jr.: *History of the Chicago Artesian Well – A demonstration of the truth of the spiritual philosophy; with an essay on the origin and use of petroleum*, Chicago, 1865.

Sidgwick, E.M. and A.S.: *H.S.: A Memoir*, London, 1906.

Sidgwick, Mrs Henry: 'Results of a personal investigation into the physical phenomena of spiritualism', SPR *Proceedings*, 1886–7, Vol. IV, pp. 48ff.

Sinclair, Upton: *Mental Radio*, Springfield, Ill., 1930.

Sitwell, Osbert: *Left Hand, Right Hand*, London, 1945.

Spiritual Magazine, The, London, 1860–5.

Stacey, C.P.: *A Very Double Life – the Private World of Mackenzie King*, Toronto, 1977.

Stead, Estelle: *My Father*, London, 1912.

Stead, W.T.: *Real Ghost Stories*, London, 1897.

Strong, George Templeton: *Diaries* (ed. Allen Nevins and Milton Halsey Thomas), New York, 1952.

Symonds, John: *Madame Blavatsky – Medium and Magician*, London, 1959.

Tabori, Paul: *Harry Price, the Biography of a Ghost Hunter*, London, 1950.

Taylor, Bayard: 'Confessions of a Medium', *Atlantic Monthly*, December 1860, pp. 699–715.

Thomson, Mortimer: *The Witches of New York, as Encountered by Q.K. Philander Doesticks. P.B.*, New York, 1859.

Tolstoi (tr. E.J. Dillon): *The Fruits of Enlightenment*, London, 1891.

Truesdell, John W.: *The Bottom Facts concerning the Science of Spiritualism*, New York, 1892.

Tuckett, Ivor: *The Evidence for the Supernatural*, London, 1911.

Twain, Mark, and W.D. Howells: *The Correspondence of Samuel L. Clemens and William Dean Howells 1872–1910* (ed. Henry Nash Smith and William M. Gibson), Cambridge, Mass., 1960.

Underhill, Leah: *The Missing Link in Modern Spiritualism*, New York, 1885.

Wallace, Alfred Russel: *My Life*, London, 1905.

Wallace, Alfred Russel: *On Miracles and Modern Spiritualism*, London, 1875.

Wallace, Alfred Russel: *The Scientific Aspect of the Supernatural*, London, 1866.

Webb, James: *The Flight from Reason*, London, 1981.

Wells, H.G., Julian Huxley and G.P.Wells: *The Science of Life*, London, 1931.

Willson, Beckles – *Occultism and Common-Sense*, London, 1908.

Witte, Count: *Memoirs*, London, 1921.

Wright, Richardson: *Forgotten Ladies : nine portraits from the American family album*, Philadelphia, 1928.

Wyndham, Horace: *Mr Sludge the Medium*, London, 1937.

Yeats, W.B.: *Memoirs* (ed. Denis Donoghue), London, 1972.

Yusupov, Feliks Feliksovich: *The End of Rasputin*, London, 1927.

Zancig, Julius: *Adventures in Many Lands*, London, 1924.

Zollner, Johann Carl Friedrich: *Transcendental Physics*, London, 1882.

Index

NOTE: *Persons who make only spiritual appearances are given in quotes.*

Kane, Dr Elisha (Ly) Kent (*contd*)
  family objects to Maggie 30, 31–2
  form of marriage with Maggie 34
  visits England, Havana, dies 34–5
  family cheats Maggie 35–6
Kellar, Harry: levitation on stage 272–3
'King, John' (*alias* of Sir Henry Morgan) 103,
    256, 258
  and Blavatsky 104
  and Eusapia 134
  and Herne and Williams 105, 108–9
  and Nelson Holmeses 103–4
'King, Katie,' (daughter of 'John')
  and Florence Cook 109–13, 116–18, 121
  and Nelson Holmeses 103–4
  exposed 104
Koestler, Arthur: Lamarckian 91
Kubler-Ross, Dr Elisabeth: sexual intercourse
    with spirits as therapy 123

Lamarck, Jean-Baptiste de 88–91
Lang, Andrew 138, 242, 256
Lecky, William
  History of Rationalism, Sidgwick on 88
Leonard, Mrs Osborne, Lodges visit 215
levitation
  Eusapia 130
  Home 71–6
  as illusion 74–5, 263, 271–3
Light on S.P.R. 87
Lindsay, Master of
  and Home seance 68–9
  levitation 71–5, 263
Livermore, Mr and 'Bella'
  and Kate Fox 103, 114
  withdraws help from Kate 229–30
Livingstone, Dr David, premature spirit visit
    by 47–8
Lodge, Sir Oliver, (physicist)
  investigates Eusapia 132–5
    with Maskelyne 256–7
  investigates Mrs Piper 209–12
  'Raymond' (dead son) 214–15
    description of the other side 216–18, 221
    Doyle on 221–2
  and S.P.R. 190, 205, 213
Lodge, Lady, (wife of Sir Oliver)
  and death of son 214–17
Lombroso, Prof. Cesare, (inventor of
    criminology), and Eusapia 130
London Dialectical Society 111, 250, 269
Longfellow, H.W., 41
Lund, Mr, on Mrs Piper seance 211–12
Lytton, Bulwer: convert 57, 61

McDougall, Dr William, (Prof. Psychology,
    Harvard)
  and American S.P.R. and Rhine 94

investigates Crandons 175, 177
  Doyle on 186
  denounces Margery 187
  suggests 'dual personality' 188
Mach, Ernst 240–1
'Magnetic Girl' 45
'magnetism, animal' 11–12
Margery *see* Crandon, Margery
marriages
  and collusion 188–9
  broken, of mediums 32–3
Marshall, Mrs, and Dr Livingstone 47–8
Marthe *see* Béraud, Marthe
Maskelyne, J.N.,
  and Blavatsky 237
  on: Eusapia's methods 138, 256–9
    scientists as testers 138
    spirit photograph 223
  Wallace on 168
  believes in table-turning 166
materialization (ectoplasm; emanations)
  Leah starts full-form 98–9
  Eusapia's 134, 148–50
  Eva C.'s 153–4
  Golighers' 150–1
  techniques of 279–81
  words for 131
  see also faces; medium, techniques of;
    pseudopodia
Medhurst, Dr, with Mrs Goldney on Florence
    Cook 231–2
Medium and Daybreak, The 110
mediums, gifts of (?) 49–51
mediums, techniques of 46–8, 273–6
  Blue Book 46, 276
  How to be a Medium by W.H. Evans 98–9
  instructions in *The Spiritualist* 43
  training school for mediums 48–9
  seances
    blank sittings 269–70
    distraction 267–70
    'fishing' 47, 210–12
    freeing hand and foot 282–3
    furniture moving 281
    giving dead man's name 275
    rappings 282; Fox sisters 2, 6–7, 17–18,
        23–4, 230–1
    reading messages 46–7
  gadgets 276–9
    false fingers 283
    marketing of 45–6
    telescopic rods 45, 277
    shoes, prepared 45–6
  levitation 74–5, 263, 271–3
  materialization 98–9, 100–2
    hiding places 159
    regurgitation 158–9
    Showers describes 125–6
    see also cabinet